THE NEGRO IN AMERICA:

A BIBLIOGRAPHY

THE NEGRO IN AMERICA:
A BIBLIOGRAPHY

Compiled by Elizabeth W. Miller

for the American Academy of Arts and Sciences

With a Foreword by Thomas F. Pettigrew

Harvard University Press

Cambridge, Massachusetts

1966

FOREWORD

This volume constitutes an important and overdue contribution to the understanding of American race relations. Not since the definitive treatment of the issue by Gunnar Myrdal in An American Dilemma, now a generation old, have we had such an extensive and searching bibliographical collection. In addition to its obvious value as a sourcebook for information and references, this modern bibliography chronicles the latest chapter in the long and curious history of American thinking about the Negro—a history that deserves brief mention in order to place this work in temporal perspective.

American racial thought was initially shaped by slavery. The peculiar institution posed a serious dilemma for early America: How could slaveholders treat human beings as mere property and at the same time uphold the lofty American ideal of human equality? The answer is that many never did rest easily with this glaring contradiction, though they tried as best they could to rationalize and excuse the conflict. Built around the firm insistence that slavery was a "positive good," these rationalizations took three basic forms: religious, cultural, and racial.

First, slavery was defended as a religiously ordained system—an effective method to Christianize and civilize African heathen. But, in time, this claim lost most of its potency. To begin with, it conflicted with the racist notion that the Negro was incapable of acculturation. And by the nineteenth century it was seriously undermined by the increasing numbers of slaves who had become Christians and thus no longer needed to be converted. More enduring were the biblical defenses of slavery. Virtually all pro-slavery spokesmen employed literal interpretations of the Old Testament to prove that the institution had Christian sanction. God had willed that the black man forever serve the white man, according to the especially popular interpretation of a drunken man's curse in Genesis 9. In fact, the whole array of Old Testament arguments assembled in the defense of slavery is still heard in the South today as a defense of segregation.

Second, slavery was justified as a cultural necessity. As fiery antislavery attacks from the North began to find their mark in the 1820's and 1830's, slave interests countered that the system fostered a superior culture. Great scholars, great writers, great statesmen were made possible, contended slaveholders, when an institution such as slavery gave them the wealth and leisure to develop their talents. After all, the South was only following the examples set by the slaveholding societies of ancient Greece and Rome. Already the results of this noble experiment were evident. Did not the planter class possess a patrician charm and gentility not to be found in the hustle and bustle of the crudely materialistic, urbanizing North? Indeed, an angry finger could be pointed at the labor evils right under the sensitive noses of the Abolitionists. Was it not true that the factory workers in the North and in England were mere "wage slaves"? Could the critics of the South deny that their own laborers suffered from miserable living and working conditions without even the "security" provided by chattel slavery? How could Northern and English Abolitionists dare to question the "benign" system of slavery upon which the South was building a great culture at precisely the time when their own societies were deep in the quagmire of cultural decay?

This cultural argument encountered two major obstacles. Any glorification of a despotic system directed by a special elite had to come to terms with the American dream. Most slavery spokesmen avoided meeting this conflict head on; they tried to maintain both the rationalization and the dream by claiming that only in a slave society could real freedom and opportunity exist for them. Moreover, the analogy with ancient Greece and Rome suffered from a fundamental difference between modern and earlier forms of slavery, for in the New World the institution was totally identified with one specific group. And, as Frank Tannenbaum comments in his Slave and Citizen, this difference "spelled the death knell of slavery itself within the European cultural area." Previously, slavery had been a condition anyone might suffer, and so it was regarded as a misfortune, but when the slave status came to be occupied solely by Negroes, the question naturally arose: Why the Negro? This query made slavery a moral problem for the first time.

Why the Negro? The cultural arguments did not provide a straightforward reply to this question; consequently, the slaveholders still relied on the Bible. By the 1830's, however, a third defense for slavery began to appear, a defense clothed in the respectability of "science." Rather than depend upon biblical revelation, the new ethnological arguments relied upon "natural law." Negroes were slaves because they comprised a separate, inferior species; their lowly rank was merely a reflection of the natural relations among the "races" of man. The basic tenet of this theory was that the various races had had distinctly different origins, for a common origin was assumed to mean equal endowment for all races. And unequal racial endowments were substantiated by an odd variety of historical and anatomical data ranging from Egyptology to the size and shape of skulls. The leaders in this thinking were actually such prominent Northern scientists as Samuel Morton and Louis Agassiz, though the most vocal and vociferous proponents were pro-slavery Southerners.

Yet two features of this early "scientific" doctrine kept it from gaining critical importance in the slavery debate. First, the more technical features of the theory were too complex to be widely read and understood. And, second, the full doctrine flew in the face of the South's most cherished religious beliefs. In particular, the concept of diverse origins conflicted with the insistent scriptural interpretation that all men arose from a common Adam-and-Eve beginning. Attractive as it was, "The Theory of the Diversity of Man," writes William Stanton in The Leopard's Spots, "tossed the religious into a theological bramble patch." Thus, most Southern spokesmen rejected the full "scientific" theory of race. Only those who liked both to dabble in "science" and engage in "parson-skinning" consistently made use of the most intellectually respectable defense of slavery.

The crowning irony came in 1859 with the publication of On the Origin of Species. Going over much of the same ethnological ground, Charles Darwin arrived at the conclusion of the Church—the common origin of man. Religion had been vindicated by a man whose acceptance by it would require generations. And the "scientists" had been proven wrong by one of their own. Our chief interest today in this historical backwater is that it marks the national beginning of a formal, articulate doctrine of white superiority. Even more than the other rationalizations of slavery, aspects of this doctrine are with us today. In fact, though repeatedly repudiated by modern research, portions of the antebellum "evidence" for Negro inferiority are still to be found in the popular racist tracts of our own times listed in this volume (see references to the work of Garrett, George, Putnam, Shuey, and Weyl).

At the popular level these elaborate theories about racial origins and scientific proofs were not appreciated or needed, but the general ideas of "race" and Negro "racial" inferiority were accepted and utilized. In the early days slaveowners had simply assumed Negro inferiority and the new doctrine comfortably supported this view. Only a few thoughtful men such as James Bowdoin, mentioned in the Preface which follows, raised the possibility of environmental influences. By the early nineteenth century, increasing numbers of white Americans accepted the idea that Negroes formed a distinct and lower type of humanity. Thus, in 1857, Chief Justice Roger Taney could confidently claim in his Dred Scott opinion that Negroes were "... so far inferior, that they had no rights which the white man was bound to respect... "

Naive and vicious as this doctrine appears today in the light of the vast advances of recent years in the biological and social sciences, Taney's racist reasoning seemed logical to many of his contemporaries. All one had to do was to look around. Were not slaves obviously inferior to their masters in intelligence and manners? And if such things were all biologically determined, was this not proof that whites were racially superior to Negroes? Such was the simple argument, for the sweeping importance of environment and opportunity were not well understood by the scientists of this period much less the laymen.

Despite Emancipation and Reconstruction, the late nineteenth century witnessed little fundamental change in the prevailing ideas about race. To be sure, as C. Vann Woodward and others have documented, there were notable, if brief, instances of biracial egalitarianism during these times—in the Reconstruction state governments, even occasionally in the Redeemer state governments, and in some segments of the Populist revolt. Nevertheless, this period culminated in the most explicitly racist era of American history, 1890 to 1910. This is the period Rayford Logan calls the "nadir" of Negro-American history. These years marked the establishment of the modern form of de jure racial segregation, a trend sanctioned by such key Supreme Court decisions as Louisville, New Orleans, and Texas Railroad v. Mississippi (1890), Plessy v. Ferguson (1896), and Cumming v. Board of Education (1899). This was also the period of American colonialism. Indeed, it was the expansion of the United States into the Phillipines that led to the unhappy phrase, "our little brown brothers."

Intellectual thought about race at the turn of the century reflected these events. Had the American Academy of Arts and Sciences commissioned a racial bibliography in 1910, it would have bulged with articles and books written from a heavily Darwinistic viewpoint. Undaunted by Darwin's blow to earlier racist notions, many believers in white racial superiority utilized biological Darwinism to argue that Negroes had evolved later than Caucasians and were therefore less "advanced." Social Darwinism, led by Yale's William Graham Sumner, completed the dominant reasoning of the period. In essence, Social Darwinists claimed government was in large part helpless to correct the desperate situation in which the Negro found himself. Stateways could not change folkways; if national traditions placed the Negro in a status of social inferiority, there was little that law and decree could do about it.

World War I shook the nation violently and sharply altered the racial scene. The mass movement of Negroes from the rural South to the nation's largest urban areas began; and "the Harlem Renaissance" of the 1920's signaled a new era of American race relations, an era in which the sophisticated and militant Negro of the cities began to replace the backward and subservient Negro of the open country. The psychological literature of the period, however, did not reflect the shift. World War I had shown the utility of intelligence tests, and many psychologists found themselves with an instrument more developed than their abilities to interpret its results. With few exceptions, the large majority of racial studies in psychology during the 1920's supported racist theories of white superiority. Empirically inadequate and theoretically naive, the racial literature of the decade was characterized by intelligence-test studies of white and Negro Americans that uncritically interpreted the usually higher white I.Q. means as evidence of inherent intellectual differences between the races.

The 1930's, however, witnessed a remarkable change in the dominant interpretation of such findings. Psychologists began to consider systematically the effects of environment and opportunity upon performance in their tests. Though still crude in some respects, a new series of more rigorous racial studies appeared in the social science literature. Certainly one of the most important and influential landmarks among these newer investigations was Otto Klineberg's Negro Intelligence and Selective Migration (1935). Do Negro children who migrate from the South improve their test performance as they remain in the North? This was the basic question Klineberg answered affirmatively, together with a demonstration that selective migration of brighter Negroes to the North was not an explanation of his critical results.

More carefully controlled research on Negro Americans over the past generation has duplicated and confirmed the fundamental findings and conclusions of the 1930's. The critical significance of environmental factors in shaping and altering human behavior is now clearly recognized. Indeed, social scientists are no longer interested in testing environmental versus heredity questions. The new conception requires a specification of how environment and heredity complexly interact to produce behavior. "Race" and all of the distorted notions surrounding this concept are simply not productive ways to approach the central scientific issues. Inherent differences between Negro and white Americans may exist, but superiority-inferiority claims have no validity in modern scientific thinking. In addition, users of this volume are cautioned that just because many differences are discernible among "races" does not necessarily mean that such differences are due to "race."

Interestingly, this advance in American social science thought appears to have been both a cause and a result of a comparable general shift in American racial thought. Consider the data collected by the National Opinion Research Center in reply to the question: "In general, do you think that Negroes are as intelligent as white people—that is, can they learn things just as well if they are given the same education and training?" In 1942, only two out of five white Americans thought Negroes equal in intelligence to whites; by 1956, almost four out of five thought so. Even more dramatic has been the change in the white South. In 1942, only one in five white Southerners agreed that Negroes were of equal intelligence to whites; by 1963, three out of five agreed.

The full force of these sweeping alterations in American thought on race will impress those who utilize this bibliography. Not just the cited books, but even more the abstracted articles serve as definitive documentation of this new and refreshing look at Negro Americans. The reader will note, too, that this view pervades material of all kinds—from fiction and biography through sociology and psychology. Indeed, this modern conception requires for its understanding insights from many diverse directions; and this need is comprehensively met in this significant volume.

Thomas F. Pettigrew
Harvard University
December 1965

PREFACE

When James Bowdoin was inducted into office as the first president of the American Academy of Arts and Sciences, he presented "A Philosophical Discourse Publickly Addressed" to that body on the eighth of November, 1780. He recited many reasons why the members should find, in the new nation, rich materials for their investigations. In common with other patriots of the day, he celebrated the unique advantages enjoyed by the citizens of the Republic, where, unfettered by tradition, by feudal forms, by the chains of custom, a new kind of society would make its contributions to mankind. Among his speculations on that occasion was one as to the "greater or less degree of natural knowledge and improvements" to be distinguished in the inhabitants of various parts of the globe. Referring to the difference between Europeans and Africans, he raised the question whether, if an inequality of "natural faculties" were observed between them, it might not "in a great measure be accounted for, by the operation of natural causes." He suggested that "there may be a variety of things, on which... [equality of capacity] ... may depend: such as education, religion, government, and other circumstances," and that "the human faculties, by reason of sameness of situation and other circumstances, might in general be equal." During the years between the Supreme Court Decision of May 17, 1954, and the enactment of the Voting Rights Bill in August 1965, his question has assumed dimensions as extensive as the nation itself, and the Negro citizens of America now demand that they at last be allowed to enjoy a "sameness of situation" with their white fellow Americans.

The present bibliography concentrates on works appearing within this time span, although many instances have arisen where, for the purpose of illuminating the background, of explaining attitudes or the direction of developments, it has appeared useful to include older sources. It is hoped that by embracing many fields, many types of publications—the polemical, the scholarly, the clinical, the prescriptive, the journalistic—the bibliography may not only aid those working in the several areas, but may point up gaps in knowledge and to some extent the relative urgency of problems, may even, in a sense, tell a story of the Negro in America during the most recent past.

The first section, on Background, includes general studies and those that have become classics in the field, historical works, general demographic analyses, biographies and autobiographies. The second section, Definition and Description, is divided into five subsections, on race and the idea of race, social institutions and conditions, individual characteristics, health, and literature and folklore. Of these the second, on social institutions and conditions, is the most extensive, embracing works on major aspects of Negro life—the family, religion, social structures and community life, the Negro press as the voice of that community life, as well as materials on the assimilative social process of racial intermarriage.

The third main section, on Intergroup Relations, scrutinizes both the prejudice that breeds discrimination, group hatreds and group fears, and the techniques for resolving these fears, for dissipating anxieties, for restraining group antagonisms. There follow sections on Rural Problems and on Urban Problems, the latter covering such topics as in-migration, the ghetto, crime and delinquency, and race violence. The major areas of housing, jobs, and schools are treated in separate sections which deal with wider aspects of these problems than the exclusively urban. A section on the Economic Status and Problems of the Negro within the national economy is followed by the sections on Employment, Housing, and Education, each of which includes material on the law, the courts, and regulatory action, as do subsequent sections on Public Accommodations and Political Rights and Suffrage.

The section on the Freedom Revolution is, understandably, the most contemporaneous in the bibliography. A subsection on civil rights and wrongs—the law, the courts, the operations of justice—is followed by analyses of the protest movement as it has grown and changed, the development of strategies and tactics, the issues involved, the demands on leadership, the responses generated both North and South, the involvement of the churches. A final main section is concerned with Black Nationalism which, perhaps because the Black Muslims constitute the largest element, remains somewhat distinct from the Freedom Revolution. Tools for Further Research are suggested in conclusion.

This is a selective bibliography. In view of the torrent of words printed during the past few years on the problems and purposes of the Negro, it would be neither possible nor useful to attempt all-inclusiveness. Nor has it been possible, because of the number of items, to annotate each entry. Such notations as are included are intended to indicate the scope or special significance of particular works, or to clarify titles which are not self-explanatory. There is an author index. Inevitably omissions will be noted, some from design, some from inadvertence, some from ignorance. The Academy will welcome both general comments from readers on the organization of the bibliography, and any suggestions of works or topics which should be included in future editions.

It is now two years since <u>Daedalus</u>, the journal of the American Academy of Arts and Sciences, under the editorship of Stephen R. Graubard embarked on preparatory work for the publication of two issues on the Negro in America, which appeared in the Autumn of 1965 and the Winter of 1966. The compilation of the bibliography was originally initiated by Mr. Graubard as a part of a study of the Negro in America undertaken by the Academy and eventuating in the <u>Daedalus</u> issues. The Carnegie Corporation of America generously supported this entire project, for which the deepest appreciation of everyone associated with the enterprise is here expressed. My personal indebtednesses are many, to members of the faculties of Harvard University who have answered appeals, to the reference librarians of the several Harvard libraries who have resolved many queries out of the riches of the Harvard collections. A number of Harvard and Radcliffe students at various times scanned periodicals and verified references. I should particularly like to thank Daniel Horowitz for his resourceful and highly knowledgeable contributions in the early stages of the task. Susanne Bodenheimer, at a later stage, gave dedicated assistance. Members of the staff of <u>Daedalus</u> have furnished unfailing support. Finally, Ann Orlov of the Harvard University Press so quickly transcended her role as editor that I can only express my warmest gratitude to her as collaborator.

Elizabeth W. Miller
Cambridge, Massachusetts
December 1965

CONTENTS

I.   Background   1

    1. General   1
    2. History   5
    3. Demography   8
    4. Biography   9

II. Definition and Description   11

    1. Race   14
    2. Social Institutions and Conditions   16

        a. Family and Child-Rearing   16
        b. Religious Life and Negro Churches   18
        c. Social Class   20
        d. Community Life, Leaders, and Organizations   21
        e. The Press   24
        f. Intermarriage   24

    3. Individual Characteristics   25

        a. Personality   25
        b. Intelligence   30

    4. Health   33

        a. Genetic   33
        b. Mental   34
        c. Patterns and Diseases   36
        d. Services   37

    5. Literature and Folklore   39

III. Intergroup Relations   45

    1. Studies of Prejudice   45
    2. Overcoming Prejudice   51

IV. Rural Problems   56

V.   Urban Problems   58

    1. General Surveys   58
    2. In-migration and Population   60

		3. The Ghetto	62
		4. Delinquency, Crime, and Police Practices	63
		5. Race Violence	66

VI.   Economic Status and Problems   68

1. General   68
2. The Poor   71
3. The Negro as Consumer   72
4. The Negro as Entrepreneur   73

VII. Employment   74

1. The Law, the Courts, and Regulatory Action   74
2. Patterns and Conditions   76
3. The Negro and the Labor Movement   81
4. Efforts to Integrate   83

VIII. Housing and Urban Renewal   87

1. The Law, the Courts, and Regulatory Action   87
2. Patterns and Conditions   89
3. Efforts to Integrate   93

IX.   Education   98

1. The Law, the Courts, and Regulatory Action   99
2. Patterns and Conditions   105

    a. General   105
    b. North   107
    c. South   109
    d. Negro Colleges and Higher Education   111
    e. Achievement and Deprivation   113
    f. Guidance and Occupational Choice   114

3. The Desegregation Effort   115

    a. General   115
    b. North   118
    c. South   120

X.   Public Accommodations   124

XI.   Political Rights and Suffrage   126

1. The Law, the Courts, and Regulatory Action   127
2. Patterns and Conditions   129

XII. The Freedom Revolution   134

    1. Civil Rights and Wrongs   136
    2. Protest: Theory and Practice   140
    3. Response and Resistance   148
    4. The Role of the Churches   155

XIII. Black Nationalism   163

XIV. Tools for Further Research   166

INDEX OF AUTHORS   171

THE NEGRO IN AMERICA:
A BIBLIOGRAPHY

I. BACKGROUND

In this section are listed works of several different types which, despite their diversity, may together provide a useful background against which students may focus individual approaches to the subject of the Negro in America. Here are such works as E. Franklin Frazier's The Negro in the United States, and Rayford W. Logan's The Negro in American Life and Thought. Here also are general population studies which present data on the composition, disposition, and racial differentials of the people of the United States. In this section, too, is a selection of historical works with particular relevance for any study of the Negro's experience in America. The comparative method so effectively employed by Frank Tannenbaum in Slave and Citizen and by Stanley Elkins in Slavery provides illuminating insights into the development of certain characteristics of the Negro identify in this country. In recent years a number of historians, among them C. Vann Woodward, John Hope Franklin, and Kenneth Stampp, by looking anew at the evidence of the past, have in many cases quite altered our perspectives on the Negro's role in that past. A limited selection of biographical and autobiographical writings are listed for their representative value. Finally, certain classic older works appear here, among them Myrdal's An American Dilemma, Wilbur Cash's The Mind of the South, John Dollard's Caste and Class in a Southern Town. To turn to them is to become strikingly aware of the dearth of recent studies of comparable distinction.

1. GENERAL

Berelson, Bernard, and Gary A. Steiner, Human Behavior: An Inventory of Scientific Findings. New York: Harcourt, Brace, 1964. A convenient summation of findings in the main areas of psychological research, including a chapter on ethnic relations, with references to classic and recent studies. One conclusion: "All races possess the abilities to participate . . . in modern technological civilization."

Blair, Lewis H., A Southern Prophecy: The Prosperity of the South Dependent Upon the Elevation of the Negro. Boston: Little, Brown, 1964. Originally published in Richmond in 1889, the book was written by a Southern businessman who had served in the Confederate Army. C. Vann Woodward has edited it, with an introduction in which he presents the work as a strong and realistic argument for civil rights.

Broom, Leonard, and Norval D. Glenn, Transformation of the Negro American. New York: Harper, 1965. A summary, drawn chiefly from other sources, of information about the present position of the Negro in the U.S.

Brown, Ina Corinne, The Story of the American Negro. New York: Friendship Press, 1936; 2nd rev. ed. 1957.

Caldwell, Erskine, In Search of Bisco. New York: Farrar, 1965. Southern life and attitudes as presented in conversations with both black and white Southerners.

Cash, W. J., The Mind of the South. New York: Knopf, 1941; reissued, Doubleday Anchor Book, 1954. An extraordinarily penetrating picture of the origins of the Southern point of view, the background of Southern romanticism, the growth of violence as an instrument of legality. Author's approach is literary and psychological, but the book is more rather than less illuminating for that reason.

Clark, Thomas D., The Emerging South. New York: Oxford University Press, 1961. The author reviews economic and cultural changes that have occurred, the shift from a rural to an industrialized society, the impact of federal aid, and then proceeds to a discussion of Southern strategies of resistance and the techniques of Negro civil rights protest. Bibliography.

Cole, Stewart G., and Mildred Wiese Cole, Minorities and the American Promise. New York: Harper, 1954.

Cox, Oliver Cromwell, Caste, Class and Race. Garden City, N. Y.: Doubleday, 1948. A Marxist criticism of the caste-class interpretation of American race relations.

Davie, Maurice, Negroes in American Society. New York: McGraw-Hill, 1949. A comprehensive textbook, with bibliography, covering all aspects of the experience of the Negro in America.

Davis, Allison W., and John Dollard, Children of Bondage. Washington, D. C.: American Council on Education, 1940. A detailed examination of the social classes into which Negroes are divided in the South within the Negro caste.

Dollard, John, Caste and Class in a Southern Town. New Haven: Yale University Press, 1937. The third edition of this important study was published by Doubleday Anchor Books in 1957. In his preface to that edition, the author, while reiterating that "the caste device for placing Negroes must be abandoned," and acknowledging present dangers, maintains that "If white men can solve the color problem, the United States is in an excellent position to do it."

Dover, Cedric, American Negro Art. London: Studio, and Greenwich, Conn.: 1960; 3rd ed. 1965. Author relates painting, sculpture, and crafts to the changing role of the Negro in American life. Bibliography, including a listing of catalogues of exhibits by Negro artists.

Drake, St. Clair, "Recent Trends in Research on the Negro in the United States," International Social Science Bulletin, UNESCO, vol. 9, no. 4, pp. 475-492 (1957). Evaluative summaries of developments in sociological research.

Drake, St. Clair, "The Social and Economic Status of the Negro in the United States," Daedalus 94:771-814 (Fall 1965). A survey of the extent of the victimization experienced by the Negro in America today.

DuBois, W. E. B., The Souls of Black Folk: Essays and Sketches. Chicago: McClurg, 1903; frequently reprinted, most recently, New York: Fawcett, 1961. Desire for a militant Negro movement.

DuBois, W. E. B., Black Reconstruction. New York: Harcourt, Brace, 1935; reissued, New York: Russell & Russell, 1964. From a Marxian point of view.

Emerson, Rupert, and Martin Kilson, "The American Dilemma in a Changing World: The Rise of Africa and the Negro American," Daedalus 94: 1055-1084 (Fall 1965).

Fein, Rashi, "An Economic and Social Profile of the Negro American," Daedalus 94:815-846 (Fall 1965). A profile based on comparison between the Negro and other Americans, using data as to the positions of the two groups at different moments in time. Extremely useful concluding note on sources, particularly U.S. government publications.

Frazier, E. Franklin, The Negro in the United States. New York: Macmillan, 1949; rev. ed., 1957. A major work, of wide historical understanding. Extensive bibliography.

Frazier, E. Franklin, Race and Culture Contacts in the Modern World. New York: Knopf, 1957. An analysis of racial relations with a worldwide perspective. In his treatment of the Negro in America the author discusses patterns of migration, economic status, political status, the caste system of the South, prejudice, problems of assimilation, and so forth.

Furnas, J.C., Goodbye to Uncle Tom. New York: Sloane, 1956. Partly an attack on Uncle Tom's Cabin, partly a documentary social history on what conditions and customs were really like, the author's conclusion is that the only practical solution to the interracial problem is to let the Negro find his own level in society, without "caste pressures." Bibliography.

Ginzberg, Eli, and Alfred S. Eichner, The Troublesome Presence: American Democracy and the Negro. New York: Free Press, 1964. A fact-crammed work which surveys the impact of the Negro on America and of America on the Negro, and assesses the cost to the nation of continuing to deny the Negro his rights.

Grimes, Alan P., Equality in America. New York: Oxford University Press, 1964. Chapter 2, "Race," discusses reasons for the difficulty of solving racial problems, traces the history of white supremacist theories, analyzes the rise of civil rights movement, the effect of Brown vs. Board of Education, protest tactics, and related matters.

Guzman, Jessie P., ed., Race Relations in the South--1963. Tuskegee, Ala.: Tuskegee Institute, March 12, 1964. A report covering legal action on the federal, state, and local levels in the areas of education, employment, recreation, registration and voting, transportation, public accommodations. Provides data on compliance and noncompliance, on voluntary group action, and on violence.

Handlin, Oscar, Race and Nationality in American Life. Boston: Little, Brown, 1957.

Hero, Alfred O., Jr., The Southerner and World Affairs. Baton Rouge: Louisiana State University Press, 1965. An examination of changing Southern attitudes toward participation by the U.S. in international undertakings, which at the same time constitutes a profile of the Southerner, both black and white, and of developing relationships, interregional as well as interracial. Extensive "Observations on Selected Sources."

Herskovits, Melville J., The Myth of the Negro Past. New York: Harper, 1941; reissued by Beacon Press Paperbacks in 1958, with new preface by the author. The outstanding work on Africanisms in the New World.

Highsaw, Robert B., ed., The Deep South in Transformation. University of Alabama Press, 1965. Discussions of social, political, economic, and cultural problems. Contributors include O. C. Carmichael, Everett C. Hughes, Louis Rubin, and Luther H. Hodges.

Hughes, Everett C., "Race Relations and the Sociological Imagination," American Sociological Review 28:879-890 (December 1963).

Hughes, Everett C., "Anomalies and Projections," Daedalus 94:1133-1147 (Fall 1965). The author considers, "at this time of actual and impending great change in the relations of Negro with other Americans, what is likely to be the general effect on our institutions and conduct."

Isaacs, Harold R., "World Affairs and U. S. Race Relations: A Note on Little Rock," Public Opinion Quarterly 22:364-396 (Fall 1958).

Isaacs, Harold R., The New World of Negro Americans. New York: Day, 1963. Subtitled "The impact of world affairs on the race problem in the United States and particularly on the Negro, his view of himself, his country, and Africa." Based on 107 interviews with American Negroes, the author provides an impressive analysis of the ways in which the growing importance and power of nonwhite, particularly African, nations has affected the life and thinking of American Negroes.

Jocher, Katherine, Guy B. Johnson, George L. Simpson, and Rupert B. Vance, eds., Folk, Region, and Society: Selected Papers of Howard W. Odum. Chapel Hill: University of North Carolina Press, 1964. Excellent collection of Odum's papers. Odum had arrived at conviction that "the earlier verdict of organic and composite race difference was wrong," and in his "Agenda for Integration" (1954) declared "'gradualism' is out." Also contains a collection of Negro folk songs, and a trilogy on Left-Wing Gordon.

Lerche, Charles O., The Uncertain South: Its Changing Patterns of Politics in Foreign Policy. Chicago: Quadrangle Books, 1964. Discusses extent to which Southern positions on foreign policy reflect Southern racial attitudes: e.g., resistance of Southern congressmen to foreign aid to underdeveloped countries.

Morris, Willie, ed., The South Today: 100 Years After Appomattox. New York: Harper, 1965. A composite picture of Southern life, developed from a Harper's Magazine supplement.

Mphahlele, Ezekiel, The African Image. New York: Praeger, 1962. The author, a South African-born poet and novelist, writes about how African and American feel about each other, as well as about intergroup relationships in general. He also discusses the black nationalists.

Myrdal, Gunnar, An American Dilemma. 2 vols., New York: Harper, 1944; 20th anniversary ed., Harper, 1963, with a new preface by Myrdal and a 10,000-word "Postscript Twenty Years Later" by Arnold Rose. This monumental work, with the basic theme of inequality and its impact on every phase of Negro life and personality, has not forfeited its classic dimensions despite inevitable modifications and injection of new factors during intervening years.

Nicholls, William H., Southern Tradition and Regional Progress. Chapel Hill: University of North Carolina Press, 1960. The effect of developing industrialization on Southern values and behavior, including a comparison of the attitudes of the rural elites and the new urban managerial, commercial, and professional classes.

"Notes From the Academy: Transcript of the American Academy Conference--May 14-15, 1965," Daedalus 95:287-441 (Winter 1966). Contributors to Fall 1965 and Winter 1966 issues of Daedalus on the Negro in America met with specialists from several fields to discuss and criticize drafts of papers in advance of publication.

Odum, Howard W., Southern Regions of the United States. Chapel Hill: University of North Carolina Press, 1936. Presented as an index of regional culture, this monumental study has as its principal focus the economic deficiencies of the South, its essentially "colonial" economy, that progressively exploited natural resources and cheap labor without any appreciable accumulation of capital.

"One Tenth of a Nation," Reporter 22:14-22 (March 31, 1960). Special section.

Park, Robert Ezra, Race and Culture. Glencoe, Ill.: Free Press, 1950. On the whole, the papers of this distinguished scholar and teacher take a more optimistic view of a parallel Negro and white rise than has been proved by the event.

Parsons, Talcott, "Full Citizenship for the Negro American: A Sociological Problem," Daedalus 94:1009-1054 (Fall 1965). The author suggests that the resolution of the Negro's predicament as the most stigmatized American minority group lies in his inclusion as a full participant in a pluralistic societal situation.

The Portrayal of the Negro in American Painting. Brunswick, Maine: Bowdoin College Museum of Art, 1964. Catalogue of a distinguished exhibition of works of art covering the period from 1710 to the present. Informative notes by Sidney Kaplan.

Preu, James, ed., The Negro in American Society. Florida State University Studies, no. 28, Tallahassee: Florida State University, 1958.

"Race in America," Christianity and Crisis 21:83-100 (May 29, 1961).

Reid, Ira de A., "The American Negro," in Joseph B. Gittler, ed., Understanding Minority Groups. New York: Wiley, 1956. Traces changing relation to the white majority, and outlines major movements through which Negro has sought to improve his status.

"The Relative Status of the Negro in the United States," Journal of Negro Education 22:221-451 (Summer 1953). Entire issue.

Roche, John P., The Quest for the Dream: The Development of Civil Rights and Human Relations in Modern America. New York: Macmillan, 1963. A social history, in which the author examines the development of--and threats to--American liberties since 1900. Ethnic and religious intolerance, the Negroes' awakening sense of identity and community, the confrontation of the American conscience concerning the Negro are among the themes treated.

Rohrer, J. H., and M. S. Edmonson, The Eighth Generation. New York: Harper, 1960. This study is a follow-up twenty years later of the people described by Davis and Dollard in Children of Bondage.

Rose, Arnold M., The Negro in America. New York: Harper, 1948. A condensation of Myrdal's American Dilemma.

Schermerhorn, R. A., "Power as a Primary Concept in the Study of Minorities," Social Forces 35:53-56 (October 1956).

Schermerhorn, R. A., "Minorities: European and American," Phylon 20:178-185 (Summer 1959).

Tussman, Joseph, ed., The Supreme Court on Racial Discrimination. New York: Oxford University Press, 1963. The full texts of significant Supreme Court decisions in the following areas: segregation in education, segregation while traveling and dining, race and freedom of speech, discrimination and livelihood, restrictive covenants, discrimination and the jury, voting. Extremely useful.

Wagley, Charles W., "The Situation of the Negro in the United States," International Social Science Bulletin, UNESCO, vol. 9, no. 4, pp. 427-438 (1957). Comparison of the caste system in the United States with the freer Latin American system.

Wagley, Charles W., and Marvin Harris, Minorities in the New World. New York: Columbia University Press, 1958. Prepared for UNESCO, this book offers a comparative analysis of six minority groups in the Western Hemisphere. Included is a study of the historical development of barriers to the integration of Negroes into U. S. society.

Walker, H. J., "Changes in the Status of the Negro in American Society," International Social Science Bulletin, UNESCO, vol. 9, no. 4, pp. 438-474 (1957). Covers economic developments, changes in politics and government, urbanization, increased voter registration, etc.

Weyl, Nathaniel, The Negro in American Civilization. Washington, D. C.: Public Affairs Press, 1960. Beginning with an examination of the historical background of American efforts to define relationship of the Negro to the nation, the author concludes that the Supreme Court decisions of 1875-1900 were liberal on racial matters. He finds significant differences between the African and European brain which he accounts for by speculations about man in torrid climates, and insists that the issue in the present "crisis" is one of individual liberty rather than of equality.

"White-Nonwhite Differentials in Health, Education, and Welfare," Health, Education, and Welfare Indicators, February-October, 1965. Prepared by the Office of Under Secretary, U. S. Department of Health, Education, and Welfare.

"The White Problem in America," Ebony 20:27+ (August 1965). Special Issue. Statement by John H. Johnson, editor and publisher: "The white man has been trying to solve the race problem through studying the Negro. We feel the answer lies in a more thorough study of the man who created the problem. In this issue we, as Negroes, look at the white man today with the hope that our effort will tempt him to look at himself more thoroughly."

2. HISTORY

Aptheker, Herbert, ed., A Documentary History of the Negro People in the United States. 2 vols., New York: Citadel, 1951; reissued 1962, 1964. A readable selection from a wide variety of sources. Vol. I covers the period through the Civil War; vol. II, from Reconstruction to 1910.

Beals, Carleton, War Within a War: The Confederacy Against Itself. Philadelphia: Chilton, 1965. A revisionary treatment of the legend of Confederate gallantry, fidelity, and unity, which brings together evidence of disaffection and desertion within the South during the Civil War.

Bennett, Lerone, Jr., Before the Mayflower: A History of the Negro in America, 1619-1962. Chicago: Johnson, 1962. A popularized history, based on a series of articles originally published in Ebony, it traces the history of Negro life from the Jamestown slaves to the "Second Reconstruction" of Martin Luther King, Jr., and the sit-in generation.

Burchard, Peter, One Gallant Rush. New York: St. Martin's, 1965. Biography of Robert Gould Shaw and his black regiment in the Civil War.

"A Century of Struggle," Progressive 26:3-58 (December 1962). Entire issue in celebration of the anniversary of the Emancipation Proclamation, with articles by Adlai Stevenson, James Baldwin, Harry Golden, Martin Luther King, C. Vann Woodward, Murray Kempton.

Christman, Henry M., ed., The South As It Is 1865-1866. New York: Viking, 1965. Republication of a report by John Richard Dennett to The Nation magazine on life in seven Southern states at the beginning of Reconstruction. Documents Southern hopes of keeping Negroes in condition resembling slavery.

Cook, Samuel DuBois, "A Tragic Conception of Negro History," Journal of Negro History 45:219-240 (October 1960).

Cox, La Wanda, and John H. Cox, Politics, Principle and Prejudice, 1865-1866: Dilemma of Reconstruction America. New York: Free Press, 1963. A detailed study of the early Reconstruction, including party congressional politics on civil rights issues.

Donald, David, The Politics of Reconstruction, 1863-1867. Baton Rouge: Louisiana State University Press, 1965.

Duberman, Martin B., In White America: A Documentary Play. Boston: Houghton Mifflin, 1964. A dramatized representation of historical episodes in American Negro history.

Eaton, Clement, The Growth of Southern Civilization. New York: Harper, 1961. The author demonstrates the growing pressure of race relations on public affairs.

Elkins, Stanley M., Slavery: A Problem in American Institutional and Intellectual Life. Chicago: University of Chicago Press, 1959; reissued, New York: Universal Library, 1963. Using both comparative and social science data, Elkins' major theme is the development of a unique and more thorough form of slavery in America because of the lack of structured institutions. Minor themes are the influence of this fact on the Negro's personality and the nature of the opposition to slavery. Virtually a classic from date of publication, the book has relevance for many contemporary issues. The footnotes constitute an extensive bibliography.

Franklin, John Hope, From Slavery to Freedom: A History of American Negroes. New York: Knopf, 1947: 2nd ed., 1956. The second edition of this comprehensive historical work has been revised and enlarged, with a long classified bibliographical essay.

Franklin, John Hope, "History of Racial Segregation in the United States," Annals of the American Academy of Political and Social Science 304:1-9 (March 1956).

Franklin, John Hope, The Militant South. Cambridge: Harvard University Press, 1956. While primarily concerned with the period 1800-1861, the author delineates persisting traits and patterns of violence that have continued into the present.

Franklin, John Hope, "The New Negro History," Journal of Negro History 42:89-97 (April 1957).

Franklin, John Hope, Reconstruction After the Civil War. University of Chicago Press, 1961.

Franklin, John Hope, The Emancipation Proclamation. Garden City, N. Y.: Doubleday, 1963. By placing the Proclamation in its historical setting, the author essays to give its proper evaluation to a document of American freedom which he believes has been greatly neglected.

Franklin, John Hope, "The Two Worlds of Race: A Historical View," Daedalus 94:899-920 (Fall 1965).

Gara, Larry, The Liberty Line: The Legend of the Under-Ground Railroad. Lexington: University of Kentucky Press, 1961. The legend is revealed as largely melodrama. The work of rescue was chiefly carried out by free Negroes, not abolitionists. Valuable as showing how the legend grew.

Garraty, John A., ed., Quarrels that have Shaped the Constitution. New York: Harper, 1964. Included: C. Vann Woodward (Plessy v. Ferguson); Bruce Catton (Dred Scott); Alfred H. Kelly (Brown v. Board of Education).

Genovese, Eugene D., The Political Economy of Slavery: Studies in the Economy and Society of the Slave South. New York: Pantheon, 1965.

Ginzberg, Eli, and Hyman Berman, The American Worker in the Twentieth Century: A History Through Biographies. New York: Free Press, 1963. An attempt to portray American labor history through the words of the workers themselves. Includes some life histories of Negro workers, especially from the years since 1941.

Hughes, Langston, and Milton Meltzer, eds., A Pictorial History of the Negro in America. New ed., rev., New York: Crown, 1963. A startling and sharply revealing collection.

Kirwan, Albert D., Revolt of the Rednecks: Mississippi Politics, 1876-1925. Lexington: University of Kentucky Press, 1951; New York: Harper Torchbook, 1965. Demonstrates, among other themes, how the rise of white democracy, of the "rednecks," in the Lower South was regularly accompanied by the rise of racism.

Litwack, Leon F., North of Slavery: The Negro in the Free States, 1790-1860. University of Chicago Press, 1961. How the North resolved, or failed to resolve, its integration problems in the antebellum period. The author effectually shows that the haven to which the North Star beckoned the fugitive slave was a Jim Crow haven. Contains a bibliographical essay.

Logan, Rayford W., The Negro in American Life and Thought: The Nadir, 1877-1901. New York: Dial, 1954. Concerned chiefly with political and economic developments in the post-Reconstruction period, the author follows the steps by which Northern desires for peace with the South and for a free hand in Northern economic expansion were realized at the expense of relegating the Negro to second-class citizenship. Bibliographical references in footnotes.

Logan, Rayford W., The Negro in the United States: A Brief Review. Princeton, N. J.: Van Nostrand, 1957. Part I consists of a concise history of the Negro from 1619. Part II is a useful compilation of 25 documents of significance for that history, mostly key court decisions and executive orders from 1873 to 1954.

McPherson, James M., Abolitionists and the Negro in the Civil War and Reconstruction. Princeton University Press, 1964.

McPherson, James M., The Negro's Civil War: How American Negroes Felt and Acted During the War for the Union. New York: Pantheon, 1965. Impressive marshaling of evidence from which the Negroes emerge as vigorous participants on both the battle and intellectual fronts.

Mannix, Daniel P., Black Cargoes: The Story of the Atlantic Slave Trade: 1518-1865. New York: Viking, 1962. Critical bibliography.

Meier, August, Negro Thought in America, 1880-1915: Racial Ideologies in the Age of Booker T. Washington. Ann Arbor: University of Michigan Press, 1964. In this period, as a result of the conflict between adherents of DuBois and of Washington, Negro thought became dichotomized into an ideology of integration and an ideology of separation. Bibliography.

Quarles, Benjamin, The Negro in the American Revolution. Chapel Hill: University of North Carolina Press, 1961.

Record, Wilson, "The Development of the Communist Position on the Negro Question in the United States," Phylon 19:306-326 (Fall 1958).

Record, Wilson, Race and Radicalism: The NAACP and the Communist Party in Conflict. Ithaca: Cornell University Press, 1964. The author demonstrates that the Communist line in the 1930's had no more appeal to the Negroes than the back-to-Africa movement had in the 1830's, and that what the Negro wants is simply to be part of America.

Reimers, David M., White Protestantism and the Negro. New York: Oxford University Press, 1965. Covers the period from the eighteenth century to early 1960's.

Rose, Arnold M., "History with a Present Meaning," Commentary 24:542-546 (December 1957). A review of recent revisionist works on the Negro.

Savage, Henry, Jr., Seeds of Time, The Background of Southern Thinking. New York: Holt, 1959. An informal, somewhat impressionistic history of the South by a moderate native. Readable, but no new perceptions or views.

Scheiner, Seth M., Negro Mecca: A History of the Negro in New York City, 1865-1920. New York: New York University Press, 1965.

Sellers, Charles Grier, ed., The Southerner as American. Chapel Hill: University of North Carolina Press, 1960. Saunders Redding: "In this group of essays, the re-evaluation of Southern history and of the Southern mind, which W. J. Cash began and Vann Woodward has lifted to academic excellence, begins to prove its influence on historical thought and scholarship in the South."

Singletary, Otis A., Negro Militia and Reconstruction. Austin: Texas University Press, 1957.

Sloan, Irving J., The American Negro: A Chronology and Fact Book. Dobbs Ferry, N. Y.: Oceana Publications, 1965. Significant events in Negro life from Spanish explorations to the present.

Stampp, Kenneth M., The Peculiar Institution: Slavery in the Ante-Bellum South. New York: Knopf, 1956. The author begins by denying the dogma of the inferiority of the race, and proceeds, using a wide choice of records and documents, to a complete revision of the history of the "peculiar institution."

Stampp, Kenneth M., The Era of Reconstruction: 1865-1877. New York: Knopf, 1965. The author's purpose is to expose the falsehood of the Southern version of Reconstruction and to demonstrate both the discriminatory strategies of the South and the genuine concern of the Radical Republicans for Negro rights and welfare.

Tannenbaum, Frank, Slave and Citizen: The Negro in the Americas. New York: Knopf, 1947. An analysis of differences in treatment and development of Negroes in North and South America, effectively employing the comparative method.

Thorpe, Earl E., Negro Historians in the United States. Baton Rouge, La.: Fraternal Press, 1958.

Thorpe, Earl E., The Mind of the Negro: An Intellectual History of Afro-Americans. Baton Rouge, La.: Ortlieb Press, 1961. A social as well as an intellectual history, this book has as its thesis the proposition that the central theme of Negro thought has been the quest for freedom and equality. The author ranges from cultural ties with Africa, through nineteenth-century protest movements, the Washington-DuBois controversy, patterns of political behavior, down to contemporary Negro cultural life.

Wade, Richard C., Slavery in the Cities: The South, 1820-1860. New York: Oxford University Press, 1965. The author demonstrates that while slavery in urban areas was vastly different from that on the plantation, it was equally degrading, enforced by harsh municipal codes, restrictions on Negro association (e.g., in their churches), segregation, and fear. The majority were household slaves, but hotels, factories, railroads, and municipalities maintained large holdings whom they hired out for short-term jobs.

Weisberger, Bernard A., "The Dark and Bloody Ground of Reconstruction Historiography," Journal of Southern History 25:427-447 (November 1959). Bibliography in footnotes.

Wiley, Bell Irvin, Southern Negroes 1861-1865. New Haven: Yale University Press, 1938. Remains a very useful general treatment.

Woodson, Carter G., and Charles H. Wesley, The Negro in Our History. Washington, D. C.: Associated Publishers, 1922; 10th ed. rev. and enlarged. 1962. A work which remains of great usefulness.

Woodward, C. Vann, Origins of the New South, 1877-1913. Baton Rouge: Louisiana State University Press, 1951. The growth of the importance of industrial, commercial, and professional elements in Southern urban areas, and the effect on Southern thought and behavior. Extensive bibliography.

Woodward, C. Vann, The Strange Career of Jim Crow. New York: Oxford University Press, 1955; 2nd rev. ed. and Galaxy paperback, 1966. The strangeness of the case residing in the fact that Jim Crow was actually a late comer on the scene and not an immemorial character in the sanctified Southern "way of life." The revised edition contains new material on civil rights legislation, public accommodations and school segregation demonstrations, and racial clashes in Birmingham, Selma, Little Rock, Harlem, Los Angeles.

Woodward, C. Vann, The Burden of Southern History. Baton Rouge: Louisiana State University Press, 1960. Eight essays on the recent and contemporary South, the impact of urbanization and industrialization, the struggle over integration.

Woodward, C. Vann, "Flight From History: The Heritage of the Negro," Nation 201:142-146 (September 20, 1965). In 100th Anniversary Issue.

Woofter, Thomas J., Southern Race Progress: The Wavering Color Line. Washington, D. C.: Public Affairs Press, 1957. Autobiography of a Southerner covering racial events since the 1890's. The story of changing race relations, with emphasis on racial cooperation for regional progress.

Wright, Richard, Twelve Million Black Voices. New York: Viking, 1941. Informal folk history.

3. DEMOGRAPHY

Beshers, James M., "Delineation of Demographic Areas and the Contiguity Ratio," Proceedings of the Social Statistics Section, American Statistical Association. Washington, D. C., 1958.

Bogue, Donald J., The Population of the United States. Glencoe, Ill.: Free Press, 1959. Deals with period 1940-1958. See particularly chapter 7, "Color-Nativity-Race Composition," and chapter 26 for projections into the future.

Calef, Wesley C., and Howard J. Nelson, "Distribution of Negro Population in the United States," Geographical Review 46: 82-97 (January 1956).

Ezell, John Samuel, The South Since 1865. New York: Macmillan, 1963. Geographical, demographic, and social composition of the South.

Glick, Paul C., American Families. New York: Wiley, 1957. A volume in the Census Monograph Series. A demographic analysis of census data on American families, with most of the information gathered since 1944. Includes differentials between whites and nonwhites in marriage age, family composition, women in the labor force, marriage rates, separation, divorce, and widowhood statistics.

Hauser, Philip M., "Demographic Factors in the Integration of the Negro," Daedalus 94: 847-877 (Fall 1965).

Jackson, Eureal Grant, "Some Tendencies in Demographic Trends in Maryland, 1950-1956," Journal of Negro Education 26:514-519 (Fall 1957).

Lieberson, Stanley, Ethnic Patterns in American Cities. Glencoe, Ill.: Free Press, 1963.

Lyman, S.M., "Sepctrum of Color," Social Research 31:364-373 (Fall 1964). Concerning racial hybrids who inhabit the Eastern, Midwestern, and Southern United States.

"The Relative Status of the Negro Population in the United States," Journal of Negro Education 22:221-451 (Summer 1953). Entire issue; a general demographic survey.

Smith, T. Lynn, "The Changing Number and Distribution of the Aged Negro Population in the United States," Phylon 18:339-354 (Fall 1957).

Taeuber, Conrad, and Irene B. Taeuber, The Changing Population of the United States. New York: Wiley, 1958. A volume in the Census Monograph Series, prepared for the Social Science Research Council in cooperation with the Department of Commerce. With emphasis on the period 1890-1950, white-nonwhite differentials are presented on such matters as rates of growth, migrations and urbanization of nonwhites, marital status, families, education, fertility, and mortality.

Taeuber, Irene B., "Migration, Mobility and the Assimilation of the Negro," American Negro at Mid-Century, Population Bulletin, Population Reference Bureau, Inc., November 1958. The fundamental change in the Negro population has been not so much movement from South to North as the concentration in industrial areas in all sectors of the country.

Taeuber, Karl E., and Alma F. Taeuber, "Changing Character of Negro Migration," American Journal of Sociology 70:429-441 (January 1965).

Valien, Preston, "General Demographic Characteristics of the Negro Population in the United States," Journal of Negro Education 32:329-336 (Fall 1963).

Wattenberg, Ben, This U. S. A.: An Unexpected Family Portrait of 194,067,296 Americans Drawn From the Census. Garden City, N. Y.: 1965. Based on 1965 Census Bureau statistics and in collaboration with Richard M. Scammon, Director, U. S. Bureau of the Census. See particularly chs. 15 and 16.

4. BIOGRAPHY

Adams, Russell L., Great Negroes, Past and Present. Chicago: Afro-American Publishing Co., 1963.

The Autobiography of Malcolm X. New York: Grove, 1965. Prepared with the assistance of Alex Haley, who also supplies an epilogue.

Bennett, Lerone, Jr., What Manner of Man: A Biography of Martin Luther King, Jr. Chicago: Johnson, 1964. Assesses the King achievement through 1964, and considers various criticisms of his tactics.

Bontemps, Arna, One Hundred Years of Negro Freedom. New York: Dodd, Mead, 1961. Presented through the lives of Negro leaders from the Civil War to the present.

Broderick, Francis L., W. E. B. DuBois, Negro Leader In a Time of Crisis. Stanford, Calif.: Stanford University Press, 1959.

Brown, Claude, Manchild in the Promised Land. New York: Macmillan, 1965. The autobiography of a young man whose Harlem childhood and "education" included belonging to a gang, being sent to a school for "emotionally disturbed" boys and subsequently to a reform school, and who now, just graduated from Howard University, plans to study law. Good writing.

Cayton, Horace R., Long Old Road: An Autobiography. New York: Trident, 1965. Life of a distinguished sociologist, co-author of Black Metropolis and Black Workers.

Cherry, Gwendolyn, Ruby Thomas, and Pauline Willis, Portraits in Color: The Lives of Colorful Negro Women. Patterson, N. J.: Pageant, 1962.

Cronon, E. D., Black Moses. Madison, Wis.: University of Wisconsin Press, 1955. Biography of Marcus Garvey.

Davis, Sammy, Jr., with Jane and Burt Boyar, Yes I Can. New York: Farrar, 1965. Autobiography of a highly successful entertainer who has both surmounted his own racial struggles and contributed greatly to the cause of his fellow Negroes.

Douglass, Frederick, Narrative of the Life of Frederick Douglass, an American Slave, Written by Himself. Boston: Anti-Slavery Office, 1845; Cambridge, Mass.: Harvard University Press, 1960.

Gregory, Dick, with Robert Lipsyte, Nigger: An Autobiography. New York: Dutton, 1964. The vivid life story of a Negro entertainer who has actively engaged in the Negro protest movement.

Griffin, John H., Black Like Me. New York: Signet Books, 1962. The author, white, becomes cosmetically black to discover what it is like to be a Negro in the South.

Hawkins, Hugh, Booker T. Washington and His Critics: Problem of Negro Leadership. Boston: Heath, 1962. Bibliography.

Hedgeman, Anna Arnold, The Trumpet Sounds: A Memoir of Negro Leadership. New York: Holt, Rinehart, 1964. Fascinating account of the early--and recent-- years of the civil rights movement. The author deals chiefly with experiences of segregation in the North.

Hickey, Neil, and Ed Edwin, Adam Clayton Powell and the Politics of Race. New York: Fleet, 1965.

Holt, Rackham, George Washington Carver. Garden City, N. Y.: Doubleday, 1943; reissued 1963.

Holt, Rackham, Mary McLeod Bethune, A Biography. Garden City, N. Y.: Doubleday, 1964.

Isaacs, Harold R., "DuBois and Africa," Race 2:3-23 (November 1960).

Johnson, James Weldon, The Autobiography of an Ex-Colored Man. New York: Knopf, 1912; reissued New York: New American Library, 1948.

Johnson, James Weldon, Along My Way. New York: Viking, 1933. Memoirs.

Ottley, Roi, The Lonely Warrior: The Life and Times of Robert S. Abbott. Chicago: Regnery, 1955.

Reddick, Lawrence D., Crusader Without Violence. New York: Harper, 1959. Biography of Martin Luther King by a member of the faculty of Alabama State College and a witness of the Montgomery bus boycott.

Redding, Jay Saunders, On Being Negro in America. New York: Bobbs-Merrill, 1951; reissued 1962.

Redding, Jay Saunders, The Lonesome Road. Garden City, N. Y.: Doubleday, 1958. The story of the Negro's part in America told through the life stories of a number of Negroes, from Daniel Payne to Thurgood Marshall.

Rowan, Carl, Go South to Sorrow. New York: Random House, 1957. Life of a Negro journalist and diplomat.

Rudwick, Elliott M., W.E.B. DuBois: A Study in Minority Group Leadership. Philadelphia: University of Pennsylvania Press, 1960.

Washington, Booker T., Up From Slavery. New York: Doubleday, 1902; frequently republished, mostly recently Garden City, N. Y.: Doubleday, 1963. Washington's theme is the need for the Negro to seek economic rather than social advance.

White, Walter, How Far the Promised Land? New York: Viking, 1955. White's two most notable campaigns as executive secretary of the NAACP were for federal anti-lynching legislation and against President Hoover's nomination of anti-Negro Judge John J. Parker to the Supreme Court.

Who's Who in Colored America. New York: Who's Who in Colored America Corporation, 1927; 7th (and last) ed. 1950.

Williams, John A., This is My Country Too. New York: New American Library, 1965. Account of author's trip by automobile back and forth across the country, and of what, as a Negro, he encountered.

Wright, Richard, Black Boy. New York: Harper, 1937; New York: New American Library paperback, 1950. Harrowing record of the author's childhood and youth in Chicago.

II. DEFINITION AND DESCRIPTION

Any definition of the Negro in America inevitably begins with the subject of race. It would clearly serve no useful purpose to present here an extensive listing of works on general anthropology. Only a representative selection of such recent studies as may indicate the nature of current concern has been included. To be noted, perhaps, is the emergence of a new "racism," a trend which one cannot doubt is in large part reflex to the increasing impact on segregationists, in the North as well as in the South, of the pressure for racial equality in America. Wesley Critz George, professor of anatomy, emeritus, of the University of North Carolina and hardly a new racist, wrote his The Biology of the Race Problem (1962) for the purpose of supporting the Southern white-supremacist position, and Carleton Putnam's Race and Reason (1961), with its blunt assertions concerning the Negroes' inherent low capacity for civilization, has been one of the most publicized statements of white racial superiority. To the great majority of scientists, however, such purportedly "scientific" pronouncements represent merely a frantic effort to shore up discredited rationalizations for a decaying caste system, and a forceful repudiation of the entire racist position, particularly of Mr. Putnam's volume, was issued by the American Association for the Advancement of Science as a special report, "Science and the Race Problem," in the November 1963 issue of Science. It is doubtful that the work of Franz Boas will all have to be done over again, but obviously Thomas F. Gossett's intellectual history of the idea of race in America may require a sequel, particularly since legal challenges to miscegenation and intermarriage statutes and the processes of social assimilation can hardly fail to increase the incidence of ethnic hybridization--or mongrelization, as the white-supremacist terms interracial marriage.

The crucial point of departure for any social definition of the Negro must be the family, since it is from the family that the child gets his identity, his values, his goals. The large number of households headed by women, the devaluation of the male role, family disintegration due to joblessness, father absence, illegitimacy--too often this is the paradigm of the Negro family, especially in the cities, where for the immigrant the strains of dislocation act most disruptively on the family unit. Increasingly social scientists are insisting that the tasks of strengthening the Negro family and the Negro male role as protector and head of his family are two of the most imperative to be undertaken.

In the social organization of the Negro community, no institution has played so important a role as the Negro church. Franklin Frazier wrote

that "the Negro church has left its imprint upon practically every aspect
of Negro life." The Negro Freedom Movement has centered largely in the
churches, especially in the South, and Negro ministers, always looked to
as leaders by their communities, have played impressive parts in that
movement. The impulse of the aroused Christian conscience is now to
decry segregated churches, Negroes have engaged in "pray-ins," and
Joseph Washington, in his Black Religion, calls for the complete assimilation of Negroes with their white co-religionists. Not all Negroes hold
this position, however. There are Negro laymen who would lament the
loss of a fellowship that has meant much to them; there are Negro ministers who see themselves demoted in their social role, perhaps even deprived of pulpits.

In the examination of the larger Negro community, its organization and
social structures, Kenneth Clark has complained that too many social
scientists display "a preoccupation with trivia," and Whitney Young, writing in Ebony for September 1963, called for "new, current, and objective
research on the whole phenomenon of Negro class structure in this country, its existence, role, and behavior patterns." While there is a seem-
ingly endless stream of discussion of the "new Negro," talk of the role of
the growing middle class, the problems of Negro professional people, of
competition among leaders of the Negro community, it remains true that
there are no recent works of the comprehensiveness or the authoritative-
ness, not only of the massive Myrdal undertaking, but of such studies as
Franklin Frazier's on The Negro in the United States.

One of the often neglected sources of knowledge of the Negro community
has been the Negro press. Several cities support a number of Negro newspapers, and such a venerable institution as the Baltimore Afro-American,
or the influential Amsterdam News of New York, the Chicago Defender,
the Pittsburgh Courier, for example, would repay more consistent study
than they have received. The years since World War II have seen a tre-
mendous increase in the number and distribution of popular Negro magazines. Recently Ebony, the largest of these, celebrated its twentieth anniversary, announcing its circulation as 900,000, and the Negro Digest,
Jet, and Tan are regularly to be found on metropolitan newsstands.

Everett C. Hughes is fond of asking what he calls the "science-fiction"
question: "Suppose that tomorrow morning Americans were to wake up
blind to all the distinguishing marks of race; what would be the long- and
the short-term results?" The final subsection under Social Institutions
and Conditions can be said to address itself to considering the distinguished sociologist's question since it presents materials on intermarriage.

What it is to be the individual Negro, the "invisible man," the "black
boy," the "Bronzeville girl," must be examined from as wide a perspective

as the Negro community. In their recent volume, <u>Human Behavior: An Inventory of Scientific Findings</u>, Bernard Berelson and Gary Steiner observe that discrimination against a group leads to deprivations that in turn create characteristics in the deprived individuals which trigger further discrimination. The damage to the personality of the Negro child, the reinforcement of self-depreciation, were adduced by the Supreme Court as supporting grounds for finding public school segregation unconstitutional. To be a Negro is not simply to be a member of a minority group. It is to have been crippled by self-hatred, by a caste status no other American, no matter how lowly, ever experiences. For this reason examinations of Negro personality, evaluations of Negro intelligence, interpretation of Negro motivations and aspirations must be undertaken, as Thomas F. Pettigrew has pointed out, with a broadly social-psychological methodology.

Closely related to the total configuration of Negro life as well as to individual characteristics are matters of health, particularly of mental health. To these are added genetic health, certain disease patterns, health habits, questions of the accessibility and type of medical services available to the Negro, in addition to the issue of the nature and extent of discrimination against Negroes in the medical professions.

The final section under "Definition and Description" is on literature and folklore, so located because these works are vivid sources for knowledge of what it is to be a Negro. The themes of Negro novelists during the last few years have largely reflected present moods, present strife. There have been novels of race conflict North and South, of the Negro search for a new identity, of exile and return, of voter registration drives and of interracial housing: publishers are increasingly hospitable to the "strong" Negro book. Furthermore, white Americans are impelled by both curiosity and anxiety to find out what they can about these dark fellow Americans. There is an audience for the Negro poet, polemicist, playwright, but it has been remarked that the Negro writer has lacked a truly helpful audience, one that is both sympathetic and receptive and at the same time critical. Serious critical examination on any extensive scale has simply not been recently undertaken. For that reason, perhaps, one still turns to the earlier studies by Sterling Brown which are here included.

In addition we must note the close relation between sophisticated Negro literature and folk literature, including the spirituals, work songs, and the blues--and it is impossible entirely to separate either from music (for which reason we list one or two such works as LeRoi Jones's <u>Blues People</u>). The folk literature presents an extraordinarily dense picture of Negro experience, aspirations, and tragic sense of existence, as well as giving rich provision of sociological, psychological, and historical data.

We do well, however, to remember, in Ralph Ellison's words, that it is "an art form and thus a transcendence of those conditions created within the Negro community by the denial of social justice."

1. RACE

Alpenfels, Ethel, Sense and Nonsense About Race. New York: Friendship Press. 1957.

Barnicot, N., "Coon's Theory of Evolution," Observer Weekend Review, May 26, 1963.

Berry, Brewton, Race and Ethnic Relations. Boston: Houghton Mifflin, 1951; 3rd ed., 1965. A comparative view of racial and ethnic interaction which examines recent events in the United States and abroad from a sociological point of view.

Berry, Brewton, Almost White: A Study of Certain Racial Hybrids in the Eastern United States. New York: Macmillan, 1963.

Black, I., "Race and Unreason: Anti-Negro Opinion in Professional and Scientific Literature Since 1954," Phylon 26:65-79 (Spring 1965).

Boyd, William C., Genetics and the Races of Man. Boston: Little, Brown, 1954.

Boyd, William C., "Genetics and the Human Race," Science 140:1057-1064 (June 7, 1963).

Coon, Carleton S., The Origin of Races. New York: Knopf, 1962. A work which aroused much controversy for positing a theory of the stage of evolution at which various races have arrived.

Coon, Carleton S., with Edward E. Hunt, Jr., The Living Races of Man. New York: Knopf, 1965. Presenting a theory of the division of Man, as he is today, into five races.

Crowe, C. Lawson, "Race and Reason: A Study in Frustration," Christianity and Crisis July 9, 1962. Review of Carleton Putnam, Race and Reason: A Yankee View.

Dobzhansky, Theodosius, Mankind Evolving: The Evolution of the Human Species. New Haven: Yale University Press, 1962. Chapters on biology and culture in human evolution, environmentalism vs. hereditarianism, natural selection and survival of the fittest, evolution in process and in the future. Includes a discussion of race theories and categories, with critical suggestions as to the need to reformulate our thinking about such concepts.

Dobzhansky, Theodosius, "A Debatable Account of the Origin of the Races," Scientific American 208:169-172 (February 1963).

Dobzhansky, Theodosius, Heredity and the Nature of Man. New York: Harcourt, Brace, 1964. A distinguished philosopher of science warns against faddist "science" that presumes to find superiority or inferiority in individuals of one race or another, reminding the reader of scientists' inability to agree on what constitutes a race, and that it is not genes or color that carry the cultural heritage of a society.

Frazier, E. Franklin, "Racial Problems in World Society," in Jitsuichi Masuoka and Preston Valien, eds., Race Relations: Problems and Theory, Chapel Hill: University of North Carolina Press, 1961.

Garn, Stanley, Human Races. Springfield, Ill.: Thomas, 1961.

George, Wesley Critz, The Biology of the Race Problem. New York: Putnam Letters Committee, 1962. A work sponsored by a commission appointed by the Governor of Alabama.

Giles, E., and O. Elliot, "Race Identification from Cranial Measurements," Journal of Forensic Science 7:147 (April 1962).

Glass, Bentley, "On the Unlikelihood of Significant Admixture of Genes from the North American Indians in the Present Composition of the Negroes of the United States," American Journal of Human Genetics 7:368-385 (December 1955).

Gossett, Thomas F., Race: The History of an Idea in America. Dallas, Tex.: Southern Methodist University Press, 1963. The author traces the development of ideas on race in the United States from the seventeenth century to the present, drawing on evidence from literature, politics, the social sciences, and religion, and presents a survey both of race theory and of bigotry.

Haller, Mark H., Eugenics, Hereditarian Attitudes in American Thought. New Brunswick, N.J.: Rutgers University Press, 1963. Including attitudes toward Negroes. Bibliography.

Hernton, Calvin C., Sex and Racism in America. Garden City, N.Y.: Doubleday, 1965. Thesis: the race problem in America is inextricably bound up with sex. Purportedly a serious sociological study, but lacking substantial documentation and objectivity.

Herskovits, Melville J., The Anthropometry of the American Negro. New York: Columbia University Press, 1930. Estimates that 71 percent of American Negroes have some white ancestry.

Howells, William W., "Our Family Tree," New York Times Book Review Section, December 9, 1962. Review of Carleton Coon's The Origin of Races.

Hughes, Everett C., "The Nature of Racial Frontiers," in Jitsuichi Masuoka and Preston Valien, eds., Race Relations: Problems and Theory, Chapel Hill: University of North Carolina Press, 1961.

Ingle, Dwight J., "Racial Differences and the Future," Science 146:375-379 (October 16, 1964). "There is no sound structure of evidence and logic which compels a conclusion" on the issue of race and intelligence. "The concept of equality is meaningful only as it relates to civil rights and opportunities."

Isaacs, Harold R., "Blackness and Whiteness," Encounter 21:8-21 (August 1963).

Karrick, D. B., "What Constitutes a Negro: A Review of Legal Statutes," Journal of the National Medical Association 51:211-214 (May 1959).

Landes, Ruth, "Biracialism in American Society: A Comparative View," American Anthropologist 57:1253-1263 (December 1955).

"Legal Definition of Race," Race Relations Law Reporter 3:571 (June 1958).

Mangum, Charles S., Jr., The Legal Status of the Negro. Chapel Hill: University of North Carolina Press, 1940. See particularly chapter 1, "Who Is a Negro."

Mayer, Milton, "The Issue is Miscegenation," Progressive 23:8-18 (September 1959).

Mead, Margaret, "The Student of Race Problems Can Say. . . ," Race 3:3-9 (November 1961). Poses the question of whether our scientific knowledge of race differences is improving.

Morant, D.M., The Significance of Racial Differences. Paris: UNESCO, 1952.

Morrison, J. L., "Illegitimacy, Sterilization and Racism: A North Carolina Case History," Social Service Review 39:1-10 (March 1965).

Muse, Benjamin, "A Virginia View of 'Race and Reason,'" New South 16:12-16 (December 1961). A review of Carleton Putnam's book.

The Myths of Racial Integration. New York: American Jewish Congress. 1960.

Newby, I. A., Jim Crow's Defense: Anti-Negro Thought in America. 1900-1930. Baton Rouge: Louisiana State University Press, 1965. The rise and fall of the concept of innate Negro inferiority among scientists, social scientists, historians, and theologians.

Pollitzer, W. S., "The Negroes of Charleston: A Study of Hemoglobin Types, Serology, and Morphology," American Journal of Physical Anthropology 16:241 (1958).

Pollitzer, W. S., "Review of Coon's 'The Origin of Races,'" American Journal of Human Genetics 15:216-218 (June 1963).

Putnam, Carleton, Race and Reason: A Yankee View. Washington, D.C.: Public Affairs Press, 1961. Proclaims the inherent inferiority of Negroes to whites in their capacity for civilization.

Race and Science: The Race Question in Modern Science. New York: Columbia University Press, 1961. Includes a statement prepared by a conference convened by UNESCO on "The Nature of Race and Race Differences."

Redfield, Robert, "Ethnic Relations, Primitive and Civilized," in Jitsuichi Masuoka and Preston Valien, eds., Race Relations: Problems and Theory, Chapel Hill: University of North Carolina Press, 1961.

Schneider, Louis, "Race, Reason and Rubbish Again," Phylon 23:149-155 (Summer 1962). Review of Putnam's Race and Reason.

"Science and the Race Problem: A Report of the AAAS Committee on Science in the Promotion of Human Welfare," Science 142:558-561 (November 1963). In refutation of racism and specifically of Putnam's Race and Reason, the report concludes "that the available evidence on the measurable differences among racial groups cannot properly support a challenge to the principle of human equality which is assured by the Constitution of the United States."

Shapiro, M., "Blood Groups and Skin Colour in Human Anthropology," Journal of Forensic Medicine 1:2-10 (July-September 1953).

Smith, Samuel Stanhope, An Essay on the Causes of the Variety of Complexion and Figure

in the Human Species. Cambridge, Mass.: Harvard University Press, 1965. Edited and
with an introduction by Winthrop D. Jordan. Originally published in 1787, this essay by a
Presbyterian clergyman and president of the College of New Jersey (now Princeton
University) was an attempt to show that physical variety among the peoples of the world
was due to natural causes, and that all men belong to a single creation.

Snyder, Louis L., The Idea of Racialism: Its Meaning and History. Princeton, N.J.: Van
Nostrand, 1962. History of theories of racial differences.

Stanton, William, The Leopard's Spots: Scientific Attitudes Toward Race in America, 1815-
1859. Chicago: University of Chicago Press, 1960.

Stern, Curt, "The Biology of the Negro," Scientific American 191:81-85 (October 1954).

Thompson, Edgar T., and Everett C. Hughes, eds., Race: Individual and Collective Behavior.
Glencoe, Ill.: Free Press, 1958; reissued New York: Free Press paperback, 1965. An
anthology of readings directed to "the problem of understanding and dealing with an idea,
the idea of race" as related to "concrete social, political, demographic, and biological
problems." An extensive bibliography is of great value.

Tyler, Leona E., The Psychology of Human Differences. New York: Appleton, 1956. A
textbook which deals to some extent with race and nationality differences, especially in
chapter 5.

Van Den Berghe, Pierre L., "Hypergamy, Hypergenation, and Miscegenation," Human
Relations 13:83-91 (February 1960).

Washburn, Sherwood L., "The Study of Race," American Anthropologist 65:521-531 (June
1963). Bibliography.

"Who is a Negro?" University of Florida Law Review 11:235 (Summer 1958).

Wirth, Louis, and Herbert Goldhamer, "The Hybrid and the Problem of Miscengenation," in
Otto Klineberg, ed., Characteristics of the American Negro, New York: Harper, 1944.

Workman, P. L., B. S. Blumberg, and A. J. Cooper, "Selection, Gene Migration and Polymorphic Stability in a U.S. White and Negro Population," American Journal of Human
Genetics 15:429-437 (December 1963).

2. SOCIAL INSTITUTIONS AND CONDITIONS

a. Family and Child Rearing

Bell, R. R., "Lower Class Negro Mothers' Aspirations for their Children," Social Forces
43:493-500 (May 1965).

Billingsley, Andrew, and Amy Tate Billingsley, "Negro Family Life in America," Social
Service Review 39:310-319 (September 1965).

Blau, Zena Smith, "Exposure to Child-Rearing Experts: A Structural Interpretation of
Class-Color Differences," American Journal of Sociology 69:596-608 (May 1964).

Blood, Robert O., and Donald M. Wolfe, Husbands and Wives: The Dynamics of Married
Living. New York: Free Press, 1963. An investigation of the differences between white
and Negro families in respect of the relative "power" of men and women.

Brody, Eugene B., "Color and Identity Conflict in Young Boys: Observations of Negro
Mothers and Sons in Urban Baltimore," Psychiatry, May 1963.

Burton, R. V., and J. W. M. Whiting, "The Absent Father and Cross-Sex Identity," Merrill-
Palmer Quarterly 7:85-95 (April 1961).

Cavan, Ruth Shonle, "Negro Family Disorganization and Juvenile Delinquency," Journal of
Negro Education 28:230-239 (Summer 1959).

D'Andrade, R. G., "Father Absence and Cross-sex Identification," unpub. doc. diss., Harvard University, 1962.

Davis, Allison W., and Robert J. Havighurst, The Father of the Man: How Your Child Gets
His Personality. Boston: Houghton Mifflin, 1947. Study of child-rearing practices among
Negroes at the lower-class and middle-class levels in Chicago.

Deasy, Leila C., and Olive W. Quinn, "The Urban Negro and Adoption of Children," Child
Welfare, November 1962.

Derbyshire, R. L., et al., "Family Structure of Young Adult Negro Male Mental Patients: Preliminary Observations from Urban Baltimore," Journal of Nervous and Mental Disease 136:245-251 (March 1963).

Edwards, G. Franklin, "Marriage and Family Life Among Negroes," Journal of Negro Education 32:451-465 (Fall 1963).

Erikson, Erik, "Memorandum on Identity and Negro Youth," Journal of Social Issues 20:29-42 (October 1964).

Frazier, E. Franklin, "Ethnic Family Patterns: The Negro Family in the United States," American Journal of Sociology 54:432-438 (May 1948).

Frazier, E. Franklin, The Negro Family in the United States. Chicago: University of Chicago Press, 1939; revised and abridged edition, with a new introduction by Nathan Glazer, 1966. Vivid accounts of the lower-class Negro world and the family system. Published in many editions since 1939, it is still the major work on the subject.

Frazier, E. Franklin, "Problems and Needs of Negro Children," Journal of Negro Education 19:269-277 (Summer 1950).

Frazier, E. Franklin, "The Negro Family in Chicago," in E. W. Burgess and D. J. Bogue. eds., Contributions to Urban Sociology. Chicago: University of Chicago Press, 1964.

Frumkin, Robert M., "Attitudes of Negro College Students Toward Intrafamily Leadership and Control," Marriage and Family Living 16: 252-253 (August 1954).

Ginzberg, Eli, ed., The Nation's Children: Vol. I, The Family and Social Change; Vol. II, Development and Education; Vol. III, Problems and Prospects. New York: Columbia University Press, 1960. Essays and articles written for Golden Anniversary White House Conference on Children and Youth.

Gipson, Theodore H., "Educational Status of the Negro Family in Louisiana," Journal of Educational Sociology 32:83-89 (October 1958).

Gould, Flo, and Richard K. Kerckhoff, "Family Life Education for the Biracial Community," Journal of Negro Education 29:187-190 (Spring 1960).

"Growing Up Negro," American Child, January 1963. Entire issue.

Himes, Joseph S., "Interrelation of Occupational and Spousal Roles in a Middle Class Negro Neighborhood," Marriage and Family Living 22:362 (November 1960).

Himes, Joseph S., "Some Work-Related Cultural Deprivations of Lower-Class Negro Youths," Journal of Marriage and the Family 26:447-449 (November 1964).

Illegitimacy and its Impact on the Aid to Dependent Children Program. Washington, D.C.: Bureau of Public Assistance, U.S. Department of Health, Education and Welfare, 1960.

Jenkins, Wesley W., "An Experimental Study of the Relationship of Legitimate and Illegitimate Birth Status to School and Personal and Social Adjustment of Negro Children," American Journal of Sociology 64:169-173 (September 1958).

Kunstadter, Peter, "A Survey of the Consanguine or Matrifocal Family," American Anthropologist 65:56-66 (February 1963).

Lewis, Hylan, "The Changing Negro Family," in Eli Ginzberg, ed., The Nation's Children, vol. I. New York: Columbia University Press, 1960. Points out that the new task of the Negro family is to prepare its members to live in a desegregated world.

Lincoln, C. Eric, "The Absent Father Haunts the Negro Family," New York Times Magazine, November 28, 1965.

Middleton, Russell, and Snell Putney, "Dominance in Decisions in the Family: Race and Class Differences," American Journal of Sociology 65:605-609 (May 1960).

Moynihan, Daniel Patrick, "Employment, Income, and the Ordeal of the Negro Family," Daedalus 94:745-770 (Fall 1965).

Moynihan, Daniel Patrick, The Negro Family: The Case for National Action. Washington, D.C.: G.P.O., 1965. Prepared for Office of Policy Planning and Research of the Department of Labor, the author documents and describes the destructive effects of the breakdown of the Negro family, particularly in urban ghettos.

"Negro Families in Rural Wisconsin: A Study of their Community Life," Madison, Wis.: Governor's Commission on Human Rights, 1959.

Nordlie, Esther B., and Sheldon C. Reed, "Follow-up Adoption Counseling for Children of Possible Racial Admixture," Child Welfare, September 1962.

Opler, Marvin K., "The Influence of Ethnic and Class Structures on Child Care," Social Problems 3:12-21 (July 1955).

Orshansky, Mollie, "Children of the Poor," Social Science Research Council Bulletin, July 1963.

Radin, Norma, and Constance K. Kamii, "The Child-Rearing Attitudes of Disadvantaged Negro Mothers and Some Educational Implications," Journal of Negro Education 34:138-146 (Spring 1965).

Rainwater, Lee, "Crucible of Identity: The Negro Lower-Class Family," Daedalus 95:172-216 (Winter 1966).

Reiss, I. L., "Premarital Sexual Permissiveness Among Negroes and Whites," American Sociological Review 29:688-698 (October 1964).

Rovere, Richard, "Letter from Washington," New Yorker September 11, 1965. Review of the findings of the report The Negro Family: The Case for National Action by Daniel Patrick Moynihan.

Ryan, William, "Savage Discovery: The Moynihan Report," The Nation 201:380-384 (November 22, 1965).

Schwartz, M., "Northern United States Negro Matriarchy: Status Versus Authority," Phylon 26:18-24 (Spring 1965).

Setleis, Lloyd, "Civil Rights and the Rehabilitation of the AFDC [Aid to Families with Dependent Children] Clients," Social Work 9:3-9 (April 1964).

Smith, Howard P., and Marcia Abramson, "Racial and Family Experience Correlates of Mobility Aspirations," Journal of Negro Education 31:117-124 (Spring 1962).

Strodtbeck, Fred L., "The Poverty-Dependency Syndrome of the ADC Female-Based Negro Family," American Journal of Orthopsychiatry 34:216-217 (March 1964). Analysis of the "progressive estrangement of indigent female-based Negro families in urban centers."

Tietze, C., and S. Lewit, "Patterns of Family Limitation in a Rural Negro Community," American Sociological Review 18:563-564 (October 1953).

Vincent, Clark, Unmarried Mothers. Glencoe, Ill., Free Press, 1961. Vincent reports that 64 percent of all illicit live births in America are to Negro mothers.

Wakin, E., Portrait of a Middle-Class Negro Family at the Edge of Harlem. New York: Morrow, 1965.

Weinstein, E. A., and P. N. Geisel, "Family Decision Making over Desegregation," Sociometry 25:21-29 (March 1961).

Woods, Sister Frances Jerome, and Alice Cunningham Lancaster, "Cultural Factors in Negro Adoptive Parenthood," Social Work, October 1962.

b. Religious Life and Negro Churches

Bardolph, Richard, "Negro Religious and Educational Leaders in 'Who's Who in America,' 1936-1955," Journal of Negro Education 26:182-192 (Spring 1957).

Beynon, Erdmann Doane, "The Voodoo Cult Among Negro Migrants in Detroit," American Journal of Sociology 43:894-907 (May 1938).

Bontemps, Arna, "Rock, Church, Rock," in Sylvester C. Watkins, ed., Anthology of American Negro Literature, New York: Random House, 1944. On Gospel Singers and their religious orientation.

Brewer, J. Mason, The Word on the Brazos. Austin: University of Texas Press, 1953. Negroes' reactions to their preachers.

Burr, Nelson R., Critical Bibliography of Religion in America. Princeton: Princeton University Press, 1961. See pp. 348-381 for "The Negro Church."

Cantril, Hadley, The Psychology of Social Movements. New York: Wiley, 1941. Good section on Father Divine and his "kingdom."

Cayton, Horace, "E. Franklin Frazier: A Tribute and a Review," Review of Religious Research 5:137-142 (Spring 1964). Review of Frazier's posthumously published The Negro Church.

Clark, Elmer T., The Small Sects in America. Nashville, Tenn.: Abingdon, 1937; rev. ed. 1949. Chapter 4 deals in detail with Negro sects, distinguishing five types of "charismatic" sects, most of them offshoots of regular churches, and all of them characterized by revivalism, emotionalism, and evangelism.

Daniel, Vattel E., "Ritual and Stratification in Chicago Negro Churches," American Sociological Review 7:353-358 (June 1942). Describes types of behavior in ecstatic cults.

Drake, St. Clair, and Horace Cayton, Black Metropolis. New York: Harcourt, Brace, 1945; Harper Torchbook, 1963. Chapter on religion has good descriptive material, as well as useful treatment of Negro ministers in a Northern urban community.

Fauset, Arthur H., Black Gods of the Metropolis. Philadelphia: University of Pennsylvania Press, 1944. Most valuable study of Negro cults in the city.

Frazier, E. Franklin, The Negro Church in America. New York: Schocken, 1963. Gunnar Myrdal: "His posthumous work on the Negro is a brief but brilliant analysis of the historical origin and the present situation of a crucially important institution of the American Negro people." Wise and humane.

Gillard, John T., Colored Catholics in the United States. Baltimore, Md.: The Josephite Press, 1941.

Glenn, Norval D., "Negro Religion and Negro Status in the United States," in Louis Schneider, ed., Religion, Culture, and Society. New York: Wiley, 1964.

Gustafson, James M., "The Clergy in the United States," Daedalus 92:724-744 (Fall 1963). Includes material on the unsatisfactory state of Negro Protestant ministry and their inadequate education.

Haynes, Leonard L., The Negro Community Within American Protestantism. Boston: Christopher, 1953.

Herskovits, Melville J., "Social History of the Negro," in C. Murchison, ed., Handbook of Social Psychology, Worcester, Mass.: Clark University Press, 1935. Contains material on place of song in Negro religious service.

Herskovits, Melville J., The Myth of the Negro Past. New York: Harper, 1941; Boston: Beacon, 1958. Chapter 7, "The Contemporary Scene: Africanisms in Religious Life," is most important for the subject of religion.

James, Willis Laurence, "The Romance of the Negro Folk Cry in America," Phylon 16:15-30 (Spring 1955). Material on the rise and amazing spread of Gospel singing.

Johnson, Benton, "Do Holiness Sects Socialize in Dominant Values?" Social Forces 39:309-316 (May 1961).

Johnson, Charles S., Growing Up in the Black Belt. Washington, D.C.: American Council on Education, 1941. Contains excellent section on the rural church.

Johnson, James Weldon, God's Trombones. New York: Viking, 1927. Contains striking descriptions of Negro sermons.

Johnston, Ruby F., The Development of Negro Religion. New York: Philosophical Library, 1954.

Johnston, Ruby F., The Religion of Negro Protestants. New York: Philosophical Library, 1956.

Jones, Raymond J., A Comparative Study of Religious Cult Behavior Among Negroes with Special Reference to Emotional Conditioning Factors. Howard University Studies in the Social Sciences, vol. 2 no. 2, Washington, D.C.: Howard University Graduate School, 1940. Classifies different types of cults from standpoint of whether they are faith-healing, or holiness, or claiming Islamic origins, etc.

Lee, J. Oscar, "Religion Among Ethnic and Racial Minorities," Annals of the American Academy of Political and Social Science 332:112-124 (November 1960).

Lenski, Gerhard, The Religious Factor: A Sociologist's Inquiry. Garden City, N.Y.: Doubleday, 1961. Religion and ethnic factors.

McLaughlin, Wayman B., "Symbolism and Mysticism in the Spirituals," Phylon 24:69-77 (Spring 1963).

Mays, Benjamin E., and Joseph W. Nicholson, The Negro's Church. New York: Institute of Social and Religious Research, 1933. A thorough and searching account not only of the Negro's church but of its role in the Negro community.

Muelder, Walter, "Recruitment of Negroes for Theological Studies," Review of Religious Research 5:152-156 (Spring 1964).

Murray, Florence, ed., The Negro Handbook. New York: Macmillan, 1949. Lists (pp. 288-289) numbers of members of Negro Baptist, Methodist, Presbyterian, Lutheran denominations as of date.

Niebuhr, H. Richard, The Social Sources of Denominationalism. New York: Holt, 1929. Contains material on early Negro churches in America.

Parker, Robert A., The Incredible Messiah. Boston: Little, Brown, 1937. Father Divine. New Day was the weekly publication of the movement.

Pope, Liston, "Caste in the Church," Survey Graphic 36:59-60, 101-104 (January 1947).

Pope, Liston, The Kingdom Beyond Caste. New York: Friendship, 1957. Contains material on the religious affiliations of American Negroes.

Pope, Liston, "The Negro and Religion in America," Review of Religious Research 5:142-152 (Spring 1964).

Powdermaker, Hortense, After Freedom: A Cultural Study in the Deep South. New York: Viking, 1939. Contains interesting accounts of Negro revivals.

Rasky, Frank, "Harlem's Religious Zealots," Tomorrow 9:11-17 (November 1949). Elder Lightfoot Solomon Michaux, "Happy Am I Prophet," and Mother Rosa Artimus Horne, "Pray for Me Priestess."

Reid, Ira De Augustine, "Let Us Prey!" Opportunity 4:274-278 (September 1926). On Negro churches in the city.

Sweet, William W., The American Churches. New York: Abingdon, 1948. Contains material on the religious affiliations of American Negroes.

Thurman, Howard, Deep River: Reflections on the Religious Insight of Certain of the Negro Spirituals. New York: Harper, 1955.

Washington, Joseph R., Jr., "Are American Negro Churches Christian?" Theology Today 20:76-86 (April 1963).

Washington, Joseph R., Jr., Black Religion: The Negro and Christianity in the United States. Boston: Beacon, 1964. This book is a combination of empirical and historical data concerning the churches of the Negro in America and a tract for the times urging the "assimilation" of the Negro into the "mainstream" of the Christian "mission."

Weatherford, Willis Duke, American Churches and the Negro: An Historical Study from Early Slave Days to the Present. Boston: Christopher, 1957.

Winter, Gibson, The Suburban Captivity of the Churches. Garden City, N.Y.: Doubleday, 1961. Contains section on middle-class Negro churches.

Woodson, Carter G., The History of the Negro Church. Washington, D.C.: Associated Publishers, 1921. A most important general study. Continues to be basic to study of the Negro church.

c. Social Class

Back, Kurt W., and Ida Harper Simpson, "The Dilemma of the Negro Professional," Journal of Social Issues 20:60-70 (April 1964). Data collected from students at Howard Medical School, to find out what kind of students sought protection by functioning in a Negro environment.

Bloom, R., et al., "Race and Social Class as Separate Factors Related to Social Environment," American Journal of Sociology 70:471-476 (January 1965).

Blue, John J., Jr., "Patterns of Racial Stratification: A Categoric Typology," Phylon 20:364-371 (Winter 1959).

Davidson, William, "Our Negro Aristocracy," Saturday Evening Post 235:9-16 (January 13, 1962).

Dykeman, Wilma, and James Stokely, "New Southerner: The Middle Class Negro," New York Times Magazine, August 9, 1959.

Edwards, G. Franklin, The Negro Professional Class. Glencoe, Ill.: Free Press, 1959. A study of occupational mobility among Negroes in professions and its influence on development of a differentiated middle class. Emphasis on generational picture and occupational goals.

Edwards, G. Franklin, "The Changing Status and Self-Image of Negroes in the District of Columbia," Journal of Intergroup Relations, Winter 1962-1963.

Frazier, E. Franklin, "The Status of the Negro in the American Social Order," Journal of Negro Education 4:293-307 (July 1935).

Frazier, E. Franklin, "The Negro Middle Class and Desegregation," Social Problems 4:291-301 (April 1957).

Frazier, E. Franklin, Black Bourgeoisie. Glencoe, Ill.: Free Press, 1957; reissued with new preface by the author, New York: Collier, 1962. A social and political tract, in which the author castigates the Negro middle class.

Frumkin, Robert M., "Race, Occupation, and Social Class in New York," Journal of Negro Education 27:62-65 (Winter 1958).

Glenn, Norval D., "Some Changes in the Relative Status of American Negroes," Phylon 24:109-122 (Summer 1963).

Glenn, Norval D., "Negro Prestige Criteria: A Case Study in the Bases of Prestige," American Journal of Sociology 68:645-657 (November 1963). Education the most important prestige criterion.

Hill, M. C., and T. D. Ackiss, "Social Classes: A Frame of Reference for the Study of Negro Society," Social Forces 22:92-98 (October 1943).

King, Charles E., "The Process of Social Stratification Among an Urban Southern Minority Population," Social Forces 31:352-355 (May 1953). How urban Negroes in a North Carolina city (21 percent Negro) stratify themselves socially.

Kleiner, R. J., and H. Taylor, Social Status and Aspirations in Philadelphia's Negro Population. Philadelphia: Commission on Human Relations, 1962.

Lees, Hannah, "The Making of a Negro Middle Class," Reporter 31:41-44 (October 8,1964).

Lincoln, C. Eric, "The Negro's Middle-Class Dream," New York Times Magazine, October 25, 1964.

Meier, August, "Negro Class Structure and Ideology in the Age of Booker T. Washington," Phylon 23:258-266 (Fall 1962).

Meier, August, and David Lewis, "History of the Negro Upper Class in Atlanta, Georgia, 1890-1958," Journal of Negro Education 28:128-139 (Spring 1959).

Montague, Joel B., and Edgar G. Epps, "Attitudes Toward Social Mobility as Revealed by Samples of Negro and White Boys," Pacific Sociological Review 1:81-84 (Fall 1958).

Parker, Seymour, and Robert J. Kleiner, "Status Position, Mobility, and Ethnic Identification of the Negro," Journal of Social Issues 20:85-102 (April 1964).

Record, Wilson, "Social Stratification and Intellectual Roles in the Negro Community," British Journal of Sociology 8:235-255 (September 1957). Bibliography.

Solzbacher, Regina, "Occupational Prestige in a Negro Community," American Catholic Sociological Review 22:250-257 (Fall 1961).

Warner, W. Lloyd, American Life: Dream and Reality. Rev. ed., Chicago: University of Chicago Press, 1962. Includes chapter on "Social Class and Color Caste in America," which presents general formulation of the problem as well as results from widely contrasting field studies.

Warner, W. Lloyd, and Leo Srole, The Social Systems of American Ethnic Groups. New Haven: Yale University Press, 1946.

Young, Whitney M., Jr., "The Role of the Middle-Class Negro," Ebony 18:66-71 (September 1963). The author gives his specifications for future Negro leaders. They must be equipped "to understand and cope with the complex psychological, socio-economic factors in our society that create poverty, ignorance, prejudice and deprivation. Social scientists can best fulfill this role."

d. Community Life, Leaders, and Organizations

"America's One Hundred Most Influential Negroes," Ebony 18:228-232 (September 1963)

Babchuk, Nicholas, and Ralph V. Thompson, "The Voluntary Associations of Negroes," American Sociological Review 27:647-655 (October 1962).

Bardolph, Richard, The Negro Vanguard. New York: Rinehart, 1959. An historical study of leading Negroes, emphasizing their origins and careers. Organized chronologically, the final section, 1936-1959, describes the acculturation process of large numbers of achieving Negroes, their approach to white middle-class values, attitudes, and behavior.

Barth, Ernest A. T., and Baha Abu-Laban, "Power Structure and the Negro Sub-Community," American Sociological Review 24:69-76 (February 1959).

Beattie, Walter M., Jr., "The Aging Negro: Some Implications for Social Welfare Services," Phylon 21:131-135 (Summer 1960).

Bell, Daniel, The End of Ideology. Glencoe, Ill.: Free Press, 1959; New York: Collier, 1960. An eminently readable as well as illuminating work which, although only incidentally concerned with the Negro, casts important light on the relation of the Negro community to the whole society.

Bennett, Lerone, Jr., The Negro Mood. Chicago: Johnson, 1964; Ballantine paperback, 1965. In one essay, "The Black Establishment," the author considers the Negro elites, their social organizations, their community roles, and the relationships of this establishment to the world of white power.

Bittle, William E., and Gilbert Geis, "Racial Self-Fulfillment and the Rise of an All-Negro Community in Oklahoma," Phylon 18:247-260 (Fall 1957).

Blalock, H. M., and Ann P. Blalock, "Situational Factors and Negro Leadership Activity in a Medium-Sized Community," Journal of Negro Education 29:85-90 (Winter 1960).

Breed, Warren, "Group Structure and Resistance to Desegregation in the Deep South," Social Problems 10:84-94 (Summer 1962).

Burgess, M. Elaine, Negro Leadership in a Southern City. Chapel Hill: University of North Carolina Press, 1962. Case histories of public issues and of Negro participation in them. In general, Negro civic leaders in the South tend to be in greater agreement on goals and to receive greater support from their followers than in the North.

Claye, Clifton M., "Leadership Behavior Among Negro School Principals," Journal of Negro Education 31:521-526 (Fall 1962).

Coleman, J. S., "Community Disorganization," in R. K. Merton and R. A. Nisbet, eds., Contemporary Social Problems. New York: Harcourt, Brace, 1961.

Diggs, C., Jr., "Negro Congressmen," Negro History Bulletin 27:114+ (February 1964).

DuBois, W. E. B., Economic Cooperation Among American Negroes. Atlanta, Ga.: Atlanta University Press, 1907. For historical retrospect. Economic cooperation among Negroes began with church groups after the Civil War.

Edwards, G. Franklin, "Community and Class Realities: The Ordeal of Change," Daedalus 95:1-23 (Winter 1966).

Fogel, David, "Social Work and Negroes," Phylon 18:277-285 (Fall 1957).

Gerber, Irwin, "The Effects of the Supreme Court's Desegregation Decision on the Group Cohesion of New York City's Negroes," Journal of Social Psychology 58:295-303 (December 1962).

Geschwender, J. A., "Social Structure and the Negro Revolt: An Examination of Some Hypotheses," Social Forces 43:248-256 (December 1964).

Gulley, William H., "Relative Effectiveness in Negro and White Voluntary Associations," Phylon 24:172-183 (Summer 1963).

Handlin, Oscar, The Newcomers: Negroes and Puerto Ricans in a Changing Metropolis. Cambridge: Harvard University Press, 1959. See especially chapter on the "Forms of Social Action" for discussion of problem of leadership and social action in Negro (and Puerto Rican) groups.

Heer, David M., "The Attractiveness of the South to Whites and Nonwhites: An Ecological Study," American Sociological Review 28:101-108 (February 1963).

Henderson, E. B., "Washington Who's Who: Pigskin Club," Negro History Bulletin 26:190-195 (March 1963). On Negro clubs.

Himes, Joseph, "Changing Social Roles in the New South," Southwestern Social Science Quarterly 37:234-242 (December 1956). Because of growing Negro militancy.

Himes, Joseph, "Negro Teen-Age Culture," Annals of the American Academy of Political and Social Science 338:91-101 (November 1961).

Himes, Joseph, and Margaret L. Hamelett, "The Assessment of Adjustment of Aged Negro Women in a Southern City," Phylon 23:139-147 (Summer 1962).

Hunter, Floyd, Community Power Structure: A Study of Decision Makers. Chapel Hill: University of North Carolina Press, 1953. The "Regional City" which the author studies is Atlanta, Ga.; his conclusion, that "none of the leaders in the Negro community may operate in the same echelons of power as the top leaders in the total community."

Johnson, Charles S., "A Southern Negro's View of the South," Journal of Negro Education 26:4-9 (Winter 1957).

Killian, Lewis M., and Charles Grigg, "Negro Perceptions of Organizational Effectiveness," Social Problems 11:380-388 (Spring 1964). Organizations Negroes prefer to look to for help are, according to Florida sample, NAACP, Democratic Party, federal government, Urban League, Negro church, labor unions, in that order.

Killian, Lews M., and Charles Grigg, Racial Crisis in America: Leadership in Conflict. Englewood, N.J.: Prentice-Hall, 1964. With Southern cities as their setting, the authors examine the attitudes of both white and Negro leaders, the operation and effectiveness of community biracial committees, and the significance of the Negro repudiation of accommodation in favor of militant protest under new, young leaders.

Killian, Lewis M., and Charles U. Smith, "Negro Protest Leaders in a Southern Community," Social Forces 38:253-257 (March 1960).

Kirkhart, Robert O., "Minority Group Identification and Group Leadership," Journal of Social Psychology 59:111-117 (February 1963).

Larkins, John R., Patterns of Leadership Among Negroes in North Carolina. Raleigh, N.C.: Irving-Stone, 1959.

Lewis, Hylan, "Innovations and Trends in the Contemporary Southern Community," Journal of Social Issues 10:19-27 (January 1954). A class analysis of Southern Negroes emphasizing the changes brought about by increasing urbanization.

Lewis, Hylan, Blackways of Kent. Chapel Hill: University of North Carolina Press, 1955. A distinguished study of Negroes in a small South Carolina mill town. The author has done some of the most creative work in the area of racial culture patterns. Rejecting the idea that there is such a thing as a distinctively "Negro culture," he finds class status, economic status the more powerful determinants.

Lewis, Hylan, and Mozell Hill, "Desegregation, Integration, and the Negro Community," Annals of the American Academy of Political and Social Science 304:116-123 (March 1956).

Lohman, Joseph D., and D. C. Reitzes, "Deliberately Organized Groups and Racial Behavior," American Sociological Review 19:342-344 (June 1954).

Ottenburg, Simon, "Leadership and Change in a Coastal Georgia Negro Community," Phylon 20:7-18 (Spring 1962).

Pfautz, Harold W., "The Power Structure of the Negro Sub-Community: A Case Study and a Comparative View," Phylon 23:156-166 (Summer 1962).

Pfautz, Harold W., "The New 'New Negro': Emerging American," Phylon 24:360-368 (Winter 1963).

Rohrer, John H., and Munro S. Edmonson, eds., The Eighth Generation: Cultures and Personalities of New Orleans Negroes. New York: Harper, 1960. Designed as a follow-up to Davis and Dollard, The Children of Bondage.

Rose, Arnold M., "Voluntary Associations Under Conditions of Competition and Conflict," Social Forces 34:159-163 (December 1955).

Rose, Arnold M., "New and Emerging Negro Problems," Journal of Intergroup Relations 1:71-75 (Spring 1960). The author considers that gaining acceptance, training for higher types of employment, and acculturation are the newer problems for Negroes, especially in the North.

Smuts, Robert W., "The Negro Community and the Development of Negro Potential," Journal of Negro Education 26:456-465 (Fall 1957). The chief responsibility of the Negro community is to broaden the horizon of Negro youth by fighting for better education and thus stimulating their motivation.

Thompson, Daniel C., The Negro Leadership Class. Englewood Cliffs, N.J.: Prentice-Hall, 1963. With his focus on New Orleans from 1940 to 1960, the author traces the origins of Negro leaders, the influences that have formed the leadership class, and the rapidly changing patterns of that leadership, and furnishes detailed and candid data on the problems of the Negro leader both within and outside his own society.

Walker, Jack L., "The Functions of Disunity: Negro Leadership in a Southern City," Journal of Negro Education 32:227-236 (Summer 1963).

Williams, Avon, "Negro Subculture, The White Man's Problem," New South 16:7-9 (October 1961).

Wilson, James Q., Negro Politics: The Search for Leadership. Glencoe, Ill.: Free Press, 1960. A valuable study of contemporary Negro politics in Northern cities, this volume is an examination of the leadership level of Negro community life, with the main emphasis on Chicago.

Wilson, James Q., "The Strategy of Protest: Problems of Negro Civic Action," Journal of Conflict Resolution 5:291-303 (September 1961). The author examines 17 issues involving Negroes in Chicago between 1958 and 1960.

Woodson, Carter G., The Negro Professional Man and the Community. Washington, D.C.: Association for the Study of Negro Life and History, 1934. Most comprehensive study in this field up to date of publication, and still very useful.

e. The Press

N. W. Ayer & Sons, <u>Directory of Newspapers and Periodicals</u>, Philadelphia, 1965, pp. 1406-1407. Published annually.

Bayton, J. A., and E. Bell, "An Exploratory Study of the Role of the Negro Press," <u>Journal of Negro Education</u> 20:8-15 (Winter 1951).

Bennett, Lerone, Jr., "Founders of the Negro Press," <u>Ebony</u> 19:96-98+ (July 1964).

Brooks, Maxwell R., <u>The Negro Press Re-examined: Political Content of Leading Negro Newspapers.</u> Boston: Christopher, 1959.

Brown, Warren, comp., <u>Check List of Negro Newspapers in the United States, 1827-1946.</u> Jefferson City, Mo.: School of Journalism, Lincoln University, 1946.

"Negro Press Marks 135th Anniversary," <u>Editor and Publisher</u> 95:13 (March 17, 1962).

"The Negro Press: 1955," <u>Time</u> 66:64+ (November 7, 1955).

Ottley, Roi, <u>The Lonely Warrior: The Life and Times of Robert S. Abbott.</u> Chicago: Regnery, 1955. Vivid picture of a Negro newspaperman, founder of the Chicago <u>Defender</u>, with some discussion of the role of the Negro press in strengthening Negro racial consciousness.

Rinder, Irwin D., "A Sociological Look into the Negro Pictorial," <u>Phylon</u> 20:169-177 (Summer 1959).

Rosen, Bernard C., "Attitude Changes Within the Negro Press Toward Segregation and Discrimination," <u>Journal of Social Psychology</u> 62:77-84 (February 1964).

Waters, Enoc P., "The Negro Press: A Call for Change," <u>Editor and Publisher</u> 95:67-68 (May 12, 1962).

f. Intermarriage

Annella, Sister M., "Some Aspects of Interracial Marriage in Washington, D.C.," <u>Journal of Negro Education</u> 25:380-391 (Fall 1956).

Barron, Milton L., <u>People Who Intermarry.</u> Syracuse, N.Y.: Syracuse University Press, 1948.

Barron, Milton L., "Research on Intermarriage: A Survey of Accomplishments and Prospects," <u>American Journal of Sociology</u> 57:249-255 (November 1951).

Broderick, C. B., "Social Heterosexual Development Among Urban Negroes and Whites," <u>Journal of Marriage and the Family</u> 27:200-203 (May 1965).

Burma, John H., "Research Note on the Measurement of Interracial Marriage," <u>American Journal of Sociology</u> 57:587-589 (May 1952). In California after annulment of anti-miscegenation law.

Burma, John H., "Interethnic Marriage in Los Angeles, 1948-1959," <u>Social Forces</u> 42:156-165 (December 1963). Study of marriage license records of Los Angeles County: Negro-white and Filipino-white most common. Rates at the end of the period triple those at beginning.

Clark, Henry, "Thinking About the Unthinkable in Race Relations," <u>Social Action</u> 30:17-22 (May 1964).

"The Constitutionality of Miscegenation Statutes," <u>Howard Law Journal</u> 1:87-100 (January 1955).

Cummins, J. D., and J. L. Kane, Jr., "Miscegenation, the Constitution, and Science," <u>Dicta</u> 38:24 (February 1961).

Doherty, J. F., <u>Moral Problems of Interracial Marriage.</u> Washington, D.C.: Catholic University of America Press, 1949.

Ehrenzweig, A. A., "Miscegenation in the Conflict of Laws," <u>Cornell Law Quarterly</u> 45:659 (Summer 1960).

Golden, Joseph, "Characteristics of the Negro-White Intermarried in Philadelphia," <u>American Sociological Review</u> 18:177-183 (April 1953).

Golden, Joseph, "Patterns of Negro-White Intermarriage," <u>American Sociological Review</u> 19:144-147 (April 1954).

Golden, Joseph, "Social Control of Negro-White Intermarriage," <u>Social Forces</u> 36:267-269 (March 1958).

Golden, Joseph, "Facilitating Factors in Negro-White Intermarriage," <u>Phylon</u> 20:273-284 (Fall 1959).

Gordon, Albert I., Intermarriage: Interfaith, Interracial, Interethnic. Boston: Beacon, 1964.
    A survey dealing with prospects and problems of intermarriage in America.
Harte, Thomas J., "Trends in Mate Selection in a Tri-Racial Isolate," Social Forces
    37:215-221 (March 1959).
"Intermarriage and the Race Problem," U.S. News and World Report 55:84-93 (November
    18, 1963).
Larsson, Clotye M., Marriage Across the Color Line. Chicago: Johnson, 1965.
Lewis, Anthony, "Race, Sex and the Supreme Court," New York Times Magazine November
    22, 1964. On sex and the Southern caste system as exemplified in the case, McLaughlin
    v. Florida.
"Marriage Across Racial Lines," statement of the Council for Christian Social Action,
    United Church of Christ (New York, 1960).
"Racial Intermarriage--A Constitutional Problem," Western Reserve Law Review 11:93
    (December 1959).
"Racial Intermarriage--A Symposium," Social Progress 4:3-35 (February 1960). Presented
    by the United Presbyterian Church.
Riley, L. H., "Miscegenation Statutes: A Re-evaluation of their Constitutionality in Light of
    Changing Social and Political Conditions," Southern California Law Review 32:28 (Fall
    1958).
Shaffer, Helen B., "Mixed Marriage," Editorial Research Reports 1:381-398 (May 24, 1961).
Walton, Edmund L., Jr., "Present Status of Miscegenation Statutes," William and Mary Law
    Review 4:28-35 (January 1963).
Weinberger, Andrew D., "A Reappraisal of the Constitutionality of Miscegenation Statutes,"
    Cornell Law Quarterly 42:208 (Winter 1957).
Wilharm, John H., Jr., "Racial Intermarriage--a Constitutional Problem," Western
    Reserve Law Review 11:93 (December 1959).
Zabel, William D., "Interracial Marriage and the Law," Atlantic 216:75-79 (October 1965).

3. INDIVIDUAL CHARACTERISTICS

a. Personality

Allport, Gordon W., Pattern and Growth in Personality. New York: Holt, 1961.
Anastasi, Anne, "Psychological Research and Educational Desegregation," Thought 35:421-
    429 (Fall 1960).
Ausubel, D. P., "Ego Development Among Segregated Negro Children," Mental Hygiene
    42:362-369 (July 1958).
Axline, Virginia M., "Play Therapy and Race Conflict in Young Children," Journal of
    Abnormal and Social Psychology 18:300-310 (July 1948).
Axline, Virginia M., "Play Therapy Procedures and Results," American Journal of Ortho-
    psychiatry 25:618-626 (July 1955).
Ball, J. C., "Comparison of MMPI Profile Differences Among Negro-White Adolescents,"
    Journal of Clinical Psychology 16:304-307 (July 1960).
Bandure, A., and R. H. Walters, Adolescent Aggression. New York: Ronald, 1959.
Beck, Samuel J., et al., "Segregation-Integration: Some Psychological Realities," American
    Journal of Orthopsychiatry 28:12-35 (January 1958). In order to remedy the damages of
    segregation, "the indicated pattern of therapeutic intervention is prompt and effective
    action for integration."
Berdie, R. F. B., "Playing the Dozens," Journal of Abnormal and Social Psychology 42:120-
    121 (January 1947). Examination of an aggressive type of behavior, especially charac-
    teristic of Negroes, which follows a formalized pattern of exchange of insults.
Berger, E. M., "Relationships Among Acceptance of Self, Acceptance of Others, and MMPI
    Scores," Journal of Counseling Psychology 2:279-284 (Winter 1955).
Brewster, Edward E., and Martelle D. Trigg, "Moral Values Among Negro College Students:
    A Study of Cultural and Racial Determinants," Phylon 23:286-293 (Fall 1962).

Brody, Eugene B., "Color and Identity Conflict in Young Boys, II," Archives of General Psychiatry 10:354-360 (April 1964).

Burton, R. V., and J. W. M. Whiting, "The Absent Father and Cross-Sex Identity," Merrill-Palmer Quarterly 7:85-95 (April 1961).

Butcher, James, Brenda Ball, and Eva Ray, "Effects of Socio-economic Level on MMPI Differences in Negro-white College Students," Journal of Counseling Psychology 11:83-87 (Spring 1964).

Butts, Hugh F., "Skin Color Perception and Self-Esteem," Journal of Negro Education 32:122-128 (Spring 1963).

Chein, Isidor, "What are the Psychological Effects of Segregation Under Conditions of Equal Facilities?" International Journal of Opinion and Attitude Research 3:229 (1949). Cited in 1954 decision Brown v. Board of Education.

Clark, Kenneth B., "Effect of Prejudice and Discrimination on Personality Development," Midcentury White House Conference on Children and Youth, 1950. Cited in 1954 decision Brown v. Board of Education.

Clark, Kenneth B., Prejudice and Your Child, Boston: Beacon, 1955; 2nd ed. enlarged, Beacon paperback, 1963.

Clark, Kenneth B., "Color, Class, Personality and Juvenile Delinquency," Journal of Negro Education 28:240-251 (Summer 1959).

Clark, Kenneth B., and J. Barker, "The Zoot Effect in Personality: A Race Riot Participant," Journal of Abnormal and Social Psychology 40:143-148 (April 1945).

Clark, Kenneth B., and Mamie P. Clark, "Racial Identification and Preference in Negro Children," in Eleanor Maccoby, et al., eds., Readings in Social Psychology, New York: Holt, 1958.

Clinard, Marshall B., and Donald L. Noel, "Role Behavior of Students from Negro Colleges in a Non-Segregated University Situation," Journal of Negro Education 27:182-188 (Spring 1958).

Coles, Robert, "Racial Identity in School Children," Saturday Review 46:56-57+ (October 19, 1963).

Coles, Robert, "Southern Children Under Desegregation," American Journal of Psychiatry 120:332-344 (October 1963).

Coles, Robert, "Racial Conflict and a Child's Question," American Journal of Ortho-psychiatry 34:218-219 (March 1964).

Coles, Robert, "Public Evil and Private Problems: Segregation and Psychiatry," Yale Review 54:513-531 (June 1965).

Coles, Robert, "'It's the Same, but It's Different,'" Daedalus 94:1107-1132 (Fall 1965). What it means to be a Negro examined through the study of Negro school children and of migrant workers in the South.

Conyers, James E., and T. H. Kennedy, "Negro Passing: To Pass or Not To Pass," Phylon 24:215-223 (Fall 1963).

Cook, Stuart W., "Desegregation: A Psychological Analysis," American Psychologist 12:1-13 (January 1957).

Dai, Bingham, "Problems of Personality Development Among Negro Children," in Clyde Kluckhohn and Harry A. Murray, eds., Personality in Nature, Society and Culture. New York: Knopf, 1953.

D'Amico, Louis A., "Problem Behavior in Negro Schools," Journal of Negro Education 26:72-74 (Winter 1957). Review of recent research.

Davis, Arthur P., "Jesse B. Semple: Negro American," Phylon 15:21-28 (Spring 1954). Semple is Langston Hughes' "Simple." He exemplifies the pressures of Jim Crow living, and his responses show his confused racial thinking, his inconsistent role playing, etc.

Derbyshire, Robert L., and Eugene B. Brody, "Social Distance and Identity Conflict in Negro College Students," Sociology and Social Research 48:301-314 (April 1964).

Deutscher, Isaac, and Isidor Chein, "The Psychological Effects of Enforced Segregation: A Survey of Social Science Opinion," Journal of Psychology 26:259-287 (October 1948). Cited in 1954 decision Brown v. Board of Education.

Dreger, R. M., "Comparative Psychological Studies of Negroes and Whites in the United States: A Reclarification," Psychological Bulletin 60:35-39 (January 1963).

Dreger, R. M., and K. S. Miller, "Comparative Psychological Studies of Negroes and Whites in the United States," Psychological Bulletin 57:361-402 (September 1960).

Epps, Edgar G., Irwin Katz, and Leland Axelson, "Relation of Mother's Employment to Intellectual Performance of Negro College Students," Social Problems 11:414-418 (Spring 1964). Among Southern Negro college students, sons of working mothers are more strongly motivated and achieve more highly.

Erikson, Erik H., "The Concept of Identity in Race Relations: Notes and Queries," Daedalus 95:145-171 (Winter 1966).

Fishman, Jacob R., and Solomon, Frederic, "Youth and Social Action, I: Perspectives on the Student Sit-in Movement," American Journal of Orthopsychiatry 33:872-882 (October 1963). The effects of social change and crisis on personality and identity formation.

Fishman, Jacob R., and Solomon, Frederic, "Youth and Social Action, II: Action and Identity Formation in the First Student Sit-in Demonstration," Journal of Social Issues 20:36-45 (April 1964). A case study of one student.

Fishman, Joshua A., "Childhood Indoctrination for Minority Group Membership," Daedalus 90:329-349 (Spring 1961).

Fontinell, Eugene, "The Identity of James Baldwin," Interracial Review 35:194-199 (September 1962).

Frazier, E. Franklin, Negro Youth at the Crossways. Washington, D.C.: American Council on Education, 1940. A study which describes the experiences of Negro boys and girls living in Washington, D.C., and Louisville, Ky., in terms of how these experiences determine personality development.

Gaier, Eugene L., and Helen S. Wambach, "Self-Evaluation of Personality Assets and Liabilities of Southern White and Negro Students," Journal of Social Psychology 51:135-143 (February 1960).

Gist, Noel P., and William S. Bennett, Jr., "Aspirations of Negro and White Students," Social Forces 42:40-48 (October 1963).

Gordon, D.N., "Note on Negro Alienation," American Journal of Sociology 76:477-478 (January 1965).

Gore, Pearl M., and J. B. Rotter, "A Personality Correlate of Social Action," Journal of Personality 31:58-64 (March 1963). An experimental testing of student willingness to participate in protest action.

Grossack, Martin M., "Psychological Effects of Segregation in Buses," Journal of Negro Education 25:71-74 (Winter 1956).

Grossack, Martin M., "Group Belongingness Among Negroes," Journal of Social Psychology 43:167-180 (February 1956).

Grossack, Martin M., "Some Personality Characteristics of Southern Negro Students," Journal of Social Psychology 46:125-131 (August 1957).

Grossack, Martin M., "Group Belongingness and Authoritarianism in Southern Negroes--A Research Note," Phylon 18:261-266 (Fall 1957).

Haggstrom, Warren C., "Segregation, Desegregation, and Negro Personality," Integrated Education 1:19-23 (October-November 1963).

Hammer, E. F., "Frustration-Aggression Hypothesis Extended to Socioracial Areas: Comparison of Negro and White Children's H-T-P's," Psychiatric Quarterly 27:597-607 (1953).

Hayakawa, S. I., "The Semantics of Being Negro," Review of General Semantics 10:163-175 (1953). Address to the Urban League of St. Louis, February 12, 1953.

Hayakawa, S. I., Symbol, Status, and Personality. New York: Harcourt, Brace, 1963. Distortion of language for various purposes, among them to encourage suspicion of Negro for white. See especially chapter 6.

Hindman, Baker M., "The Emotional Problems of Negro High School Youth Which are Related to Segregation and Discrimination in a Southern Urban Community," Journal of Educational Sociology 27:115-127 (September 1953).

Hokanson, J. E., and G. Calden, "Negro-white Differences on the MMPI," Journal of Clinical Psychology 16:32-33 (January 1960).

Hughes, J. H., and G. C. Thompson, "A Comparison of the Value Systems of Southern Negro and Northern White Youth," Journal of Educational Psychology 45:300-309 (July 1954).

Iscoe, Ira, Martha Williams, and Jerry Harvey, "Age, Intelligence, and Sex as Variables in the Conformity Behavior of Negro and White Children," Child Development 35:451-460 (June 1964).

Jackson, Esther Merle, "The American Negro and the Image of the Absurd," Phylon 23:359-371 (Winter 1962).

Johnson, Edwina C., "The Child in the Prestige Vacuum," Integrated Education 1:13-26 (December 1963-January 1964).

Johnson, Robert B., "Negro Reactions to Minority Group Status," in Milton L. Barron, ed., American Minorities, New York: Knopf, 1957. A study of an upstate New York community of 60,000 population, 3 percent Negro.

Kardiner, Abram, and Lionel Ovesey, The Mark of Oppression: Explorations in the Personality of the American Negro. New York: Norton, 1951; Cleveland: World, 1962, a Meridian reprint. A study of Negro personality based on psychoanalytic investigation of 25 Negroes.

Karon, Bertram P., The Negro Personality: A Rigorous Investigation of the Effects of Culture. New York: Springer, 1958. The book addresses itself to the question: "What does it feel like to live as a member of a caste in an otherwise democratic society?" A substantial--and readable--work which includes a study of the differences between Northern and Southern Negroes. Useful statistics.

Katz, Irwin, and Charles Greenbaum, "Effects of Anxiety, Threat, and Racial Environment on Task Performance of Negro College Students," Journal of Abnormal and Social Psychology 66:562-567 (June 1963).

Kerckhoff, A. C., and T. C. McCormick, "Marginal Status and Marginal Personality," Social Forces 34:48-55 (October 1955).

Killens, John Oliver, "Explanation of the 'Black Psyche,'" New York Times Magazine, June 7, 1964. Repudiates "Gunga Din" role--which he considers more accurate epithet than "Uncle Tom."

Kvaraceus, William C., Negro Self-Concept: Implications for School and Citizenship. Medford, Mass.: Lincoln Filene Center for Citizenship and Public Affairs, Tufts University, 1964.

Lapouse, Rema, and Mary A. Monk, "Behavior Deviations in a Representative Sample of Children: Variation by Sex, Age, Race, Social Class and Family Size," American Journal of Orthopsychiatry 34:436-446 (April 1964).

Levin, David, "James Baldwin's Autobiographical Essays: The Problem of Negro Identity," Massachusetts Review 5:239-247 (Winter 1964).

Luchins, Abraham S., and Edith H. Luchins, "Personality Impressions from Communications Reflecting Attitudes Toward Segregation," Journal of Social Psychology 58:315-330 (December 1962).

Middleton, Russell, "Alienation, Race, and Education," American Sociological Review 28:973-977 (December 1963).

Middleton, Russell, and John Moland, "Humor in Negro and White Sub-Cultures: A Study of Jokes Among University Students," American Sociological Review 24:61-69 (February 1959).

Miller, C., C. Wertz, and S. Counts, "Racial Differences on the MMPI," Journal of Clinical Psychology 17:159-161 (April 1961).

Millstein, G., "A Negro Says It With Jokes," New York Times Magazine, April 30, 1961.

Milner, Esther, "Some Hypotheses Concerning the Influence of Segregation on Negro Personality Development," Psychiatry 16:291-297 (August 1953).

Mischel, W., "Preference for Delayed Reinforcement and Social Responsibility," Journal of Abnormal and Social Psychology 62:1-7 (January 1961).

Mischel, W., "Delay of Gratification, Need for Achievement, and Acquiescence in Another Culture," Journal of Abnormal and Social Psychology 62:543-552 (May 1961).

Mischel, W., "Father-Absence and Delay of Gratification: Cross-Cultural Comparisons," Journal of Abnormal and Social Psychology 63:116-124 (July 1961).

Mitchell, Lonnie E., "Aspiration Levels of Negro Delinquent, Dependent, and Public School Boys," Journal of Negro Education 26:80-85 (Winter 1957).

Morland, J. Kenneth, "Racial Recognition by Nursery School Children in Lynchburg, Virginia," Social Forces 37:132-137 (December 1958).

Morland, J. Kenneth, "Racial Self-Identification: A Study of Nursery School Children," American Catholic Sociological Review 24:231-242 (Fall 1963).

Mussen, Paul, and Luther Distler, "Masculinity, Identification, and Father-Son Relationships," Journal of Abnormal and Social Psychology 59:350-356 (September 1959).

Myers, Henry J., and Leon Yochelson, "Color Denial in the Negro," Psychiatry 11:39-46 (February 1948).

"Negro American Personality," Journal of Social Issues 20:1-145 (April 1964). Entire issue, edited by Thomas F. Pettigrew and Daniel C. Thompson. See particularly Pettigrew's article, "Negro American Personality: Why Isn't More Known?" for exposition of problem.

Palermo, D. S., "Racial Comparisons and Additional Normative Data on the Children's Manifest Anxiety Scale," Child Development 30:53-57 (March 1959).

Pennington, Stewart, and Lonnie E. Mitchell, "Sex Differences in Reactions to Minority Group Status," Journal of Negro Education 28:35-41 (Winter 1959).

Pettigrew, Thomas F., A Profile of the Negro American. Princeton, N.J.: Van Nostrand, 1964. A work which brings together an impressive amount of clinical material on the Negro personality, together with studies of behavioral traits. The author demonstrates the need for the development of a broad social psychological theory of Negro American personality. Extensive bibliography.

Powdermaker, Hortense, "The Channeling of Negro Aggression by the Cultural Process," American Journal of Sociology 48:750-758 (May 1943). Discusses concealment of aggression by two nonaggressive roles Negroes have been assigned: the faithful slave and the faithful, meek Negro.

Price, Arthur Cooper, "A Rorschach Study of the Development of Personality Structure in White and Negro Children in a Southeastern Community," Genetic Psychology Monographs 65:3-52 (1962).

Prothro, James W., and Charles U. Smith, "The Psychic Cost of Segregation," Adult Education 5:179-181 (1955).

Prothro, James W., and Charles U. Smith, "Ethnic Differences in Authoritarian Personality," Social Froces 35:334-338 (May 1957). Bibliography.

Psychiatric Aspects of School Desegregation: Report No. 37. New York: Group for the Advancement of Psychiatry Publications Office, 1957.

Radzinski, J. M., "The American Melting Pot: Its Meaning to Us," American Journal of Psychiatry 115:873-886 (April 1959).

Rohrer, J. H., and M. S. Edmonson, The Eighth Generation. New York: Harper, 1960. This study is a follow-up twenty years later of the people described by Davis and Dollard in Children of Bondage. Problems of racial identification and individual identity stressed throughout.

Rosen, Bernard C., "Race, Ethnicity, and the Achievement Syndrome," American Sociological Review 24:47-60 (February 1959).

Secord, P. F., and E. S. Berscheid, "Stereotyping and the Generality of Implicit Personality Theory," Journal of Personality 31:65-78 (March 1963).

Seeman, Melvin, "Intellectual Perspective and Adjustment to Minority Status," Social Problems 4:142-153 (January 1956).

Singer, S. L., and B. Stefflre, "A Note on Racial Differences in Job Values and Desires," Journal of Social Psychology 43:333-337 (May 1956).

Smith, Charles U., and James W. Prothro, "Ethnic Differences in Authoritarian Personality," Social Forces 35:334-338 (May 1957).

Spock, Benjamin, "Children and Discrimination," Redbook 123:30+ (September 1964).

Stevenson, H. W., and E. C. Stewart, "A Developmental Study of Racial Awareness in Young Children," Child Development 29:399-409 (September 1958).

Taylor, Dalmas A., "The Relationship Between Authoritarianism and Ethnocentrism in Negro College Students," Journal of Negro Education 31:455-459 (Fall 1962).

Trent, Richard D., "The Relation Between Expressed Self-Acceptance and Expressed Attitudes Toward Negroes and Whites Among Negro Children," Journal of Genetic Psychology 91:25-31 (September 1957).

Vaughan, Graham M., "Concept Formation and the Development of Ethnic Awareness," Journal of Genetic Psychology 103:93-103 (September 1963).

Vaughan, Graham M., "Ethnic Awareness in Relation to Minority Group Membership," Journal of Genetic Psychology 105:119-130 (September 1964).

Veroff, J., J. W. Atkinson, Shiela C. Feld, and G. Gurin, "The Use of Thematic Apperception to Assess Motivation in a Nationwide Interview Study," Psychological Monographs 74:12:1-12 (1960).

Volkan, U., "Five Poems by Negro Youngsters Who Faced a Sudden Desegregation," Psychiatric Quarterly 37:607-617 (October 1963).

Vontress, Clemmont E., "The Negro Against Himself," Journal of Negro Education 32:237-242 (Summer 1963).

Weaver, E. K., "How Do Children Discover They Are Negroes?" Understanding the Child 24:108-112 (1955).

Witmer, Helen, and Ruth Kotinsky, eds., Personality in the Making. New York: Harper, 1952. Fact-finding report of the Midcentury White House Conference on Children and Youth. Chapter 6 was cited in 1954 decision Brown v. Board of Education.

Woronoff, Israel, "Negro Male Identification Problems," Journal of Educational Sociology 36:30-32 (September 1962).

Yarrow, Marian R., and Bernard Lande, "Personality Correlates of Differential Reactions to Minority Group-Belonging," Journal of Social Psychology 38:253-272 (November 1953).

b. Intelligence

Anastasi, Anne, "Intelligence and Family Size," Psychological Bulletin 53:187-209 (May 1956).

Anastasi, Anne, and Rita D'Angelo, "A Comparison of Negro and White Pre-School Children in Language Development and Goodenough Draw-a-Man I.Q.," Journal of Genetic Psychology 81:147-165 (December 1952).

Bloom, Benjamin S., Stability and Change in Human Characteristics. New York: Wiley, 1964. See review by Bruno Bettelheim in New York Review, September 10, 1964, and flurry of rejoinders by Dr. Robert Coles, Susan Bove, and Dr. Melvin Rubenstein in issue of October 22. At issue: whether deprived child's achievement levels can be altered after 4 or 5 years.

Bond, Horace Mann, "Cat on a Hot Tin Roof," Journal of Negro Education 27:519-523 (Fall 1958). A review of Audrey Shuey's judgments on Negro intelligence and a general consideration of intelligence tests and the Negro.

Carson, Arnold S., and A. I. Rabin, "Verbal Comprehension and Communication in Negro and White Children," Journal of Educational Psychology 51:47-51 (April 1960).

Deutsch, Martin, "The Disadvantaged Child and the Learning Process: Some Social, Psychological and Developmental Considerations," in A. H. Passow, ed., Education in Depressed Areas. New York: Teachers College Bureau of Publications, Columbia University, 1963.

Deutsch, Martin, and Bert Brown, "Social Influences in Negro-White Intelligence Differences," Journal of Social Issues 10:24-35 (April 1964).

Deutsch, Martin, et al., "Guidelines for Testing Minority Group Children," Journal of Social Issues 20:129-148 (April 1964).

"Did you find that there was much difference in the ability of Negro children to receive and profit by instruction?" Southern Regional Council Report No. L-13, December 15, 1959.

Edmonds, William S., "Oh, That Median Score--The Bane of Negro Pupils," Journal of Negro Education 31:75-77 (Winter 1962).

Fulk, Byron E., and Thomas W. Harrell, "Negro-White Army Test Scores and Last School Grade," Journal of Applied Psychology 36:34-35 (February 1952).

Garfunkel, F., and B. Blatt, "Standardization of Intelligence Tests on Southern Negro School Children," Training School Bulletin 60:94-99 (August 1963).

Garrett, Henry E., "Klineberg's Chapter on Race and Psychology: A Review," Mankind Quarterly 1:15-22 (1960).

Garrett, Henry E., "The Equalitarian Dogma," Mankind Quarterly 1:253-257 (1961). The "equalitarian dogma" is a hoax, embraced for purely ideological purposes, and its supporters ignore the "scientific facts that would prove Negroes as a group are intellectually inferior to whites."

Garrett, Henry E., "The SPSSI and Racial Differences," American Psychologist 17:260-263 (May 1962).

Gustafson, Lucille, "Relationship Between Ethnic Group Membership and the Retention of Selected Facts Pertaining to American History and Culture," Journal of Educational Sociology 31:49-56 (October 1957). The minority group will remain unretentive to the extent that it is kept outside the larger group.

Hammer, E. F., "Comparison of the Performances of Negro Children and Adolescents on Two Tests of Intelligence, One an Emergency Scale," Journal of Genetic Psychology 84: 85-93 (March 1954).

Higgins, C., and Cathryne Sivers, "A Comparison of Stanford-Binet and Colored Raven Progressive Matrices I.Q.'s for Children with Low Socioeconomic Status," Journal of Consulting Psychology 22:465-468 (December 1958).

Hobart, Charles W., "Underachievement Among Minority Group Students: An Analysis and a Proposal," Phylon 24:184-196 (Summer 1963).

Horton, Carrell P., and E. Perry Crump, "Growth and Development XI. Descriptive Analysis of the Backgrounds of 76 Negro Children Whose Scores are Above or Below Average on the Merrill-Palmer Scale of Mental Tests at Three Years of Age," Journal of Genetic Psychology 100:225-265 (June 1962).

Hunt, J. M., Intelligence and Experience. New York: Ronald, 1951. Intelligence not an inherited capacity, genetically fixed, but a set of processes that, within wide hereditary limits, is subject to experiential factors.

Iscoe, Ira, and John Pierce-Jones, "Divergent Thinking, Age, and Intelligence in White and Negro Children," Child Development 35:785-798 (September 1964).

Jensen, Arthur R., "A Statistical Note on Racial Differences in the Progressive Matrices," Journal of Consulting Psychology 23:273-274 (June 1959).

John, Vera P., "The Intellectual Development of Slum Children: Some Preliminary Findings," American Journal of Orthopsychiatry 33:813-822 (October 1963). Patterns of linguistic and cognitive behavior.

Johnson, Granville B., Jr., "A Comparison of Two Evaluation Instruments for the Analysis of Academic Potential of Negro Children," Phylon 20:44-47 (Spring 1959).

Kennedy, Wallace A., and Ronald S. Lindner, "A Normative Study of the Goodenough Draw-a-Man Test on Southeastern Negro Elementary School Children," Child Development 35:33-62 (March 1964).

Kennedy, W. A., et al., "Use of the Terman-Merrill Abbreviated Scale on the 1960 Stanford-Binet Form L-M on Negro Elementary School Children of the Southeastern United States," Journal of Consulting Psychology 27:456-457 (October 1963).

Kennedy, W. A., et al., "A Normative Sample of Intelligence and Achievement of Negro Elementary School Children in the Southeastern United States," Monographs of the Society for Research in Child Development 28:1:1-112 (1963).

Klineberg, Otto, Race and Psychology. Paris: UNESCO, 1951. Pamphlet.

Klineberg, Otto, "Negro-White Differences in Intelligence Test Performance: A New Look at an Old Problem," American Psychologist 18:198-203 (April 1963). "The science of psychology can offer no support to those who see in the accident of inherited skin color or other physical characteristics any excuse for denying to individuals the right to full participation in American democracy."

Klineberg, Otto, ed., Characteristics of the American Negro. New York: Harper, 1944. Although dated, these six essays present useful summaries of psychological studies up to 1944, and indicate techniques out of which later, and more accurate, methods have developed.

Klineberg, Otto, et al., "On Race and Intelligence: A Joint Statement," American Journal of Orthopsychiatry 27:420-422 (April 1957). On the untenability of any theory of inherent racial inequality.

Knobloch, Hilda, and B. Pasamanick, "Further Observations on the Behavioral Development of Negro Children," Journal of Genetic Psychology 83:137-157 (September 1953).

Krech, David, and Richard Crutchfield, Elements of Psychology. New York: Knopf, 1958. Includes some discussion of racial differences in intelligence.

Lee, Everett S., "Negro Intelligence and Selective Migration: A Philadelphia Test of the Klineberg Hypothesis," American Sociological Review 16:227-233 (April 1951). In the main, substantiated by independent evidence in Philadelphia.

Long, Howard Hale, "The Relative Learning Capacities of Negroes and Whites," Journal of Negro Education 26:121-134 (Spring 1957).

McCord, William M., and Nicholas J. Demerath, III, "Negro Versus White Intelligence: A Continuing Controversy," Harvard Educational Review 28:120-135 (Spring 1958). Bibliography.

McGurk, Frank, "On White and Negro Test Performance and Socio-economic Factors," Journal of Abnormal and Social Psychology 48:448-450 (July 1953).

McGurk, Frank, "Socio-economic Status and Culturally Weighted Test Scores of Negro Subjects," Journal of Applied Psychology 37:276-277 (August 1953).

McGurk, Frank, "Psychological Tests: A Scientist's Report on Race Differences," U.S. News and World Report 41:92-96 (September 21, 1956).

McGurk, Frank, "Negro vs. White Intelligence--An Answer," Harvard Education Review 29: 54-62 (Winter 1959). The author, professor of Psychology at Villanova University, has, as his purpose, to show that "Negroes as a group do not possess as much capacity as whites as a group."

McGurk, Frank, "Psychological Test Score Differences and the 'Culture Hypothesis,'" Mankind Quarterly 1:165-175 (January 1961).

McQueen, Robert, and Browning Churn, "The Intelligence and Educational Achievement of a Matched Sample of White and Negro Students," School and Society 88:327-329 (September 24, 1960).

Norman, Arthur, "A New Approach to Negro Education," Journal of Negro Education 30:35-40 (Winter 1961). On the relation between cultural enrichment and I.Q.

North, Robert D., "The Intelligence of American Negroes," Anti-Defamation League Research Reports vol. 3, no. 2 (November 1956). A scholarly evaluation of the research literature. Includes a bibliography of published research dealing with Negro-white intelligence differentials.

Osborne, R. T., "Racial Differences in Mental Growth and School Achievement: A Longitudinal Study," Psychological Reports 7:233-239 (1960).

Pasamanick, Benjamin, "A Comparative Study of the Behavioral Development of Negro Infants," Journal of Genetic Psychology 69:3-44 (September 1946).

Pasamanick, Benjamin, and Hilda Knobloch, "Early Language Behavior in Negro Children and the Testing of Intelligence," Journal of Abnormal and Social Psychology 59:401-402 (May 1955).

Pasamanick, Benjamin, and Hilda Knobloch, "The Contribution of Some Organic Factors to School Retardation in Negro Children," Journal of Negro Education 27:4-9 (Winter 1958). "Prenatal and paranatal factors consequent to socio-economic circumstance" are often responsible for large numbers of "organically injured Negro children," who are thus handicapped to contend.

Peters, James S., II, "A Study of the Wechsler-Bellevue Verbal Scores of Negro and White Males," Journal of Negro Education 29:7-16 (Winter 1960). Extensive bibliography.

Peterson, J., and L. H. Lanier, "Studies in the Comparative Abilities of Whites and Negroes," Mental Measurement Monograph no. 5, 1929.

Pettigrew, Thomas F., "Negro American Intelligence: A New Look at an Old Controversy," Journal of Negro Education 32:6-25 (Winter 1963).

Plotkin, Lawrence, "Racial Differences in Intelligence," American Psychologist 14:526-527 (August 1959).

Robinson, Mary L., and M. Meenes, "The Relationship Between Test Intelligence of Third Grade Negro Children and the Occupations of their Parents," Journal of Negro Education 16:136-141 (Spring 1947).

Rosen, S. R., "Personality and Negro-White Intelligence," Journal of Abnormal and Social Psychology 61:148-160 (July 1960).

Rowe, Allen S., and Willard E. Caldwell, "The Somatic Apperception Test," Journal of General Psychology 68:59-69 (January 1963). Perception of their own size by a group of Negro adolescents.

Schultz, Raymond E., "A Comparison of Negro Pupils' Ranking with those Ranking Low in Educational Achievement," Journal of Educational Sociology 31:265-270 (March 1958).

Semler, Ira J., and Ira Iscoe, "Comparative and Developmental Study of the Learning Abilities of Negro and White Children Under Four Conditions," Journal of Educational Psychology 54:38-44 (February 1963).

Shuey, Audrey, The Testing of Negro Intelligence. Lynchburg, Va.: Bell, 1958. Author is a psychologist at Randolph-Macon College, who marshals her evidence to demonstrate that there is a "native difference between Negroes and whites as determined by intelligence tests."

Smart, Mollie S., "Confirming Klineberg's Suspicion," American Psychologist 18:621 (September 1963).

Sperrazzo, Gerald, and Walter L. Wilkins, "Racial Differences in the Progressive Matrices," Journal of Consulting Psychology 23:273-274 (June 1959). A reply to Jensen's note in same issue, q.v.

Teahan, John E., and Elizabeth M. Drews, "A Comparison of Northern and Southern Negro Children on the WISC," Journal of Consulting Psychology 26:292 (June 1962).

Tuddenham, R. D., "The Nature and Measurement of Intelligence," in L. Postman, ed., Psychology in the Making. New York: Knopf, 1962.

Tumin, Melvin M., ed., Race and Intelligence: An Evaluation. New York: Anti-Defamation League, 1963.

Woodring, Paul, "Ability Grouping, Segregation, and the Intellectual Elite," School and Society 87:164-165 (April 11, 1959).

Woods, Walter, and Robert Toal, "Subtest Disparity of Negro and White Groups Matched for I.Q.'s on the Revised Beta Test," Journal of Consulting Psychology 21:136-138 (April 1957).

See also Chapter IX, section 2e on Achievement and Deprivation.

4. HEALTH

a. Genetic

Baker, P. T., "American Negro-White Differences in the Thermal Insulative Aspects of Body Fat," Human Biology 31:316-324 (December 1959).

Bass, L. N., and H. B. Yaghmai, "Report of a Case of Hemophilia in a Negroid Infant," Journal of the National Medical Association 54:561-562 (September 1962).

Blumberg, B. S., ed., Genetic Polymorphisms and Geographic Variations in Disease. New York: Grune and Stratton, 1961.

Bullock, W. H., J. B. Johnson, and T. W. Davis, "Hemophilia in Negro Subjects," American Medical Association Archives of Internal Medicine 100:759-764 (November 1957).

Cooper, A. J., et al., "Biochemical Polymorphic Traits in a U.S. White and Negro Population," American Journal of Human Genetics 15:420-428 (December 1963).

Dublin, T. R., and B. S. Blumberg, "An Epidemiologic Approach to Inherited Disease Susceptibility," Public Health Reports 76:499-505 (June 1961). On possession of hemoglobin S trait.

Fuller, J. L., and W. R. Thompson, Behavior Genetics. New York: Wiley, 1960.

Goldstein, Marcus S., "Longevity and Health Status of Whites and Non-Whites in the United States," Journal of the National Medical Association 46:83-104 (March 1954).

Goldstein, Marcus S., "Longevity and Health Status of the Negro American," Journal of Negro Education 32:337-348 (Fall 1963).

Grabill, Wilson H., Clyde V. Kiser, and Pascal K. Whelpton, The Fertility of American Women. New York: Wiley, 1958. Based on censuses of 1950 and earlier, this book is basically a statistical study of population as related to race, age, mobility, etc.

Guralnick, Lillian, Mortality by Occupation and Industry Among Men 20 to 64 Years of Age: United States, 1950. Vital Statistics Special Reports, Vol. LII, No. 2, Washington, D.C.: GPO, 1962.

Harper, P. A., L. K. Fischer, and R. V. Rider, "Neurological and Intellectual Status of Prematures at Three to Five Years of Age," Journal of Pediatrics 55:679-690 (December 1959). Includes data on Negro cases.

Horton, C. P., and E. P. Crump, "Changes in Skin Color of Fifty-one Negro Infants from Birth Through Three Years of Age, as Related to Skin Color of Parents, Socioeconomic Status, and Developmental Quotient," American Medical Association Archives of Dermatology 80:421-426 (October 1959).

Iampietro, P. F., R. F. Goldman, E. R. Buskirk, and D. E. Bass, "Response of Negro and White Males to Cold," Journal of Applied Psychology 14:798-800 (September 1959).

"Improved Mortality Among Colored Policyholders," Statistical Bulletin, Metropolitan Life Insurance Company 43:6-8 (August 1962). This company insures about one fifth of the entire Negro population.

Ivy, A. C., "Physiological Differences Produced by Race and Diet," Hawaii Medical Journal
   and Inter-Island Nurses' Bulletin 16:21-25 (September-October 1956).
Karpinos, B. D., "Racial Differences in Visual Acuity," Public Health Reports 95:1045-1050
   (November 1960). Negro Americans, on average, have superior visual acuity.
Kitagawa, Evelyn M., and Philip M. Hauser, "Trends in Differential Fertility and Mortality
   in a Metropolis--Chicago," in E. W. Burgess and D. J. Bogue, eds., Contributions to
   Urban Sociology, Chicago: University of Chicago Press, 1964. A Summary of five studies
   of fertility and mortality in Chicago made over a period of 40 years.
Lee, Everett S., and Anne S. Lee, "The Differential Fertility of the American Negro,"
   American Sociological Review 17:437-447 (August 1952).
Lee, Everett S., and Anne S. Lee, "The Future Fertility of the American Negro," Social
   Forces 37:228-231 (March 1959).
National Office of Vital Statistics, Death Rates for Selected Causes by Age, Color, and Sex:
   United States and Each State, 1949-1951. Washington, D.C.: GPO, 1959.
Pettigrew, Thomas F., and Ronald L. Nuttall, "Negro American Perception of the Irradia-
   tion Illusion," Perceptual and Motor Skills 17:98 (August 1963).
Scott, R. B., et al., "Growth and Development of Negro Infants: V. Neuromuscular Patterns
   of Behavior during the First Year of Life," Pediatrics 16:24-30 (July 1955).
Vincent, M., and J. Hugon, "Relationships between Various Criteria of Maturity at Birth,"
   Biologica Neonatorum (Basel) 4:223-279 (1962).
Willie, Charles V., and William B. Rothney, "Racial, Ethnic, and Income Factors in the
   Epidemiology in Neonatal Mortality," American Sociological Review 27:522-526 (August
   1962).

b. Mental

Bernard, Viola W., "Psychoanalysis and Members of Minority Groups," Journal of the
   American Psychoanalytic Association 1:256-267 (April 1953).
Brody, Eugene B., "Social Conflict and Schizophrenic Behavior in Young Adult Negro
   Males," Psychiatry 24:337-346 (November 1961).
Clausen, J. A., "Drug Addiction," in R. K. Morton and R. A. Nisbet, eds., Contemporary
   Social Problems, New York: Harcourt, Brace, 1961. Negroes constitute 60 percent of
   addicts.
Crawford, R. R., G. W. Hellins, and R. L. Sutherland, "Variations between Negroes and
   Whites in Concepts of Mental Illness and its Treatment," Annals of the New York
   Academy of Science 84:918-937 (December 8, 1960).
Derbyshire, R. L., et al., "Family Structure of Young Adult Negro Male Mental Patients:
   Preliminary Observations from Urban Baltimore," Journal of Nervous and Mental
   Disease 136:245-251 (March 1963).
Deutsch, A., "The First U.S. Census of the Insane (1840) and Its Use as Pro-Slavery
   Propaganda," Bulletin of the History of Medicine 15:469-482 (December 1944). Presented
   data that the rate of mental illness among Negroes was much higher in the North than in
   the South.
Dorfman, Elaine, and Robert J. Kleiner, "Race of Examiner and Patient in Psychiatric
   Diagnosis and Recommendations," Journal of Consulting Psychology 26:393 (August 1962).
Faris, R. E. L., and H. W. Dunham, Mental Disorder in Urban Areas. Chicago: University
   of Chicago Press, 1939. Negroes have higher rates of schizophrenia than manic depression.
Fein, Rashi, Economics of Mental Illness. Joint Commission on Mental Illness and Health,
   Monograph Series, no. 2, New York: Basic Books, 1958. An economist estimates and
   discusses the significance of direct and indirect costs of mental illness in the U.S. Not
   specifically concerned with the Negro, it nonetheless has relevance in view of the high
   incidence of Negro mental illness.
Frumkin, Robert M., "Race and Major Mental Disorders: A Research Note," Journal of
   Negro Education 23:97-98)Winter 1954). A study undertaken in 1949-1950 of Negro v.
   white rates of admission to Ohio state mental hospitals showed the Negro percentage to
   be higher.

Grossack, Martin M., ed., Mental Health and Segregation. New York: Springer-Verlag, 1963. Included are studies of the consequences of segregation on personality, school adjustment, mental health in both Northern and Southern states, problems of guidance and treatment, experimental studies, and case reports.

Hansen, Carl F., "Mental Health Aspects of Desegregation," Journal of the National Medical Association 51:450-456 (November 1959).

Henton, C. L., "The Effect of Socio-Economic and Emotional Factors on the Onset of Menarche Among Negro and White Girls," Journal of Genetic Psychology 98:255-264 (June 1961). Negro girls experienced more severe emotional reaction; their mothers were less alert to their needs.

Hollingshead, A. B., and F. C. Redlich, Social Class and Mental Illness: A Community Study. New York: Wiley, 1958. Study conducted in New Haven, Conn.

Ivins, S. P., "Psychoses in the Negro: A Preliminary Study," Delaware State Medical Journal 22:212-213 (August 1950).

Jaco, E. G., The Social Epidemiology of Mental Disorders. New York: Russell Sage Foundation, 1960.

Jahoda, Marie, Race Relations and Mental Health. New York: Columbia University Press, 1960.

Keeler, Martin H., and Mintauts M. Vitols, "Migration and Schizophrenia in North Carolina Negroes," American Journal of Orthopsychiatry 33:554-557 (April 1963).

Kleiner, Robert J., and Seymour Parker, "Migration and Mental Illness: A New Look," American Sociological Review 24:687-690 (October 1959).

Kleiner, Robert J., and Seymour Parker, "Goalstriving, Social Status, and Mental Disorder: A Research Review," American Sociological Review 28:189-203 (April 1963).

Kleiner, Robert J., Jacob Tuckman, and Martha Lavell, "Mental Disorder and Status Based on Religious Affiliation," Human Relations 12:273-276 (August 1959).

Kleiner, Robert J., Jacob Tuckman, and Martha Lavell, "Mental Disorder and Status Based on Race," Psychiatry 23:271-274 (August 1960).

Malzberg, Benjamin, "Mental Disease Among Native and Foreign-Born Negroes in New York State," Journal of Negro Education 25:175-181 (Spring 1956).

Malzberg, Benjamin, and Everett S. Lee, Migration and Mental Disease. New York: Social Science Research Council, 1956.

Pasamanick, Benjamin, "Mental Subnormality," New England Journal of Medicine 266:1092-1097 (May 24, 1962).

Pasamanick, Benjamin, "Some Misconceptions Concerning Differences in the Racial Prevalence of Mental Disease," American Journal of Orthopsychiatry 33:72-86 (January 1963). The author is sceptical of conclusions that Negroes have higher rates of psychoses.

Pasamanick, Benjamin, "Myths Regarding Prevalence of Mental Disease in the American Negro: A Century of Misuse of Mental Hospital Data and Some New Findings," Journal of the National Medical Association 56:6-17 (January 1964).

Pasamanick, Benjamin, and P. H. Knapp, eds., Social Aspects of Psychiatry. Washington, D.C.: American Psychiatric Association, 1958.

Pasamanick, Benjamin, and Hilda Knobloch, "Race, Complications of Pregnancy, and Neuropsychiatric Disorders," Social Problems 5:267-278 (Winter 1957-1958).

Prange, A. J., Jr., and M. M. Vitols, "Jokes Among Southern Negroes: the Revelation of Conflict," Journal of Nervous and Mental Disease 136:162-167 (February 1963).

Riese, H., "Group Therapeutical Experience with Antisocial and Prepsychotic Negro Children," Acta Psychotherapeutica et Psychosomatica (Basel), Supplement to vol. 7: 319-327 (1959).

Rose, Arnold M., "Psychoneurotic Breakdown Among Negro Soldiers in Combat," Phylon 17:61-69 (Spring 1956).

Rosen, H., and J. D. Frank, "Negroes in Psychotherapy," American Journal of Psychiatry 119:456-460 (November 1962).

Sabagh, Georges, F. Dingman, George Tarjan, and Stanley W. Wright, "Social Class and Ethnic Status of Patients Admitted to a State Hospital for the Retarded," Pacific Sociological Review 2:76-80 (Fall 1959).

Schermerhorn, R. A., "Psychiatric Disorders Among Negroes: A Sociological Note," American Journal of Psychiatry 112:878-882 (1956).

Sclare, A., "Cultural Determinants in the Neurotic Negro," British Journal of Medical Psychology 26:278-288 (Part 4 1953).

Shane, M., "Some Subcultural Consideration in the Psychotherapy of a Negro Patient," Psychiatric Quarterly 34:9-27 (January 1960).

Stewart, D. D., "Posthospital Social Adjustment of Former Mental Patients from Two Arkansas Counties," Southwestern Social Sciences Quarterly 35:317-323 (March 1955).

Strayer, R., "A Study of the Negro Alcoholic," Quarterly Journal of Studies on Alcohol 22: 111-123 (March 1961).

Vitols, Mintauts M., "The Significance of the Higher Incidence of Schizophrenia in the Negro Race in North Carolina," North Carolina Medical Journal 22:147-158 (April 1961).

Vitols, Mintauts M., H. G. Waters, and Martin H. Keeler, "Hallucinations and Delusions in White and Negro Schizophrenics," American Journal of Psychiatry 120:472-476 (November 1963). The incidence of hallucinations is greater among Negroes.

Wilson, D. C., and Edna M. Lantz, "The Effect of Culture Change on the Negro Race in Virginia as Indicated by a Study of State [Mental] Hospital Admissions," American Journal of Psychiatry 114:25-32 (July 1957).

c. Patterns and Diseases

Adams, M. S., et al., "Iron-Deficiency Anemia in Negro Infants and Children in the Metropolitan Area of the District of Columbia," Medical Annals of the District of Columbia 32:391-393 (October 1963).

Alter, S. M., "Multiple Sclerosis in the Negro," Archives of Neurology 7:83-91 (August 1962).

Anderson, R. S., and Laurie M. Gunter, "Sex and Diabetes Mellitus: A Comparative Study of 26 Negro Males and 26 Negro Females Matched for Age," American Journal of the Medical Sciences 242:481-486 (October 1961).

Baumgartner, Leona, "Urban Reservoirs of Tuberculosis," American Review of Tuberculosis 79:687-689 (May 1959).

Berry, L. H., "Black Men and Malignant Fevers," Journal of the National Medical Association 56:43-47 (January 1964).

Cavusoglu, M., and L. H. Levine, "Gout in the Negro Female," New York Journal of Medicine 60:2597-2600 (August 15, 1960).

Christopherson, W. M., and J. E. Parker, "A Study of the Relative Frequency of Carcinoma of the Cervix in the Negro," Cancer 13:711-713 (July-August 1960).

Commission on Chronic Illness, Chronic Illness in the United States. Vol. IV, Chronic Illness in a Large City: The Baltimore Study. Cambridge: Harvard University Press, 1957.

Comstock, G. W., "An Epidemiologic Study of Blood Pressure Levels in a Biracial Community in the Southern United States," American Journal of Hygiene 65:271-315 (May 1957).

Cultural Considerations in Changing Health Attitudes. Washington, D.C.: Department of Preventive Medicine and Public Health, Howard University, 1961.

Deschin, Celia S., Teen-Agers and Venereal Disease. Atlanta, Ga.: U.S. Department of Health, Education, and Welfare, 1961.

Goldstein, M. S., "Longevity and Health Status of the Negro American," Journal of Negro Education 32:337-348 (Fall 1963).

Grant, F. W., and D. Groom, "A Dietary Study among a Group of Southern Negroes," Journal of the American Dietetic Association 35:910-918 (September 1959).

Groom, D., et al., "Coronary and Aortic Atherosclerosis in the Negroes of Haiti and the United States," Annals of Internal Medicine 51:270-289 (August 1959).

Hardy, Janet, Tuberculosis in White and Negro Children. 2 vols., Cambridge: Harvard University Press, 1958.

Herring, B. D., "Pernicious Anemia and the American Negro," American Practitioner 13: 544-548 (August 1962).

Hilleboe, H. E., and B. W. Larimore, eds., Preventive Medicine. Philadelphia: Saunders. 1962. Includes data on parasitic diseases of Negro Southerners.

Hingson, R. A., "Comparative Negro and White Mortality During Anesthesia, Obstetrics and Surgery," Journal of the National Medical Association 49:203-211 (July 1957).

Matsuda, R., "Relative Growth of Negro and White Children in Philadelphia," Growth 27: 271-284 (December 1963).

Nichaman, M. Z., E. Boyle, Jr., T. P. Lesesne, and H. I. Sauer, "Cardiovascular Disease Mortality by Race, Based on a Statistical Study in Charleston, South Carolina," Geriatrics 17:724-737 (November 1962).

Payton, E., E. P. Crump, and C. P. Horton, "Growth and Development VII: Dietary Habits of 571 Pregnant Southern Negro Women," Journal of the American Dietetic Association 37:129-136 (August 1960).

Pettigrew, Ann Hallman, and Thomas F. Pettigrew, "Race, Disease, and Desegregation: A New Look," Phylon 24:315-333 (Winter 1963). A valuable survey leading to the conclusion that "the 'racial differences' in health that do exist provide further evidence of the societal need for desegregation and improved living conditions for all Americans." Extensive bibliographical footnotes.

Phillips, J. H., and G. E. Burch, "Cardiovascular Diseases in the White and Negro Races," American Journal of the Medical Sciences 238:97-124 (July 1959).

Roberts, H. J., "The Syndrome of Narcolepsy and Diabetogenic Hyperinsulinism in the American Negro: Its Relationship to the Pathogenesis of Diabetes Mellitus, Obesity, Dysrhythmias, and Accelerated Cardiovascular Disease," Journal of the National Medical Association 56:18-42 (January 1964).

Rose, G., "Cardiovascular Mortality Among American Negroes," Archives of Environmental Health 5:412-414 (November 1962).

Russell, A. L., and P. Ayres, "Periodontal Disease and Socioeconomic Status in Birmingham, Ala.," American Journal of Public Health 50:206-214 (February 1960).

Seltzer, A. P., "The Incidence of Otosclerosis among Negroes," Journal of the National Medical Association 53:502-503 (September 1961).

Stamler, J., et al., "Racial Patterns of Coronary Heart Disease," Geriatrics 16:382-396 (August 1961).

Steiner, P. E., "Cancer and Race, with Emphasis on the American and African Negroes and on the Mexican," Unio Internationalis Contra Cancrum (Louvain) 13:959-966 (1957).

d. Services

Altenderfer, Marion E., and Beatrice Crowther, "Relationship Between Infant Mortality and Socio-economic Factors in Urban Areas," Public Health Reports 64:331-339 (March 18, 1949).

Babow, Irving, "Minority Group Integration in Hospitals: A Sample Survey," Hospitals 35: 47-48 (February 1961).

Brown, L. G., "Experience with Racial Attitudes of the Medical Profession in New Jersey," Journal of the National Medical Association 55:66-68 (January 1963).

Calvet, Ivis, "Integration in Hospitals," Interracial Review 35:163+ (July 1962).

Carnegie, M. E., "Impact of Integration on the Nursing Profession: Historical Sketch," Negro History Bulletin 28:154-155+ (April 1965).

Cobb, W. M., "The Negro Physician and Hospital Staffs," Hospital Management 89:22-24 (March 1960).

Cobb, W. M., ed., "Integration in Medicine: A National Need," Journal of the National Medical Association 49:1-71 (January 1957). Entire issue. Articles listed separately.

Cornely, P. B., "Trend in Racial Integration in Hospitals in the United States," Journal of the National Medical Association 49:8-10 (January 1957).

Cowles, Wylda, and Steven Polgar, with collaboration of Leonard Simmons and John Switzer, "Health and Communication in a Negro Census Tract," Social Problems 10:228-236 (Winter 1963).

Davis, M. M., and H. H. Smythe, "Providing Adequate Health Service to Negroes," Journal of Negro Education 18:305-317 (Summer 1949).

Dummett, C. O., "Dental Health Problems of the Negro Population," Journal of the American Dental Association 61:308-314 (September 1960).

Engel, Leonard, "We Could Save 40,000 Babies a Year," New York Times Magazine, November 17, 1963. On high U.S. infant mortality rate. High rate for Negroes based on New York Health Department records.

Friedsam, N. J., C. D. Whatley, and A. L. Rhodes, "Some Selected Aspects of Judicial

Commitments of the Mentally Ill in Texas," Texas Journal of Science 6:27-30 (1954). Negroes are more quickly committed to mental institutions than whites. Once committed, they are less likely to receive advanced therapy.

Goldstein, R. L., "Negro Nurses in Hospitals," American Journal of Nursing 60:215-217 (February 1960).

Grannum, E. S., "Medical Economics and the Negro Physician," Journal of the National Medical Association 55:426-429 (September 1963).

Gunter, L. M., "The Effect of Segregation on Nursing Students," Nursing Outlook 9:74-76 (February 1961).

Hentoff, Nat, "Doctor Nyswander," New Yorker 41:32-34+ (June 26, 1965); 41:32-34+ (July 3, 1965). Account of one woman's effective, if unorthodox, efforts to aid narcotics addicts.

Hirsch, E. F., "The Hospital Care of Negroes and the Appointment of Negro Physicians to Medical Staffs of Hospitals in Chicago," Proceedings of the Institute of Medicine of Chicago 23:156-159 (November 15, 1960).

Kenney, J. A., Jr., "What the NMA Can Do About the Shortage of Physicians," Jouranl of the National Medical Association 55:46-48 (January 1963).

Kenney, J. A., Jr., "Medical Civil Rights," Journal of the National Medical Association 55: 430-432 (September 1963).

Kitagawa, Evelyn M., and Philip M. Hauser, "Trends in Differential Fertility and Mortality in a Metropolis--Chicago," in E. W. Burgess and D. J. Bogue, eds., Contributions to Urban Sociology. Chicago: University of Chicago Press, 1964. By 1950 most of the difference between white and nonwhite fertility rates could be attributed to differences in socioeconomic status. As for differential mortality, gradual convergence in mortality differentials by color and socioeconomic status indicates rising accessibility of all groups to good medical care.

Langer, E., "Hospital Discrimination: HEW Criticized by Civil Rights Groups," Science 149:355-357 (September 17, 1965).

McLean, F. C., "Negroes and Medicine in Chicago," Proceedings of the Institute of Medicine of Chicago 23:2-6 (January 15, 1960).

Morris, H. H., Jr., K. E. Appel, and J. L. Procope, "Psychiatric, Community, and Racial Integration in a General Hospital," American Journal of Psychiatry 119:1049-1054 (May 1963).

Morris, J. P., "The Denial of Staff Positions to Negro Physicians: A Violation of the Sherman Act," Journal of the National Medical Association 52:211-215 (May 1960).

Morris, R. G., Jr., "The Problem in Securing Hospital Staff Appointments for Negro Physicians in Chicago," Journal of the National Medical Association 52:194-197 (May 1960).

Motley, C. B., "Desegregation: What It Means to the Medical Professions and the Responsibilities It Places on the Negro Professionals," Journal of the National Medical Association 55:441-443 (September 1963).

National Urban League, Report of the Hospital Committee. Washington, D.C., 1963.

New Opportunities for Negroes in Medicine. 34-page pamphlet, Chicago: National Medical Fellowships, 1962.

Pierce, H. E., Jr., "Surgical Planning for Cosmetic Defects in the Negro," Journal of the National Medical Association 51:190-198 (May 1959).

Ravitz, M. J., "Integration of Nurses: A Latent Function of Hospital Discrimination," Phylon 16:295-301 (Fall 1955).

Reitzes, Dietrich C., Negroes and Medicine. Cambridge: Harvard University Press, 1958. Part I is a study of medical education for Negro students, with emphasis on factors limiting their entry into the profession. Part II covers care by and for Negroes in fourteen communities, with emphasis on factors affecting integration of Negro doctors into the larger medical community. A substantial work on medical services for and by Negroes.

Reitzes, Dietrich C., and H. Reitzes, "Factors which Block or Facilitate Integration in the Field of Medicine," Interracial Review, September 1960.

Scholz, B. W., "Medicine in the Slums," New York State Journal of Medicine 63:2132-2138 (July 15, 1963).

Shanahan, T. J., "Negroes in Nursing Education: A Report on Catholic Schools," Hospital Progress 42:100-102 (July 1961).

Smith, Earl B., "Practical Aspects of Hospital Integration," Journal of the National Medical Association 52:367-368 (September 1960).

Smith, Earl B., "Medical Justice and Injustice," Interracial Review 35:254-255 (November 1962).

Snyder, J. D., "Race Bias in Hospitals: What the Civil Rights Commission Found," Hospital Management 96:52-54 (November 1963).

Stevens, Rutherford B., "Interracial Practices in Mental Hospitals," Mental Hygiene 36:56-65 (January 1952).

Thompson, W. A., et al., "The Negro in Medicine in Detroit," Journal of the National Medical Association 55:475-481 (November 1963).

Williams, Philip F., "Material Welfare and the Negro," Journal of American Medical Association 132:611-614 (November 16, 1946).

5. LITERATURE AND FOLKLORE

Baldwin, James, Notes of a Native Son. Boston: Beacon, 1955; Beacon, Bantam (New York) paperbacks. Essays.

Baldwin, James, Giovanni's Room. New York: Dial, 1956; New York: Dell, Apollo (Morrow) paperbacks. Novel set in Paris concerning conflicting heterosexual and homosexual relations.

Baldwin, James, Nobody Knows My Name. New York: Dial, 1961; New York: Dell, Delta paperbacks. Essays.

Baldwin, James, Another Country. New York: Dial, 1962; New York: Dell paperback. Novel with New York as setting.

Baldwin, James, Go Tell It On the Mountain. New York: Dial, 1963; New York: Dell, Grossett, New American Library paperbacks. Novel about growing up in Harlem.

Baldwin, James, Blues for Mister Charlie. New York: Dial, 1964; New York: Dell paperback. Play about a young Negro who is slain by a white Southern bigot. Baldwin has said that the play is based "distantly" on the case of Emmet Till.

Baldwin, James, Going to Meet the Man. New York: Dial, 1965. Eight short stories.

Barksdale, Richard K., "Trends in Contemporary Poetry," Phylon 19:408-416 (Winter 1958).

Barrett, William E., Lillies of the Field. Garden City, N.Y.: Doubleday, 1962. Novel of a Negro youth who finds himself building a chapel for a small group of German nuns. Later made into a prize-winning film.

Beechwood, Mary, Memphis Jackson's Son. Boston: Houghton Mifflin, 1956. Novel of corruption and redemption of a Howard University student from the rural South.

Bone, Robert A., The Negro Novel in America. New Haven: Yale University Press, 1958; rev. ed. Yale Paperbound, 1965. A history of novels by Negroes since 1953. Bone favors "art-centered novels" like Ellison's Invisible Man rather than more socially inspired materials.

Bontemps, Arna Wendell, ed., American Negro Poetry. New York: Hill & Wang, 1963.

Braithwaite, William S., "Alain Locke's Relationship to the Negro in American Literature," Phylon 18:166-173 (Summer 1957). A eulogy of Locke and his gift of "soul" to Negro writers of the twenties and thirties.

Breman, Paul, ed., Sixes and Sevens. London: Paul Breman, 1962. Poems by 13 Negro poets.

Brewer, J. Mason, Worser Days and Better Times: The Folklore of the North Carolina Negro. Chicago: Quadrangle Books, 1965. Preface and notes by Warren E. Roberts, drawings by R. L. Toben.

Brooks, Gwendolyn, A Street in Bronzeville. New York: Harper, 1945. Poems which convey with great success the authentic flavor of Negro community life in Chicago.

Brooks, Gwendolyn, Annie Allen. New York: Harper, 1949. Poems. Miss Brooks received the Pulitzer Prize for poetry in 1950.

Brooks, Gwendolyn, Maud Martha. New York, Harper, 1953. Novel.

Brooks, Gwendolyn, The Bean Eaters. New York: Harper, 1960. Poems.

Brooks, Gwendolyn, Selected Poems. New York: Harper, 1963; also Harper paperback. Selections from earlier volumes of verse, plus a number of new poems.

Brown, Frank L., Trumbull Park. Chicago: Regnery, 1959. A novel of race conflict which powerfully conveys the mood of tension developing in a public housing project.

Brown, Sterling A., "Negro Character as Seen by White Authors," Journal of Negro Education 2:180-201 (January 1933). An important essay. Brown describes seven stereotypes of the Negro used by white authors, beginning with pre-Civil War literature.

Brown, Sterling A., The Negro in American Fiction. Washington, D.C.: Associates in Negro Folk Education, 1937.

Brown, Sterling A., Negro Poetry and Drama. Washington, D.C.: Associates in Negro Folk Education, 1937. One of the "Bronze Booklets." An excellent study of the development of Negro poetry from the eighteenth century. In the section on drama, Brown discusses white characterizations of the Negro as well as plays by Negroes.

Brown, Sterling A., "Negro Folk Expression," Phylon 14:50-60 (Spring 1953). Observations on the uniqueness of Negro spirituals, seculars, and work-songs.

Brown, Sterling A., Arthur P. Davis, and Ulysses Lee, eds., The Negro Caravan. New York: Dryden, 1941. Still a very useful source book, with an excellent introduction.

Butcher, Margaret Just, The Negro in American Culture, Based on Materials Left by Alain Locke. New York: Knopf, 1956; New York: New American Library paperback, 1965. Basic survey of contribution of Negroes to the arts in America.

Chastain, Thomas, Judgment Day. Garden City, N.Y.: Doubleday, 1962. Novel of Southern race conflict.

Clarke, John Henrik, "Transition in the American Negro Short Story," Phylon 21:360-366 (Winter 1960). Shallow in its interpretation, this article is a list of short story writers from slave narratives to the present.

Cothran, Tilman C., "White Stereotypes in Fiction by Negroes," Phylon 11:252-256 (Autumn 1950). An analysis of novels of the 1940 vintage, demonstrating the Negro response to white conceptions of the Negro.

Coles, Robert, "Baldwin's Burden," Partisan Review 31:409-416 (Summer 1964). Critical of Baldwin's romanticism and of his contradictory generalizations about love and hate, this is an impressively probing essay.

Collier, Eugenia W., "James Weldon Johnson: Mirror of Change," Phylon 21:351-359 (Winter 1960). An intelligent, if not too detailed, discussion of Johnson's development away from the use of Negro dialect in his poetry while still retaining his folk subject. Central to the piece is a comparison with Paul Dunbar.

Courlander, Harold, Negro Folk Music, U.S.A. New York: Columbia University Press, 1963. A comprehensive and scholarly work.

Davis, Arthur P., "The Alien-and-Exile Theme in Countee Cullen's Racial Poems," Phylon 14:390-400 (Winter 1953). A study of poems of the Renaissance of the 1920's, with particular emphasis on African themes.

Davis, Arthur P., "Integration and Race Literature," Phylon 17:141-146 (Summer 1956). A discussion of the effect of integration in turning the Negro author away from protest literature immediately after 1954 Supreme Court decision.

Davis, Christopher, First Family. New York: Coward-McCann, 1961. A novel of a Negro family in white suburbia.

Davis, Ossie, Purlie Victorious. New York: French, 1961. Play which ridicules both Negro and Southern stereotypes.

Davis, Russell F., Anything for a Friend. New York: Crown, 1963. A "hip" first-person novel, the discovery of love, life, and integration at the high school level.

Demby, William, The Catacombs. New York: Pantheon, 1965. Autobiographical novel of the return of a Negro writer from Rome to America to seek his true identity.

DeVegh, Elizabeth, Knot of Roots. New York: Random House, 1958. A novel of the inter-related worlds of a Negro and a white.

Dorson, Richard M., "Negro Witch Stories on Tape," Midwest Folklore 2:229-241 (Winter 1952) and "A Negro Storytelling Session on Tape," ibid., 3:201-212 (Winter 1953). Stories heard in Calvin Township, Cass County, Michigan, in a Negro enclave within a white farm area, where Negroes have lived and owned farms since 1840.

Dorson, Richard M., "Negro Tales," Western Folklore 13:77-97 (April 1954) and 13:160-169 (July 1954). Dorson has considerable skill in describing his storytellers, their surroundings and circumstances, with the result that the reader learns much of how his Negro subjects live.

Dorson, Richard M., ed., <u>Negro Folktales in Michigan</u>. Cambridge: Harvard University Press, 1956.

Dorson, Richard M., ed., <u>Negro Tales from Pine Bluff, Arkansas, and Calvin, Michigan</u>. Bloomington: Indiana University Press, 1958.

Echeruo, M. J. C., "American Negro Poetry," <u>Phylon</u> 24:62-68 (Spring 1963). Interesting, though slight, account of the effect of race conflict upon the poetry of the Negro. Compares American Negro and African poetry.

Edwards, Junius, <u>If We Must Die</u>. Garden City, N.Y.: Doubleday, 1963. One day in the life of a Negro Korean War veteran who has returned to his Southern home. The author does not quite succeed in bringing his character to life, and hence leaves the reader unmoved.

Ellison, Ralph, <u>The Invisible Man</u>. New York: Random House, 1952. A distinguished and angry novel about what white society does to the Negro in America.

Ellison, Ralph, "The World and The Jug," <u>New Leader</u>, December 9, 1963.

Ellison, Ralph, "On Becoming a Writer," <u>Commentary</u> 38:57-60 (October 1964). An essay by a writer who has from the beginning refused to think of himself only as a Negro writer.

Ellison, Ralph, <u>Shadow and Act</u>. New York: Random House, 1964. Twenty essays (and two interviews), the best and most personal of which show a writer concerned to understand and to make the reader understand what it is to be an American Negro today.

Ellison Ralph, " 'Tell It Like It Is, Baby,' " <u>Nation</u> 201:129-136 (September 20, 1965). In 100th Anniversary Issue.

Fair, Ronald L., <u>Many Thousand Gone</u>. New York: Harcourt, Brace, 1965. Subtitled <u>An American Fable</u>, this short novel tells a savage and yet compassionate tale of Negro revolt in an imaginary Mississippi county.

Feibleman, Peter S., <u>A Place Without Twilight</u>. Cleveland: World, 1958. A novel of a mulatto girl in New Orleans.

Fisher, Miles M., <u>Negro Slave Songs in the United States</u>. Ithaca: Cornell University Press, 1953. Spirituals seen as revolutionary protests.

Fontaine, William T., "Toward a Philosophy of the American Negro Literature," <u>Présence Africaine</u>, Engl. ed., no's. 24-25:164-176 (February-May 1959). Impressionistic but interesting glance at Negro literature, especially at Wright's <u>Native Son</u>.

Ford, Nick Aaron, "Battle of the Books: A Critical Survey of Books By and About Negroes Published in 1960," <u>Phylon</u> 22:119-134 (Summer 1961).

Ford, Nick Aaron, "The Fire Next Time? A Critical Survey of Belles Lettres By and About Negroes Published in 1963," <u>Phylon</u> 25:123-134 (Summer 1964).

Friedenberg, Edgar Z., "Another Country for an Arkansas Traveler," <u>New Republic</u> 147: 23-26 (August 27, 1962). Observations on Baldwin's <u>Another Country</u> and its implications for the South.

Gaines, Ernest J., <u>Catherine Carmier</u>. New York: Atheneum, 1964. A young Negro returns to teach in the South after ten years in the North. A creditable first novel.

Gloster, Hugh M., <u>Negro Voices in American Fiction</u>. Chapel Hill: University of North Carolina Press, 1948. Valuable survey of literature through World War II; often concerned with the social setting of the writer rather than strictly with his literary output.

Goyen, William, <u>The Fair Sister</u>. Garden City, N.Y.: Doubleday, 1963. Novel about a female evangelist with a night-club background.

Hansberry, Lorraine, <u>A Raisin in the Sun</u>. New York: Random House, 1959. Text of the Broadway play, which received the New York Critics Circle Award.

Hayden, Robert, <u>A Ballad of Remembrance</u>. London: Paul Breman, 1962. Poems.

Hill, Herbert, ed., <u>Soon, One Morning: New Writing by American Writers, 1940-1962</u>. New York: Knopf, 1963. A collection of essays, fictions, poems, "to display the range of contemporary writing."

Himes, Chester B., <u>Third Generation</u>. Cleveland: World, 1954. Novel.

Howe, Irving, "Black Boys and Native Sons," <u>Dissent</u> 10:353-368 (Fall 1963).

Howe, Irving, and Ralph Ellison, "The Writer and the Critic--An Exchange," <u>New Leader</u> February 3, 1964. The last stage of a running controversy which began with Howe's article in <u>Dissent</u> Fall 1963, followed by Ellison's reply in the <u>New Leader</u> December 9, 1963, as to possibility of the Negro's writing about any subject independently of the protest movement.

Hughes, Carl Milton, The Negro Novelist: A Discussion of the Writings of American
    Negro Novelists, 1940-1950. New York: Citadel, 1953. Basically a sequel to Gloster's
    Negro Voices.
Hughes, Langston, Montage of a Dream Deferred. New York: Holt, 1951.
Hughes, Langston, Simple Stakes a Claim. New York: Rinehart, 1957. The Simple stories
    have repeatedly been highly praised.
Hughes, Langston, Selected Poems. New York: Knopf, 1959.
Hughes, Langston, Ask Your Mama. New York: Knopf, 1961. Poems set in a pattern of jazz
    music.
Hughes, Langston, The Best of Simple. New York: Hill & Wang, 1961. Selections from a
    number of Hughes's "Simple" tales.
Hughes, Langston, Something in Common and Other Stories. New York: Hill & Wang, 1963.
Hughes, Langston, Simple's Uncle Sam. New York: Hill & Wang, 1965. Forty-six stories
    about Hughes's famous character, Jesse B. Semple, which bring his observations up to
    date on current affairs.
Hughes, Langston, ed., Reader. New York: Braziller, 1958. Anthology of poems, plays,
    and short stories, including new material.
Hughes, Langston, ed., New Negro Poets U.S.A. Bloomington: Indiana University Press,
    1964. Thirty-seven poets are represented, few in more than one or two poems. Their
    verses are widely various, from deeply personal lyric to harsh protest.
Hughes, Langston, ed., The Book of Negro Humor. New York: Dodd, Mead, 1966.
Hughes, Langston, and A. Bontemps, The Poetry of the Negro. Garden City, N.Y.:
    Doubleday, 1949.
Hughes, Langston, LeRoi Jones, and John A. Williams, "Problems of the Negro Writer,"
    Saturday Review 46: 19-21, 40 (April 20, 1963). Three short essays.
Isaacs, Harold, "Five Writers and their African Ancestors," Phylon 21:243-265 (Fall
    1960) and 21:317-336 (Winter 1960). Fascinating reflections on the African heritage of
    the American Negro in the works of Langston Hughes, Richard Wright, Ralph Ellison,
    James Baldwin, and Lorraine Hansberry. The last three were interviewed.
Jackson, Blyden, "The Blithe Newcomers: A Résumé of Negro Literature in 1954," Phylon
    16:5-12 (Spring 1955).
Jackson, Blyden, "The Continuing Strain: Résumé of Negro Literature in 1955," Phylon
    17:35-40 (Spring 1956).
Jacobson, Dan, "James Baldwin as Spokesman," Commentary 32:497-502 (December 1961).
    A study of Baldwin by a South African Jew, who sees Baldwin's reluctance to aim for
    power in brute terms as characteristically American.
James, Willis Laurence, "The Romance of the Negro Folk Cry in America," Phylon
    16:15-30 (Spring 1955). An essay on the religious expression of folk music and on the
    Gospel Singers.
Johnson, James Weldon, ed., The Book of American Negro Poetry. New York: Harcourt,
    Brace, 1922.
Johnson, James Weldon, God's Trombones. New York: Viking, 1927.
Johnson, James Weldon, ed., The Book of American Negro Spirituals. New York: Viking,
    1947.
Jones, LeRoi, "Myth of a Negro Literature," Saturday Review 46:20-21 (April 20, 1963).
Jones, LeRoi, Blues People: Negro Music in White America. New York: Morrow, 1963.
    Ralph Ellison, in New York Review, February 6, 1964, objects that the "tremendous
    burden of sociology which Jones would place upon this body of music is enough to give
    even the blues the blues."
Jones, LeRoi, The System of Dante's Hell. New York: Grove, 1965. A novel about youth in
    the Negro slums of Newark.
Kelley, William Melvin, A Different Drummer. Garden City, N.Y.: Doubleday, 1962.
    A novel about the effect of a mass Negro exodus from the South on the lives of the white
    Southerners left behind.
Kelley, William Melvin, Dancers on the Shore. Garden City, N.Y.: Doubleday, 1964.
    Sixteen short stories which, in spite of firm writing and control of form, are not quite
    up to the quality of his A Different Drummer.
Killens, John O., Youngblood. New York: Dial, 1954. Novel of a Georgia Negro family
    during the early twentieth century.

Killens, John O., And Then We Heard the Thunder. New York: Knopf, 1963. Story of a
Negro soldier in World War II who becomes progressively more involved in the battle
for equality. An impressive novel.

Killens, John O., et al., The American Negro Writer and his Roots. New York: American
Society of African Culture, 1960. Papers from 1959 conference of AMSAC by Killens,
Saunders Redding, Samuel Allen, John Henrik Clarke, Julian Mayfield, Arthur Davis,
Langston Hughes, William Branch, Arna Bontemps, Loften Mitchell.

Kolb, Avery E., Jigger Whitchet's War. New York: Simon & Schuster, 1959. Novel of Negro
soldier in World War II.

Lash, John, "A Long Hard Look at the Ghetto: A Critical Summary of Literature by and
about Negroes in 1956," Phylon 18:7-24 (Spring 1957).

Lash, John, "The Conditioning of Servitude: A Critical Summary of Literature by and
about Negroes in 1957," Phylon 19:143-152 (Summer 1958).

Lash, John, "Dimension in Racial Experience: A Critical Summary of Literature by and
about Negroes in 1958," Phylon 20:115-131 (Summer 1959).

Lash, John, "Expostulation and Reply: A Critical Summary of Literature by and about
Negroes in 1959," Phylon 21:111-123 (Summer 1960).

Locke, Alain, The New Negro. New York: Boni, 1925. Author was guiding figure in Negro
Renaissance of the 1920's.

McIlwain, William, The Glass Rooster. Garden City, N.Y.: Doubleday, 1960. A heavily
stereotyped novel of a Northern Negro's return to the South.

MacInnes, Colin, "Dark Angel: The Writings of James Baldwin," Encounter 21:22-33
(August 1963). A thoughtful essay, giving careful attention to each of Baldwin's books.

McKay, Claude, Home to Harlem. New York: Harper, 1928; Pocket Books, Inc., 1965.

McKay, Claude, Selected Poems. New York: Bookman, 1953.

Maddux, Rachel, Abel's Daughter. New York: Harper, 1960. Novel of interracial friendship
in the Deep South.

Marcus, Steven, "The American Negro in Search of Identity," Commentary 16:456-463
(November 1953). An early appreciation of the differences among Wright's The Outsider,
Ellison's Invisible Man, and Baldwin's Go Tell It On The Mountain.

Marshall, Paule, Soul Clap Hands and Sing. New York: Atheneum, 1961. Four short stories,
with settings in Barbados, Brooklyn, British Guiana, and Brazil.

Martin, Ralph, Skin Deep. New York: McKay, 1964. The story of four American Negro
expatriates who attempt to escape the problem of race in America by living in the
"liberal" atmosphere of Paris, only to discover they cannot escape.

Maund, Alfred, The Big Boxcar. Boston: Houghton Mifflin, 1957. Chaucerian tales by
Negro pilgrims from the South.

Mayfield, Julian, The Hit. New York: Vanguard, 1957. Novel about a Harlem Negro and
the policy racket.

Mayfield, Julian, Long Night. New York: Vanguard, 1958. Novel of a youth in Harlem.

Mayfield, Julian, The Grand Parade. New York: Vanguard, 1961. Novel of politics in a
city along the Mason-Dixon line.

Miller, Warren, Cool World. Boston: Little, Brown, 1959. Vivid and powerful novel of
the depths of Harlem life, subsequently made into a movie.

Miller, Warren, The Siege of Harlem. New York: McGraw-Hill, 1964. A novel describing
the organization of a separate Harlem government sometime in the future.

Milner, Jay, Incident at Ashton. New York: Appleton, 1961. Novel about Negro attempts to
register to vote in a Delta town.

"The Negro in Literature: The Current Scene," Phylon 11:297-394 (Winter 1950). The
entire issue devoted to the subject, and constituting an important summary of the work
of Negro writers through 1950. Articles of special interest are those by Sterling Brown,
Nick A. Ford, Ulysses Lee, Charles H. Nichols, Jr., William G. Smith, and Margaret
Walker.

Nilon, Charles H., Faulkner and the Negro. Boulder: University of Colorado Press, 1962.
This work, No. 8 in the series of University of Colorado Studies in Language and
Literature, presents a restrained, scholarly examination of Faulkner's treatment of
the Negro-white community.

Norris, Hoke, All the Kingdoms of the Earth. New York: Simon & Schuster, 1956. Novel
depicting a Negro community in the South.

Oliver, Clinton, "The Name and Nature of American Negro Literature: An Interpretive
Study in Genres and Ideas," unpub. doc. diss., Harvard University, 1965. Includes a
useful section on bibliography, pp. 336-357.

Parks, Gordon, The Learning Tree. New York: Harper, 1963. Novel of Negro youth
growing up in a small Kansas town during the 1920's.

Pool,Rosey,ed.,Beyond the Blues: New Poems by American Negroes. London: Headley,
1962. Collection of poems, chiefly by younger poets.

Porter, Dorothy P., "Early American Negro Writings: A Bibliographical Study," Papers
of the Bibliographical Society of America 39:192-268 (January 1945).

Redding, Jay Saunders, To Make a Poet Black. Chapel Hill: University of North Carolina
Press, 1939. An important study of Negro literature.

Redding, Jay Saunders, Stranger and Alone. New York: Harcourt, Brace, 1950. Sensitive
novel of the education of a young Negro intellectual.

Rexroth, Kenneth, "Panelizing Dissent: Report on Conference on the Negro Writer in the
United States," Nation 199:97-99 (September 7, 1964). Seminar sponsored by University
of California.

Rogers, Lettie Hamlett, Birthright. New York: Simon & Schuster, 1957. Novel of integration crisis.

Russell, Beth Duvall, On Earth As It Is. Boston: Christopher, 1963. Poems.

Russell, Ross, The Sound. New York: Dutton, 1961. Novel of jazz musicians.

Saxton, Alexander Plaisted, Bright Web in the Darkness. New York: St. Martin's, 1958.
Novel of industrial works in World War II.

Schomburg, Arthur Alfonso, A Bibliographical Checklist of American Negro Poetry. New
York: Heartman, 1916. The extensive Schomburg Collection in the New York Public
Library provides a wealth of material for the scholar.

Simmons,Herbert,Corner Boy. Boston: Houghton Mifflin,1957. Novel of juvenile delinquency.

Smalley, Webster, ed., Five Plays by Langston Hughes. Bloomington: Indiana University
Press, 1963. Includes "Mulatto," "Soul Gone Home," "Little Ham," "Simply Heavenly,"
"Tambourines to Glory."

Smith, William Gardner, South Street. New York: Farrar, Straus, 1954. Novel of
Philadelphia Negroes.

Smith, William Gardner, The Stone Face. New York: Farrar, Straus, 1963. Novel.

Stone, Alma, The Bible Salesman. Garden City, N.Y.: Doubleday, 1962. Novel set in New
York City Negro neighborhood.

Watkins, Sylvester C., ed., Anthology of American Negro Literature. New York: Random
House, 1944.

Wheeler, Keith, Peaceable Lane. New York: Simon & Schuster, 1960. Novel of the Negro's
entrance into a New York suburb.

Whiteman, Maxwell, A Century of Fiction by American Negroes, 1853-1952. Philadelphia:
Saifer, 1955. A comprehensive descriptive bibliography which not only attempts to list
all fiction by Negroes during this period, but corrects mistaken attributions to Negroes
of a number of books.

Williams, John A., Night Song. New York: Farrar, Straus, 1961. Novel of the jazz world.

Williams, John A., Sissie. New York: Farrar, Straus, 1963. Novel of Negro family life.

Wilson, Neill Compton, Freedom Song. New York: Holt, 1955. Novel of a Negro folk
musician in the antebellum South.

Wright, Charles, The Messenger. New York: Farrar, Straus, 1963. Novel of a messenger's
experiences on every level of New York life, from Wall Street to the Bowery.

Wright, Richard, Native Son. New York: Harper, 1940; New York: New American Library
paperback, 1962. Titanic story of Bigger Thomas from the Chicago ghetto, his struggle
to survive, and his doom.

Wright, Richard, White Man--Listen! Garden City, N.Y.: Doubleday, 1957; also Doubleday
Anchor Book. A personal interpretation of how the white man looks to nonwhite eyes.

Wright, Richard, Long Dream. Garden City, N.Y.: Doubleday, 1958. Novel of a Mississippi
Negro who seeks salvation by expatriation in France.

Wright, Richard, Eight Men. Cleveland: World, 1961; New York: Avon paperback, 1962.
Short stories, published posthumously, on the theme of the Negro's conflict with white
society.

Wright, Richard, Lawd Today. New York: Walker, 1963; New York: Avon paperback.
Novel, written before Native Son, about one sordid day in the life of a Negro postal
clerk in depression Chicago. Similar to Native Son in atmosphere, but weaker as a novel.

III. INTERGROUP RELATIONS

In the words of Whitney Young, Jr., "Race relations is no longer a spectator sport." In this section are included not only works on race relations, but works on the operations of prejudice and discrimination, as well as on the techniques for easing intergroup conflicts and on the problems attendant on the desegregation process. In any consideration of these problems, a useful caveat is provided by Bruno Bettelheim: "It is high time we began to bring clarity into our complex white-Negro relations by recognizing what belongs to class as such, irrespective of history or skin color."

This closer attention to class and class conflict is exemplified in such a work as Milton Gordon's Assimilation in American Life. Indeed, increasingly, behavioral scientists are stressing ways of modifying discriminatory intergroup and interclass practices as opposed to an earlier concentration on the reduction of prejudice as the road to racial amity. Evidence continues to mount that, contrary to the cherished cliché, "You cannot legislate morality," the law can and does change the hearts and minds of men. It does so by way of the intermediate step of regulating behavior, restraining discriminatory practices, punishing unjust acts. Over and over again it is being demonstrated that once behavior is changed--in school rooms, at lunch counters, in court houses--attitudes do begin to change. It is for this reason that Negroes press for federal civil rights action, and that social scientists explore techniques for changing situations as mechanisms for altering discriminatory action.

1. STUDIES OF PREJUDICE

Allman, Reva White, "A Study of the Social Attitudes of College Students," Journal of Social Psychology 53:33-51 (February 1961).

Allport, Gordon, The Nature of Prejudice. Cambridge, Mass.: Addison-Wesley, 1954; Garden City, N.Y.: Doubleday Anchor Book, abridged, 1958. A basic work.

Allport, Gordon W., and B. M. Kramer, "Some Roots of Prejudice," Journal of Psychology 22:9-39 (July 1946).

Antonovsky, Aaron, "The Social Meaning of Discrimination," Phylon 21:81-95 (Spring 1960).

Athey, K. R., Joan E. Coleman, Audrey P. Reitman, and Jenny Tang, "Two Experiments Showing the Effect of the Interviewer's Racial Background on Response to Questionnaires Concerning Racial Issues," Journal of Applied Psychology 44:244-246 (August 1960).

Axelrod, Morris, Donald R. Matthews, and James W. Prothro, "Recruitment for Survey Research on Race Problems in the South," Public Opinion Quarterly 26:254-262 (Summer 1962).

Banks, W.S.M., II, "The Rank Order of Sensitivity to Discrimination of Negroes in Columbus, Ohio," American Sociological Review 15: 529-534 (August 1950). Conclusion: Myrdal's order of discrimination hypothesis is by and large an accurate portrayal of sensitivity of Negroes in Columbus.

Banton, Michael, "Sociology and Race Relations," Race 1:3-14 (November 1959).

Barron, Milton L., ed., American Minorities: A Textbook of Readings in Intergroup Relations. New York: Knopf, 1957.

Barth, Ernest A. T., "The Language Behavior of Negroes and Whites," Pacific Sociological Review 4:69-72 (Fall 1961). Language behavior reinforces social distance.

Berry, Brewton, Race and Ethnic Relations. Boston: Houghton Mifflin, 1951; 3rd ed., 1965. A comparative view of racial and ethnic interaction which examines recent events in the United States and abroad from a sociological point of view.

Bettelheim, Bruno, "Class, Color and Prejudice," Nation 197:231-234 (October 19, 1963). Presents thesis that the conflict in white-Negro relations stems from unwillingness to separate a class problem from a race or caste problem.

Bettelheim, Bruno, and Morris Janowitz, Social Change and Prejudice. New York: Free Press, 1964. A reissue of The Dynamics of Prejudice, together with a reassessment as of 1964.

Blalock, Hubert M., Jr., "Per Cent Non-White and Discrimination," American Sociological Review 22:677-682 (December 1957).

Blalock, Hubert M., Jr., "A Note on Adjusting Discrimination Rates for Per Cent Non-White," Journal of Negro Education 27:66-68 (Winter 1958).

Blalock, Hubert M., Jr., "A Power Analysis of Racial Discrimination," Social Forces 39:53-59 (October 1960).

Blumer, Herbert, "Race Prejudice as a Sense of Group Position," Pacific Sociological Review 1:3-7 (Spring 1958).

Boylan, Francis T., and O'Meara Byrns, "Stereotype and Inquiry Concerning Southern Born Negro Pupils in Chicago," Journal of Educational Sociology 32:76-82 (October 1958).

Breed, Warren, and Thomas Ktsanes, "Pluralistic Ignorance in the Process of Opinion Formation," Public Opinion Quarterly 25:382-392 (Fall 1961). Relationship between attitudes to segregation and ignorance.

Brody, Eugene B., et al., "Prejudice in American Negro College Students, Mental, Status, Antisemitism, and Antiforeign Prejudice," Archives of General Psychiatry 9:619-628 (December 1963).

Brophy, Ira N., "The Luxury of Anti-Negro Prejudice," Public Opinion Quarterly 9: 456-466 (Winter 1945-1946).

Brooklyn Association for the Study of Negro Life and History, "A Report on the Treatment of Minorities in Elementary School Textbooks." Brooklyn, N.Y., 1963.

Burnstein, E., and Adie V. McRae, "Some Effects of Shared Threat and Prejudice in Racially Mixed Groups," Journal of Abnormal and Social Psychology 64:257-263 (April 1962).

Campbell, Byram, Race and Social Revolution: Twenty-one Essays on Racial and Social Problems. New York: Truth Seeker, 1958.

Campbell, Ernest Q., "Moral Discomfort and Racial Segregation--An Examination of the Myrdal Hypothesis," Social Forces 39:228-234 (March 1961).

Christie, Richard, and Peggy Cook, "A Guide to Published Literature Relating to the Authoritarian Personality Through 1956," Journal of Psychology 45:171-199 (April 1958).

Christie, Richard, and Marie Jahoda, eds., Studies in the Scope and Method of "The Authoritarian Personality." Glencoe, Ill.: Free Press, 1954.

Clark, Kenneth B., Prejudice and Your Child. Boston: Beacon, 1955; 2nd ed. enlarged, Beacon paperback, 1963.

Cooper, Joseph B., "Prejudicial Attitudes and the Identification of their Stimulus Objects: A Phenomenological Approach," Journal of Social Psychology 48:15-23 (February 1958).

Curry, Andrew E., "The Negro Worker and the White Client: A Commentary on the Treatment Relationship," Social Casework 45:131-136 (March 1964).

Dicks, H. V., "Psychological Factors in Prejudice," Race 1:27-40 (November 1959).

Eboine, Alvin E., and Max Meenes, "Ethnic and Class Preferences Among College Negroes," Journal of Negro Education 29:128-133 (Spring 1960). Study based on a Howard University sample.

Edmunds, Edwin R., "The Myrdalian Thesis: Rank Order of Discrimination," Phylon 15: 297-313 (Summer 1954). This study, conducted in Texas and Oklahoma, concludes that the Myrdalian hypothesis is not accurate in the Southwest.

Ehrlich, Howard J., "The Study of Prejudice in American Social Science," Journal of Intergroup Relations, Spring 1962.

Ehrlich, Howard J., "Stereotyping and Negro-Jewish Stereotypes," Social Forces 41: 171-176 (December 1962).

Erskine, Hazel G., "The Polls: Race Relations," Public Opinion Quarterly 26:137-148 (Spring 1962).

Fineberg, S. Andhil, "Deflating the Professional Bigot," Journal of Intergroup Relations 1:47-53 (Winter 1959-1960).

Fishman, Joshua A., "An Examination of the Process and Function of Social Stereotyping," Journal of Social Psychology 43:26-64 (February 1956). Including racial stereotyping.

Fitzpatrick, Joseph P., "Attitudes of Puerto Ricans Toward Color," American Catholic Sociological Review 20:219-233 (Fall 1959).

Foster, L. H., "Race Relations in the South, 1960: A Tuskegee Institute Report," Journal of Negro Education 30:138-149 (Spring 1961).

Frazier, E. Franklin, "Sociological Theory and Race Relations," American Sociological Review 12:265-271 (June 1947).

Glazer, Nathan, "Negroes and Jews: The New Challenge to Pluralism," Commentary 38:29-34 (December 1964).

Goddard, David, "Letter to an American Friend," Race 5:30-37 (January 1964). Experiences of an Englishman with a Puerto Rican wife in the Southern states.

Gray, J. S., and A. J. Thompson, "Ethnic Prejudices of White and Negro College Students," Journal of Abnormal and Social Psychology 48:311-313 (April 1953).

Greenberg, Herbert, Jerome Pierson, and Stanley Sherman, "The Effects of Single-Session Education Techniques on Prejudice Attitudes," Journal of Educational Sociology 31:82-86 (October 1957).

Grossack, Martin M., "Perceived Negro Group Belongingness and Social Rejection," Journal of Psychology 38:127-130 (July 1954).

Hamblin, Robert L., "The Dynamics of Racial Discrimination," Social Problems 10: 103-120 (Fall 1962).

Hentoff, Nat, "Race Prejudice in Jazz," Harper's Magazine 218:72-77 (June 1959). Observations on the two-way prejudice in what seems outwardly the most integrated of the performing arts.

Higdon, Hal, "The Troubled Heart of Sigma Chi," New York Times Magazine, November 14, 1965. On the pressure being put on all white-only fraternities to open their doors to Negroes, particularly on Sigma Chi, whose national organization has blocked all efforts to liberalize policies.

Himelstein, P., and J. C. Moore, "Racial Attitudes and the Action of Negro and White Background Figures as Factors in Petition-Signing," Journal of Social Psychology 61:267-272 (December 1963).

Hites, Robert W., and Edward P. Kellogg, "The F and Social Maturity Scales in Relation to Racial Attitudes in a Deep South Sample," Journal of Social Psychology 62:189-196 (April 1964).

Hope, John, II, "Trends in Patterns of Race Relations in the South Since May 17, 1954," Phylon 17:103-118 (Summer 1956).

Jahoda, Marie, "What Is Prejudice?" Look 24:93-94 (May 26, 1960).

Janowitz, Morris, "Social Change and Prejudice," in E. W. Burgess and D. J. Bogue, eds., Contributions to Urban Sociology, Chicago: University of Chicago Press, 1964.

Javits, Jacob K., Discrimination--U.S.A. New York: Harcourt, Brace, 1960. A detailed and concrete review of discrimination in voting, housing, and schooling, which emphasizes the effectiveness of law as a force for progressive social change in race relations.

Johnson, Guy B., "The Course of Race Conflicts and Racial Movements in the South," in Jitsuichi Masuoka and Preston Valien, eds., Race Relations: Problems and Theory, Chapel Hill: University of North Carolina Press, 1961.

Kasoff, Allen, "The Prejudiced Personality: A Cross Cultural Test," Social Problems 6:59-67 (Summer 1958).

Katz, Irwin, and L. Benjamin, "Effects of White Authoritarianism in Biracial Work Groups," Journal of Abnormal and Social Psychology 61:448-456 (September 1960).

Kelly, James G., Jean E. Ferson, and Wayne H. Holtzman, "The Measurement of Attitudes Toward the Negro in the South," Journal of Social Psychology 48:305-317 (November 1958).

Kelman, Herbert C., and Thomas F. Pettigrew, "How to Understand Prejudice,"
    Commentary 28:436–441 (November 1959). Reply to William Petersen, "Prejudice in
    American Society," ibid. 26:342-348 (October 1958).
Killian, Lewis M., and Charles M. Grigg, "Rank Order of Discrimination of Negroes and
    Whites in a Southern City," Social Forces 39:235-239 (March 1961).
Koenig, Frederick W., and Morton B. King, Jr., "Cognitive Simplicity and Prejudice,"
    Social Forces 40:220-222 (March 1962).
Koenig, Frederick W., and Morton B. King, Jr., "Cognitive Simplicity and Out-Group
    Stereotyping," Social Forces 42:324-327 (March 1964).
Kutner, Bernard, Carol Wilkins, and Penny R. Yarrow, "Verbal Attitudes and Overt
    Behavior Involving Racial Prejudice," Journal of Abnormal and Social Psychology 47:
    649-652 (July 1952).
Lee, Frank F., "The Race Relations Patterns by Areas of Behavior in a Small New
    England Town," American Sociological Review 19:138-143 (April 1954).
Lee, Frank F., Negro and White in a Connecticut Town: A Study in Race Relations. New
    York: Bookman Associates, 1961.
Lee, J. Oscar, "Racism: Effects, Origins, Remedies," Christian Century 80:907-909
    (July 17, 1963).
Lief, Harold I., "Development of Attitudes in Respect to Discrimination: An Atypical
    Stereotype of the Negroes' Social Worlds," American Journal of Orthopsychiatry 32:
    86–88 (January 1962).
Livson, Norman, and Thomas F. Nichols, "Social Attitude Configurations in an Adolescent
    Group," Journal of Genetic Psychology 91:3-23 (September 1957).
McDaniel, Paul A., and Nicholas Babchuk, "Negro Conceptions of White People in a
    Northeastern City," Phylon 21:7-19 (Spring 1960).
Mann, John H., "The Influence of Racial Prejudice on Sociometric Choices and Perceptions,"
    Sociometry 21:150-158 (June 1958).
Mann, John H., "The Relationship Between Cognitive, Affective, and Behavioral Aspects
    of Racial Prejudice," Journal of Social Psychology 49:223-228 (May 1959).
Marcus, Lloyd, The Treatment of Minorities in Secondary School Textbooks. New York:
    Anti-Defamation League, 1961.
Marney, Carlyle, Structures of Prejudice. New York: Abingdon, 1961.
Martin, James G., "Group Discrimination in Organizational Membership Selection,"
    Phylon 22:186-192 (June 1959).
Martin, James G., "Intergroup Tolerance--Prejudice," Journal of Human Relations 10:
    197-204 (Winter-Spring, 1962).
Mason, Philip, An Essay on Racial Tension. New York: Oxford University Press, 1954.
    What can be learned from biological sciences and other disciplines concerning racial
    tension.
Masuoka, Jitsuichi, and Preston Valien, eds., Race Relations: Problems and Theory.
    Chapel Hill: University of North Carolina Press, 1961. Articles listed separately.
Medalia, Nahum Z., "Myrdal's Assumptions on Race Relations: A Conceptual Commentary,"
    Social Forces 40:223-227 (March 1962).
Mendelson, Wallace, Discrimination: Based on the Report of the United States Commission
    on Civil Rights. Englewood Cliffs, N.J.: Prentice-Hall, 1962.
Merz, Louise E., and Leonard I. Pearlin, "The Influence of Information on Three Dimen-
    sions of Prejudice Toward Negroes," Social Forces 95:344-351 (May 1957).
Middleton, Russell, "Ethnic Prejudice and Susceptibility to Persuasion," American
    Sociological Review 25:679-686 (October 1960).
Miyamoto, S. Frank, "The Process of Intergroup Tension and Conflict," in E. W. Burgess
    and D. J. Bogue, eds., Contributions to Urban Sociology, Chicago: University of
    Chicago Press, 1964.
Nelson, Harold A., "Expressed and Unexpressed Prejudices Against Ethnic Groups in a
    College Community," Journal of Negro Education 31:125-131 (Spring 1962).
Neprash, Jerry A., "Minority Group Contacts and Social Distance," Phylon 14:207-212
    (June 1953). Conclusion: prejudice flourishes in absence of personal contacts. Thus the
    existence of segregation is a condition of its perpetuation.
Noel, Donald L., and Alphonso Pinkney, "Correlates of Prejudice: Some Racial Differences
    and Similarities," American Journal of Sociology 69:609-622 (May 1964).

O'Shea, Harriet E., and Gerald Engel, "Some Current Student Attitudes Toward Presidential Candidates of Different Categories (Racial and Religious)," Journal of Psychology 51: 233-246 (January 1961).

Palmer, Roderick, "The Incidence of Race in Social Action," Journal of Negro Education 31:188-190 (Spring 1962).

"Papers and Proceedings of a Conference on Negro-Jewish Relations in the United States," Jewish Social Studies 27:3-66 (January 1965). Entire issue. Includes both race and attitude studies, Jewish involvement in civil rights struggle, and economic relations between Jews and Negroes.

Petersen, William, "Prejudice in American Society: A Critique of Some Recent Formulations," Commentary 26:342-348 (October 1958).

Pettigrew, Thomas F., "Personality and Socio-Cultural Factors in Intergroup Attitudes: A Cross-National Comparison," Journal of Conflict Resolution 2:29-42 (March 1958).

Pettigrew, Thomas F., "Regional Differences in Anti-Negro Prejudice," Journal of Abnormal and Social Psychology 59:28-36 (July 1959).

Pinkney, Alphonso, "Prejudice Toward Mexican and Negro Americans: A Comparison," Phylon 24:353-359 (Winter 1963).

Podhoretz, Norman, "My Negro Problem--and Ours," Commentary 35:93-101 (February 1963).

Raab, Earl, and Seymour M. Lipset, Prejudice and Society. New York: Anti-Defamation League, 1959.

Raab, Earl, ed., American Race Relations Today. Garden City, N.Y.: Doubleday, 1962. Ten essays on factors other than discrimination which complicate the process of achieving an integrated society. Among the contributors: Seymour M. Lipset, Morton Grodzins, Nathan Glazer, Joseph Himes, James B. Conant.

Record, Wilson, Minority Groups and Intergroup Relations in the San Francisco Bay Area. Berkeley: Institute of Governmental Studies, University of California, 1963.

Reitzes, Dietrich C., "Institutional Structure and Race Relations," Phylon 20:48-66 (Spring 1959).

Rhyne, Edwin Hoffman, "Racial Prejudice and Personality Scales: An Alternative Approach." Social Forces 41:44-53 (October 1962); 42:242-246 (December 1963).

Richmond, Anthony H., "Sociological and Psychological Explanations of Racial Prejudice," Pacific Sociological Review 4:63-68 (Fall 1961).

Roberts, Harry W., "Prior-service Attitudes Toward Whites of 219 Negro Veterans," Journal of Negro Education 22:455-465 (Fall 1953).

Robinson, James H., and Kenneth B. Clark, "What Negroes Think About Jews," Anti-Defamation League Bulletin 14:4-8 (December 1957).

Rose, Arnold M., "Intergroup Relations vs. Prejudice," Social Problems 4:173-176 (October 1956). Suggests attitudes are not necessarily related to action patterns.

Rose, Arnold M., ed., Race Prejudice and Discrimination. New York: Knopf, 1951. Sections on minority problems in the United States, kinds of discrimination, group identification and the minority community, perceptions of the minority and the causes of prejudice, and proposed techniques for eliminating minority problems.

Rose, Arnold M., and Caroline Rose, eds., The Minority Problem: A Book of Readings. New York: Harper, 1965. Such problems as residential segregation, fair employment, intergroup relations examined in the context of theories of prejudice and discrimination.

Rousseve, Ronald J., Discord in Brown and White: Nine Essays on Intergroup Relations in the United States, by a Negro-American. New York: Vantage, 1961.

Rudwick, Elliott M., "Race Labeling and the Press," Journal of Negro Education 31:177-181 (Spring 1962).

Sheatsley, Paul B., "White Attitudes Toward the Negro," Daedalus 95:217-238 (Winter 1966).

Sheppard, Harold L., "The Negro Merchant: A Study of Negro Anti-Semitism," American Journal of Sociology 53:96-99 (September 1947).

Simon, W. B., "Race Relations and Class Structures," Journal of Social Psychology 60:187-193 (August 1963).

Simpson, George Eaton, and J. Milton Yinger, Racial and Cultural Minorities: An Analysis of Prejudice and Discrimination. New York: Harper, 1953; rev. ed., 1958. A study of majority-minority relations in the context of the whole area of sciences of human behavior. Both great breadth of view and an impressive breadth of scholarship are evident in their work. Excellent bibliography.

Simpson, Richard, "Negro-Jewish Prejudice: Authoritarianism and Some Social Variables as Correlates," Social Problems 7:138-146 (Fall 1959).

Star, Shirley, "An Approach to the Measurement of Interracial Tension," in E. W. Burgess and D. J. Bogue, eds., Contributions to Urban Sociology, Chicago: University of Chicago Press, 1964.

Steckler, G.A., "Authoritarian Ideology in Negro College Students," Journal of Abnormal and Social Psychology 54:396-399 (May 1957).

Stouffer, Samuel A., "Quantitative Methods in the Study of Race Relations," in Jitsuichi Masuoka and Preston Valien, eds., Race Relations: Problems and Theory, Chapel Hill: University of North Carolina Press, 1961.

Stuart, Irving R., "Minorities vs. Minorities: Cognitive, Affective and Conative Components of Puerto Rican and Negro Acceptance and Rejection," Journal of Social Psychology 59:93-99 (February 1963). In labor unions.

Suchman, Edward A., et al., "Hypotheses and Prospects for Opinion Research in Desegregation," Public Opinion Quarterly 22:190-191 (Summer 1958).

Tabachnick, B. Robert, "Some Correlates of Prejudice Toward Negroes in Elementary Age Children," Journal of Genetic Psychology 100:193-203 (June 1962)

Thompson, Daniel C., "Development of Attitudes in Respect to Discrimination: The Formation of Social Attitudes," American Journal of Orthopsychiatry 32:74-85 (January 1962).

Thompson, Edgar T., "Language and Race Relations," in Jitsuichi Masuoka and Preston Valien, eds., Race Relations: Problems and Theory, Chapel Hill: University of North Carolina Press, 1961.

Trent, Richard D., "The Color of the Investigator as a Variable in Experimental Research with Negro Subjects," Journal of Social Psychology 40:281-287 (November 1954).

Triandis, Harry C., and Leigh Mintern Triandis, "Race, Social Class, Religion, and Nationality as Determinants of Social Distance," Journal of Abnormal and Social Psychology 61:110-118 (July 1960).

Vander Zanden, James W., American Minority Relations: the Sociology of Race and Ethnic Group. New York: Ronald, 1963. A well-written and well-ordered study drawing on research in many fields. Discusses the operation of prejudice and discrimination in intergroup relations, and the function of social change in affecting dominant-minority group relations.

Weiss, Walter, "An Examination of Attitude Toward Negroes," Journal of Social Psychology 55:3-21 (October 1961).

Westie, Frank R., and Margaret L. Westie, "The Social-Distance Pyramid: Relationships Between Caste and Class," American Journal of Sociology 63:190-196 (September 1957).

Wilkins, Roy, "Jewish-Negro Relations: An Evaluation," American Judaism, Spring 1963.

Williams, Robin M., Jr., et al., Strangers Next Door: Ethnic Relations in American Communities. Englewood Cliffs, N.J.: Prentice-Hall, 1964. Sociological and social-psychological studies made between 1948 and 1956 in Elmira, N.Y.; Steubenville, Ohio; Bakersfield, Calif.; and Savannah, Ga.

Wills, Garry, "In Defense of Uncle Toms: The Semantics of Racism," Commonweal 83: 178-180 (November 1965).

Wolfe, John B., "Incidents of Friction Between Negroes and Whites in Southeastern U.S.A.," Mankind Quarterly 2:122-127 (October-November 1961). A catalogue of nearly 2000 interviews to determine what incidents involving a person of the same or of different race are the most irritating.

Works, Ernest, "The Prejudice-Interaction Hypothesis from the Point of View of the Negro Minority Group," American Journal of Sociology 67:47-52 (July 1961).

Worsnop, Richard L., "Racism in America," Editorial Research Reports 1964 vol. 1: 343-360 (May 13, 1964).

Wright, Richard, The Outsider. New York: Harper, 1953. A personal interpretation of how the white man looks to nonwhite eyes.

2. OVERCOMING PREJUDICE

Annals of the American Academy of Political and Social Science 304:1-143 (March 1956).
Entire issue on "Racial Desegregation and Integration." Articles listed separately.

Babbit, Thelma W., and Arthur W. Chickering, "The Conference as a Resource," Journal of Intergroup Relations 3:12-20 (Winter 1961-1962).

Balfour, Brickner, New Jewish Initiatives in the Field of Race. New York: Union of American Hebrew Congregations, 1963.

Banks, Waldo R., "Changing Attitudes Towards the Negro in the United States: The Primary Causes," Journal of Negro Education 30:87-93 (Spring 1961).

Bloch, Herman D., "Recognition of Negro Discrimination: A Solution," Journal of Social Psychology 48:291-295 (November 1958).

Blumer, Herbert, "Social Science and the Desegregation Process," Annals of the American Academy of Political and Social Science 304:137-143 (March 1956).

Bogardus, Emory S., "Stages in White-Negro Relations in the United States: An Outline," Society and Social Research, October 1960.

Bond, Marjorie H., "Teenage Attitudes and Attitude Change as Measured by the Q-Technique," Journal of Educational Sociology 36:10-16 (September 1962). A description of Brotherhood, U.S.A., an intergroup education workshop for southern California youth.

Burgess, Ernest W., "Social Planning and Race Relations," in Jitsuichi Masuoka and Preston Valien, eds., Race Relations: Problems and Theory, Chapel Hill: University of North Carolina Press, 1961.

Campbell, Ernest Q., "On Desegregation and Matters Sociological," Phylon 22:135-145 (Summer 1961).

Campbell, John D., Leon J. Yarrow, and Marian R. Yarrow, "A Study of Adaptation to a New Social Situation," Journal of Social Issues 14:3-7 (January 1958). Group adaptation as observed in a two-weeks' camp of Negro and white children.

Carleton, William G., "Negro Rights in the South: Making Haste Slowly," Teachers College Record 62:18-26 (October 1960). Author finds that racial attitudes are softening, and that there have been gains in acceptance of desegregation.

Carter, Elmer, "Policies and Practices of Discrimination Commissions," Annals of the American Academy of Political and Social Science 304:62-77 (March 1956).

Carter, Marion Elizabeth, "Human Relations in the Course Offerings of the District of Columbia Teachers College," Journal of Negro Education 27:69-78 (Winter 1958).

Clark, Dennis, "Leadership Education in an All-White Neighborhood," Journal of Intergroup Relations, Winter 1961-1962.

Clark, Kenneth B., ed., "Desegregation: An Appraisal of the Evidence," Journal of Social Issues 9:2-76 (Fall 1953).

Coleman, A. Lee, "Social Scientists' Predictions About Desegregation, 1950-1955," Social Forces 38:258-262 (March 1960).

Cook, Lloyd A., and Elaine Cook, Intergroup Education. New York: McGraw-Hill, 1954.

Cook, Stuart W., "Desegregation: A Psychological Analysis," American Psychologist 12:1-13 (January 1957). Address by the president of the New York State Psychological Association, January 28, 1956.

Dabbs, James McBride, "The South's Man Across the Table," New South 12:3-9 (June 1957). Confronting Negroes in community conferences a new experience for Southern whites.

Daly, Victor R., " A Decade of Progress in Race Relations in the Nation's Capital," Journal of Intergroup Relations 2:252-258 (Summer 1961).

Dean, John P., and Alex Rosen, A Manual of Intergroup Relations. Chicago: University of Chicago Press, 1955. The authors outline several "propositions" that can be applied in intergroup relations to minimize prejudiced behavior, with special emphasis on changing situations as mechanisms for altering discriminatory actions.

De Fleur, Melvin L., and Frank R. Westie, "The Interpretation of Interracial Situations: An Experiment in Social Perception," Social Forces 38:17-23 (October 1959).

Eddy, Elizabeth M., "Attitudes Toward Desegregation Among Southern Students on a Northern Campus," Journal of Social Psychology 62:285-302 (April 1964).

Epstein, Charlotte, "A Plan for Coordination of Intergroup Relations Services," Journal of Intergroup Relations 1:32-36 (Summer 1960).

Fen, Sing-Nan, "The Learning of Social Relations in School," Journal of Negro Education 32:87-91 (Winter 1963).

Frank, John P., "Legal Developments in Race Relations," in Allan P. Sindler, ed., Change in the Contemporary South, Durham: Duke University Press, 1963.

Frazier, E. Franklin, "Desegregation as an Object of Sociological Study," in Arnold M. Rose, ed., Human Behavior and Social Processes. Boston: Houghton, Mifflin, 1962.

Gordon, Milton M., Assimilation in American Life. New York: Oxford University Press, 1964. The author has "chosen to focus on the nature of group life itself in the United States as constituting the social setting in which relationships among persons of differing race, religion, and national origin take place." He concludes that the American social structure will continue to consist of a series of ethnic subcommunities crisscrossed by social class, and that secondary group relationships across ethnic lines will increasingly occur in urbanized industrial society.

Greenberg, Herbert, A. L. Chase, and T. M. Cannon, Jr., "Attitudes of White and Negro High School Students in a West Texas Town Toward School Integration," Journal of Applied Psychology 41:27-31 (February 1957).

Greenberg, Herbert, and Dolores Hutto, "The Attitudes of West Texas College Students Toward School Integtration," Journal of Applied Psychology 42:301-304 (October 1958). A study indicating that while the attitudes of white students were generally positive, they were influenced by negative attitude toward desegregation by their parents.

Greene, Robert J., "Some Proposals Looking Toward Cooperation Among Public and Private Intergroup Relations Agencies," Journal of Intergroup Relations 3:21-27 (Winter 1961-1962).

Grossack, Martin M., "Attitudes Towards Desegregation of Southern White and Negro Children," Journal of Social Psychology 46:299-306 (November 1957).

Grossack, Martin M., "Segregation and Power Relationships," American Psychologist 16:652-653 (October 1961). Resistance to integration as much dependent on power relationships within the social system as to prejudice. Questions Pettigrew's "latent liberal concept."

Hager, Don J., "Social and Psychological Factors in Integration," Journal of Educational Sociology 31:57-63 (October 1957). Importance of community-wide efforts in all areas of social contact.

Hyman, Herbert H., and Paul B. Sheatsley, "Attitudes Toward Desegregation," Scientific American 195:26, 35-39 (December 1956).

Hyman, Herbert H., and Paul B. Sheatsley, "Attitudes Toward Desegregation--Seven Years Later," Scientific American 211:14, 16-23 (July 1964).

Hyman, Herbert H., and Paul B. Sheatsley, "How Whites View Negroes, 1942-1963," New York Herald-Tribune, November 19, 1963.

Holtzman, W. H., "Attitudes of College Men Toward Non-Segregation in Texas Schools," Public Opinion Quarterly 20:559-569 (Fall 1956).

Iskander, Michel G., "The Neighborhood Approach," Journal of Intergroup Relations 3:80-86 (Winter 1961-1962).

Johnson, Charles S., "Introduction: From Race Relations to Human Relations," in Jitsuichi Maᵤoka and Preston Vailen, eds., Race Relations: Problems and Theory, Chapel Hill: University of North Carolina Press, 1961.

Johnson, Guy B., "A Sociologist Looks at Racial Desegregation in the South," Social Forces 32:1-10 (October 1954).

Johnson, Robert B., "Changing Status of the Negro in American Life," Journal of Inter-group Relations 1:56-70 (Spring 1960).

Katz, Irwin, Conflict and Harmony in an Adolescent Interracial Group. New York: New York University Press, 1955.

Katz, Irwin, and Melvin Cohen, "The Effects of Training Negroes upon Cooperative Problem Solving in Biracial Teams," Journal of Abnormal and Social Psychology 64:319-325 (May 1964).

Kohn, M. L., and Robin Williams, Jr., "Situational Patterning in Intergroup Relations," American Sociological Review 21:164-174 (April 1956). Report of an experiment which consisted in initiating unpatterned situations of integration and studying the responses of participants, and the processes by which participants redefined or modified responses.

Lamanna, Richard, "Ecological Correlates of Attitude Toward Desegregation," American Catholic Sociological Review 22:242-249 (Fall 1961).

Lieberson, Stanley, "Comparative Segregation and Assimilation of Ethnic Groups," unpub. doc. diss., University of Chicago, 1960.

Lippman, Leopold, "Public Relations for Better Race Relations," Public Relations Journal 16:18-19 (February 1960). Prepared for Seattle Urban League.

Lombardi, Donald N., "Factors Affecting Changes in Attitudes Toward Negroes Among High School Students," Journal of Negro Education 32:129-136 (Spring 1963).

Long, Heiman, "Community Research and Intergroup Adjustment," in Jitsuichi Masuoka and Preston Valien, eds., Race Relations: Problems and Theory, Chapel Hill: University of North Carolina Press, 1961.

Long, Herman H., "Some Major Issues of Intergroup Relations for the Sixties," Journal of Intergroup Relations 1:5-11 (Fall 1960). Objectives: equal opportunities in all areas and eradication of group victimization of Negroes.

Loth, David, and Harold C. Fleming, Integration North and South. Santa Barbara, Calif.: Fund for the Republic, 1956. Survey of desegregation progress.

Lott, Bernice E., and Albert J. Lott, Negro and White Youth: A Psychological Study in a Border State Community. New York: Holt, 1963. A study of High School students in a Kentucky community tending to demonstrate there is a "community culture" which penetrates the barrier of segregation.

McKee, James B., "Community Power and Strategies in Race Relations: Some Critical Observations," Social Problems 6:195-203 (Winter 1958-1959).

Mann, John H., "The Effect of Inter-Racial Contact on Sociometric Choices and Perceptions," Journal of Social Psychology 50:143-152 (August 1959).

Marciniak, Edward, "Interracial Councils in Chicago," America 99:640-642 (September 20, 1958).

Marrow, Alfred J., Changing Patterns of Prejudice: A New Look at Today's Racial, Religious, and Cultural Tensions. Philadelphia: Chilton, 1962. The former chairman of New York City's Commission on Intergroup Relations (1955-1960) presents his views on the work of a municipal intergroup commission, relates examples of how effective the one in New York was, and discusses intergroup problems in America in general.

Marsh, B. L., "Easing Community Tensions," Public Management 45:194-198 (September 1963). In a suburban community.

Mason, Philip, "An Approach to Race Relations," Race 1:41-52 (November 1959).

Mausner, Bernard, "Desegregation and Integration," American Psychologist 16:317-318 (June 1961).

Maxey, Alva, "The Block Club Movement in Chicago," Phylon 18:124-131 (Summer 1957). How community activities within small areas can foster an integrative spirit.

Mays, Benjamin E., "A Plea for Straight Talk Between the Races," Atlantic 206:85-86 (December 1960). Author is president of Atlanta's Morehouse College, and an authority on the Negro church.

Nichols, Lee, Breakthrough on the Color Front. New York: Random House, 1954. History of the integration of the armed forces. Conclusion: the military was a spearhead toward integration in the United States at large.

Ogburn, William Fielding, "Social Change and Race Relations," in Jitsuichi Masuoka and Preston Valien, eds., Race Relations: Problems and Theory, Chapel Hill: University of North Carolina Press, 1961.

Organizations and Personnel Engaged in Human Relations Activities in the South: Special Report. Atlanta, Ga.: Southern Regional Council, May 1, 1957.

Pettigrew, Thomas F., "Desegregation and Its Chances for Success: Northern and Southern Views," Social Forces 35:339-344 (May 1957).

Pettigrew, Thomas F., "Demographic Correlates of Border-State Desegregation," American Sociological Review 22:683-689 (December 1957).

Pettigrew, Thomas F., "Social Psychology and Desegregation Research," American Psychologist 16:105-112 (March 1961). On the importance of directing research to the attitudes of the "latent liberal," "one who has the personality potentiality of becoming liberal once the norms of the culture change."

Pettigrew, Thomas F., "Complexity and Change in American Racial Patterns: A Social
    Psychological View," Daedalus 94: 974-1008 (Fall 1965). The author's prognosis for
    1984 is that racial patterns will most differ from today's "in the employment realm and
    least in the areas of housing and family." He points out that "The whole issue of de facto
    segergation in schools, churches, and other neighborhood-based institutions revolves
    around residential segregation," and that this is the most difficult problem to solve.
Pettigrew, Thomas F., and Richard M. Cramer, "The Demography of Desegregation,"
    Journal of Social Issues 15:61-71 (October 1959).
Pierce, C.M., "A Psychiatric Approach to Present Day Racial Problems," Journal of the
    National Medical Association 51:207-210 (May 1959).
Robbins, Richard, "Local Strategy in Race Relations: The Illinois Experience With
    Community Human Relations Commissions and Councils," Journal of Intergroup
    Relations 2:311-324 (Fall 1961).
Roberts, Harry W., "The Impact of Military Service Upon the Racial Attitudes of Negro
    Servicemen in World War II," Social Problems 1:65-69 (October 1953).
Root, Robert, Progress Against Prejudice. New York: Friendship Press, 1965. Reports of
    recent developments in improving race relations, principally in the North and border
    states.
Shelley, J., "Biracial Citizens' Committee Works Toward Integration," Public Manage-
    ment 45:277 (December 1963).
Sherif, Muzafer, "Superordinate Goals in the Reduction of Intergroup Conflicts,"
    American Journal of Sociology 63:349-356 (January 1958).
Sherif, Muzafer, ed., Intergroup Relations and Leadership. New York: Wiley, 1962.
Sherif, Muzafer, O. J. Harvey, B. J. White, and W. R. Hood, Intergroup Conflict and
    Cooperation: The Robbers Cave Experiment. Norman, Okla.: Institute of Group Rela-
    tions, 1961.
Sherif, Muzafer, and Carolyn Sherif, Groups in Harmony and Tension. New York: Harper,
    1953. Largely theoretical. Chapters 2, 4, and 5 more particularly directed to problems
    concerning Negroes.
Simpson, George Eaton, and J. Milton Yinger, "The Changing Patterns of Race Relations,"
    Phylon 15:327-345 (December 1954). The authors predict that changes in economic
    conditions in the South, increased Negro voting, legal changes, and increased oppor-
    tunities for higher education will be most effective means of advancing the Negro and
    spurring desegregation rather than efforts to decrease prejudice.
Smith, Charles U., "Race, Human Relations and the Changing South," Phylon 23:66-72
    (Spring 1962).
Smith, Lillian, Now is the Time. New York: Viking, 1955. Both polemic and account of
    race relations since the 1954 Supreme Court decision. The author gives a list of what
    whites can do to improve race relations. A bibliography "for the layman."
"Sports Integration is Setting Example," New South 13:3-9 (April 1958). On the basis of a
    survey of professional and college sports, the evidence is that when barriers fall in
    sport, other barriers give way.
"Statement on Integration," American Journal of Orthopsychiatry 34:421-422 (April 1964).
    Prepared by Social Issues Committee of the American Orthopsychiatric Association on
    the need for joint effort by all behavioral scientists to help Negro solve integration
    problems.
Stember, Charles Herbert, Education and Attitude Change: The Effect of Schooling on
    Prejudice Against Minority Groups. New York: Institute of Human Relations, 1961.
Stetler, Henry G., Attitudes Toward Racial Integration in Connecticut. Hartford: Com-
    mission on Civil Rights of the State of Connecticut, 1961.
Suchman, Edward A., et al., Desegregation: Some Propositions and Research Suggestions.
    New York: Anti-Defamation League, 1958. Outlines of problem areas and suggestions
    for further research, together with lists of some studies already undertaken.
Teacher Education for Human Relations in the Classroom: A Report from 1,108 College
    Professors. Chicago: North Central Association, 1962.
Thompson, Richard, Race and Sport. London: Oxford University Press, 1964. Issued under
    the auspices of the Institute of Race Relations.
Tumin, Melvin M., "Exposure to Mass Media and Readiness for Desegregation," Public
    Opinion Quarterly 21:237-251 (Summer 1957).

Tumin, Melvin M., Desegregation: Resistance and Readiness. Princeton: Princeton University Press, 1958. Suggests that propensities to unlawfulness bear an inverse relationship to improvements in social class and occupational status.

Tumin, Melvin M., and Robert Rotberg, "Leaders, the Led, and the Law: A Case Study in Social Change," Public Opinion Quarterly 21:355-370 (Fall 1957).

Tumin, Melvin M., and Robert Rotberg, "Readiness and Resistance to Desegregation: A Social Portrait of the Hard Core," Social Forces 36:256-263 (March 1958).

Tumin, Melvin M., and Robert Rotberg, "Sociological Aspects of Desegregation," American Journal of Orthopsychiatry 29:180-185 (January 1959). "A good deal of discrimination has been eliminated without a matching reduction in . . . prejudice." Therefore we should focus on behavior.

Tumin, Melvin M., Robert Rotberg, Paul Barton, and Bernie Burrus, "Education, Prejudice and Discrimination: A Study in Readiness for Desegregation," American Sociological Review 23:41-49 (February 1958).

Warner, W. Lloyd, and Leo Srole, "Differential Assimilation of American Ethnic Groups," in Milton L. Barron, ed., American Minorities, New York: Knopf, 1957.

Watts, Lewis G., "Social Integration and the Use of Minority Leadership in Seattle, Washington," Phylon 21:136-143 (Summer 1960).

Weaver, Robert C., "The Changing Status of Racial Groups," Journal of Intergroup Relations 2:6-17 (Winter 1960-1961).

Webster, Staten W., "The Influence of Interracial Contact on Social Acceptance in a Newly Integrated School," Journal of Educational Psychology 52:292-296 (December 1961).

Williams, Lorraine A., "The Interracial Conference of the National Council of Negro Women," Journal of Negro Education 26:204-206 (Spring 1957).

Williams, Robin M., Jr., The Reduction of Inter-Group Tensions. New York: Social Science Research Council Bulletin No. 57, 1947. Education alone has little effect in reducing deep prejudice.

Wilner, Daniel M., Rosabelle Price Walkley, and Stuart W. Cook, Human Relations in Interracial Housing: A Study of the Contact Hypothesis. Minneapolis: University of Minnesota Press, 1955.

Winder, Alvin, "White Attitudes Toward Negro-White Interaction in a Number of Community Situations," Journal of Social Psychology 44:15-32 (August 1956).

Yarrow, Marian R., ed., "Interpersonal Dynamics in a Desegregation Process," Journal of Social Issues 14:3-63 (Winter 1958).

Yarrow, Marian R., John D. Campbell, and Leon J. Yarrow, "Acquisition of New Norms: A Study of Racial Desegregation," Journal of Social Issues 14:8-28 (Winter 1958).

Young, R. K., W. M. Benson, and W. H. Holtzman, "Changes in Attitudes Toward the Negro in a Southern University," Journal of Abnormal and Social Psychology 60:131-133 (January 1960).

IV. RURAL PROBLEMS

The rapid urbanization of the Negro during recent years has led to a tendency to overlook the problems of the Negroes who are still a part of the farm population. The statistician announces, "In the South more than half of the Negroes are city dwellers." He is less apt to emphasize that one fifth of the Negroes in the United States are in agriculture, and that nearly half of all Southern Negroes are still engaged in rural occupations, including migrant labor, and that the poverty, the disease, the disabilities of all kinds of which they are the victims are among the most stubborn and intractable problems faced by the Negro people in any region of the country.

Anderson, C. Arnold, "Economic Status Differentials Within Southern Agriculture," Rural Sociology 19:50-67 (March 1954).

Anderson, C. Arnold, and M. J. Bowman, Tenure Changes and the Agricultural Ladder in Southern Agriculture. Bulletin 634, Kentucky Agricultural Experiment Station, 1955.

Bertrand, Alvin L., Agricultural Mechanization and Social Change in Rural Louisiana. Baton Rouge: Louisiana State University Agricultural Experiment Station Bulletin No. 458, 1957. Result: decreased need for plantation agricultural labor and hence increased Negro migration to cities.

Better Homes for Negro Farm Families: A Handbook for Teachers Outlining an Educational Program in Housing. Washington, D.C.: U.S. Office of Education, Agricultural Education Branch, 1947. Prepared jointly by Agricultural Education Service and Home Economics Education Service.

Bird, Alan R., Poverty in Rural Areas of the United States: Agricultural Economic Report No. 63. Washington, D.C.: U.S. Department of Agriculture, June 1965.

Brown, Morgan C., "Selected Characteristics of Southern Rural Negroes Exchanged to a Southern Urban Center," Rural Sociology 27:64-70 (March 1962).

Coles, Robert, "What Migrant Farm Children Learn," Saturday Review 48:73-74+ (May 15, 1965).

Cowhig, James D., and Calvin L. Beale, "Socioeconomic Differences Between White and Nonwhite Farm Populations of the South," Social Forces 42:354-362 (March 1964). Study from census data of 1950 and 1960 shows improvement for both groups, but also difference widening.

Hill, Herbert, No Harvest for the Reaper: The Story of the Migratory Agricultural Worker in the United States. New York: NAACP, 1960.

Hilsheimer, G. von, "Child Care and the Migrant Farm Hand," Journal of Nursing Education 18: 262-266 (September 1963).

Johnson, Charles S., Growing Up in the Black Belt. Washington, D.C.: American Council on Education, 1941. A study of the personality development of rural Negro youth as affected by their cultural environment in the South. Part I consists of ten brief sketches of youths from different rural settings. Part II examines the rural South which made up their environment, economic institutions, patterns of social life, family life.

Jones, Lewis W., "The Negro Farmer," Journal of Negro Education 22:322-332 (Summer 1953).

Mayo, Selz C., and C. Horace Hamilton, "The Rural Negro Population of the South in Transition," Phylon 24:160-171 (Summer 1963). The authors examine population growth rates and distribution, Negro fertility rates, age groups, occupations, education. Their data show that 43 percent of rural Negroes have had less than five grades of school and are functional illiterates.

Mayo, Selz C., and C. Horace Hamilton, "Current Population Trends in the South," Social Forces 42:77-88 (October 1963).

Mirel, E., "Rural Negroes Need Help," Science News Letter 84:214 (October 5, 1963). Especially Negro youth.

Moore, Truman E., The Slaves We Rent. New York: Random House, 1965. A description of the life of migrant workers, a vivid picture of rural slum life. Illustrated.

"Negro Families in Rural Wisconsin: A Study of their Community Life," Madison, Wis.: Governor's Commission on Human Rights, 1959.

"Negro Farmers Get Unfair Deal," Farm Journal, 89:78 (April 1965).

"New Hope for Rural Dixie: Firms in Carolinas Create Jobs for Negroes," Ebony 19:50+ (June 1964).

Palley, Howard A., "The Migrant Labor Problem--Its State and Interstate Aspects," Journal of Negro Education 32:35-42 (Winter 1963).

Payne, Raymond, "Organizational Activities of Rural Negroes in Mississippi," Mississippi State College Agricultural Experiment Station Circular No. 192, Starkville, Miss., 1953. Southern Negroes unlikely to participate actively in organizations other than churches and fraternal groups.

Pederson, H.A., "Mechanized Agriculture and the Farm Laborer," Rural Sociology 19: 143-151 (June 1954).

Pellegrin, Roland J., and Vernon J. Parenton, "The Impact of Socio-Economic Change on Racial Groups in a Rural Setting," Phylon 23:55-60 (Spring 1962).

Peter, Emmet, Jr., "On the Outside Looking Out," New Republic 152:18 (June 26, 1965). On the position of Negro farmers.

Pomfret, John D., "Negro Farm Workers in Florida Fight Poverty Every Day," New York Times, April 20, 1964.

"Racial Bias in Workings of U.S. Farm Aid is Criticized by Federal Civil Rights Unit," Wall Street Journal, March 1, 1965. Negroes in the South as a rule simply frozen out by local agencies of Department of Agriculture.

Record, C. Wilson, "Negroes in the California Agriculture Labor Force," Social Problems 6:354-361 (Spring 1959). An attempt to account for the few Negroes in this field.

Rogers, W. W., "Negro Alliance in Alabama," Journal of Negro History 45:38-44 (January 1960). Account of the Colored Farmers' National Alliance and Cooperative Union.

Rubin, Morton, Plantation County. Chapel Hill: University of North Carolina Press, 1951; New Haven: College and University Press, 1963. Observations on the social structure and cultural values of a typical Southern county, in effect constituting a companion work to Blackways of Kent, Hylan Lewis's study of a Southern mill town.

Rubin, Morton, "Social and Cultural Change in the Plantation Area," Journal of Social Issues 10:28-35 (January 1954).

Rubin, Morton, "Localism and Related Values Among Negroes in a Southern Rural Community," Social Forces 36:263-267 (March 1958).

Rubin, Morton, "Migration Patterns of Negroes from a Rural Northeastern Mississippi Community," Social Forces 39:59-66 (October 1960).

Ruttan, Vernon W., "Farm and Non-Farm Employment Opportunities for Low Income Farm Families," Phylon 20:248-255 (Fall 1959).

Sargent, F. O., "Economic Adjustments of Negro Farmers in East Texas," Southwestern Social Science Quarterly 42:32-39 (June 1961).

Smith, P. M. "Personal and Social Adjustment of Negro Children in Rural and Urban Areas of the South," Rural Sociology 26:73-77 (March 1961).

United States Commission on Civil Rights, Equal Opportunity in Farm Programs. Washington, D.C.: GPO, 1965.

Wright, Dale, They Harvest Despair: The Migrant Farm Worker. Boston: Beacon, 1965.

V. URBAN PROBLEMS

It becomes increasingly evident that we have done our best to bring out the worst in the urban Negro. As Kenneth B. Clark has recently written, "The dark ghetto is institutionalized pathology." The pattern of Negro migration continues to be from country to city, Southern as well as Northern, from smaller to larger city, from slum fringes to inner-city ghettos. Here all the Negroes' problems become most evident, poverty, crime, lack of education, decayed housing, exploitation by demagogic leaders, racial conflict.

The urban Negro's three greatest problems are jobs, schools, and housing. His continued relegation to congested slums inevitably means joblessness, substandard segregated schools, and neighborhood environments that foster disease and human degradation; separate sections on Employment (VII), Housing (VIII), and Education (IX) cover these areas of special concern. These are all disabilities that cannot be removed by the passage of civil rights and voting rights legislation, that cannot be significantly affected by welfare operations. In the city, and particularly in the Northern city, the Negro predicament cannot be isolated from the total issue of urban organization. Deteriorating inner cities, diminishing employment opportunities for all the unskilled poor, overburdened city finances, municipal administrations no longer commensurate with the requirements of megalopolis--these are the ingredients of what Robert Weaver has called "The Urban Complex," in which the Negro will continue to be ghetto-bound until some massive approach to urban dilemmas is undertaken.

1. GENERAL SURVEYS

Abrams, Charles, The City is the Frontier. New York: Harper, 1965.

Allen, James Egert, The Negro in New York. New York: Exposition Press, 1964. Foreword by Arthur Levitt.

An American City in Transition: The Baltimore Community Self-Survey of Inter-Group Relations. Maryland Commission on Interracial Problems and Relations, and Baltimore Commission on Human Relations, 1955.

Anthony, Daniel S., and Walter D. Chambers, Newark: A City in Transition. Newark, N.J.: Mayor's Commission on Group Relations, 1959. Vol. I, Characteristics of the Population; Vol. II, Residents' Views on Inter-Group Relations & Statistical Tables; Vol. III, Summary and Recommendations.

Banfield, Edward C., The Case of the Blighted City. Chicago: American Foundation for Continuing Education, 1959. Told as a story, or case study, for use by informal groups as basis for discussion, the book includes city politics, urban redevelopment, housing, and Negroes.

Beshers, James M., Urban Social Structure. New York: Free Press, 1962. A study of the over-all network of social relations which emphasizes social distance. Analysis centers on both belief and behavior and such factors as residence and marriage, and how these have implications for urban social structure.

Blalock, H. M., Jr., "Urbanization and Discrimination in the South," Social Problems 7:146-152 (Fall 1959).

Burgess, E. W., and Donald J. Bogue, eds., Contributions to Urban Sociology. Chicago: University of Chicago Press, 1964. Several useful articles on the urban Negro are listed separately.

Carter, Wilmoth A., "Negro Main Street as a Symbol of Discrimination," Phylon 21:234-242 (Fall 1960).

Carter, Wilmoth A., The Urban Negro in the South. New York: Vantage, 1962. Title misleading since this is an analysis of one street in one city, Raleigh, N.C. The author does not use the most recent data (1960 census), although she does have an appendix on the sit-ins.

Church in Metropolis. Quarterly publication of the Joint Urban Program, Episcopal Church Center, 815 Second Avenue, New York, N.Y. 10017.

Coke, James G., "The Lesser Metropolitan Areas of Illinois," Illinois Government, No. 15, November 1962. Urbana: Institute of Government and Public Affairs, University of Illinois. Shows that, with respect to Illinois, large city problems, such as unsatisfactory racial relations, are duplicated in small cities.

Drake, St. Clair, and Horace R. Cayton, Black Metropolis: A Study of Negro Life in a Northern City. New York: Harcourt, Brace, 1945; New York: Harper Torchbook, 2 vols., 1963. The Harper edition has been enlarged by a new chapter, "Bronzeville 1961," an appendix, "Black Metropolis 1961," and "Suggestions for Collateral Reading, 1962." The classic study of urban Negro life, it is a great social survey as well as a systematic analysis of social organization.

Dulaney, William L., "The Negro and the City," Journal of Negro Education 31:198-201 (Spring 1962).

Egan, John J., "The Human Side of Neighborhoods," Integrated Education 1:20-25 (June 1963).

Fact Book on Youth in New York City. Community Council of Greater New York, 1956.

Frazier, E. Franklin, "The Urban Ordeal of Negroes," Negro Digest 12:26-32 (December 1962).

Gist, Noel P., and L. A. Halbert, Urban Society. New York: Crowell, 1956.

Glazer, Nathan, and Daniel Patrick Moynihan, Beyond the Melting Pot. Cambridge: M.I.T. Press and Harvard University Press, 1963. A study of the five largest ethnic groups in New York City: Negroes, Puerto Ricans, Jews, Italians, Irish. Full bibliographical notes and index.

Green, Constance McLaughlin, Washington: Capital City, 1879-1950. Princeton: Princeton University Press, 1963. The author devotes significant portion of the book to the vicissitudes of the Negro community. She describes the policy of the potent Board of Trade as one of "tightening racial segregation and controlling the city's pattern of growth by every financial and political means."

Green, Constance McLaughlin, The Rise of Urban America. New York: Harper, 1965. See particularly last chapter for Negro urban minorities today.

Grier, Eunice, and George Grier, Negroes in Five New York Cities: A Study of Problems, Achievements, and Trends. New York State Commission Against Discrimination, 1958.

Grodzins, Morton, The Metropolitan Area as a Racial Problem. Pittsburgh: University of Pittsburgh Press, 1958.

Horne, Frank S., "The Open City--Threshold to American Maturity," Phylon 38:133-139 (Summer 1957).

Johnson, James Weldon, Black Manhattan. New York: Knopf, 1930. Valuable retrospectively, especially for description of the gradual takeover of Harlem by the Negroes.

Killian, Lewis M., and Charles M. Grigg, "Urbanism, Race, and Anomia," American Journal of Sociology 67:661-665 (May 1962).

Lieberson, Stanley, Ethnic Patterns in American Cities. Glencoe, Ill.: Free Press, 1963.

Martin, Roscoe C., Metropolis in Transition: Local Government Adaptation to Changing Urban Needs. Washington, D.C.: Housing and Home Finance Agency, September 1963.

The Negro in Cleveland. Cleveland Urban League, June 1964.

New York City in Crisis: A Study in Depth of Urban Sickness. New York: McKay, 1965. Prepared by the staff of the New York Herald-Tribune.

Schlivek, Louis B., Man in Metropolis. Garden City, N.Y.: Doubleday, 1965. Contains accounts of the difficulties Negroes have in finding homes in suburbia, with the result that Negro workers in suburban plants face long commutes to city ghettos.

Schnore, Leo F., The Urban Scene: Human Ecology and Demography. New York: Free Press, 1965.

Silberman, Charles E., "The City and the Negro," Fortune 65:88+ (March 1962).

Vance, Rupert B., and Nicholas J. Demerath, eds., The Urban South. Chapel Hill: University of North Carolina Press, 1954. A useful collection. Articles listed separately.

Weaver, Robert C., The Urban Complex: Human Values in Urban Life. New York: Doubleday, 1964. Chapter 4, "Urbanization of the Negro," takes the position that despite glaring evils, the move to the city has resulted in net gain for the Negro.

Weaver, Robert C., Dilemmas of Urban America, Cambridge, Mass.: Harvard University Press, 1965. On new trends in suburbia, urban renewal, and problems of racial policy.

Weissbourd, Bertram, Segregation, Subsidies, and Megalopolis. Santa Barbara, Calif.: Center for the Study of Democratic Institutions, 1964. The effects of federal housing policies.

White, Theodore H., "Negro in the Big Cities: Part I," Life 55:100+ (November 22, 1963); "Part II," ibid. 55:78+ (November 29, 1963).

Whyte, William H., Jr., "Are Cities Un-American?" Fortune 56:122-127+ (September 1957).

2. IN-MIGRATION AND POPULATION

Bogue, Donald J., Components of Population Change in Standard Metropolitan Areas. Oxford, Ohio: Scripps Foundation, Miami University, and Population Center, University of Chicago, 1957.

Bogue, D. J., and D. P. Dandekar, Population Trends and Prospects for the Chicago-Northwestern Indiana Consolidated Metropolitan Area: 1960-1990. Population Research and Training Center, University of Chicago, March 1962.

Chapin, F. Stuart, and Shirley F. Weiss, eds., Urban Growth Dynamics. New York: Wiley, 1962.

Chicago Commission on Human Relations, Solving the Problem of Chicago's Population Growth, 1957. Report on a conference of community leaders.

Coe, Paul F., "Non-White Population Increases in Metropolitan Areas," Journal of American Statistical Association 50:283-308 (June 1955). Chiefly on population movements 1940-1950.

Coe, Paul F., "The Nonwhite Population Surge to Our Cities," Land Economics 35:195-210 (August 1959). A useful article; see especially footnote references for bibliography.

Duncan, Otis D., and Beverly Duncan, Chicago's Negro Population. Monograph Series of the Chicago Community Inventory, Chicago: University of Chicago Press, 1956.

Grier, Eunice S., Understanding Washington's Changing Population. Washington, D.C.: Washington Center for Metropolitan Studies, 1961.

Grier, Eunice, and George Grier, Race Relations in Broome County: A Profile for 1958. New York State Commission Against Discrimination, 1958. Race relations in Binghamton, Endicott, Johnson, where Negro influx has been numerically insignificant.

Grier, George, with Eunice Grier, "The Negro Migration: Doubled Populations in a Decade Pose Urgent Problems for Northern Cities," Housing Yearbook, Washington, D.C.: National Housing Conference, 1960.

Grier, George, with Eunice Grier, The Impact of Race on Neighborhood in the Metropolitan Setting. Washington, D.C.: Washington Center for Metropolitan Studies, May 1961.

Hamilton, C. Horace, "Educational Selectivity of Net Migration from the South," Social Forces 38:33-42 (October 1959).

Hauser, Philip M., Total and Metropolitan Population of the United States as the Sixties Begin. New York: Lawrence, 1960. All of these works by Mr. Houser have great relevance for understanding the problems of Negroes in urban situations.

Hauser, Philip M., On the Impact of Population and Community Changes on Local Government. Pittsburgh: Pittsburgh University Press, 1961.

Hauser, Philip M., Population Perspectives. New Brunswick: Rutgers University Press, 1961.

Hauser, Philip M., Rapid Growth: Key to Understanding Metropolitan Problems. Washington, D.C.: Washington Center for Metropolitan Studies, 1961.

Hauser, Philip M., ed., Population Dilemma: A Policy for America. New York: Spectrum-Prentice Hall, 1963.

Kahl, Joseph A., The American Class Structure. New York: Rinehart, 1957. Chapter 8, "Ethnic and Race Barriers," deals with the movement of Negroes into cities and into industry.

Knapp, Robert B., Social Integration in Urban Communities: A Guide for Educational Planning. New York: Bureau of Publications, Teachers College, Columbia University, 1960.

Meadow, Kathryn P., "Negro-White Differences Among Newcomers to a Transitional Urban Area," Journal of Intergroup Relations 3:320-330 (Fall 1962).

Miller, Loren, "The Changing Metro-Urban Complex," Journal of Intergroup Relations 3:55-64 (Winter 1961-1962).

Mugge, Robert H., "Differentials in Negro Migration to Atlanta," in E. W. Burgess and D.J. Bogue, eds., Contributions to Urban Sociology, Chicago: University of Chicago Press, 1964.

"Negroes in the City of New York," Commission on Intergroup Relations, City of New York, 1961.

"New Census Look at Cities and Race," Washington Post, March 26, 1961.

New York State Commission Against Discrimination, Non-Whites in New York's Four 'Suburban' Counties: An Analysis of Trends. New York, 1959.

Newman, Dorothy K., "The Negro's Journey to the City--Part I," Monthly Labor Review 88:502-507 (May 1965). Brief survey of what Negro migrant experiences in housing, occupations, earnings and income, education.

Newman, Dorothy K., "The Negro's Journey to the City--Part II," Monthly Labor Review 88:644-649 (June 1965). Comparison of Negro experience with that of white immigrant minorities demonstrates tragic discrepancy in their degree of acceptance and inclusion.

Rames, Jose, "Racial Anatomy of a City," New University Thought 3:20-34 (September-October 1963). Detroit.

Reid, Ira De Augustine, The Negro Immigrant, His Background Characteristics and Social Adjustment, 1899-1937. New York: Columbia University Press, 1949.

Schmid, Calvin F., and Wayne W. McVey, Jr., Growth and Distribution of Minority Races in Seattle, Washington. Seattle: Seattle Public Schools, 1964.

Schmid, Calvin F., and Vincent A. Miller, Impact of Recent Negro Migration on Seattle Schools. Office of Population Research, University of Washington, 1959.

Schnore, Leo F., and Harry Sharp, "Racial Changes in Metropolitan Areas, 1950-1960," Social Forces 41:241-253 (March 1963).

Shannon, Lyle W., "The Public's Perception of Social Welfare Agencies and Organizations in an Industrial Community," Journal of Negro Education 32:276-285 (Summer 1963).

Shannon, Lyle W., and Elaine Krass, "The Urban Adjustment of Immigrants: The Relationship of Education to Occupation and Total Family Income," Pacific Sociological Review 6:37-42 (Spring 1963). Anglos, Mexican-Americans, and Negroes compared.

Taeuber, Karl E., and Alma F. Taeuber, "Is the Negro an Immigrant Group?" Integrated Education 1:25-28 (June 1963). Raises the question whether Negroes who migrate to Northern cities will be assimilated in same way as European immigrant groups have become, or whether the second-generation urban Negro will remain in same relative position as his parents.

Taeuber, Karl E., and Alma F. Taeuber, "The Negro as an Immigrant Group: Recent Trends in Racial and Ethnic Segregation in Chicago," American Journal of Sociology 69:374-382 (January 1964).

Zimmer, Basil G., "The Adjustment of Negroes in a Northern Industrial Community," Social Problems 9:378-386 (Spring 1962).

3. THE GHETTO

Baldwin, James, "The Harlem Ghetto: Winter 1948," Commentary 5:165-170 (February 1948).

Bell, Wendell, "A Probability Model for the Measurement of Ecological Segregation." Social Forces 32:357-364 (May 1954).

Bell, Wendell, and Ernest M. Willis, "The Segregation of Negroes in American Cities," Social and Economic Studies 6:59-75 (March 1957).

Brown, Claude, "Harlem, My Harlem," Dissent 8:371-382 (Summer 1961).

Clark, Dennis, The Ghetto Game. New York: Sheed and Ward, 1962.

Clark, Kenneth B., Dark Ghetto. New York: Harper, 1965. Taking his departure from the HARYOU report Youth in the Ghetto, the author here goes on to examine the ugly facts of the ghetto everywhere and for all its denizens, and to articulate the minimum requirements for a genuine obliteration of ghetto barriers.

DeMott, Benjamin, "An Unprofessional Eye: Project for Another Country," American Scholar 32:451-457 (Summer 1963). On Domestic Peace Corps pilot project in Harlem.

English, W. H., "Minority Group Attitudes of Negroes and Implications for Guidance," Journal of Negro Education 26:99-107 (Spring 1957). A study of the Negro minority in Springfield, Mass., to determine why the Negroes, as a group, seemed so unwilling "to participate in many activities open to them as residents," why they were so unaggressive. (In 1965, Springfield was the scene of intense Negro protest.)

Grodzins, Morton, "Metropolitan Segregation," Scientific American 198:33-41 (October 1957).

Grodzins, Morton, The Metropolitan Area as a Racial Problem. Pittsburgh: University of Pittsburgh Press, 1958. Development of central city into a lower-class Negro slum and its consequences.

Harrington, Michael, "Harlem Today," Dissent 8:371-382 (Summer 1961).

Hunter, David R., The Slums: Challenge and Response. New York: Free Press, 1964.

Keller, Suzanne, "The Social World of the Urban Slum Child," American Journal of Orthopsychiatry 33:823-831 (October 1963). Comparison of Negro and white children.

Lyford, Joseph P., "The Talk of Vandalia," in The Negro as an American. Santa Barbara, Calif.: Center for the Study of Democratic Institutions, 1963. Preliminary report of a study of Manhattan's West Side, with both Negro and Puerto Rican minorities.

McKay, Claude, Harlem: Negro Metropolis. New York: Dutton, 1940.

Osofsky, Gilbert, The Making of a Ghetto. New York: Harper, 1966. Traces the change in Harlem from an elegant white neighborhood to a slum and center of Negro population.

Sexton, Patricia Cayo, Spanish Harlem: Anatomy of Poverty. New York: Harper, 1965. The author argues for organizing the poor to organize themselves and to use their political power to effect social change.

Silberman, Charles E., "Up From Apathy--The Woodlawn Experiment: Self-Help in a Slum Neighborhood," Commentary 37:51-58 (May 1964).

Stringfellow, William, "Christianity, Poverty and the Practice of the Law," Harvard Law School Bulletin 10:4-7+ (June 1959). On "the need for the law and the lawyer to be really immersed in life as it is." Harlem as case study.

Stringfellow, William, "Race, Religion, and Revenge," Christian Century, February 14, 1962. Negroes in Harlem.

Stringfellow, William, My People is the Enemy: An Autobiographical Polemic. New York: Holt, 1964. A young white lawyer and Episcopal layman, who lived and worked among the Harlem poor, gives a vivid picture of ghetto life.

Taeuber, Karl E., "Residential Segregation," Scientific American 213:12-19 (August 1965). The author finds that the principal cause of Negro segregation in urban ghettos is discrimination and that there is "no basis for anticipating major changes . . . until patterns of housing discrimination can be altered."

Taeuber, Karl E., and Alma F. Taeuber, Negroes in Cities. Chicago: Aldine, 1965. An important study based on calculation of the segregation indices for 207 American cities.

Weaver, Robert C., The Negro Ghetto. New York: Harcourt, Brace, 1948.

Weaver, Robert C., "Non-White Population Movements and Urban Ghettos," Phylon 20: 235-241 (Fall 1959).

Weaver, Robert C., The Urban Complex: Human Values in Urban Life. Garden City, N.Y.:

Doubleday, 1964. The author presents in dramatic focus the near impossibility for any sizable number of Negroes to escape from the urban ghettos. His remedy: for the federal government to take more aggressive leadership in urban renewal.

Williamson, Stanford W., With Grief Acquainted. Chicago: Follett, 1964. Negro life on Chicago's South Side.

Wirth, Louis, The Ghetto. Chicago: University of Chicago Press, 1928. Describes ghetto-formation as inevitable end product of successive stages.

Youth in the Ghetto: A Study of the Consequences of Powerlessness and a Blueprint for Change. New York: Harlem Youth Opportunities Unlimited, 1964. HARYOU report presented to the President's Committee on Juvenile Delinquency, April 1964.

4. DELINQUENCY, CRIME, AND POLICE PRACTICES

Annual Reports, Department of Correction, City of New York, 1958-1963. Figures by race on criminal offenders are included.

Axelrad, Sidney, "Negro and White Male Institutionalized Delinquents," American Journal of Sociology 62:569-574 (May 1952).

Bacon, Margaret K., I. L. Child, and H. Barry, III, "A Cross-Cultural Study of Correlates of Crime," Journal of Abnormal and Social Psychology 66:291-300 (April 1963).

Barker, Gordon H., and W. Thomas Adams, "Negro Delinquents in Public Training Schools in the West," Journal of Negro Education 32:294-300 (Summer 1963).

Bates, William, "Caste, Class and Vandalism," Social Problems 9:349-353 (Spring 1962).

Beattie, R. H., "Criminal Statistics in the United States," Journal of Criminal Law, Criminology, and Police Science 51:49-65 (May-June 1960).

Bensing, R. C., and O. Schroeder, Jr., Homicide in an Urban Community. Springfield, Ill.: Thomas, 1960.

Bohannon, P., ed., African Homicide and Suicide. Princeton: Princeton University Press, 1960.

Brown, L. P., "Black Muslims and the Police," Journal of Criminal Law, Criminology and Police Science 56:119-126 (March 1965).

Caldwell, M. G., "Personality Trends in the Youthful Male Offender," Journal of Criminal Law, Criminology and Police Science 49:405-416 (January-February 1959).

Cavan, Ruth Shonle, "Negro Family Disorganization and Juvenile Delinquency," Journal of Negro Education 28:230-239 (Summer 1959).

Chein, Isidor, Donald L. Gerard, Robert S. Lee, and Eva Rosenfeld, The Road to H: Narcotics, Delinquency and Social Policy. New York: Basic Books, 1964.

Clark, Kenneth B., "Color, Class, Personality and Juvenile Delinquency," Journal of Negro Education 28:240-251 (Summer 1959).

Cloward, Richard A., and Lloyd E. Ohlin, Delinquency and Opportunity: A Theory of Delinquent Gangs. Glencoe, Ill.: Free Press, 1960. An important book in the contemporary reconsideration of gangs which is changing the perspective from delinquency as an attribute of individuals to that of a larger social system.

Cohen, A. K., Delinquent Boys: The Culture of the Gang. Glencoe, Ill.: Free Press, 1955.

Cohen, A. K., and J. F. Short, Jr., "Research in Delinquent Subcultures," Journal of Social Issues 14:20-37 (Summer 1958).

Cohen, A. K., and J. F. Short, Jr., "Juvenile Delinquency," in R. K. Merton and R. A. Nisbet, eds., Contemporary Social Problems, New York: Harcourt, Brace, 1961.

Coles, Robert, "The Question of Negro Crime," Harper's Magazine 228:134-136, 139 (April 1964).

Cressey, Donald R., "Epidemiology and Individual Conduct: A Case from Criminology," Pacific Sociological Review 3:47-58 (Fall 1960).

Cressey, Donald R., "Crime," in R. K. Merton and R. A. Nisbet, eds., Contemporary Social Problems. New York: Harcourt, Brace, 1961.

Cross, G.J., "Negro, Prejudice, and the Police," Journal of Criminal Law, Criminology, and Police Science 55:405 (September 1964).

Daniel, Walter G., "The Role of Youth Character-Building Organizations in Juvenile Delinquency Prevention," Journal of Negro Education 28:310-317 (Summer 1959).

Diggs, Mary H., "Some Problems and Needs of Negro Children as Revealed by Comparative Delinquency and Crime Statistics," Journal of Negro Education 19:290-297 (Summer 1950).

Dobbins, D. A., and B. M. Bass, "Effects of Unemployment on White and Negro Prison Admissions in Louisiana," Journal of Criminal Law, Criminology, and Police Science 48:522-525 (January-February 1958).

Douglass, Joseph H., "The Extent and Characteristics of Juvenile Delinquency Among Negroes in the United States," Journal of Negro Education 28:214-229 (Summer 1959).

Epstein, Charlotte, Intergroup Relations for Police Officers. Baltimore: Williams & Wilkins, 1962.

Federal Bureau of Investigation, Uniform Crime Reports, 1960-1961. Washington, D.C.: GPO, 1961-1962.

Federal Bureau of Prisons, National Prisoner Statistics: Prisoners in State and Federal Institutions, 1950. Leavenworth, Kan.: U.S. Penitentiary, 1954.

Federal Bureau of Prisons, National Prisoner Statistics: Prisoners Released from State and Federal Institutions, 1951. Atlanta, Ga.: U.S. Penitentiary, 1955.

Federal Bureau of Prisons, National Prisoner Statistics: Prisoners Released from State and Federal Institutions, 1952 and 1953. Atlanta, Ga.: U.S. Penitentiary, 1957.

Federal Bureau of Prisons, "Executions, 1961," in National Prisoner Statistics, No. 28 (April 1962).

Finestone, Harold, "Cats, Kicks, and Color," Social Problems 5:3-13 (July 1957). Suggestions as to the origin and function of a style of life among lower-class Negro heroin users.

Fox, Vernon, and Joann Volakakis, "The Negro Offender in a Northern Industrial Area," Journal of Criminal Law, Criminology and Police Science 46:641 (January-February 1956).

Franklin, J. C., "Discriminative Value and Patterns of the Wechsler-Bellevue Scales in the Examination of Delinquent Negro Boys," Educational and Psychological Measurement 5:71-85 (Spring 1945).

Geis, Gilbert, "Statistics Concerning Race and Crime," Crime and Delinquency 11:142-150 (April 1965).

Glueck, Sheldon, and Eleanor T. Glueck, Unraveling Juvenile Delinquency. New York: Commonwealth Fund, 1950.

Gold, M., "Suicide, Homicide, and the Socialization of Aggression," American Journal of Sociology 63:651-661 (May 1958).

Henry, A. F., and J. F. Short, Jr., Suicide and Homicide. Glencoe, Ill.: Free Press, 1954.

Henton, Comradge L., and Charles Washington, "Differential Studies of Recidivism Among Negro and White Boys," Journal of Genetic Psychology 98: 247-253 (June 1961).

Hill, Mozell C., "The Metropolis and Juvenile Delinquency Among Negroes," Journal of Negro Education 28:277-285 (Summer 1959).

Hypps, Irene C., "The Role of the School in Juvenile Delinquency Presentation (with Especial Reference to Pupil Personnel Services)," Journal of Negro Education 28:318-328 (Summer 1959).

Jenkins, Herbert T., "Police, Progress, and Desegregation in Atlanta," New South 17: 10-13 (June 1962). Author is Atlanta Chief of Police.

Johnson, Guy B., "The Negro and Crime," in Martin E. Wolfgang, Leonard Savitz, and Norman Johnston, The Sociology of Crime and Delinquency. New York: Wiley, 1962. While based on a prewar study, this paper is still a useful discussion of such factors as subordination, insecurity, etc., in Negro crime, as well as of the caste structure of the administration of justice in the South.

Kephart, William M., "The Negro Offender," American Journal of Sociology 60:46-50 (July 1954).

Kephart, William M., "Integration of Negroes into the Urban Police Force," Journal of Criminal Law, Criminology and Police Science 45:325-333 (September-October 1954)

Kephart, William M., Racial Factors and Urban Law Enforcement. Philadelphia: University of Pennsylvania Press, 1957. Based on extensive research on the Philadelphia Police Force.

Kramer, S. A., "Predicting Juvenile Delinquency Among Negroes," Sociology and Social Research 48:478-489 (July 1964).

Kvaraceus, William C., "The Nature of the Problem of Juvenile Delinquency in the United States," Journal of Negro Education 28:191-199 (Summer 1959).

Lewis, Hylan, "Juvenile Delinquency Among Negroes: A Critical Summary," Journal of Negro Education 28:371-387 (Summer 1959).

Lohman, Joseph D., The Police and Minority Groups. Chicago, 1947. A manual prepared by Lohman, sheriff of Cook County, and the supervisory officers of the division of police for use in the Chicago Park District Training School.

Lohman, Joseph D., "Juvenile Delinquency: A Social Dimension," Journal of Negro Education 28:286-299 (Summer 1959).

London, Nathaniel J., and Jerome K. Myers, "Young Offenders: Psychopathology and Social Factors," Archives of General Psychiatry 4:274-282 (March 1961). A report of research conducted by the Connecticut State Department of Mental Health in New Haven County Jail on all young white and Negro male offenders in jail for more than ten days. Psychiatric diagnoses, socioeconomic background, and education taken into account for each subject.

McCloskey, Mark A., "State and Municipal Youth Authorities or Commissions and Their Role in Juvenile Delinquency Prevention," Journal of Negro Education 28:339-350 (Summer 1959).

McCormick, Ken, Sprung: The Release of Willie Calloway. New York: St. Martin's, 1964. Articles written by the author for the Detroit Free Press helped to produce new witnesses and obtain a new trial for Calloway, wrongfully sentenced to life imprisonment.

McManus, George P., "Human Relations Training for Police," Interracial Review 35:98-99 (April 1962).

Maccoby, Eleanor E., Joseph P. Johnson, and Russell M. Church, "Community Integration and the Social Control of Juvenile Delinquency," Journal of Social Issues 14:38-51 (Summer 1958).

Mays, Benjamin E., "The Role of the 'Negro Community' in Delinquency Prevention Among Negro Youth," Journal of Negro Education 28:366-370 (Summer 1959).

Miller, Carroll L., "Educational Level and Juvenile Delinquency Among Negroes," Journal of Negro Education 28:268-276 (Summer 1959).

Morgan, Charles, Jr., "Integration in the Yellow Chair," New South 18:11-16 (February 1963). On segregated justice except in the "yellow chair."

Pettigrew, Thomas F., and Rosalind B. Spier, "The Ecological Structure of Negro Homicide," American Journal of Sociology 67:621-629 (May 1962).

Porterfield, Austin L., and Robert H. Talbert, "Crime in Southern Cities," in Rupert B. Vance and Nicholas J. Demerath, eds., The Urban South, Chapel Hill: University of North Carolina Press, 1954.

Reiss, Albert J., and Albert Lewis Rhodes, "Are Educational Norms and Goals of Conforming, Truant and Delinquent Adolescents Influenced by Group Position in American Society," Journal of Negro Education 28:252-267 (Summer 1959).

Robinson, Sophia M., "How Effective Are Current Delinquency Preventive Programs?" Journal of Negro Education 28:351-365 (Summer 1959).

Roebuck, Julian B., "The Negro Drug Addict as an Offender Type," Journal of Criminal Law, Criminology and Police Science 53:36-43 (March 1962).

Roebuck, Julian B., "Negro Numbers Man as a Criminal Type: The Construction and Application of a Typology," Journal of Criminal Law, Criminology and Police Science 54:48-60 (March 1963).

Roebuck, Julian B., and M. L. Cadwallader, "The Negro Armed Robber as a Criminal Type: The Construction and Application of a Typology," Pacific Sociological Review 4:21-26 (Spring 1961).

Rudwick, Elliott M., "Police Work and the Negro," Journal of Criminal Law, Criminology and Police Science 50:596-599 (March-April 1960).

Rudwick, Elliott M., "Negro Policemen in the South," Journal of Criminal Law, Criminology and Police Practice 51:273 (July-August 1960).

Rudwick, Elliott M., "Negro Police Employment in the Urban South," Journal of Negro Education 30:102-108 (Spring 1961).

Rudwick, Elliott M., "The Southern Negro Policeman and the White Offender," Journal of Negro Education 30:426-431 (Fall 1961).

Salisbury, Harrison, The Shook-Up Generation. New York: Harper, 1958. Illuminating
    study of New York gangs, including Negro gangs.
Samuels, Gertrude, "Who Shall Judge a Policeman?" New York Times Magazine, August
    2, 1964. Following upon 1964 Negro riots, persistent charges of police brutality bring
    demands for a civilian review board.
Savitz, Leonard, Delinquency and Migration. Philadelphia: Commission on Human Re-
    lations, 1960.
Schmid, C. F., "Urban Crime Areas, Part I," American Sociological Review 25:527-542
    (August 1960); "Part II," ibid. 25:655-678 (October 1960).
Schultz, Leroy G., "Why the Negro Carries Weapons," Journal of Criminal Law, Crimi-
    nology and Police Science 53:476-481 (December 1962).
Sherif, Muzafer, and Carolyn Sherif, Reference Groups: Explorations in Conformity and
    Deviance of Adolescents. New York: Harper, 1964.
Short, James F., Jr., and Fred L. Strodtbeck, Group Process and Gang Delinquency.
    Chicago: University of Chicago Press, 1965. Negro groups considered passim.
Spergel, Irving, "Male Young Adult Criminality, Deviant Values, and Differential
    Opportunities in Two Lower Class Negro Neighborhoods," Social Problems 10:237-250
    (Winter 1963).
"A Statement of Recommended Police Policy Resulting from the New York University
    Graduate School of Public Administration Conference on 'The Challenge of Desegregation
    for the American Police Executive,'" Interracial Review 35:115 (May 1962).
Teeters, Negley K., and David Matza, "The Extent of Delinquency in the United States,"
    Journal of Negro Education 28:200-213 (Summer 1959).
Thomas, Rose C., "Family and Child Welfare Agencies and Juvenile Delinquency Pre-
    vention," Journal of Negro Education 28:300-309 (Summer 1959).
Towler, Juby E., The Police Role in Racial Conflicts. Springfield, Ill.: Charles C. Thomas,
    1965. A handbook by the Chief of Detectives of Danville, Va., on how to use the law as
    an instrument by which one race may subject another.
Tufts, Edith Miller, "The Role of the Children's Bureau and Other Federal Agencies in
    Juvenile Delinquency Prevention," Journal of Negro Education 28:329-338 (Summer
    1959).
Vontress, Clemmont E., "Patterns of Segregation and Desegregation: Contributing Factors
    to Crime Among Negroes," Journal of Negro Education 31:108-116 (Spring 1962).
Wilson, James, Q., "Generational and Ethnic Differences among Career Police Officers,"
    American Journal of Sociology 69:522-528 (March 1964).
Wolfgang, Marvin E., Patterns in Criminal Homicide. Philadelphia: University of Pennsyl-
    vania Press, 1958. A valuable study strongly suggesting that racial discrimination
    exists both North and South in the conviction and sentencing of those accused of criminal
    homicide. Careful research on black-white differentials with reference to socioeconomic
    factors, choice of victim, style.
Zeitz, L., "Survey of Negro Attitudes Toward Law," Rutgers Law Review 19:288-316
    (Winter 1965).

5. RACE VIOLENCE

Bart, Peter, "Panel on Watts Riots Warns of Further Racial Violence," New York Times,
    December 7, 1965. Analysis and summary of report by McCone Commission to Governor
    Edmund G. Brown of California concerning Los Angeles riots in summer of 1965.
Brown, Earl L., Why Race Riots? Lessons from Detroit. New York: Public Affairs
    Committee, 1944. Pamphlet on the 1943 Detroit riots.
Clark, Kenneth B., "Group Violence: A Preliminary Study of the Attitudinal Pattern of its
    Acceptance and Rejection--a Study of the 1943 Harlem Riots," Journal of Social
    Psychology 19:319-337 (August 1944).
Curry, J. E., and Glen D. King, Race Tensions and the Police. Springfield, Ill.: Thomas,
    1962.

"Does Anyone Really Care? Negroes Who Rioted in Los Angeles," <u>Christian Century</u> 82:1148 (September 22, 1965).

"F.B.I. Report on Racial Disturbances During the Past Summer," <u>America</u> 111:414-415 (October 10, 1964).

Goodman, George W., Jr., "Watts, U.S.A.: A Post Mortem," <u>Crisis</u> 72:487-492,532 (October 1965).

Grimshaw, Allen D., "Lawlessness and Violence in America and their Special Manifestations in Changing Negro White Relations," <u>Journal of Negro History</u> 44:52-72 (January 1959).

Grimshaw, Allen D., "A Study in Social Violence: Urban Race Riots in the United States," unpub. doc. diss., University of Pennsylvania, 1959.

Grimshaw, Allen D., "Urban Racial Violence in the United States: Changing Ecological Considerations," <u>American Journal of Sociology</u> 66:109-119 (September 1960). Importance of police attitudes in current events in the South.

Grimshaw, Allen D., "Relationships Among Prejudice, Discrimination, Social Tension, and Social Violence," <u>Journal of Intergroup Relations</u> 2:302-310 (Fall 1961).

Grimshaw, Allen D., "Negro-White Relations in the Urban North: Two Areas of High Conflict Potential," <u>Journal of Intergroup Relations</u> 3:146-158 (Spring 1962). Specifically, housing and recreation.

Grimshaw, Allen D., "Factors Contributing to Colour Violence in the United States and Great Britain," <u>Race</u> 3:3-19 (May 1962).

Grimshaw, Allen D., "Police Agencies and the Prevention of Racial Violence," <u>Journal of Law, Criminology and Police Science</u> 54:110 (March 1963).

Grimshaw, Allen D., "Three Major Cases of Colour Violence in the United States," <u>Race</u> 5:76-87 (July 1963). Tulsa riot of 1921 as Southern style; Chicago, 1919, as Northern style; and East St. Louis, 1917, as mixed type.

Grimshaw, Allen D., "Actions of Police and the Military in American Race Riots," <u>Phylon</u> 26:271-289 (Fall 1963). Historical résumé.

"Harlem Diary," <u>Ramparts</u> 3:14-28 (October 1964). A special report on the Harlem riots of 1964, largely in the form of a taped record by Lez Edmond, who was present throughout the period.

McMillan, George, "Racial Violence and Law Enforcement," <u>New South</u> 15:4-32 (November 1960).

McWilliams, Carey, "Watts: The Forgotten Slum," <u>Nation</u> 201:89-90 (August 30, 1965).

Miller, Alexander, "Crisis Without Violence," Anti-Defamation League, 1964. Pamphlet. Account of how New Rochelle, N.Y., avoided violence despite a crisis situation in race relations.

"Negro After Watts" Time Essay," <u>Time</u> 86:16-17 (August 27, 1965).

Nieburg, H. L., "The Threat of Violence and Social Change," <u>American Political Science Review</u> 56:865-873 (December 1962).

Rudwick, Elliott M., <u>Race Riot at East St. Louis, July 2, 1917</u>. Carbondale: Southern Illinois University Press, 1964. An historical case study with strong contemporaneous interest.

Sanders, Stanley, "Riot as a Weapon: The Language of Watts," <u>Nation</u> 201:490-493 (December 20, 1965). The author argues that failure to recognize the "genuine differences" between the way white and Negro communities think and react, and to understand what the differences mean, "will inevitably lead to more riots."

Shapiro, Fred C., and James W. Sullivan, <u>Race Riots New York 1964.</u> New York: Crowell, 1964. Authors are staff reporters for the New York <u>Herald Tribune.</u>

<u>Violence in the City -- An End or a Beginning?</u> A Report by the (California) Governor's Commission on the Los Angeles Riots (December 2, 1965). The commission, headed by John McCone, former head of the CIA, found the summer riots symptomatic of a serious urban sickness which,if not attacked with energetic new measures,will become endemic.

Waskow, Arthur L., <u>From Race Riot to Sit In, 1919 and the 1960's</u>. Garden City, N.Y.: Doubleday, 1966. The story of two periods of racial clashes in the United States. The author explores the possibility that violent conflict can be replaced by nonviolent means.

Witcover, Jules, "Rochester Braces for Another July," <u>Reporter</u> 33:33-35 (July 15, 1965).

VI. ECONOMIC STATUS AND PROBLEMS

Not every Negro is poor, and in this country there are more white families in the poverty class than Negro families, but the Negro poor constitute a disproportionately large element of their total population. Crucially handicapped by his economic weakness at the time of Emancipation, the Negro has ever since been consistently inhibited by discriminatory practices that have denied him credit, restricted the area of his business opportunities, forced him to compete on unequal terms, and so far as possible relegated him to menial jobs. The business opportunities open to him have been largely limited to insurance, service trades, some real estate and banking, and publishing for his fellow Negro Americans. Awareness has been growing that to ignore the economic health of this large segment of the population is not only inhumane but dangerous. Both the Small Business Bureau and private groups are moving more aggressively than in the past to assist Negro business, and clearly much of the urgency behind President Johnson's poverty program stems from the need to take quick action against rising unrest caused by poverty.

At the same time recognition of the importance of Negroes as consumers has been growing, not just because of their numbers, but because an expanding Negro middle class is evidence that more and more individuals are being enabled to participate in American business and professional life. Here the trade press has shown itself in many instances more alert than the scholarly journals to the Negro's economic importance, whether as producer, consumer, or burden on the community. While their interest stems chiefly either from the desire to capture their share of the Negro market or from concern over how to integrate work forces in conformity with government regulations, trade publications do reflect vividly many of the actualities of the Negro's experience in business and industry.

1. GENERAL SURVEYS

Batchelder, A. B., "Economic Forces Serving the Ends of the Negro Protest," Annals of the American Academy of Political and Social Science 357:80-88 (January 1965).

Becker, Gary S., The Economics of Discrimination. Chicago: University of Chicago Press, 1957. An interesting study of the economic consequences of discrimination. The author's purpose is "to develop a theory of non-pecuniary motivation and to apply it quantitatively to discrimination in the market place."

Blalock, H.M., "Economic Discrimination and Negro Increase," American Sociological Review 21:584-588 (October 1956).

Brown, Robert, and Franklin M. Fisher, "Negro-White Savings Differentials and the Modigliani-Brumberg Hypothesis," Review of Economics and Statistics 40:79-81 (February 1958).

Drake, St., Clair, "The Social and Economic Status of the Negro in the United States," Daedalus 94:771-814 (Fall 1965).

Denison, Edward F., The Sources of Economic Growth in the United States and the Alternative Before Us. Washington, D.C.: Committee on Economic Development, 1962. Has relevance for participation of the Negro.

Fein, Rashi, "An Economic and Social Profile of the Negro American," Daedalus 94:815-846 (Fall 1965).

Frazier, E. Franklin, "The Status of the Negro in the American Social Order," Journal of Negro Education 4:293-307 (July 1935). On the hypothesis that the Negro's status has been bound up with his role in the economic system, the author concludes, "In the urban environment he is showing signs of understanding the struggle for power between the proletariat and the owning classes, and is beginning to cooperate with white workers in this struggle which offers the only hope of his complete emancipation." A fascinating presentation of the thinking of the 1930's.

Ginzberg, Eli, The Negro Potential. New York: Columbia University Press, 1956. A publication of Columbia's Conservation of Human Resources Project. Premises are that "It is never sensible or right for a nation to waste valuable human resources through failure to develop or utilize them," and that "the best hope for the Negro's speedy and complete integration into American society lies in . . . a strong and virile economy."

Ginzberg, Eli, "Segregation and Manpower Waste," Phylon 21:311-316 (Winter 1960).

Ginzberg, Eli, ed., The Negro Challenge to the Business Community. New York: McGraw-Hill, 1964. Highlights of an American Assembly conference at Arden House in January 1964, a rigorous discussion by Whitney Young, Thomas F. Pettigrew, Kenneth B. Clark, Daniel P. Moynihan, and others.

Guscott, Kenneth I., "NAACP Views Conditions," Industry 28:12-13, 29 (July 1963).

Haynes, Marion, "A Century of Change: Negroes in the U.S. Economy, 1860-1960," Monthly Labor Review 85:1359-1365 (December 1962).

Henderson, G., "The Negro Recipient of Old-Age Assistance: Results of Discrimination," Social Casework 46:208-214 (April 1965).

Henderson, Vivian W., "The Economic Imbalance: An Enquiry into the Economic Status of Negroes in the United States, 1935-1960, with Implications for Negro Education," Quarterly Review of Higher Education Among Negroes 28:84-98 (January 1960).

Henderson, Vivian W., "Economic Dimensions in Race Relations," in Jitsuichi Masuoka and Preston Valien, eds., Race Relations: Problems and Theory, Chapel Hill: University of North Carolina Press, 1961.

Henderson, Vivian W., The Economic Status of Negroes: In the Nation and In the South. Atlanta, Ga.: Southern Regional Council, 1963. Thorough and revelatory.

Hill, Herbert, "Recent Effects of Racial Conflict on Southern Industrial Development" Phylon 20:319-326 (Winter 1959).

Hughes, Emmet John, "The Negro's New Economic Life," Fortune 54:126-131+ (September 1956).

Kessler, Matthew A., "Economic Status of Nonwhite Workers, 1955-1962," Monthly Labor Review 86:780-788 (July 1963).

Kosa, J., and Nunn, C. Z., "Race, Deprivation and Attitude toward Communism," Phylon 25:337-346 (Winter 1964).

Krueger, A. O., "The Economics of Discrimination," Journal of Political Economy 71:481-486 (October 1963). Economic effects of discrimination, how the majority profit from discrimination against the minority, with minority unable to retaliate.

Lane, R. E., "The Fear of Equality," American Political Science Review 53:33-51 (March 1959). On resistance to economic, or income, equality, not only to Negroes specifically, but of all groups.

Lang, Gladys Engel, "Minority Groups and Economic Status in New York State," in Aaron Antonovsky and Lewis L. Lorwin, eds., Discrimination and Low Incomes. New York: New School for Social Research, 1959 (multi.).

Lipset, Seymour M., and Reinhard Bendix, Social Mobility in Industrial Society. Berkeley: University of California Press, 1959. Emphasizing that it is the rate of economic expansion which is most significant in determining the extent of social mobility in a society, the authors point out the factors inhibiting the Negro from sharing the opportunities presented by such expansion.

Miller, Helen Hill, "Private Business and Education in the South," Harvard Business Review 38:75-88 (July-August 1960).

Miller, Helen Hill, "Business Citizenship in the Deep South," Business Horizons 5:61-66 (Spring 1962).

Miller, Herman Phillip, Income of the American People. New York: Wiley, 1955. Prepared for the Social Science Research Council in cooperation with the U.S. Department of Commerce, Bureau of the Census.

Miller, Herman Phillip, Trends in the Income of Families and Persons in the United States, 1947-1960. Washington, D.C.: U.S. Department of Commerce, Bureau of the Census, 1963.

Miller, Herman Phillip, Rich Man, Poor Man. New York: Crowell, 1964. The author, an economic statistician with long experience at the Bureau of the Census, analyzes the characteristics of the poor, the Negro-white income differential over time, and the relative economic advantage of education for Negroes and whites. Tables and statistics with commentary intelligible to the general reader.

"More Race Pressure on Business," Business Week 1706:130, 132 (May 12, 1962).

Morgan, Frank, "The Price of Strife: Race Turmoil Threatens to Stifle Mississippi's Economic Development," Wall Street Journal, February 2, 1965. Racial tensions causing a slump in plant building and in tourism. Negro consumer boycotts raise growing fears.

National Urban League, Economic and Social Status of the Negro in the U.S. Washington, D.C., 1961.

Needham, Maurice d'Arlan, Negro Orleanian: Status and Stake in a City's Economy and Housing. New Orleans: Tulane Publications, 1962.

Nicholls, William H., "The South as a Developing Area," Journal of Politics 26:22-40 (February 1964).

Perlo, Victor, "Trends in the Economic Status of the Negro People," Science and Society 16:115-150 (Spring 1952). Continuing trend since war, despite great Negro gains in economic and social status, has been for living costs of Negroes to rise more rapidly than those of whites, and for living standards of Negroes in cities to be cut very sharply.

"The Price of Defiance," Business Week 1727:31-32 (October 6, 1962). Mississippi, the race problem, and economic development.

Ratchford, R. U., "The Reorganization of the Southern Economy," in Jessie P. Guzman, ed., The New South and Higher Education. Tuskegee: Tuskegee Institute, 1954.

Ring, H. H., et al., Negroes in the United States: Their Employment and Economic Status. U.S. Bureau of Labor Statistics Bulleton No. 1119, 1953.

Robcock, Stefan H., "The Negro in the Industrial Development of the South," Phylon 14:319-325 (Fall 1953).

Rose, Alvin W., "The Changing Economic Background of American Race Relations," Southwestern Social Science Quarterly 31:159-173 (December 1950).

Schultz, Theodore W., "Investment in Human Capital," American Economic Review 51:1-17 (March 1961). Presidential address before American Economic Association, December 1960. Education of Negroes, and other disadvantaged groups, must be considered as investment. The cost of welfare, human deterioration too great to be borne by society.

Siegel, Paul M., "On the Cost of Being a Negro," Sociological Inquiry 35:41-57 (Winter 1965).

Singer, Herman, "Not All Black," Dissent 11:157-159 (Spring 1964). The relation between the movement for civil rights and the opportunity to share in affluence.

"South's Race Disputes Involve Businessman," Business Week 1633:32, 34 (December 17, 1960).

Sterner, Richard, The Negro's Share. New York: Harper, 1943. Still a useful study of Negro income, consumption, housing, and public assistance, it is one of a series of investigations concerning the Negro instituted and financed by the Carnegie Corporation. Contains a mass of statistical data on occupational and employment trends, family composition and incomes, expenditures and consumption, housing conditions, both rural and urban, as well as discussion of Negro's economic position in American society.

Tobin, James, "On Improving the Economic Status of the Negro," Daedalus 94:878-898 (Fall 1965). "By far the most powerful factor determining the economic status of Negroes is the over-all state of the U.S. economy. A vigorously expanding economy with a steadily tight labor market will rapidly raise the position of the Negro."

U.S. Department of Labor, The Economic Situation of Negroes in the United States. Bulletin S-3, Washington, D.C.: GPO, 1960; rev. 1962. Many Negroes felt that this bulletin, issued during the closing weeks of the 1960 presidential campaign with a Foreword by Secretary of Labor James P. Mitchell, was unrealistically optimistic about Negro gains and that its chief purpose was to attract Negro votes for the Republican ticket rather than to present the true facts of the Negroes' economic situation.

Weaver, Robert C., "Challenges to Democracy," paper given at a symposium in Chicago and published in The Negro as an American, Santa Barbara, Calif.: Center for the Study of Democratic Institutions, 1963. The author emphasizes the economic aspects of the Negro problem, and stresses the importance of the involvement of middle-class Negroes with the total Negro community.

"What 'Massive Resistance' Costs Norfolk and its Businessmen," Business Week 1518:32-34 (October 4, 1958).

2. THE POOR

Bagdikian, Ben H., In the Midst of Plenty: The Poor in America. Boston: Beacon, 1964. Deals with America's "forgotten poor" in urban and rural slums and with the Negro problem as part of problem of the poor in general.

Batchelder, Alan, "Poverty: The Special Case of the Negro," American Economic Review 55:530-540 (May 1965). Bibliography.

Bremner, Robert H., From the Depths: The Discovery of Poverty in the United States. New York: New York University Press, 1964.

Broadfield, George W., "A Different Drum," Nation 201:161-165 (September 20, 1965). 100th Anniversary Issue. Author designed and directed the country's first Domestic Peace Corps (1962-1964).

David, Martin, "Incomes and Dependency in the Coming Decades," American Journal of Economics and Sociology 3:249-267 (July 1964). A study by the Survey Research Center at the University of Michigan finds 29 percent of all families in the U.S. are "poor," and 10.4 million families need additional income for an adequate standard of living. Of these 1.4 million are nonwhite families.

"Dimensions of Poverty in New York City," Mayor's Council on Poverty, New York, March 23, 1964.

Dunne, George H., ed., Poverty in Plenty. New York: Kenedy, for Georgetown University, 1964. A symposium marking the 175th anniversary of the University.

Ferman, Louis A., Joyce L. Kornbluh, and Alan Haber, eds., Poverty in America. Ann Arbor: University of Michigan Press, 1965. A book of readings which brings together materials on the problems of the Negro poor.

Harrington, Michael, The Other America: Poverty in the United States. New York: Macmillan, 1962. Because of the disproportionately large number of Negroes who belong to the impoverished class, Negro poverty is considered throughout. Chapter 4, "If You're Black, Stay Back," is specifically concerned with the Negro.

Lampman, Robert J., "Recent Thought on Egalitarianism," Quarterly Journal of Economics 71:234-266 (May 1957).

Lampman, Robert J., The Low Income Population and Economic Growth. Joint Economic Committee of the U.S. Congress, Study Paper No. 12, Washington, D.C.: GPO, 1959.

Myrdal, Gunnar, Challenge to Affluence. New York: Pantheon, 1964. Addressing himself to problems of poverty and the rate of economic growth in the United States, the author foresees that the proletariat of the unemployed, the uneducated, and the migrant, of whom Negroes form a large proportion, will increase in number and become a permanent class unless economic growth rate rises sharply.

Office of Economic Opportunity, Congressional Presentation, April 1965. 2 vols. Washington, D.C.: GPO, 1965. Vol. I, The First Step on a Long Journey, a description of all the the programs provided for by legislation setting up the OEO; illustrated. Vol. II, Appendix, statistical details of all programs.

Orshansky, M., "Aged Negro and his Income," Social Security Bulletin 27:3-13 (February 1964).

Orshansky, M., "Counting the Poor: Another Look at the Poverty Profile," Social Security Bulletin 28:3-29 (January 1965).

Street, David, and John C. Leggett, "Economic Deprivation and Extremism: A Study of Unemployed Negroes," American Journal of Sociology 67:53-57 (July 1961).

U.S. Congress, Joint Committee on the Economic Report, Characteristics of the Low-
Income Population and Related Federal Programs. Washington, D.C.: GPO, 1955.

U.S. Congress, Joint Committee on the Economic Report, A Program for the Low-Income
Population at Substandard Levels of Living. Washington, D.C.: GPO, 1956.

3. THE NEGRO AS CONSUMER

Alexis, Marcus. "Pathways to the Negro Market," Journal of Negro Education 28:114-128
(Spring 1959).

Barnes, Nicholas L., Some Potentialities and Limitations of the Negro Market in Chicago.
Chicago: T and T, 1953.

"Birmingham's Race Conflict Has Small Effect on Sales," Advertising Age 34:88 (November
11, 1963).

Black, L. E., "Negro Market: Growing, Changing, Challenging," Sales Management 91:7
(October 4, 1963).

Bullock, Henry Allen, "Consumer Motivations in Black and White--Part I," Harvard Business Review 33:89-104 (May-June 1961); "Part II," ibid., 33:110-124 (July-August 1961).
Two thorough and thoughtful articles.

Danzig, Fred, "Negro Marketer Gets Bigger Role as Awareness of Specialized Field
Grows," Advertising Age 33:96, 98 (September 10, 1962).

Hall, Claude H., "Guide to Marketing for 1959: The Negro Market," Printers' Ink 265:
137-138 (October 31, 1958). These reports appear annually in an autumn issue of
Printers' Ink. They include bibliographies on Negro marketing information and useful
surveys.

"Heavy Buying by Negro Households Is Shown by WWRL," Advertising Age 34:242 (August
26, 1963).

Holte, C. L., "Negro Market: To Profit from It, Recognize It and Service its Needs,"
Printers' Ink 262:29-32 (April 4, 1958).

Korenvaes, P., "Negro Market," Dun's Review and Modern Industry 82:61-62 (November
1963).

"Market Basics," Sponsor 15:16-21 (October 9, 1961). A selection of articles dealing with
the Negro market and the radio.

"Marketing to the Negro Consumer: Special Report," Sales Management 84:5 (March 4,
1960).

"Negro Boycott Could Have Serious, Lasting Effect on Sales, Study Shows," Advertising Age
(September 30, 1963).

"Negro Business Pressure Grows," Business Week 1599: 31-32, 34 (April 23, 1960).

"Negro Buying Power," Southern Regional Council, Report No. L-18 Atlanta, Ga., 1960,
mimeo.

"Negro Groups Put Economic Pressure On," Business Week 1591:26-28 (February 27,
1960).

"Negro Impact on Market," Broadcasting 64:96 (June 17, 1963).

"Negro Market: Buying Power Changes Market Place," Printers' Ink 284:9 (August 30,
1963).

"Negro Market Data: Still Inadequate, but Starting to Flow," Sponsor 13:12-13 (September
26, 1959).

"Negro Marketing Basics," Sponsor 14:17-28 (September 26, 1960). Includes tables.

"The Negro's Force in the Marketplace," Business Week 1708:76 (May 26, 1962).

Sawyer, Broadus E., "An Examination of Race as a Factor in Negro-White Consumption
Patterns," Review of Economics and Statistics 44:217-220 (May 1962).

"$2 Billion Negro Furnishing Market Seen by Ebony," Advertising Age 34:88 (March 25,
1963).

"Why an Ethnic Appeal is Working," Printers' Ink 279:54-55 (June 1, 1962). In radio.

4. THE NEGRO AS ENTREPRENEUR

"Aiding Negro Businessmen: Small Business Opportunities Corporation, Philadelphia,"
   Business Week, April 18, 1964.
Asbury, Edith Evans, "Negro Businesses to Receive Advice and Financial Aid," New York
   Times, June 18, 1964. Formation of Interracial Council of Business Opportunity, co-
   sponsored by American Jewish Congress and Urban League of Greater New York.
The Census of Negro-Owned Businesses. Philadelphia: Drexel Institute of Technology,1964.
   Includes every Negro business in Philadelphia, no matter how small.
Fitzhugh, H. Naylor, ed., Problems and Opportunities in the Field of Business. Washington,
   D.C.: U.S. Department of Commerce, 1962.
Foley, Eugene P., "The Negro Businessman: In Search of a Tradition," Daedalus 95:107-
   144 (Winter 1966). An examination of why Negro business has not developed in America,
   with suggestions of steps that are most needed to encourage future development. Tables.
Harris, Abram L., The Negro as Capitalist. Philadelphia: American Academy of Political
   and Social Science, 1936. Still useful for reference.
Kinzer, Robert H., and Edward Sagarin, The Negro in American Business. New York:
   Greenberg, 1950. Examines the dilemma for Negro business of separation or integration. Statistics are out of date, but still useful as background. The authors advocate joint
   development of "the separate and the integrated philosophies of business."
Lipset, Seymour M., and Reinhard Bendix, Social Mobility in Industrial Society. Berkeley:
   University of California Press, 1960. Emphasizing that it is the rate of economic expansion which is most significant in determining extent of social mobility, the authors point
   out factors inhibiting Negroes from sharing economic opportunities of expansion.
McPeak, William, "A Plea for Cooperatives," Interracial Review 36:215-217 (November
   1963). As a means of relieving economic disabilities, Negroes should establish credit
   cooperatives, housing cooperatives, marketing cooperatives.
Patterson, William L., "Mr. A. D. Fuller and Negro Unity," Political Affairs 43:57-59
   (February 1964). Remarks on speech by Negro millionaire before the National Association
   of Manufacturers.
Pierce, J. A., Negro Business and Business Education. New York: Harper, 1947. Still useful as a general study, both for its examination, in Part I, of the characteristics and
   structure of Negro business, and for its recommendations, in Part II, for preparing
   Negroes for greater participation in business.
Trent, W. J., Jr., "Development of Negro Life Insurance Enterprises," unpub. master's
   thesis, University of Pennsylvania, 1932. Study of insurance undertakings of fraternal
   organizations and mutual aid societies.
Young, Harding B., "The Negro's Participation in American Business," Journal of Negro
   Education 32:390-401 (Fall 1963).
Young, Harding B., and James M. Hund, "Negro Entrepreneurship in Southern Economic
   Development," in Melvin L. Greenhut and W. Tate Whitman, eds., Essays in Southern
   Economic Development, Chapel Hill: University of North Carolina Press, 1964.

VII. EMPLOYMENT

The banner under which the March on Washington took place on August 28, 1963, was "Jobs and Freedom," and many Negro writers stress the economic factors that are central to the demands of the Freedom Movement. The problem of Negro employment--and unemployment--has received much public and governmental attention ever since Fair Employment Practice regulations were promulgated during World War II. Their distinctly less than impressive effectiveness has been documented by Paul H. Norgren in his Toward Fair Employment. The resistance of certain unions and of Southern employers, coupled with the fearfulness, indifference, or lack of aggressive policy on the part of Northern employers at the same time that automation is eliminating unskilled and semi-skilled jobs, have meant that the Negro predicament daily worsens, especially where Negro labor is concentrated in Northern ghettos. With seventy-five percent of all Negroes in the labor market in the three lowest occupational categories, and these the categories often drastically affected by automation, with Negro unemployment rates substantially higher than those for white workers and jobs for Negro youth virtually nonexistent, the Negro is well aware that without a job any "Freedom" he achieves will remain illusory.

Despite the urgency of the situation, studies of Negro employment have remained very largely either statistical or concerned with regulatory action. There has, for example, been little recent analysis of Negro occupational trends. One can, however, anticipate that the creation of the Office of Economic Opportunity directed toward the total problem of poverty in the United States may stimulate the kinds of studies genuinely useful for understanding the dimensions of Negro economic disabilities.

1. THE LAW, THE COURTS, AND REGULATORY ACTION

Aaron, Benjamin, "The Labor-Management Reporting and Disclosure Act of 1959," Harvard Law Review 73:858-907 (March 1960).

Bamberger, Michael A., and Nathan Levin, "The Right to Equal Treatment: Administrative Enforcement of Antidiscrimination Legislation," Harvard Law Review 74:526-589 (January 1961).

Becker, William, "After FEPC--What?" Journal of Intergroup Relations 3:337-343 (Fall 1962). Discrimination in apprenticeship programs and its effect.

Berger, Morroe, Effects of Fair Employment Legislation in States and Municipalities. Staff Report, U.S. Senate, 82nd Congress, 2nd Session, Washington, D.C.: GPO, 1952.

Berger, Morroe, Equality by Statute: Legal Controls over Group Discrimination. New York: Columbia University Press, 1952. A study based on the New York State Law against Discrimination.

Birnbaum, O., "Equal Employment Opportunity and Executive Order 10925," University of Kansas Law Review 11:17-34 (October 1962).

Bullock, Paul, Merit Employment: Non-Discrimination in Industry. Los Angeles: Institute of Industrial Relations, UCLA, 1960. A brief history of fair employment regulations, with a description of various federal and local programs.

"The Controversy Over the 'Equal Opportunity' Provisions of the Civil Rights Bill," Congressional Digest 43:67-96 (March 1964).

Cox, Archibald, "The Duty of Fair Representation," Villanova Law Review 2:151-177 (January 1957). Admonitions addressed to labor unions.

"Discrimination in Union Membership: Denial of Due Process Under Federal Collective Bargaining Legislation," Rutgers Law Review 12:543-556 (Summer 1958).

Donahue, Charles, "Equal Employment Opportunity," Federal Bar Journal 24:76-86 (Winter 1964). The author, Solicitor, Department of Labor, discusses inequities in hiring practices, and discriminative practices within certain unions.

Ellis, Greeley H., Jr., "The Constitutional Right to Membership in a Labor Union--Fifth and Fourteenth Amendments," Journal of Public Law 8:580-595 (Fall 1959).

"Employment Discrimination," Race Relations Law Reporter 5:569-592 (Summer 1960).

"Employment Discrimination: State FEPC Laws and the Impact of Title VII of the Civil Rights Act of 1964," Western Reserve Law Review 16:608 (May 1965).

"Equal Employment Opportunity," Hearings before the Special Subcommittee on Labor of the Committee on Education and Labor, October 23, 1961--January 24, 1962. U.S. House of Representatives, 87th Congress, 1st and 2nd Sessions, 1961, 1962.

"Equal Employment Opportunity in the United States: The Civil Rights Act of 1964," International Labour Review 90:377-379 (October 1964).

"Equal Opportunity in Apprenticeship Programs," Hearings before the Special Subcommittee on Labor of the Committee on Education and Labor, August 21-23, 1961. U.S. House of Representatives, 87th Congress, 1st Session, 1961.

Ginsburg, Gilbert J., "Non-discrimination in Employment: Executive Order 10925," Military Law Review 1961:141 (October 1961).

Groves, H. E., "States as 'Fair' Employers," Howard Law Journal 7:1-16 (Winter 1961).

Gutman, D., ed., "Discrimination in Employment and Housing: A Symposium," New York Law Forum 6:1+ (January 1960)

Hartman, Paul, Comparative Analysis of State Fair Employment Practices Laws. New York: Anti-Defamation League, 1962.

Hill, Herbert, et al., "Twenty Years of State Fair Employment Practice Commissions: A Critical Analysis with Recommendations," Buffalo Law Review 14:22-78 (Fall 1964).

King, Robertson L., "Protecting Rights of Minority Employees," Labor Law Journal 11:143-154 (February 1960).

Kovarsky, Irving, "Racial Discrimination in Employment and the Federal Law," Oregon Law Review 38:54-85 (December 1958).

Levitan, S. A., Youth Employment Act. Kalamazoo, Mich.: Upjohn Institute for Employment Research, 1963.

Lunden, Leon E., Antidiscrimination Provisions in Major Contracts, 1961. Washington, D.C.: U.S. Department of Labor, Bureau of Labor Statistics, Bulletin No. 1336, 1962.

Maloney, W. H., Jr., "Racial and Religious Discrimination in Employment and the Role of the NLRB," Maryland Law Review 21:219-232 (Summer 1961).

Mayhew, Leon Hinckley, "Law and Equal Opportunity: Anti-Discrimination Law in Massachusetts," unpub. doc. diss., Harvard University, 1963. A thorough examination of all ramifications of the Massachusetts Law.

Morgan, Chester A., "An Analysis of State FEPC Legislation," Labor Law Journal 8:478 (July 1957).

Norgren, Paul H., and Samuel Hill, with the Assistance of F. Ray Marshall, Toward Fair Employment. New York: Columbia University Press, 1964. An important work which includes a survey of racial discrimination arising either from management or union practices, and an examination and assessment of all FEP laws and executive orders. The authors also advance proposals for what they consider the most effective legislation, together with suggestions for improving the administration of laws and regulations.

Rabkin, Sol, "Enforcement of Laws Against Discrimination in Employment," Buffalo Law Review 14:100-113 (Fall 1964).

"Racial Discrimination and the Duty of Fair Representation," Columbia Law Review 65:273-287 (February 1965). Racial discrimination is subject to the remedies of the National Labor Relations Act.

"Racial Discrimination on the Jobsite: Competing Theories and Competing Forums," UCLA
    Law Review 12:1186 (May 1965).
"Racial Discrimination in Unions," Temple Law Quarterly 38:311 (Spring 1965).
"Racial Discrimination in Union Membership," University of Miami Law Review 13:364-
    369 (Spring 1959).
Read, F. T., "Minority Rights and the Union Shop," Minnesota Law Review 49:227
    (December 1964).
Ruchames, Louis, Race, Jobs, and Politics: The Story of FEPC. New York: Columbia Uni-
    versity Press, 1953.
Screiber, Harry N., "The Thirteenth Amendment and Freedom of Choice in Personal
    Service Occupations: A Reappraisal," Cornell Law Quarterly 49:508-514 (Spring 1964).
Shirk, E. M., "Cases are People: An Interpretation of the Pennsylvania Fair Employment
    Practice Law," Dickinson Law Review 62:289-305 (June 1958).
Shostak, Arthur, "Appeals from Discrimination in Federal Employment: A Case Study,"
    Social Forces 42:174-178 (December 1963). Study of appeals records in 27 cases, 1952-
    1962, in a Northeastern federal manufacturing center. Most of the cases involved the
    failure of Negroes to secure promotion; only one was decided in appellant's favor.
Sovern, Michael I., "The National Labor Relations Act and Racial Discrimination," Columbia
    Law Review 62:563-632 (April 1962). Author advocates continued legal pressure by
    means of federal laws on the grounds that "Substantial improvement in any sector of
    civil rights has a snowball effect."
Spitz, H., "Tailoring the Techniques to Eliminate and Prevent Employment Discrimination,"
    Buffalo Law Review 14:79-99 (Fall 1964).
"State to Punish a Union Barring Negro Members," New York Times, March 5, 1964. Ruling
    of the State Commission for Human Rights that Local 28 of the Sheet Metal Workers
    International Association, in violation of state law, has excluded Negroes for 76 years.
"Toward Equal Opportunity in Employment," Buffalo Law Review 14:1+ (Fall 1964). Entire
    issue devoted to reports of a conference held at the University of Buffalo Law School.
Tower, John, "FEPC--Some Practical Considerations," Federal Bar Journal 24:87-92
    (Winter 1964). The author, U.S. Senator from Texas, attacks general proposition that
    discrimination is illegal and maintains that FEPC has been given arbitrary power to
    "ram . . . racial quotas" down the throats of employers.
Weiss, L., "Federal Remedies for Racial Discrimination by Labor Unions," Georgetown
    Law Journal 50:457-477 (Spring 1962).
Woll, J. Albert, "Labor Looks at Equal Rights in Employment," Federal Bar Journal 24:98
    (Winter 1964). The author, general counsel for the AFL-CIO, maintains that Titles VI
    and VII of the Civil Rights Bill are reasonable and provide ample opportunity for
    voluntary compliance.

2. PATTERNS AND CONDITIONS

Amos, W. E., and Jane Perry, "Negro Youth and Employment Opportunities," Journal of
    Negro Education 32:358-366 (Fall 1963).
Antonovsky, Aaron, and Melvin J. Lerner, "Negro and White Youth in Elmira," in Aaron
    Antonovsky and Lewis L. Lorwin, eds., Discrimination and Low Incomes. New York: New
    School for Social Research, 1959 (multi.).
Antonovsky, Aaron, and Lewis L. Lorwin, eds., Discrimination and Low Incomes. New York:
    New School for Social Research, 1959 (multi.). Studies under the direction of New York
    State Commission Against Discrimination.
Apprentices, Skilled Craftsmen and the Negro: An Analysis. New York State Commission
    Against Discrimination, 1960.
Apprenticeship Training in New York Openings in 1963. New York: Workers Defense League,
    1963.
Babow, Irving, and Edward Howden, A Civil Rights Inventory of San Francisco: Part I,
    Employment. San Francisco: Council for Civic Unity, 1958.
Bancroft, Gertrude, The American Labor Force: Its Growth and Changing Composition.
    New York: Wiley, 1958. Statistics and description of trends and patterns since 1890.

Data on white and nonwhite components of the labor force considered in this changing context. A volume in the census Monograph Series, prepared for the Social Science Research Council in cooperation with the U.S. Department of Commerce.

The Banking Industry: Verified Complaints and Informal Investigations. New York State Commission Against Discrimination, 1958.

Baron, Harold, "Negro Unemployment: A Case Study," New University Thought 3:279-282 (September-October 1963).

Batchelder, A. B., "Decline in the Relative Income of Negro Men," Quarterly Journal of Economics 78:525-548 (November 1964).

Becker, Gary S., "Discrimination and the Occupational Progress of Negroes: A Comment," Review of Economics and Statistics 44:214-215 (May 1962).

Blalock, H. M., Jr., "Occupational Discrimination: Some Theoretical Propositions," Social Problems 9:240-247 (Winter 1962).

Bloch, Herman D., "Employment Status of the New York Negro in Retrospect," Phylon 20: 327-344 (December 1959).

"Bringing Better Jobs to Negroes," Business Week, November 3, 1962. An employment agency in Philadelphia which specializes in jobs for Negroes.

Buckley, Louis F., "Discriminatory Aspects of the Labor Market of the 60's," Review of Social Economy 19:25-42 (March 1961).

Buckley, Louis F., "Nonwhite Employment in the United States," Interracial Review 36:32-33 (February 1963).

Buckley, Louis F., "Youth Employment Problems," Interracial Review 36:174-175 (September 1963).

Carl, E. L., and K. R. Callahan, "Negroes and the Law," Journal of Legal Education 17:3: 250-271 (1964-1965). On the great need to increase the number of Negro Lawyers. Strong motivation, satisfactory qualifications, and likelihood of professional opportunity have in the past militated against attraction of Negro students to the law.

Chalmers, W. Ellison, and Nathaniel W. Dorsey, "Research on Negro Job Status," Journal of Intergroup Relations 3:344-359 (Fall 1962).

"Changing Status of Negro Women Workers," Monthly Labor Review 87:671-673 (June 1964).

Characteristics of 6,000 White and Nonwhite Persons Enrolled in Manpower Development and Training Act Training. Washington, D.C.: U.S. Department of Labor, Office of Manpower, Automation, and Training, 1963.

Cobb, W. Montague, "Not to the Swift: Progress and Prospects of the Negro in Science and the Professions," Journal of Negro Education 27:120-126 (Spring 1958).

Cohen, Albert K., and Harold M. Hodges, "Characteristics of the Lower-Blue-Collar Class," Social Problems 10:303-334 (Spring 1963).

Council of Economic Advisors, The High Cost of Racial Discrimination in Employment, Statement presented to the Joint Economic Committee of Congress in September, 1962; released by the Southern Regional Council, Atlanta, Ga., October 15, 1962.

Cunningham, George E., "Reasons for Belated Education: A Study of the Plight of Older Negro Teachers," Journal of Negro Education 27:195-200 (Spring 1958).

Daniel, Walter C., "Negroes as Teaching Assistants in Some Publicly-Supported Universities," Journal of Negro Education 31:202-204 (Spring 1962).

Daniel, W. G., "The Relative Employment and Income of American Negroes," Journal of Negro Education, 32:349-357 (Fall 1963).

Decker, Paul M., "A Study of Job Opportunities in the State of Florida for Negro College Graduates," Journal of Negro Education 29:93-95 (Winter 1960).

Dewey, Donald, "Negro Employment in Southern Industry," Journal of Political Economy 60:279-293 (August 1952).

Dewey, Donald, Four Studies of Negro Employment in the Upper South. Washington, D.C.: National Planning Association, 1953.

Dewey, Donald, "Southern Poverty and the Racial Division of Labor," New South 17:3-5, 11-13 (May 1962). Penetrating and thorough studies of Negro employment in the South.

Discrimination and Low Incomes. New York State Commission Against Discrimination, 1959.

Duncan, Otis D., and Beverly Duncan, The Negro Population of Chicago: A Study of Residential Succession. Chicago: University of Chicago Press, 1957. Occupational patterns also examined.

Dwyer, Robert J., "The Negro in the U.S. Army," Sociology and Social Research 38:103-112 (November 1953). Wherever the pattern of segregation has broken down, there has been a marked absence of friction or tension, and in many cases changes in the Negro's relations with the civilian community have followed.

Edwards, G. Franklin, "The Occupational Mobility of Negro Professional Workers," in E. W. Burgess and D. J. Bogue, eds., Contributions to Urban Sociology, Chicago: University of Chicago Press, 1964.

Employment in the Hotel Industry. New York State Commission Against Discrimination, 1958).

The Employment of Negroes as Driver Salesmen in the Baking Industry. New York State Commission Against Discrimination, 1960.

Employment Practices in Pennsylvania. Report of the Governor's Commission on Industrial Race Relations, Harrisburg, 1953.

Employment Study. Report (Part V) of the Governor's Advisory Commission on Civil Rights, Columbus, Ohio, 1958.

"Ethnic Survey of Municipal Employees," City Commission on Human Rights of New York, March 19, 1964.

Falls, Arthur G., "The Search for Negro Medical Students," Integrated Education 1:15-19 (June 1963).

Feldman, J. Arnold, "The 1960 Audit of Negro Veterans and Servicemen," Journal of Intergroup Relations 2:79-81 (Winter 1960-1961).

Florida Council on Human Relations, "Negro Employment in Miami," New South 17:6-10 (May 1962).

Gallaher, Art, Jr., The Negro and Employment Opportunities in the South--Houston. Atlanta, Ga.: Southern Regional Council, 1961.

Ginzberg, Eli, and Hyman Berman, "The Negro's Problem is the White's," New York Times Magazine, February 9, 1964.

Glenn, Norval D., "Changes in the American Occupational Structure and Occupational Gains of Negroes During the 1940's," Social Forces 41:188-195 (December 1962).

Glenn, Norval D., "Some Changes in the Relative Status of American Non-whites, 1940-1960," Phylon 24:109-122 (Summer 1963). Relative changes in occupation, employment, income, and educational status.

Greenwald, William, and Robert E. Weintraub, "Money Benefits of Education by Sex and Race in New York State, 1956," Journal of Educational Sociology 34:312-319 (March 1961).

Guillory, Barbara M., "The Career Patterns of Negro Lawyers in New Orleans," unpub. master's thesis, Louisiana State University, 1960.

Hare, Nathaniel, "The Changing Occupational Status of the Negro in the United States: An Intracohort Analysis," unpub. doc. diss., University of Chicago, 1962.

Harper, R. M., "Racial Contrasts in Income," Alabama Lawyer 21:257-260 (July 1960).

Harrington, Michael, "The New Lost Generation: Jobless Youth," New York Times Magazine, May 24, 1964.

Harrison, Lincoln J., "The Status of the Negro CPA in the United States," Journal of Negro Education 31:503-506 (Fall 1962).

Hart, Joe W., "Effects of Automation on the Position of Negroes in a Southern Industrial Plant," and "A Study of the Effects of Efforts to Improve Employment Opportunities of Negroes on the Utilization of Negro Workers," Journal of Human Relations 12:419-423 (Spring 1964). Two brief research notes.

Hauser, Philip M., "The Labor Force as a Field of Interest for the Sociologist," American Sociological Review 16:530-538 (August 1951).

Hawley, Langston T., Negro Employment in the Birmingham Metropolitan Area. Washington, D.C.: National Planning Association, 1954.

Hentoff, Nat, "Race Prejudice in Jazz," Harper's Magazine 218:72-77 (June 1959).

Hiestand, Dale L., Economic Growth and Employment Opportunities for Minorities. New York: Columbia University Press, 1964. Introduction by Eli Ginzberg. The author finds the labor demand factor more important for the Negro than supply. Opportunities for Negro workers tend to open up chiefly to replace white workers with better opportunities, that is, in declining occupational areas with little long-run significance. Bibliography.

Hill, Herbert, "Patterns of Employment Discrimination," Crisis 69:137-147 (March 1962).

Hill, Herbert, "Racial Discrimination in the Nation's Apprenticeship Training Program,"
Phylon 23:215-224 (Fall 1962).

Hope, John, II, "The Self-Survey of the Packing House Union," Journal of Social Issues 9:
28-36 (January 1953).

Hope, John, II, "The Employment of Negroes in the United States by Major Occupation and
Industry," Journal of Negro Education 22:307-321 (Summer 1953). Period 1940-1950.

Hope, John, II, "Equality of Employment Opportunity: A Process Analysis of Union
Initiative," Phylon 18:140-154 (Summer 1957).

Hope, John, II, "Central Role of Intergroup Agencies in the Labor Market: Changing Research and Personnel Requirements," Journal of Intergroup Relations 2:132-144 (Spring
1961).

Hope, John, II, "Equal Employment Opportunity: Changing Problems, Changing Techniques,"
Journal of Intergroup Relations 4:29-36 (Winter 1962-1963).

Hope, John, II, and E. Shelton, "The Negro in the Federal Government," Journal of Negro
Education 32:367-374 (Fall 1963).

Jefferson, Miles, "The Negro on Broadway, 1954-55," Phylon 16:303-312 (Fall 1955).
Extent of employment and type of roles (chiefly minor).

Jefferson, Miles, "The Negro on Broadway, 1955-56," Phylon 17:227-237 (Fall 1956).

"Jobs for Negroes: How Much Progress in Sight?" Newsweek 62:68-70, 72 (July 15, 1963).

"Job Outlook for Youth," Ebony 18:25-30 (May 1963).

Jobs, 1960-1970: The Changing Pattern. Albany: New York State Department of Labor, 1960.

Jones, Major J., The Negro and Employment Opportunities in the South--Chattanooga.
Atlanta, Ga.: Southern Regional Council, 1962.

Kiehl, Robert, "Negro Engineers and Students Report on their Profession," Journal of
Negro Education 27:189-194 (Spring 1958).

Kohler, Mary Conway, assisted by Marcia Freeman, Youth and Work in New York City. New
York: Taconic Foundation, March 1962.

Kuebler, Jeanne, "Negro Jobs and Education," Educational Research Reports, January 23,
1963.

Lang, Gladys Engel, "Discrimination in the Hiring Hall," in Aaron Antonovsky and Lewis L.
Lorwin, eds., Discrimination and Low Incomes. New York: New School for Social Research, 1959 (multi.).

"Manpower Report of the President and a Report on Manpower Requirements, Resources,
Utilization and Training," by U.S. Department of Labor, transmitted to the Congress
March 1964.

Marshall, Thurgood, "Summary Justice--The Negro GI in Korea," Crisis 58:297-304, 350-
355 (May 1951).

Marshall, Thurgood, Report on Korea. NAACP, 1951. The author, who went to Korea to
investigate alleged injustice in Courts Martial, found that JimCrow policies still existed
in army.

Michael, Donald, Cybernation: The Silent Conquest. Pasadena, Calif.: Center for the Study
of Democratic Institutions, 1962. Effect on length of work-week, unions, total unemployment.

Michael, Donald, The Next Generation. New York: Random House, 1965. The author
concludes that without long-term, extensive effort to eliminate the sources of low
capability, a "Negro menial, unskilled, worker society" will be perpetuated. Report
prepared for President's Committee on Juvenile Delinquency and Youth Crime.

Mihlon, Lawrence F., "Industrial Discrimination--The Skeleton in Everyone's Closet,"
Factory 70:80-87 (April 1962).

Morgan, Gordon D., "Representation of Negroes and Whites as Employees in the Federal
Prison System," Phylon 23:372-378 (Winter 1962).

Morrow, Joseph J., "American Negroes--A Wasted Resource," Harvard Business Review
35:65-74 (January-February 1957). An examination of the opportunities, problems,
advantages, and disadvantages of accelerated hiring of Negroes by business.

Moynihan, Daniel Patrick, "Behind Los Angeles: Jobless Negroes and the Boom," Reporter
33:31 (September 9, 1965).

Moynihan, Daniel Patrick, "Employment, Income, and the Ordeal of the Negro Family,"
Daedalus 94:745-770 (Fall 1965).

National Manpower Council, A Policy for Skilled Manpower. New York: Columbia University Press, 1954.

National Manpower Council, Improving the Work Skills of the Nation. New York: Columbia University Press, 1955.

National Planning Association, Committee of the South, Selected Studies of Negro Employment in the South: Report No. 6. Washington, D.C.: National Planning Association, 1953.

"Negroes in Apprenticeship: New York State," Monthly Labor Review 83:952-957 (September 1960).

"The Negro's Drive for Jobs," Business Week, August 17, 1963.

"Negro Employment Problem," Dun's Review and Modern Industry 82:59-60, 62 (August 1963).

"The Negro in [School] Administration," Overview 2:35-37 (June 1961).

The Negro Wage-Earner and Apprenticeship Training Programs. New York: NAACP, 1960.

Newton, I. E., "The Negro and the National Guard," Phylon 23:18-28 (Spring 1962).

Nicol, Helen, with Merci L. Drake, Negro Women Workers in 1960. Washington, D.C.: GPO, 1964. Prepared for the Women's Bureau, Department of Labor.

Nonwhite Unemployment in the U.S. 1947-1958. New York State Commission Against Discrimination, Division of Research, 1958.

Norgren, Paul H., Racial Discrimination in Employment: Bibliography. Princeton: Princeton University Press, 1962.

Norgren, Paul H., et al., Employing the Negro in American Industry: A Study of Management Practices. New York: Industrial Relations Counselors, 1959. A study of 44 firms. Negro employment treated within the framework of industrial relations issues, and the realization of success within this framework.

Northrup, Herbert, and Richard Rowan, eds., The Negro and Employment Opportunity. Ann Arbor: University of Michigan Bureau of Industrial Relations, 1965.

Puryear, Mahlon T., "No Time for 'Tragic Ironies,'" Interracial Review 36:34-35 (February 1963). Negroes, employment, and technological change.

Puryear, Mahlon T., "The Negro in the Labor Force,' Taconic Foundation Assessment Project, June 15, 1963.

Railroad, Employment in the New York and New Jersey. New York State Commission Against Discrimination, 1958.

Ramaker, Robert, "Negro Colleges Train Too Many Teachers, Too Few Technicians," Wall Street Journal, July 15, 1959.

Rayack, Elton, "Discrimination and the Occupational Progress of Negroes," Review of Economics and Statistics 43:209-214 (May 1961).

Reddick, L. D., "The Negro Policy of the American Army since World War II," Journal of Negro History 38:194-215 (April 1953). The Army has gone a considerable way toward abandoning Jim Crow policy, but practices have not yet caught up with policy.

Reed, Eugene T., "I Am a Controversial Dentist," Interracial Review 35:100-101 (April 1962). Professional problems of a New York Negro Catholic dentist seeking admission to the New York State Dental Society.

Roberts, Gene, Jr., "Waste of Manpower--Race and Employment in a Southern State," South Atlantic Quarterly 61:141-150 (Spring 1962).

Rose, Harold M., "The Market for Negro Educators in Colleges and Universities Outside the South," Journal of Negro Education 30:432-435 (Fall 1961).

Russell, R. D., "Experiences of Negro High School Girls with Domestic Placement Agencies," Journal of Negro Education 31:172-176 (Spring 1962).

Schiffman, J., "Employment of High School Graduates and Dropouts in 1962," Monthly Labor Review 86:772-779 (July 1963).

Schwartz, M., "Why They Don't Want to Work," Personnel Administration 27:6-10 (March 1964). Study of work motivation of Negroes.

Seidenberg, Jacob, Negroes in the Work Group. Ithaca: New York State School of Industrial and Labor Relations, Cornell University, 1950.

Silberman, Charles E., "The Businessman and the Negro," Fortune 68:97-99+ (September 1963). The author, from a survey of a number of representative firms, demonstrates that most of them have done very little to open up job opportunities for Negroes.

Steele, H. Ellsworth, "Jobs for Negroes" Some North-South Plant Studies," Social Forces 32:152-162 (December 1953).

Street, James H., The New Revolution in the Cotton Economy. Chapel Hill: University of North Carolina Press, 1957. And how it affects labor force.

Strutt, Joseph W., Survey of Non-White Employees in State Government. Harrisburg, Pa.:
    Human Relations Commission, March, 1963.
Survey of Ohio College and University Placement Offices with Regard to Job Placement of
    Minority Students. Columbus: Ohio Civil Rights Commission, 1962.
Thompson, Daniel C., "Career Patterns of Teachers in Negro Colleges," Social Forces
    36:270-276 (March 1958).
Thompson, Daniel C., Problems of Faculty Morale," Journal of Negro Education 29:37-46
    (Winter 1960).
Training of Negroes in the Skilled Trades. Hartford: Connecticut Commission on Civil
    Rights, 1954. Limited vocational education facilities available to Negroes.
Turner, Ralph H., "Relative Position of the Negro Male in the Labor Force of Large
    American Cities," American Sociological Review 16:524-529 (August 1951).
Turner, Ralph H., "Foci of Discrimination in the Employment of Non-Whites," American
    Journal of Sociology 58:247-256 (November 1952).
Turner, Ralph H., "Negro Job Status and Education," Social Forces 32:45-52 (October 1953).
Turner, Ralph H., "Occupational Patterns of Inequality," American Journal of Sociology 59:
    437-447 (March 1954).
"Two State Reports on Job Discrimination," Monthly Labor Review 81:1125-1130 (October
    1958). New York and New Jersey.
United States Commission on Civil Rights, Report, Vol. III, Employment. Washington, D.C.:
    GPO, 1961.
United States Department of Labor, Women's Bureau Bulletin No. 287, Negro Women
    Workers in 1960. Washington, D.C.: GPO, 1963.
Viorst, J., "Negroes in Science," Science News Letter 87:218-219 (April 3, 1965).
Weaver, Robert C., Negro Labor: A National Problem. New York: Harcourt, Brace, 1946.
    A Study of Negro employment opportunities through World War II. The best and most
    comprehensive work on this subject up to date of publication.
Willhelm, Sidney M., and Edwin H. Powell, "Who Needs the Negro?" Trans-Action 1:3-6
    (September-October 1964). Subtitled "From the economics of exploitation to the
    economics of uselessness." The issue today is "a search for human rights in a world of
    machines that makes so many human beings utterly dispensable."
Wilson, C. E., "Automation and the Negro: Will We Survive?" Liberator 5:8-11 (July 1965).
    Study of the consequences of automation on the economic life of black workers.

3. THE NEGRO AND THE LABOR MOVEMENT

Bain, M., "Organized Labor and the Negro Worker," National Review 14:455 (June 4, 1963).
Battle, Robert, III, and Horace Sheffield, "Trade Union Leadership Council--Experiment in
    Community Action," New University Thought 3:34-41 (September-October 1963). Civil
    rights and unions in Detroit.
Bell, Daniel, "Reflections on the Negro and Labor," New Leader 46:18-20 (January 21, 1963).
Bell, Daniel, and Seymour M. Lipset, eds., "Trade unions and Minority Problems," Journal
    of Social Issues 9:2-62 (January 1953). Entire issue.
Bloch, Herman D., "Craft Unions, A Link in the Circle of Negro Discrimination," Phylon
    18:361-372 (Winter 1957).
Bloch, Herman D., "Craft Unions and the Negro in Historical Perspective," Journal of
    Negro History 43:10-33 (January 1958).
Bloch, Herman D., "Negroes and Organized Labor," Journal of Human Relations 10:357-374
    (Summer 1962).
Boggs, James, "The American Revolution: Pages from a Negro Worker's Notebook,"
    Monthly Review 15:13-93 (July and August, 1963).
Brooks, Tom, "Negro Militants, Jewish Liberals, and the Unions," Commentary 32:209-216
    (September 1961).
Brooks, Tom, "The Negro's Place at Labor's Table," Reporter 27:38-39 (December 6,
    1962).
Carey, James B., "Race Hate: Newest Union-Busting Weapon," Progressive 22:16-18
    (January 1958).

Doyle, William, Seymour M. Lipset, Herbert Hill, Bill Goode, B. K. Johnpoll, and Daniel J.
    Schulder, "Negroes and the Labor Movement: Record of the 'Left Wing' Unions," New
    Politics 2:142-151 (Fall 1962).
Fleischman, Harry, "Is Labor Color Blind?" Progressive 23:24-28 (November 1959).
Fleishman, Harry, and James Rorty, We Open the Gates: Labor's Fight for Equality. New
    York: National Labor Service, 1958.
Greer, Scott, Last Man In: Racial Access to Union Power. Glencoe, Ill: Free Press, 1959.
Greer, Scott, "The Place of the Negro in the American Labor Movement," American Review
    1:98-109 (Winter 1961).
Grob, Gerald N., "Organized Labor and the Negro Worker, 1865-1900," Labor History 1:
    164-176 (Spring 1960).
Hill, Herbert, "Labor Unions and the Negro: The Record of Discrimination," Commentary
    28:479-488 (December 1959).
Hill, Herbert, "Organized Labor and the Negro Earner: Ritual and Reality," New Politics
    1:8-19 (Winter 1962).
Hill, Herbert, "Racism Within Organized Labor: A Report of Five Years of the AFL-CIO,
    1955-1960," Journal of Negro Education 30:109-118 (Spring 1961).
Hill, Herbert, "The ILGWU--Fact and Fiction," New Politics 2:7-27 (Winter 1963).
Hope, John, II, Equality of Opportunity: A Union Approach to Fair Employment. Washington,
    D.C.: Public Affairs, 1956.
Jacobs, Paul, The State of the Unions. New York: Atheneum, 1963. An inside look at Ameri-
    can labor, a view of its leaders and members, their problems, scandals and future. See
    particularly chapter, "The Negro Worker Asserts His Rights," pp. 174 ff.
Johnson, Oakley C., "Marxism and the Negro Freedom Struggle," Journal of Human
    Relations 13:21-39 (Autumn 1965). Expectations and failures of efforts to join working
    class and Negro causes.
Kahn, Tom, The Economics of Equality. New York: League for Industrial Democracy, 1964.
    Thesis: the uniting of the Negro and the labor movements is the key to the future of
    America as a nation.
Kornhauser, William, "The Negro Union Official," American Journal of Sociology 57:443-
    452 (March 1952).
Kornhauser, William, "Ideology and Interests," Journal of Social Issues 9:49-60 (Winter
    1953). Of the trade unions.
"Labor-Negro Division Widens," Business Week, July 9, 1960.
"Labor's 'Race Problem,'" Fortune 59:191-192, 194 (March 1959).
Litwak, Leon, The American Labor Movement. New York: Prentice-Hall Spectrum, 1962.
Marshall, Ray, "Some Factors Influencing Union Racial Practices," Proceedings of the
    Industrial Relations Research Association 1961.
Marshall, Ray, "Union Racial Practices and the Labor Market," Monthly Labor Review 85:
    269-270 (March 1962).
Marshall, Ray, "Union Racial Problems in the South," Journal of Economy and Society,
    Berkeley: University of California Institute of Industrial Relations, May, 1962.
Marshall, Ray, "Union Structure and Public Policy: The Control of Union Racial Practices,"
    Political Science Quarterly 78:444-458 (September 1963).
Marshall, Ray, "The Negro and Organized Labor," Journal of Negro Education 32:375-389
    (Fall 1963).
Marshall, Ray, "Ethnic and Economic Minorities: Unions' Future or Unrecruitable," Annals
    of the American Academy of Political and Social Science 350:63-73 (November 1963).
Marshall, Ray, "Unions and the Negro Community," Industrial Labor Relations Review 17:
    179-202 (January 1964).
Marshall, Ray, The Negro Worker and the Trade Unions: A Foot in the Door. New York:
    Wiley, 1965.
Mitchell, George S., and Horace R. Cayton, Black Workers and the New Unions. Chapel Hill:
    University of North Carolina Press, 1939. Good on impact of the CIO.
"The Philadelphia Story: Union Bias Is a Major Barrier to Equal Opportunity," Barron's
    43:1 (June 3, 1963).
Randolph, A. Philip, "The Unfinished Revolution," Progressive 26:20-25 (December 1962).
    A persuasive plea for job retraining as an answer to automation. Includes a short
    summary of Negro and labor union relations since the 1830's.

Raskin, A. H., "Civil Rights: The Law and the Unions," Reporter 31:23-28 (September 10, 1964).

Read, F. T., "Minority Rights and the Union Shop," Minnesota Law Review 49:227 (December 1964).

Rich, J. C., "The NAACP versus Labor," New Leader 45:20-21 (November 26, 1962).

Rony, Vera, "Labor Drives to Close the South's Open Shop," The Reporter 33:31-34 (November 18, 1965).

Rose, Alvin W., "The Influence of a Border City Union on the Race Attitudes of Its Members," Journal of Social Issues 9:20-24 (Winter 1953). Based on a study of Teamsters Local 688 in St. Louis, Mo., published in Union Solidarity: The Internal Cohesion of a Labour Union. Minneapolis: University of Minnesota Press, 1952. Expresses optimism about ameliorating race relations through action of union leadership.

Taft, Philip, Organized Labor in American History. New York: Harper, 1964. Chapter 50, "Organized Labor and the Negro," although brief, is good historical résumé. Bibliographies to each chapter and an index.

Trewhitt, Henry L., "Southern Unions and the Integration Issue," Reporter 15:25-28 (October 4, 1956).

Tyler, Gus, "The Truth About the ILGWU," New Politics 2:6-17 (Fall 1962).

"Union Program for Eliminating Discrimination," Monthly Labor Review 86:58-59 (January 1963).

4. EFFORTS TO INTEGRATE

"The Anti-Bias Drive Hits Construction," Engineering News-Record, May 30, 1963.

"Anti-Bias Order Cracks Down on Union," Engineering News-Record, September 26, 1963.

"Anti-Discrimination Pact Signed in Philadelphia," Publishers' Weekly 184:35-36 (October 14, 1963). In the printing industry.

"Bias Drive May Help Nonunion Forces," Engineering News-Record, July 16, 1963.

"Billion-dollar Prize Spurs Integration," Business Week, June 3, 1961. At Lockheed plant in Georgia.

Bird, C., "More Room at the Top: Company Experience in Employing Negroes in High Jobs," Management Review 52:4-16 (March 1963).

Bloch, Herman D., "Recognition of Discrimination--A Solution," Journal of Social Psychology 48:291-295 (November 1958).

Bowman, Garda W., "Employment by Merit Alone," Office Executive 36:14-15, 37 (May 1961).

Bowman, Garda W., "What Helps or Harms Promotability," Harvard Business Review 42:6-8+ (January-February 1964). A survey of executive thinking concerning management opportunities.

Brecher, Ruth, and Edward Brecher, "The Military's Limited War Against Segregation," Harper's Magazine 227:79-82,90-92 (September 1963). Army and air force bases are becoming islands of decency and progress in turbulent areas of South.

Browne, V. J., "Racial Desegregation in the Public Service, with Particular Reference to the U.S. Government," Journal of Negro Education 23:242-248 (Summer 1954).

"Builders Fear Anti-Bias Order," Engineering News-Record, July 12, 1962.

Bullock, Paul, "Combating Discrimination in Employment," California Management Review 3:18-32 (Summer 1961).

Calvet, Ivis J., "Operation Achievement," Interracial Review 36:170-172 (September 1963). Progress in New York in obtaining jobs for Negroes.

"Carrying Out a Plan for Job Integration," Business Week, April 13, 1963.

Cassell, Frank H., "Positive Action on Unemployment," Integrated Education 1:36 (June 1963).

Christopher, Maurice, "Desegregate Ads, TV, Lever Tells Agencies," Advertising Age 34:1, 8 (August 12, 1963).

Christopher, Maurice, "CORE Seeks More Integrated Ads," Advertising Age 34:128 (September 9, 1963).

"Civil Rights Groups Move on Homebuilding," Engineering News-Record, October 12, 1961.
"Commission Puts Union Bias on the Spot," Engineering News-Record, March 12, 1964.
"Contractor Group Hits Revised Equal Employment Standards," Air Conditioning, Heating, and Refrigeration News, August 5, 1963.
"Contractors Urged to Take Lead on Bias," Engineering News-Record, August 22, 1963.
"Court Halts Bias: Chicago Ironworkers Must Accept Negro Apprentices," Engineering News-Record, October 24, 1963.
Cox, T., "Counselor's Views on Changing Management Policies," Public Relations Journal 19:8-9 (November 1963). How public relations organizations can meet problem of job discrimination.
"CPI [Chemical Process Industries] Takes Lead in Antibias Drive," Chemical Week 89:77-78+ (October 21, 1961).
"Crackdown on Discrimination Begins," Engineering News-Record, July 4, 1963. In government contracts.
"Detroit Feels Brunt of Negro Pressure," Business Week, June 29, 1963.
"Detroit Groups Adopt Anti-Bias Program," Engineering News-Record, August 1, 1963.
Douglass, Joseph H., "Intergroup Relations in the Federal Service," Journal of Intergroup Relations 2:37-48 (Winter 1960-1961).
Dworkin, Martin S., "The New Negro on Screen," Progressive 24:39-41 (October 1960); 24:33-36 (November 1960); 24:34-36 (December 1960). Three short articles discussing effect of Negro demands for "equality in imagery," and the realistic use of Negro actors.
Evans, James C., and David A. Lane, Jr., "Integration in the Armed Services," Annals of the American Academy of Political and Social Science 304:78-85 (March 1956).
Fleming, Harold C., "Equal Job Opportunity: Slogan or Reality?" Personnel Administration 26:25-28 (March 1963).
Four Years on the Job in Michigan. Lansing: Michigan F.E.P.C., 1960.
"Government Issues Apprenticeship Rules," Engineering News-Record, January 2, 1964.
Gould, John, "NOW: Massachusetts Plan for Equal Employment Opportunity," Industry (Mass.) 29:10-11,34 (December 1963).
Homan, H. L., and R. A. Enion, "What Are Some Industrial Relations Approaches to Integration?" Personnel Administration 26:55-57 (November 1963).
Hope, John, II, "Industrial Integration of Negroes: The Upgrading Process," Human Organization 11:5-14 (Winter 1952). Case studies of three Southern plants of the International Harvester Company, where an active nondiscrimination policy demonstrated possibility of moving toward color-blindness in upgrading workers on basis of efficiency.
Hope, John, II, "Efforts to Eliminate Racial Discrimination in Industry--With Particular Reference to the South," Journal of Negro Education 23:262-272 (Summer 1954).
Hunton, Harold, "Implementing 'Affirmative Action' with Air Force Contractors," Interracial Review 36:36-38 (February 1963).
"Industry Acts to Bar Apprenticeship Bias," Engineering News-Record, October 3, 1963.
Integration in the Armed Services: A Progress Report. Washington, D.C., 1955. Prepared for the Office of the Assistant Secretary of Defense for Manpower and Personnel.
James, J. H., "Guidelines for Initiating Fair Employment Practices," Personnel 40:53-59 (May 1963).
"Joint Stand Rejects Racial Quotas for Plumbing Apprentices," Air Conditioning, Heating, and Refrigeration News, August 26, 1963.
Katz, Irwin, Judith Goldston, and Lawrence Benjamin, "Behavior and Productivity in Bi-Racial Work Groups," Human Relations 11:123-141 (May 1958).
Killens, John Oliver, "Hollywood in Black and White," Nation 201:157-160 (September 20, 1965). 100th Anniversary Issue.
Kopp, R. W., "Management's Concern with Recent Civil Rights Legislation," Labor Law 16:67 (February 1965).
London, Jack, and Richard Hammett, "Impact of Company Policy upon Discrimination," Sociology and Sociological Research 39:88-91 (1954). A study of two industrial plants in the Midwest. Both professed a policy of nondiscrimination, but effective results were achieved only in the plant (automotive) where management and union took positive action.
Lunden, Leon E., "Antidiscrimination Provisions in Major Contracts," Monthly Labor Review 85:643-651 (June 1962).

McManus,G. J.,"How Industry Views Integration,"Iron Age 193:44-45 (February 27, 1964).

The Management of Racial Integration in Business. New York: McGraw-Hill, 1964. A "Special Report to Management" prepared by a research team in Harvard Graduate School of Business Administration. On the basis of field interviews and case studies, the group suggests techniques for personnel managers and makes projections for the future. Useful appendices list Negro newspapers, Negro radio stations, and predominantly Negro colleges and universities. Bibliography.

"Mechanical Contractors Association of America Directors OK Construction Industry Joint Committee Standard on Apprenticeship," Air Conditioning, Heating, and Refrigeration News, November 25, 1963.

"Merit for Hire: How On-the-Job Integration has Worked Out in Leading Companies," Supervisory Management 3:8-14 (May 1958).

"Minority Worker Hiring and Referral in San Francisco," Monthly Labor Review 81:1131-1136 (October 1958).

Mitchell, James P., "The Intimate State of Man," New South 15:9-13 (February 1960). Integration and problems of the human potential.

Moffitt, Donald, "Business-Backed 'Fair' in Seattle Aims to Open More Jobs to Negroes," Wall Street Journal, January 29, 1965. On a project organized by the Chamber of Commerce to increase number and range of jobs for Negroes.

Morris, R. B., "Adopting a Human Relations Policy," Public Management 45:198-200 (September 1963). Glencoe, Ill., develops formula for equal opportunity and non-discrimination.

Morrow, Joseph J., "Integrating the Negro into the Office," Office, March 1955.

Moss, James Allen, "Negro Teachers in Predominantly White Colleges," Journal of Negro Education 27:451-462 (Fall 1958).

Moss,James Allen,"The Utilization of Negro Teachers in the Colleges of New York State," Phylon 21:63-70 (Spring 1960).

"National Association of Plumbing-Heating-Cooling Contractors Raps Latest Draft of Anti-Bias Regulations for Apprenticeship Programs," Air Conditioning, Heating, and Re-frigeration News, December 2, 1963.

"NAACP Demands Hit Snag," Broadcasting 32:42-44 (August 5, 1963). State Employees Union turns down request for adding a Negro to each crew.

"NAACP Making Headway at Film Studios," Broadcasting 32:52 (September 2, 1963).

"NAACP Sticks to Hollywood Deadline; No Set Quota for Negroes on Production Crews," Broadcasting 32:84 (September 16, 1963).

"Negroes Desire 'Integrated Ads' Researcher Finds," Advertising Age 33:28 (November 12, 1962).

"Negroes for the Jobs," Economist 205:660 (November 17, 1962).

"Negroes Score a Breakthrough," Engineering News-Record, November 15, 1962. Admitted to apprenticeships in construction industry.

"Negroes Take Aim at GM," Business Week, July 20, 1963.

"New York Strikes at Discrimination by Unions," Air Conditioning, Heating, and Refrigera-tion News, March 23, 1964. In sheet metal and plumbing trades.

Nichols, Lee, Breakthrough on the Color Front. New York: Random House, 1954. A detailed study of the desegregation of the armed forces.

"One Company's Answer to Negro Job Problem," Business Management 25:42-45 (February 1964). Pitney-Bowes, Inc., Stamford, Connecticut.

"Opportunities Industrialization Center Will Help Negroes Help Themselves," Air Conditioning, Heating, and Refrigeration News, March 16, 1964.

Patten, Thomas H., Jr., "The Industrial Integration of the Negro," Phylon 24:334-352 (Winter 1963).

Peabody, Malcolm E., Jr., "Government-Industry Unite for Civil Rights Program,"Industry (Mass.) 288:10-12,32 (August 1963).

Pearson, Leonard E., "Equal Opportunity, Equal Justice," Christian Century 75:806-807 (July 9, 1958). Job Opportunity Program of Indianapolis, Ind., Society of Friends.

Perry,John,"Business--Next Target for Integration," Harvard Business Review 41:104-115 (March-April 1963). An important article suggesting practical methods of integration and outlining aspects of the problem as they apply both to Negroes and to managers.

"Philadelphia Crafts Offer Union Apprenticeship to Any Who Qualify," Air Conditioning, Heating, and Refrigeration News, September 2, 1963.

"Plan for Equal Opportunity at Lockheed," Monthly Labor Review 84:748-749 (July 1961).
President's Committee on Equality of Treatment and Opportunity in the Armed Services, Freedom to Serve. Washington, D.C.: GPO, 1950.
"Race Demonstrations Open Union Doors," Engineering News-Record, January 2, 1964. In the New York City building trades.
"Readying for Rights Law," Chemical Week 94:77 (February 22, 1964). Preparation on hiring practices.
Robinson, Jackie, "The Racial Crisis," Sales Management 91:33-37 (August 16, 1963). Reprinted in entirety in Negro Digest, November 1963, under title "Race and Big Business."
Sawyer, David A., "Fair Employment in the Nation's Capital: A Study of Progress and Dilemma," Journal of Intergroup Relations 4:37-54 (Winter 1962-1963).
Shostak, A. B., "Human Problems in Improving Industrial Race Relations," Personnel Administration 26:28-31 (March 1963).
Speroff, B., "Problems and Approaches in Integrating Minority Group Work Forces," Journal of Social Psychology 37:271-273 (May 1953).
"A Stronger CIJC [Construction Industry Joint Conference] to Speak on Bias," Engineering News-Record, August 1, 1963.
Stuart, Irving R., "Intergroup Relations and Acceptance of Puerto Ricans and Negroes in an Immigrant's Industry," Journal of Social Psychology 56:89-96 (February 1962).
"Study Finds Anti-Bias Laws Ignored," Engineering News-Record, August 8, 1963.
"Text of Plumbing Industry's Policy Statement Rejecting Racial Quota System," Air Conditioning, Heating, and Refrigeration News, September 9, 1963.
"Treat Negro Equally to Get His Business, Marketing Men Told," Advertising Age 34:62 (October 7, 1963).
"Unions Sign Nondiscrimination Pledges," Engineering News-Record, November 22, 1962.
"URW Pushes Civil Rights; Beset by Bias Charges," Chemical Week 93:121 (September 14, 1963).
"Urban League Hits New York Agencies on Racial Discrimination in Employment," Advertising Age 34:1,96 (April 22, 1963).
"Washington Rules Out Bias in Training," Engineering News-Record, October 24, 1963. Construction industry apprenticeship program.
Weintraub, Robert, "Employment Integration and Racial Wage Differences in a Southern Plant," Industrial and Labor Relations Review 12:214-226 (January 1959).
Wheeler, J. H., "Impact of Race Relations on Industrial Relations in the South," Labor Law Journal 15:474 (July 1964).
Wood, David G., "How Businessmen Can Fight 'Big Government'--and Win," Harper's Magazine 227:77-81 (November 1963). Suggestions by a steel man that business step in and make plans to provide jobs, particularly for Negroes, and take initiative in obtaining rights for Negroes.
Wortman, M. S., Jr., and F. Luthans, "How Many Contracts Ban Discrimination in Employment?" Personnel 41:75-79 (January 1964).

VIII. HOUSING AND URBAN RENEWAL

The two principal approaches to the problem of Negro housing have been anti-discrimination enactments and community development by way of urban renewal and integrated public housing, fields that have attracted some of the most able students and public servants. While the combating of discriminatory practices, the fostering of interracial community amity, the just administration of laws continue to be goals, the plight of the ghetto Negro is only part of the total problem of the modern city.

Charles Abrams has said that housing constitutes the most serious single barrier to the Negro's advance. So long as Negroes are confined in ghettos, attempts to conquer de facto segregation of the public schools will be repeatedly frustrated, and all the attributes of slum life will continue to foster family instability, unemployment, crime, and social violence. Karl and Alma Taeuber, in their recently published Negroes in Cities (1965), have declared that discrimination is by far the strongest cause of residential segregation, and foresee little hope for its early eradication. If they are correct, the prospects are indeed dismal for a long time to come.

1. THE LAW, THE COURTS, AND REGULATORY ACTION

Abrams, Charles, "Discrimination and the Struggle for Shelter," New York Law Forum 6: 3-12 (January 1960). The author, President of the National Committee Against Discrimination in Housing, argues for a program to create decent environments, with emphasis on vacant land utilization rather than large-scale housing developments, on rental housing in small units, and on a mortgage loan program.

Abrams, Charles, "The Housing Order & Its Limits," Commentary 35:10-14 (January 1963).

Aurbach, Herbert A., John R. Coleman, and Bernard Mausner, "Restrictive and Protective Viewpoints of Fair Housing Legislation: A Comparative Study of Attitudes," Social Problems 8:118-125 (Fall 1960).

Avins, Alfred, ed., Open Occupancy vs. Forced Housing Under the 114th Amendment: A Symposium on Anti-Discrimination Legislation, Freedom of Choice, and Property Rights in Housing. New York: Bookmailer, 1963. Included are pieces by lawyers, social scientists, real estate dealers from several areas of the country. While a wide range of opinions is covered, the volume is weighted on the side of "freedom of choice."

Bittker, B. I., "The Case of the Checker-board Ordinance: An Experiment in Race Relations," Yale Law Journal 71:1387-1423 (July 1962).

Blumrosen, A. B., "Antidiscrimination Laws in Action in New Jersey: A Law-Sociology Study," Rutgers Law Review 19:189 (Winter 1965).

Branscomb, A. W., "Analysis of Attempts to Prohibit Racial Discrimination in the Sale and Rental of Publicly Assisted Private Housing," George Washington Law Review 28:758-778 (April 1960).

Carter, Robert L., Dorothy Kenyon, Peter Marcuse, and Loren Miller, with a foreword by by Charles Abrams, Equality. New York: Pantheon, 1965. The views of four legal authorities on the issue of quotas and preferential treatment for Negroes as a means of achieving racial equality.

"Civil Rights: Discrimination in Private Housing," Marquette Law Review 46:237-241 (Fall 1962).

Colley, N. S., and M. L. McGhee, "The California and Washington Fair Housing Cases," Law in Transition 22:79-92 (Summer 1962).

"Development of Open Occupancy Laws: A Survey of Legislation Against Discrimination in Housing," Gavel 24:13-20 (September 1963).

Fisher, Margaret, and Frances Levenson, Federal, State and Local Action Affecting Race and Housing. National Association of Intergroup Relations Officials, September 1962.

Frey, D. S., "'Freedom of Residence' in Illinois," Chicago Bar Record 41:9-21 (October 1959).

Ginger, A. F., "Little Democracy--Housing for America's Minorities in 1960," Lawyers Guild Review 20:6-17 (Spring 1960).

Goldblatt, Harold, and Florence Cromien, "The Effective Social Reach of the Fair Housing Practices Law of the City of New York," Social Problems 9:365-370 (Spring 1962).

Gutman, D., ed., "Discrimination in Employment and Housing: A Symposium," New York Law Forum 6:1+ (January 1960). Entire issue.

Hager, Don J., "Housing Discrimination, Social Conflict, and The Law," Social Problems 8:80-87 (Summer 1960).

Hellerstein, W. E., "Benign Quota, Equal Protection, and 'The Rule in Shelley's Case,'" Rutgers Law Review 17:531-561 (Spring 1963). On restrictive covenants.

Henkin, Louis, "Shelley v. Kramer, Notes for a Revised Opinion," University of Pennsylvania Law Review 110:473-505 (February 1962). On restrictive covenants and the constitutionality of state action in private cases.

"Integration in Housing," Lawyers Guild Review 18:1+ (Spring 1958). Special issue entirely devoted to housing problems.

"Is There a Civil Right to Housing Accommodations?" Notre Dame Lawyer 33:463-488 (May 1958).

Kaplan, M., "Discrimination in California Housing: The Need for Additional Legislation," California Law Review 50:635-649 (October 1962).

Kozol, L. H., "The Massachusetts Fair Housing Practices Law," Massachusetts Law Quarterly 47:295-305 (September 1962).

Lehman, W. W., "Discrimination in F.H.A. Home Financing," Chicago Bar Record 40:375-379 (May 1959).

Lehman, W. W., "Must I Sell My House to a Negro?" Chicago Bar Record 42:283-288 (March 1961).

McEntire, Davis, "Government and Racial Discrimination in Housing," Journal of Social Issues 13:60-67 (Fall 1957).

McGhee, M. L., and A. F. Ginger, "The House that I Live In: A Study of Housing for Minorities," Cornell Law Quarterly 46:194-257 (Winter 1961).

McGraw, B. T., "The Housing Act of 1954 and Implications for Minorities," Phylon 16:171-182 (Spring 1955).

Mayhew, Leon Hinckley, "Law and Equal Opportunity: Anti-Discrimination Law in Massachusetts," unpub. doc. diss., Harvard University, 1963.

Miller, Loren, "Supreme Court Covenant Decision--An Analysis," Crisis 55:265-266 (September 1948).

Miller, Loren, "Government's Role in Housing Equality," Journal of Intergroup Relations 1:56-61 (Winter 1959-1960).

Miller, Loren, "The Law and Discrimination in Housing," Lawyers Guild Review 20:123-136 (Winter 1960).

Moffitt, Donald, "Fair Housing Flop? Negroes' Effort to End Residential Segregation Hits Stiff Opposition," Wall Street Journal, February 1, 1965. In California, efforts to ban discrimination in sales and rentals have been consistently blocked by the voters, and federal orders have been ineffective.

Nesbitt, George B., "Federal Concerns and Responsibilities with Relocation," Phylon 19:75-76 (Spring 1958).

"New Jersey Housing Anti-bias Law: Applicability to Non-State-Aided Developments," Rutgers Law Review 12:557-581 (Summer 1958).

"New York's Anti-bias Statute of 1961 as it Affects Cooperative Apartments," New York University Intramural Law Review 18:269 (May 1963).

New York State Commission Against Discrimination, Legislation on Discrimination in Housing: Federal, State and City. Albany, 1956.

Novasky, V. S., "Benevolent Housing Quota," Howard Law Journal 6:30 (January 1960).

"Racial Discrimination in Housing," University of Pennsylvania Law Review 107:515-550 (February 1959).

"Racial Discrimination by State Lessee as State Action," Iowa Law Review 47:718 (Spring 1962).

"Racial Restriction in Leaseholds," University of Florida Law Review 11:344-351 (Fall 1958).

"Racially Restrictive Covenants in Deeds," Georgia Bar Journal 25:232-238 (November 1962).

Roberts, Richard J., "Fair Housing Laws: A Tool for Racial Equality," Social Order 12:20-34 (January 1962).

Roseman, D. M., "May Operative Builders of F.H.A. Housing be Barred from Discriminating Against Purchasers on Basis of Race?" Boston Bar Journal 3:21-24 (December 1959).

Saks, J. H., and Sol Rabkin, "Racial and Religious Discrimination in Housing: A Report of Legal Progress," Iowa Law Review 45:488-524 (Spring 1960).

Semer, Milton, and Martin Sloane, "Equal Housing Opportunities and Individual Property Rights," Federal Bar Journal 24:47-75 (Winter 1964). Authors, legal counsel for Housing and Home Finance Agency, defend constitutionality of nondiscrimination orders in housing as preserving freedom of choice, and discuss "equal protection of law" clause, restrictive covenants, federal and state fair housing acts.

Sparkman, John, "Civil Rights and Property Rights," Federal Bar Journal 24:31-46 (Winter 1964). Author, U.S. Senator from Alabama, attacks overemphasis on civil rights at expense of "natural" rights, i.e., free choice of associates, free control of property and conduct of business. Special targets: Title II, Title VI of Civil Rights Bill of 1964, and 1962 executive order on integration in federal housing.

"State Statute Prohibiting Discrimination in Private Sale of Publicly Assisted Housing Denies Equal Protection of the Laws," Harvard Law Review 75:1647-1649 (June 1962).

United States Commission on Civil Rights, Report 1961 Book IV, Housing. Washington, D.C.: GPO, 1961.

United States Commission on Civil Rights, Civil Rights U.S.A.: Housing in Washington, D.C., 1962. Washington, D.C., 1962.

United States Housing and Home Finance Agency, State Statutes and Local Ordinances and Resolutions Prohibiting Discrimination in Housing and Urban Renewal Operations. Washington, D.C.: GPO, 1962.

Van Alstyne, W. W., "Discrimination in State University Housing Programs--Policy and Constitutional Considerations," Stanford Law Review 13:60-79 (December 1960).

Van Alstyne, W. W., "The O'Meara Case and Constitutional Requirements of State Anti-Discrimination Housing Laws," Howard Law Journal 8:158-168 (Spring 1962).

"Voluntary Segregation Held not Illegal Discrimination," Ohio State Law Journal 24:412 (Spring 1963).

Vose, Clement E., "NAACP Strategy in the Covenant Cases," Western Reserve Law Review 6:101-145 (Winter 1955).

Vose, Clement E., Caucasians Only--The Supreme Court, the NAACP, and the Restrictive Covenant Cases. Berkeley: University of California Press, 1959.

2. PATTERNS AND CONDITIONS

Abrams, Charles, Forbidden Neighbors. New York: Harper, 1955. A thorough analysis of corporate practices that determine housing choice.

Abrams, Charles, The City is the Frontier. New York: Harper, 1965. A searching analysis of urban renewal in the United States. See particularly chapter 4, "The Racial Upheaval in Cities."

Abrams, Charles, "The Housing Problem and the Negro," Daedalus 95:64-76 (Winter 1966). The author emphasizes the factors which reinforce the ghettoization of the Negroes, and reminds the reader that "the poverty of people and the poverty of cities are parts of the same problem."

Anderson, Martin, The Federal Bulldozer: A Critical Analysis of Urban Renewal: 1949-
    1962. Cambridge: Massachusetts Institute of Technology Press, 1964. Including the
    impact on the Negro of urban redevelopment.
Banfield, Edward C., and Morton Grodzins, Government and Housing in Metropolitan Areas.
    New York: McGraw-Hill,1958. A Volume in ACTION's Series on Housing and Community
    Development,this work considers not only government housing operations in metropolitan
    areas, but population trends in cities, with implications for political parties and
    metropolitan reorganization.
Barth, Ernest A. T., and Sue March, "A Research Note on the Subject of Minority Housing,"
    Journal of Intergroup Relations 3:314-319 (Fall 1962).
Bauer, Catherine, "Social Questions in Housing and Community Planning," Journal of Social
    Issues 7:1-34 (Winter 1951). The author points out the class character of residential
    housing in Western countries regardless of race.
Bell, Wendell, "Comment on Cowgill's 'Trends in Residential Segregation of Nonwhites,'"
    American Sociological Review 22:221-222 (April 1957).
Bickers, J. T., "The Real Estate Broker," Phylon 19:87-88 (Summer 1958).
Blayton, J. B., "Secondary Mortgage Operations," Phylon 19:86 (Summer 1958).
Blumberg, Leonard, "Urban Rehabilitation and Problems of Human Relations," Phylon 19:
    97-105 (Spring 1958).
Commission on Race and Housing,Where Shall We Live? Berkeley: University of California
    Press, 1958. Report of a three-year study on discrimination and segregation in housing.
    Includes a bibliography of published and unpublished studies of various areas in the nation.
Cowgill, Donald D., "Trends on Residential Segregation of Non-Whites in American Cities,
    1940-1950," American Sociological Review 21:43-47 (February, 1956).
Cowgill, Donald D., "Segregation Scores for Metropolitan Areas," American Sociological
    Review 27:400-402 (June 1962). A numerical index for 21 metropolitan areas showing
    degree of residential segregation.
Discrimination in Housing in the Boston Metropolitan Area. Report of the Massachusetts
    State Advisory Committee to the United States Commission on Civil Rights, December
    1963.
Duncan, Beverly, and Philip M. Hauser, Housing a Metropolis: Chicago. Glencoe, Ill.: Free
    Press, 1961. A Cooperative research program by the Chicago Community Inventory of
    the University of Chicago and the governmental agencies of the City of Chicago. A
    general work, with one chapter on "White-nonwhite Differentials in Housing." Also
    treats of demolition and new construction, characteristics of lower-income families and
    housing, and the family cycle.
Duncan, Otis Dudley, and Beverly Duncan, "Residential Distribution and Occupational
    Stratification," American Journal of Sociology 60:493-503 (March 1955).
Duncan, Otis Dudley, and Beverly Duncan, "A Methodological Analysis of Segregation
    Indexes," American Sociological Review 20:210-217 (April 1955).
Duncan, Otis Dudley, and Beverly Duncan, The Negro Population of Chicago: A Study of
    Residential Succession. Chicago: University of Chicago Press, 1957.
Duncan, Otis Dudley, and Beverly Duncan, "Contributions to the Theory of Segregation
    Indexes," Urban Analysis Report no. 14, Chicago Community Inventory, Unitersity of
    Chicago, no date, hecto.
Duncan, Otis Dudley, and Stanley Lieberson, "Ethnic Segregation and Assimilation," Ameri-
    can Journal of Sociology 64:364-374 (January 1959). A study of residential patterns in
    Chicago 1930-1950, showing a positive relationship between assimilation and length of
    residence, along with a remarkably stable pattern of differential segregation and spatial
    separation of ethnic colonies.
Duncan, Otis Dudley, W. R. Scott, S. Lieberson, B. Duncan, and H. H. Winsborough,
    Metropolis and Region. Baltimore: Johns Hopkins Press, 1960.
Egan, John J., "Why Are We Rebuilding Our Cities?" Interracial Review 35:244-246
    (November 1962).
Foote, N. N., J. Abu-Lughod, M. M. Foley, and L. Winnick, Housing Choices and Housing
    Constraints. New York: McGraw-Hill, 1960. Factors, including personal decisions, that
    determine choice.
Freeman, Howard E., Helen M. Hughes, Robert Morris, Thomas F. Pettigrew, and Lewis G.
    Watts, The Middle-Income Negro Family Faces Urban Renewal. Waltham, Mass.:

Brandeis University, for the Department of Commerce and Development, Commonwealth of Massachusetts, 1964. A study of families in the Washington Park section of
Boston during the rehabilitation of the Neighborhood.

Friedrichs, Robert W., "Christians and Residential Exclusion: An Empirical Study of a
Northern Dilemma," Journal of Social Issues 15:14-23 (October 1959).

Gans, Herbert J., "The Failure of Urban Renewal," Commentary 39:29-37 (April 1965).

Glazer, Nathan, and Davis McEntire, eds., Studies in Housing and Minority Groups.
Berkeley: University of California Press, 1960. Independent studies of Negro housing in
Atlanta, Birmingham, San Antonio, Houston, New Orleans, Dade County (Miami area),
and Detroit.

Greeley, Andrew M., and Robert D. Crain, "Housecleaning in the Negro Community?"
Interracial Review 35:247-249 (November 1962).

Greer, Frank, "Financing Programs of the National Mortgage Association," Phylon 19:77-
81 (Spring 1958).

Grier, Eunice S., and George Grier, In Search of Housing: A Study of Experiences of Negro
Professional and Technical Personnel in New York State. New York State Commission
Against Discrimination, 1958. In upstate New York cities.

Grodzins, Morton, "Metropolitan Segregation," Scientific American 197:24, 33-41 (October
1957).

Hartman, Chester W., Low-Income Housing in the Boston Area: Needs and Proposals.
Prepared by Housing Advisory Research Committee, Massachusetts Committee on
Discrimination in Housing, July 1964.

Holmes, Bob, "A Study in Subtlety: Riverside Renewal," Interracial Review 36:118-120
(June 1963). Urban renewal and Negroes in Riverside, California.

"Housing and Minorities," Phylon 19:8-124 (Summer 1958). Entire issue, covering such
topics as urban renewal, slum clearance, relocation, community participation, public
and private financing, etc.

"Income and Ability to Pay for Housing of Nonwhite Families in New York State," New York
State Temporary Housing and Rent Commission, August, 1955.

Isaacs, Reginald R., "Are Urban Neighborhoods Possible?" Journal of Housing 5:177-180
(July 1948).

Isaacs, Reginald R., "The 'Neighborhood Unit' As an Instrument for Segregation," Journal of
Housing 5:215-219 (August 1948).

Jackson, Hubert M., "Public Housing and Minority Groups," Phylon 19:21-30 (Spring
1958).

Johnson, Reginald A., Racial Bias and Housing. New York: National Urban League, 1963.

Jones, Malcolm, "The Workable Program of a Southern Metropolis, Atlanta, Georgia,"
Phylon 19:60-63 (Spring 1958).

Keyes, Walter E., "Federal Agencies in Urban Redevelopment," Phylon 19:90-91 (Summer
1958).

Kistin, Helen, Housing Discrimination in Massachusetts. Prepared by Housing Advisory
Research Committee, Massachusetts Committee on Discrimination in Housing, May 1964.

Lee, Alfred McClung, "The Impact of Segregated Housing on Public Schools," School and
Society 88:241-243 (May 7, 1960).

Lieberson, Stanley, "The Impact of Residential Segregation on Ethnic Assimilation," Social
Forces 40:52-57 (October 1961).

McEntire, Davis, Residence and Race: Final and Comprehensive Report to the Commission
on Race and Housing by the Director. Berkeley: University of California Press, 1960.
Statistical tables are based on 1950 census, and therefore do not show gains as revealed
in 1960 census. The work contains especially valuable material on the growth of New
York Negro sections, and expresses strong belief in the efficacy of law to effect change.
Good bibliography.

McGraw, B. T., "Urban Renewal in the Interest of All People," Phylon 19:45-55 (Spring
1958).

McGraw, B. T., "Potentials for Equal Opportunity in Housing and Community Development,"
Journal of Intergroup Relations 3:126-137 (Spring 1962).

McKee, James B., "Changing Patterns of Race and Housing: A Toledo Study," Social Forces
41:253-260 (March 1963).

Maslen, Sidney, "Relocation in the Southeastern Region During the Process of Urban
Renewal," Phylon 19:70-71 (Spring 1958).

Meyerson, Martin, and Edward C. Banfield, Politics, Planning, and the Public Interest. Glencoe, Ill.: Free Press, 1955. An analysis of how decisions were reached on sites for low-rent public housing in Chicago after passage of federal public housing act of 1949, of how Negro groups react on public issues, and of the impossibility of separating housing from racial and political problems.

Meyerson, Martin, Barbara Terrett, and William Wheaton, Housing, People, and Cities. New York: McGraw-Hill, 1962. On housing and community development.

Midwestern Minority Housing Markets. Special Report by Advance Mortgage Corporation, Chicago, December 1, 1962.

Miller, Alexander F., "Levittown, U.S.A.," Phylon 19:108-112 (Spring 1958).

Miller, Mike, and Carl Werthman, "Public Housing: Tenants and Troubles," Dissent 8:282-288 (Summer 1961).

Nash, William, The Impact of Public Programs on the Housing Shortage in the Boston Area. Prepared by Housing Advisory Research Committee, Massachusetts Committee on Discrimination in Housing, April 1963.

Needham, Maurice d'Arlan, Negro Orleanian: Status and Stake in a City's Economy and Housing. New Orleans: Tulane Publications, 1962.

Nesbitt, George B., "Urban Renewal in Perspective," Phylon 19:64-68 (Spring 1958).

Nonwhite Housing In Wisconsin. Madison: Governor's Commission on Human Rights, 1953. Part I: findings of surveys of five largest cities; Part II: recommendations, with special reference to realtors, builders, and lenders.

Northwood, Lawrence K., "The Threat and Potential of Urban Renewal: A 'Workable Program' for Better Race Relations," Journal of Intergroup Relations 2:101-114 (Spring 1961).

Our Nonwhite Population and Its Housing: Changes Between 1950 and 1960. Housing and Home Finance Agency, Office of the Administrator, Washington, D.C., May 1963. Statistics on population, income, education, employment, household composition, and housing.

Papageorge, George T., "Relocation: An Essential of Urban Renewal," Phylon 19:69-70 (Spring 1958).

Race and Housing--New York City 1961: Papers Presented at the Annual Meeting October 18, 1961. New York Citizen's Housing and Planning Council, 1961.

Ravitz, Mel J., "Effects of Urban Renewal on Community Racial Patterns," Journal of Social Issues 13:38-49 (October 1957). Detroit.

Raymond, George M., Malcolm D. Rivkin, and Herbert J. Gans, "Urban Renewal," Commentary 40:72-80 (July 1965). Mr. Raymond and Mr. Rivkin present their criticisms of Mr. Gans's article in Commentary, April 1965, and Mr. Gans replies.

Richey, Elinor, "Splitsville, U.S.A.: An Ironic Tale of Urban Renewal and Racial Segregation," Reporter 28:35-38 (May 23, 1963).

Rossi, Peter H., Why Families Move. Glencoe, Ill.: Free Press, 1955. The personal decisions that affect moving.

Rothman, Jack, "The Ghetto Makers," Nation 193:222-225 (October 7, 1961).

Schwartz, Raymond J., "The Federal Housing Authority and Urban Planning," Phylon 19:89-90 (Spring 1958).

Scott, Barbara W., "The Status of Housing of Negroes in Pittsburgh. Pittsburgh Commission on Human Relations, May 1962.

Smith, Ralph L., "Racial Discrimination in Metropolitan Housing," New Leader, February 16, 1959.

Sutton, R. O., "Conventional Mortgage Financing," Phylon 19:84-86 (Spring 1958).

Taeuber, Karl E., "Residential Segregation by Color in the United States, 1940 and 1950," unpub. doc. diss., Harvard University, 1960. Using computers and census data, the author measured and analyzed the extent of racial segregation in 188 American cities with population over 50,000.

Taeuber, Karl E., "Residential Segregation," Scientific American 213:12-19 (August 1965). The author finds that the principal cause of Negro segregation in urban ghettos is discrimination and that ther is "no basis for anticipating major changes. . . until patterns of housing discrimination can be altered." An important study based on calculation of the segregation indices for 207 American cities.

Taeuber, Karl E., and Alma F. Taeuber, <u>Negroes in Cities: Residential Segregation and Neighborhood Change.</u> Chicago: Aldine, 1965. A systematic description of patterns of Negro residential segregation and the processes of urban neighborhood change.

Thompson, Robert A., "The Social Dynamics in Demographic Trends and the Housing of Minority Groups," <u>Phylon</u> 19:31-43 (Spring 1958).

"Urban Revival: Goals and Standards," <u>Annals of the American Academy of Political and Social Science</u> 352:1-151 (March 1964). Entire issue,with the majority of articles having some relevance for problem of Negro housing.

Vax, John J., "Home Financing Assistance by Voluntary Home Mortgage Credit Program," <u>Phylon</u> 19:81-82 (Spring 1958).

Von Eckardt, Wolf, "Black Neck in the White Noose," <u>New Republic</u> 149:14-17 (October 19, 1963). "The vast majority of displaced poor Negroes are worse off after urban renewal than they were before."

Warner, A. E., and Milton S. Goldberg, "Governments and Housing: Accessibility of Minority Groups to Living Space," <u>Land Economics</u> 37:369-373 (November 1961).

Weaver, Robert C., "Recent Developments in Urban Housing and Their Implications for Minorities," 16:275-282 (Fall 1955).

Weaver, Robert C., "Class, Race and Urban Renewal," <u>Land Economics</u> 36:235-251 (August 1960). The author is Administrator of the U.S. Housing and Home Finance Agency.

Wedge, E. Bruce, "The Concept 'Urban Renewal,'" <u>Phylon</u> 19:55-60 (Spring 1958).

Whitson, Edmund R., and Paul A. Brinker, "The Housing of Negroes in Oklahoma," <u>Phylon</u> 19:106-108 (Spring 1958).

Young, Whitney M., Jr., "Participation of Citizens," <u>Phylon</u> 19:96 (Spring 1958). In decisions on urban renewal.

3. EFFORTS TO INTEGRATE

Abrahamson, Julia, <u>A Neighborhood Finds Itself.</u> New York: Harper, 1959. The Hyde Park-Kenwood urban renewal effort in Chicago and its repercussions.

Abrams, Charles, <u>Equal Opportunity in Housing.</u> National Committee Against Discrimination in Housing, April 1963. A survey of the effects of the federal housing program.

Adams, Frankie V., "The Community-Wide Stake of Citizens in Urban Renewal," <u>Phylon</u> 19:92-96 (Spring 1958).

Bacon, Margaret H., "The White Noose of the Suburbs," <u>Progressive</u> 24:37-38 (October 1960). An account of the attempt of the Friends Suburban Housing Agency to establish integrated residential areas in suburban Philadelphia.

Balk, Alfred, "A Builder Who Makes Integration Pay," <u>Harper's Magazine</u> 231:94-99 (July 1965). On Morris Milgram.

"Benign Quotas: A Plan for Integrated Private Housing," <u>Yale Law Journal</u> 70:126-134 (November 1960).

Bressler, Marvin, "The Myers' Case: An Instance of Successful Invasion," <u>Social Problems</u> 8:126-142 (Fall 1960).

Caplan, Eleanor, and Eleanor P. Wolf, "Factors Affecting Racial Change in Two Middle Income Housing Areas," <u>Phylon</u> 21:225-233 (Fall 1960).

Clark, Dennis, "Strategy in Suburbia," <u>Interracial Review</u> 35:160, 164-167 (July 1962). The utilization of committees of conscience to challenge housing segregation.

Clark, Dennis, "Comeback Parish," <u>Interracial Review</u> 35:250-254 (November 1962).

Clark, Henry, <u>The Church and Residential Desegregation: A Case Study of an Open Housing Covenant Campaign.</u> New Haven, Conn: College and University Press, 1965.

Cohen, Oscar, "The Benign Quota in Housing: The Case For and Against," <u>Anti-Defamation League Bulletin</u> 16:3, 7 (January 1959).

Connecticut Commission on Civil Rights, <u>Racial Integration in Public Housing Projects in Connecticut.</u> 1955.

Connecticut Commission on Civil Rights, <u>Private Interracial Neighborhoods in Connecticut.</u> 1957.

Deutsch, Morton, and Mary Evans Collins, <u>Interracial Housing: A Psychological Evaluation of a Social Experiment.</u> Minneapolis: University of Minnesota Press, 1951. The authors conclude that public policy can change social attitudes under certain favorable circumstances.

Dodson, Dan W., "Can Intergroup Quotas Be Benign?" Journal of Intergroup Relations 1:12-17 (Fall 1960). An evaluation of means of achieving racial balance, with suggestions of alternatives to quotas.

Downs, Anthony, "An Economic Analysis of Property, Values and Race," Land Economics 36:181 (May 1960). Review of Luigi Laurenti, Property Values and Race, Berkeley: University of California Press, 1960.

Fauman, S. Joseph, "Housing Discrimination, Changing Neighborhoods, and Public Schools," Journal of Social Issues 13:21-30 (October 1957).

Fishman, Joshua A., "Some Social and Psychological Determinants of Intergroup Relations in Changing Neighborhoods: An Introduction to the Bridgeview Study," Social Forces 40:42-51 (October 1961). A Study of a New Jersey suburb, and its experience of integration. Contains a summary of recent writings on intergroup relations in changing neighborhoods.

Greenfield, Robert W., "Factors Associated with Attitudes Toward Desegregation in a Florida Residential Suburb," Social Forces 40:31-42 (October 1961).

Grier, Eunice S., "Research Needs in the Field of Housing and Race," Journal of Intergroup Relations 1:21-31 (Summer 1960). Twelve leading intergroup practitioners in the field of housing suggest research projects for study.

Grier, Eunice S., "Factors Hindering Integration in American Urban Areas," Journal of Intergroup Relations 2:293-301 (Fall 1961).

Grier, Eunice S., In Search of a Future. Washington, D.C.: Washington Center for Metropolitan Studies, 1963.

Grier, Eunice S., and George Grier, Buyers of Interracial Housing: A Study of the Market for Concord Park, Philadelphia: University of Pennsylvania Institute for Urban Studies, January, 1957. A study of an early middle-class project.

Grier, Eunice S., and George Grier, "Market Characteristics in Interracial Housing," Journal of Social Issues 13:50-67 (Fall 1957). The authors analyze Negroes and whites who seek mixed housing.

Grier, Eunice S., and George Grier, Privately Developed Interracial Housing: An Analysis of Experience. Berkeley: University of California Press, 1960. Survey based on a relatively small number of units.

Grier, Eunice, and George Grier, "Obstacles to Desegregation in America's Urban Areas," Race 6:3-17 (July 1964).

Grier, Eunice, and George Grier, "Equality and Beyond: Housing Segregation in the Great Society," Daedalus 95:77-106 (Winter 1966). Both retrospective survey and recommendations and projections for the future.

Hepburn, Richard, "White Suburbia--Token Integration Northern Style," Interracial Review 35:169-170 (July 1962).

Horne, Frank S., "Interracial Housing in the United States," Phylon 19:13-20 (Spring 1958).

Hunt, Chester L., "Negro-White Perception of Interracial Housing," Journal of Social Issues 15:24-29 (October 1959).

Hunt, Chester L., "Private Integrated Housing in a Moderate Size Northern City," Social Problems 7:195-209 (Winter 1959-1960).

Hunt, Chester L., "A Research Report on Integrated Housing in a Small Northern City," Journal of Intergroup Relations 3:65-79 (Winter 1961-1962). A study of Kalamazoo, Michigan, disclosed a strong market for mixed housing.

Johnson, Philip A., Call Me Neighbor, Call Me Friend: The Case History of the Integration of a Neighborhood on Chicago's South Side. Garden City, N.Y.: Doubleday, 1965. The account, by a Lutheran minister, of a neighborhood's progress from panic, over the entrance of one Negro family, to peaceful integration.

Kerckhoff, Richard K., "A Study of Racially Changing Neighbors," Merrill-Palmer Quarterly 3:15-49 (Fall 1957).

Ladd, W. M., "The Effect of Integration on Property Values," American Economic Review 52:801-808 (September 1962).

Laurenti, Luigi, Property Values and Race: Studies in Seven Cities. Special Research Report to the Commission on Race and Housing, Berkeley: University of California Press, 1960. Detailed study of price trends in 20 well defined neighborhoods where nonwhite entry occurred in all-white areas. The author found nonwhite entry most often associated with price improvement or stability. He detected no single or uniform pattern of nonwhite influence on property values.

Leacock, Eleanor, Martin Deutsch, and Joshua A. Fishman, "The Bridgeview Study: A Preliminary Report," Journal of Social Issues 15:30-37 (October 1959). Study of a New Jersey suburb of New York to determine reasons for the ultimate failure, after initial success, of efforts to integrate the community.

Lees, Hannah, "Making Our Cities Fit to Live In," Reporter 16:30-34 (February 21, 1957). Chiefly concerned with Philadelphia projects and progress. The success of Morris Milgram in building for open occupancy receives special note.

National Community Relations Advisory Council, A Guide to Changing Neighborhoods, New York, 1956. Designed to aid leaders in resolving problems, such as how to dispel the myth of declining values.

McDermott, John, and Dennis Clark, "Helping the Panic Neighborhood: A Philadelphia Approach," Interracial Review 28:131-135 (August 1955). In effect constitutes a guide for professionals seeking to maintain integrated communities.

Market Experience and Occupancy Patterns in Interracial Housing Developments: Case Studies of Privately Financed Projects in Philadelphia and New York City. University of Pennsylvania Institute for Urban Studies, William L. C. Wheaton, Director, 1957.

Mayer, Albert J., "Race and Private Housing: A Social Problem and a Challenge to Understanding Human Behavior," Journal of Social Issues 13:3-6 (October 1957). A brief article pointing out that the "invasion-succession" sequence of changing neighborhoods is susceptible to scientific investigation.

Mercer, N. A., "Discrimination in Rental Housing: A Study of Resistance of Landlords to Non-White Tenants," Phylon 23:47-54 (Spring 1962).

Metzger, Earl H., Jr., "Local Agency Concerns and Responsibilities," Phylon 19:71-73 (Spring 1958).

Milgram, Morris, "Commercial Development of Integrated Housing," Journal of Intergroup Relations 1:55-60 (Summer 1960). Description by the president of Modern Community Developers of several integrated projects.

Nesbitt, George B., "Dispersion of Nonwhite Residence in Washington, D.C." Land Economics 32:201-212 (August 1956).

Nesbitt, George B., "Misconceptions in the Movement for Civil Rights in Housing," Journal of Intergroup Relations 2:61-67 (Winter 1960-1961).

Nesbitt, George B., and Marian P. Yankauer, "The Potential for Equalizing Housing Opportunity in the Nation's Capital," Journal of Intergroup Relations 4:73-97 (Winter 1962-1963).

Northwood, Lawrence K., and A. T. Barth, Urban Desegregation: Negro Pioneers and Their White Neighbors. Seattle: University of Washington Press, 1965. A study of successful Negro pioneers in 15 white neighborhoods in Seattle. Includes specimen questionnaires and bibliography.

Northwood, Lawrence K., and Louise H. Klein, "The Benign Quota, an Unresolved Issue of Attitudes of Agency Personnel," Phylon 25:111 (Summer 1964). On the effectiveness of social agency campaigns in advance of Negro entry.

Palmore, Erdman, and John Howe, "Residential Integration and Property Values," Social Problems 10:52-55 (Summer 1962).

Rames, Jose, "How Not to Pass Open Occupancy," New University Thought 3:16-21 (December 1963-January 1964).

Rapkin, Chester, Market Experience and Occupancy Patterns in Interracial Housing Developments. Philadelphia: Institute for Urban Studies, University of Pennsylvania, July, 1957.

Rapkin, Chester, and William G. Grigsby, The Demand for Housing in Racially Mixed Areas: A Study of the Nature of Neighborhood Change. Berkeley: University of California Press, 1960. Factors influencing white and nonwhite demand for housing in several racially mixed areas in Philadelphia.

Reston, James, "Shaker Heights: The Middle Class Negroes and an Ohio Suburb," New York Times, November 10, 1963.

Richey, Elinor, "Kenwood Foils the Block-busters," Harper's Magazine 227:42-47 (August 1963). Action to preserve Kenwood area in Chicago as fully integrated single-home area.

Rose, Arnold M., "Inconsistencies in Attitudes Toward Negro Housing," Social Problems 8:286-292 (Spring 1961).

Rose, Arnold M., F. J. Atelsek, and L. R. McDonald, "Neighborhood Reactions to Isolated Negro Residents: An Alternative to Invasion and Succession," American Sociological Review 18:497-507 (October 1953).

Rosen, Ellsworth E., with Arnold Nicholson, "When a Negro Moves Next Door," Saturday Evening Post 231:32-33+(April 4, 1959). Account of a Baltimore neighborhood where Negroes have been welcomed and white residents have remained.

Rosen, Harry, and David Rosen, But Not Next Door. New York: Avon, 1963.

Rosenfeld, Stephen S., "Interracial Group Tries to Make Living Easier in Changing NW Neighborhood," Washington Post (Section B: City Life), January 28, 1962. An account of Neighbors, Inc., an organization of white and Negro residents of an area in Washington, D.C., working to improve intergroup relations and to preserve its integrated character.

Roshco, Bernard, "The Integration Problem and Public Housing," New Leader 43:10-13 (July 4-11, 1960).

Rossi, Peter H., and Robert A. Dentler, The Politics of Urban Renewal: The Chicago Findings. New York: Free Press, 1961. A study of the Hyde Park-Kenwood Community. Planning objectives: that Negroes in the area were to be of the same socioeconomic level as whites, and that there should be a fixed balance between races. Cf. review by H. J. Gans, Commentary, February 1963.

Rubin, Morton, "The Negro Wish to Move: The Boston Case," Journal of Social Issues 15:4-13 (October 1959).

Rubin, Morton, "The Function of Social Research for a Fair Housing Practice Committee," Journal of Intergroup Relations 2:325-331 (Fall 1961).

Rutledge, Edward, "Housing Bias in the College Community," Journal of Intergroup Relations 1:30-39 (Fall 1960).

Schietinger, E. Frederick, "Racial Succession and Changing Property Values in Residential Chicago," in E. W. Burgess and D. J. Bogue, eds., Contributions to Urban Sociology, Chicago: University of Chicago Press, 1964.

Schiltz, Michael E., "Interracial Housing," Social Order 11:276-279 (June 1961). Review of five books in the Race and Housing Studies, stressing failure of construction industry to build for lower-middle-income groups.

Shaffer, Helen B., "Residential Desegregation," Editorial Research Reports 1958:48-60 (January 15, 1958).

Shaffer, Helen B., "Interracial Housing," Editorial Research Reports 1963:87-104 (February 6, 1963).

Smith, Bulkeley, Jr., "The Reshuffling Phenomenon: A Pattern of Residence of Unsegregated Negroes," American Sociological Review 24:77-79 (February 1959).

Smith, Bulkeley, Jr., "The Differential Residential Segregation of Working-class Negroes in New Haven," American Sociological Review 24:529-533 (August 1959).

Snowden, George W., "Some Problems in the Relocation of Minority Families in the Nations's Capital," Phylon 19:73-74 (Spring 1958).

Spiegel, Hans B. C., "Tenants' Intergroup Attitudes in a Public Housing Project with Declining White Population," Phylon 21:30-39 (Spring 1960).

Stetler, Henry G., Racial Integration in Public Housing Projects in Connecticut. Hartford: Connecticut Commission on Civil Rights, 1955.

Stetler, Henry G., Racial Integration in Private Residential Neighborhoods in Connecticut. Hartford: Connecticut Commission on Civil Rights 1957.

A Study of the Resources, Capabilities for Rehabilitation, and Preferences of Families Living or Owning Property in the Lippitt Hill Rehabilitation Area and their Attitudes toward their Neighborhood and its Rehabilitation. Providence Redevelopment Agency, 1962. Study made by the Urban League of Rhode Island.

Sussman, Marvin B., "The Role of Neighborhood Associations in Private Housing for Racial Minorities," Journal of Social Issues 13:31-37 (October 1957).

Tillman, James A., Jr., "Fair Housing: A Conceptual and Analytic Frame of Reference," Journal of Intergroup Relations 1:18-29 (Fall 1960).

Tillman, James A., Jr., "The Quest for Identity and Status: Facets of the Desegregation Process in the Upper Midwest," Phylon 22:329-339 (Winter 1961). Deals with residential patterns and restrictions, and collective resistance to fair housing in non-Southern communities. Describes the Greater Minneapolis Fair Housing Program in detail.

Tillman, James A., Jr., "Morningtown, U.S.A.--A Composite Case History of Neighborhood Change," Journal of Intergroup Relations 2:156-166 (Spring 1961).

Tillman, James A., Jr., "Rationalization, Residential Mobility and Social Change," Journal of Intergroup Relations, Winter 1961-1962.

Weaver, Robert C., "The Effects of Anti-Discrimination Legislation Upon the FHA- and VA-insured Housing Market in New York State," Land Economics 31:303-313 (November 1955).

Weaver, Robert C., "Integration in Public and Private Housing," Annals of the American Academy of Political and Social Science 304:86-97 (March 1956).

Weaver, Robert C., Dilemmas of Urban America. Cambridge: Harvard University Press, 1965. On the difficulties of urban renewal, the racial problems in urban planning, and the roles of government versus private enterprise.

Weisbord, Marvin, "Homes Without Hate," Progressive 25:28-32 (January 1961). On Morris Milgram and his Modern Community Developers, Inc., established to develop open occupancy housing.

Wertz, R. C., "Power of Positive Action: Rockville, Maryland, Moves Quickly to Prevent Violence When Negro Family Moves into Suburb," National Civic Review 52:540 (November 1963).

Wolf, Eleanor P., "The Invasion-Succession Sequence as a Self-Fulfilling Prophecy," Journal of Social Issues 13:7-20 (October 1957). As seen in a Detroit suburb.

Wolf, Eleanor P., "Racial Transition in a Middle-Class Area," Journal of Intergroup Relations 1:75-81 (Summer 1960). Findings of a study of Russel Woods, near Detroit.

Works, E., "Residence in Integrated and Segregated Housing and Improvements in Self-Concepts of Negroes," Sociology and Social Research 46:294-301 (April 1962).

Wyant, William K., "Holding Action," New Leader 40:16-19 (July 8, 1957). An example of benevolent quotas aiding the stability of a racially mixed situation.

Yankauer, Marian P., and M. B. Sunderhauf, "Housing: Equal Opportunity to Choose Where One Shall Live," Journal of Negro Education 32:402-414 (Fall 1963).

IX. EDUCATION

At midday on May 17, 1954, Chief Justice Earl Warren pronounced the unanimous opinion of the Supreme Court "that in the field of public education the doctrine of 'separate but equal' has no place. Separate educational facilities are inherently unequal." His words were received as a revolutionary pronouncement, as if the decision were unprecedented, unheralded, unanticipated. It was in fact the culmination of a series of cases on segregation in education which had begun in 1938 with a case concerning the right of a Negro applicant to be admitted to the Missouri Law School. Other cases in the field of higher education followed, and in 1951 the first school case reached the court from Clarendon County, South Carolina. By 1952 this case and others from Kansas, Delaware, Virginia, and the District of Columbia were before the Court as <u>Oliver Brown et al.</u> v. <u>Board of Education of Topeka, Kansas.</u> This was the case on which the Court ruled that Monday morning. Recognizing the profound dislocations and problems of adjustment that would follow, the Court postponed its ruling on the implementation of the decision until the following May.

More than a decade after that decision of 1954, the chief problem in the South is still enforcement of compliance with the order to desegregate the public schools. Here, however, the passage of the Civil Rights Act of 1964 is beginning to bear fruit. In several hitherto recalcitrant communities, integration programs have been initiated, and public officials who for years denied the legality of opinions of the Court are now acknowledging that those opinions have been enacted into law, their conversion in large measure due to the threat of the withholding of federal funds. In Northern cities with great and growing Negro concentrations, the problem of <u>de facto</u> segregation has assumed proportions almost as great as <u>de jure</u> segregation in the South, with the added complication that as Negro urban populations increase and white migrants to the suburbs continue to form communities which turn their backs on the problem, the patterns of racial segregation of the urban public school population become more stubbornly established.

On the basis of the experience of the past ten years, it would appear that among the problems most urgently in need of study are not only how to achieve school integration North and South, but the questions of whether and what kind of preferential treatment for disadvantaged Negro children should be provided to compensate for past educational deprivations and culturally barren environments, of what can be done to prepare both communities and individuals pupils for adjustment to the integrated situation so as to minimize inevitable psychological strains and tensions, of how to stimulate motivation, to provide guidance. The very process of desegregation, furthermore, involves severe dislocations for teachers and school administrators; not unnaturally many Negro teachers are deeply concerned as to what desegregated education may mean for them and their jobs.

Then there is the problem of the Negro colleges, including many smaller church-affiliated institutions. Three yearbook issues of the Journal of Negro Education within the past decade have examined the question of Negro institutions of higher education. The Summer 1958 issue considered "The Future of the Negro College," the Summer 1960 issue "The Negro Church-Related College," and the Summer 1962 issue "The Negro Public College." Some of these institutions are very strong, in some a measure of integration has started, some have become associated with Northern colleges, as Tougaloo has with Brown University, in the effort to strengthen curricula and foster desegregation. In the case of others with meager financial resources, inadequate equipment, ill prepared faculties, they might usefully be assisted to become preparatory schools or junior colleges.

During the past decade the emphasis has been understandably on the sequence of crisis situations--in Little Rock, in Clinton, Tennessee, at the University of Mississippi--and on compiling desegregation scores. While these scores may show a quickened rate of public school desegregation, one must anticipate a continuing need for steady pressures on laggard or evasive Southern school districts. And without strenuous, innovative programs in Northern cities, it is only too likely that they will be the next scenes of public school desegregation crises.

1. THE LAW, THE COURTS, AND REGULATORY ACTION

Abraham, Henry J., "School Desegregation in the South," Current History 41:94-96 (August 1961). A study of the response of Southern courts to 1954 Supreme Court Decision, with a table showing 1961 desegregation figures.

Armstrong, Robert G., "A Reply to Herbert Wechsler's Holmes Lecture 'Toward Neutral Principles of Constitutional Law,'" Phylon 21:211-224 (Fall 1960).

Berger, Morroe, "Desegregation, Law, and Social Science," Commentary 23:471-477 (May 1957). The author seeks to assess how far Supreme Court was influenced by the findings of social science and what the role of the social sciences can and should be in jurisprudence.

Bernstein, Barton J., "Case Law in Plessy v. Ferguson," Journal of Negro History 47: 192-198 (July 1962).

Bernstein, Barton J., "Plessy v. Ferguson: Conservative Sociological Jurisprudence," Journal of Negro History 48:196-205 (July 1963).

Bickel, Alexander M., "The Original Understanding and the Segregation Decision," Harvard Law Review 69:1-34 (November 1955). The author concludes that the Court was able to reach the decision it did "because the record of history, properly understood, left the way open to, in fact invited, a decision based on the moral and material state of the nation in 1954, not 1866."

Bickel, Alexander M., The Least Dangerous Branch. Indianapolis, Ind.: Bobbs-Merrill, 1962. Namely, the judicial branch. Arguing that the basis of all law is consensual, the author finds this especially true of judge-made constitutional law.

Bickel, Alexander M., "The Decade of School Desegregation: Progress and Prospects," Columbia Law Review 64:193 (February 1964). On the assumption that the "establishment phase, characterized by permissive tokenism," is over, the author considers what enforcement policies and legal action should be pursued to obtain complete Southern compliance and resolution of the problem of Northern de facto school segregation.

Black, C. L., Jr., "Lawfulness of the Segregation Decisions," Yale Law Journal 69:421 (January 1960).

Blaustein, Albert P., Civil Rights U.S.A.: Public Schools, Cities in the North and West, 1963: Camden and Environs. Staff Report submitted to the U.S. Commission on Civil Rights, Washington, D.C., 1963.

Blaustein, Albert P., and Clarence Clyde Ferguson, Jr., Desegregation and the Law: The Meaning and Effect of the School Segregation Cases. New Brunswick, N.J.: Rutgers University Press, 1957; 2nd ed. rev. Vintage, 1962. Revision consists of addition of chapter, "The Aftermath 1957-1961." A comprehensive examination of the whole legal issue, the book contains texts of the Supreme Court opinions of 1954 and 1955, bibliographical notes to each chapter, a Table of Cases, and an index.

Bluford, Lucile H., "The Lloyd Gaines Story," Journal of Educational Sociology 32:242-246 (February 1959). Gaines and the University of Missouri Law School: a 1938 Supreme Court case.

Borinski, Ernst, "A Legal and Sociological Analysis of the Segregation Decision of May 17, 1954," University of Pittsburgh Law Review 15:622-627 (Summer 1954).

Brady, Tom P., "A Review of 'Black Monday,'" Winona, Miss.: Association of Citizens' Councils of Mississippi, no date. "Black Monday" is May 17, 1954, Supreme Court decision day. Author is Circuit Judge, 14th Judicial District, former chairman of the States' Rights Democratic Party in 1948.

Byrnes, James F., "The Supreme Court Must Be Curbed," U.S. News and World Report 40: 50-54 (May 18, 1956). Opposition voiced by a former Secretary of State, former Justice of the Supreme Court.

Cahn, Edmond, "Jurisprudence," New York University Law Review 30:150-159 (January 1955). Commenting on "the meaning of the victory," the author believes that the 1954 decision spared the nation a genuine constitutional crisis, that only the institution of judicial review could abolish "separate but equal" without both protracted delay and great conflict.

Carey, A. J., "Desegregation--Bane or Blessing?" Chicago Bar Record 44:244 (February 1963).

Carmichael, Omer, and Weldon James, The Louisville Story. New York: Simon & Schuster, 1957. Account by the Superintendent of School and a staff writer on the Louisville Courier-Journal of compliance procedures adopted in that city.

Carter, Robert L., and Thurgood Marshall, "The Meaning and Significance of the Supreme Court Decree on Implementation," Journal of Negro Education 24:397-404 (Summer 1955).

Clark, Kenneth B., "Desegregation: An Appraisal of the Evidence," Journal of Social Issues 9:2-76 (October 1953). Entire issue. The author, professor of psychology, College of the City of New York, prepared this material as part of the evidence presented to the Supreme Court in the case of Brown v. Board of Education. Topics covered: I. The Background: The Role of Social Scientists; II. The Question Posed and the Strategy for the Reply; III. Findings; IV. Some Implications for a Theory of Social Change. An impressive piece of work.

Clark, Kenneth B., "The Desegregation Cases: Criticism of the Social Scientist's Role," Villanova Law Review 5:224 (Winter 1959-1960).

"Constitutionality of De Facto School Segregation," North Dakota Law Review 41:346 (March 1965).

Cook, Eugene, and William I. Potter, "The School Segregation Cases: Opposing the Opinion of the Supreme Court," and Stumberg, G.W., "Supporting the Opinion of the Supreme Court," American Bar Association Journal 42:313-315 (April 1956).

"Declaration of Constitutional Principles," Congressional Record 102:4459 (March 12, 1956). Formulated by the Congressional delegations from the Southern states, this statement came to be known as the "Southern Manifesto."

"De Factor Segregation--The Elusive Spectre of Brown," Villanova Law Review 9:283-294 (Winter 1964).

"De Factor Segregation and the Neighborhood School," Wayne Law Review 9:514 (Spring 1963).

"De Facto Segregation--A Study in State Action," Northwestern University Law Review 57:722 (January-February 1963).

Dent, Tom, "New Law Against Tokenism," New South 18:10-15 (January 1963).

Deutsch, E. P., "Views from Many Bridges on School Segregation and Integration," American Bar Association Journal 51:233-238 (March 1965).

"Dillard Case, Desegregation and the Doctrine of Non-Integration: A Review," Virginia Law Review 49:367 (March 1963). The Dillard case arose out of the division of Charlottesville, Va., into six school districts. The schools in each were not officially segregated, but one district was all Negro. Negroes who applied for transfers were denied.

Drinan, Robert F., "Racially Balanced Schools: Psychological and Legal Aspects," Catholic Lawyer 11:16-20 (Winter 1965). Author is Dean of Boston College Law School and chairman of the Advisory Committee for Massachusetts to the U.S. Commission on Civil Rights.

Dure, Leon, "Virginia's New Freedoms," Georgia Review, vol. 18, Winter 1961. Author was an early supporter of "freedom of choice" school laws, under which school scholarships are offered to all pupils, who are then free to choose whether to go to public or private schools. His thesis: "our virtuous American governments have been destroying the freedom of assembly" since 1954.

Eastland, James O., "The Supreme Court's 'Modern Scientific Authorities' in the Segregation Cases," Congressional Record 101:7119-7122 (May 26, 1955). Speech before the U.S. Senate by the Senator from Mississippi.

"Effect of Pupil Placement Laws upon Southern Education," Albany Law Review 23:376 (May 1959).

"Effects of Segregation and the Consequences of Desegregation: A Social Science Statement," Minnesota Law Review 37:427-439 (May 1953).

Ervin, Sam J., Jr., "The Case for Segregation," Look 20:32-33 (April 3, 1956). By the Senator from North Carolina.

Fairman, Charles, "The Attack on the Segregation Cases," Harvard Law Review 70:83 (November 1956).

Faubus, Orval, "Address," Mississippi Law Journal 30:520 (October 1959).

"Federal Courts and Integration of Southern Schools: Troubled Status of the Pupil Placement Acts," Columbia Law Review 62:1448 (December 1962). Concludes by predicting "the impending obsolescence of the pupil placement acts."

Fiss, Owen M., "Racial Imbalance in the Public Schools: The Constitutional Concepts," Harvard Law Review 78:564-617 (January 1965). Thorough survey of all remedial measures already undertaken or proposed, and the responsibility of the courts to require reform.

Franklin, M., "The Constitution, the Supreme Court, and Integration," Lawyers Guild Review 18:153 (Winter 1958).

Freund, Paul A., "Storm over the American Supreme Court," Modern Law Review 21:345 (July 1958).

Gaillard, S. P., "Origin of the Races and their Development for Peace (Separate but Equal)," Alabama Lawyer 20:115 (April 1959).

Garsand, Marcel, Jr., "Public School Integration: A Call for Legislative Action," Loyola Law Review 9:2:208-218 (1958-1959).

Gates, Robbins L., The Making of Massive Resistance: Virginia's Politics of Public School Desegregation, 1954-1956. Chapel Hill: University of North Carolina Press, 1962. An examination of all the political ramifications of the resistance to the 1954 Supreme Court decision. Bibliography.

Gegan, B. E., "De Jure Integration in Education," Catholic Lawyer 11:4-15 (Winter 1965).

Gill, Robert L., "The Negro in the Supreme Court, 1962," Quarterly Review of Higher Education Among Negroes 31:77-96 (July 1963). Chiefly concerned with the Meredith case in Mississippi, but other school and public accommodations cases included.

Givens, R. A., "Impartial Constitutional Principles Supporting Brown v. Board of Education," Howard Law Journal 6:179 (June 1960).

Gordon, Milton M., "The Girard College Case: Desegregation and a Municipal Trust," Annals of the American Academy of Political and Social Science 304:53-61 (March 1956).

Gordon, Milton M., "The Girard College Case: Resolution and Social Significance," Social Problems 7:15-27 (Summer 1959). Girard College in Philadelphia is a 118-year-old privately endowed boarding school for "poor, white male orphans." It was the subject of litigation from 1954 to 1958, when Negroes twice carried unsuccessfully to the Supreme Court their fight to integrate it. New action is being prepared by NAACP under Civil Rights Act of 1964.

Greenberg, Jack, "Social Scientists Take the Stand: A Review and Appraisal of Their Testimony in Litigation," Michigan Law Review 54:953-970 (May 1956).

Gregor, A. J., "Law, Social Science, and School Segregation: An Assessment," Western Reserve Law Review 14:621 (September 1963).

Guzman, Jessie P., "Twenty Years of Court Decisions Affecting Higher Education in the South: 1938-1958," Journal of Educational Sociology 32:247-253 (February 1959).

Hamilton, Charles V., "The Constitutional Status of the 'Colored Youth' Provision in State Charters for Private Negro Colleges," Journal of Negro Education 28:467-471 (Fall 1959).

Hartman, Paul, "United States Supreme Court and Desegregation," Modern Law Review 23:353 (July 1960).

Heyman, I. M., "The Chief Justice, Racial Segregation, and the Friendly Critics," California Law Review 49:104 (March 1961).

Hyman, J. D., and W. J. Newhouse, Jr., "Desegregation of the Schools: The Present Legal Situation," Buffalo Law Review 14:208 (Winter 1964).

"Implementation of the Segregation Decision," Northwestern University Law Review 49· 557-566 (September-October 1954).

Irving, Florence B., "Segregation Legislation by Southern States," New South 12:3-8 (February 1957). To circumvent 1954 Supreme Court decision.

Jager, Melvin F., "Injunction--School Boards May Have an Affirmative Duty to End De Facto Segregation," University of Illinois Law Forum 1961:741-745 (Winter 1961).

Jansen, Donald Orville, "Private and State Actions in School Segregation," Loyola Law Review 11:1:92-99 (1961-1962). Author suspects that such devices as support of private schools by public funds will not long be permitted.

Jenkins, T. M., "Judicial Discretion in Desegregation: The Hawkins Case," Howard Law Journal 4:193 (June 1958). Concerning Negro student who attempted to enter University of Florida Law School.

Johnson, Charles S., "Some Significant Social and Educational Implications of the U.S. Supreme Court's Decision," Journal of Negro Education 23:368-369 (Summer 1954).

Jones, W. B., "I Speak for the White Race," Alabama Lawyer 18:201 (April 1957).

Kaplan, John, "Segregation Litigation and the Schools," Northwestern University Law Review 58:1 (March-April 1963).

Kaplan, John, "Segregation Litigation and the Schools--Part II: The General Northern Problem," Northwestern University Law Review 58:157 (May-June 1963).

Kaplan, John, "Comment," Columbia Law Review 64:223 (February 1964). On article by A. M. Bickel, "The Decade of School Desegregation." Author takes issue with Bickel's position, that political opposition to a judicial doctrine is legitimate and proper safety valve, on grounds that it seems to legitimize delay.

Kaplan, John, "Segregation Litigation and the Schools: The Gary Litigation," Northwestern University Law Review 59:121 (May-June 1964).

Kelly, Alfred H., "Brown v. Board of Education," in John A. Garraty, ed., Quarrels that have Shaped the Constitution. New York: Harper, 1964. Author took part in NAACP strategy conferences on these cases, and his analysis reflects his first-hand involvement.

Kilpatrick, James Jackson, The Southern Case for School Segregation. New York: Crowell, 1962. Presented as a case at law, with sections on the Evidence, the Law, and the Prayer of the Petitioner. Author's position is that the "Negro says he's the white man's equal; show me"; and "He has no right--no legal right, no moral right--to intrude upon the private institutions of his neighbors."

Laney, L. M., "State Segregation Laws and Judicial Courage," Arizona Law Review 1:102 (Spring 1959).

"The Law, the Mob, and Desegregation," California Law Review 47:126 (March 1959). Includes examination of possible legal remedies against school officials, individuals, and state officials.

Leflar, Robert A., and Wylie H. Davis, "Public School Segregation," Harvard Law Review 67:377-392 (January 1954).

Leverett, E. F., "School Segregation Cases," Georgia Bar Journal 23:9 (August 1960).

Lewis, Anthony, "Supreme Court Enlarging Role as Instrument of Social Change," New York Times, May 18, 1964.

Lewis, O. C., "Parry and Riposte to Gregor's 'The Law, Social Science, and School Segregation: An Assessment,' " Western Reserve Law Review 14:637 (September 1963).

Logan, Rayford W., "The United States Supreme Court and the Segregation Issue," Annals of the American Academy of Political and Social Science 304:10-16 (March 1956).

McKay, Robert B., "With All Deliberate Speed: Legislative Reaction and Judicial Development, 1956-1957," Virginia Law Review 43:1205 (December 1957).

McIntyre, William R., "School Integration: Fifth Year," Editorial Research Reports 1958:655-672 (August 27, 1958). Discussion of the role of the Supreme Court, of the sources of resistance, and particularly of the struggle to resist compliance in Virginia.

McWhinney, Edward, "An End to Racial Discrimination in the United States?" Canadian Bar Review 32:545-566 (May 1954). Author foresees wide ramifications of 1954 Supreme Court decision in many other areas than education.

Maryland Commission on Interracial Problems and Relations and the Baltimore Commission on Human Relations, Desegregation in the Baltimore City Schools (July 1955).

Maslow, Will, "De Facto Public School Segregation," Villanova Law Review 6:353 (Spring 1961).

Meador, D. J., "The Constitution and the Assignment of Pupils to Public Schools," Virginia Law Review 45:517 (May 1959).

Miller, Arthur S., Racial Discrimination and Private Education: A Legal Analysis. Chapel Hill: University of North Carolina Press, 1957.

Morse, O., "Policy and the Fourteenth Amendment: A New Semantics," Fordham Law Review 27:187 (Summer 1958).

Morsell, John A., "Schools, Courts, and the Negro's Future," Harvard Educational Review 30:179-194 (Summer 1960).

Murphy, J. W., "Can Public Schools be 'Private'?" Alabama Law Review 7:48-73 (Fall 1954).

Murphy, Walter F., "Desegregation in Public Education--A Generation of Future Litigation," Maryland Law Review 15:221 (Summer 1955).

Muse, Benjamin: Virginia's Massive Resistance. Bloomington: Indiana University Press, 1961.

Nabrit, James M., Jr., "Legal Inventions and the Desegregation Process," Annals of the American Academy of Political and Social Science 304:35-43 (March 1956). Formerly dean of the Law School, the author is now president of Howard University.

North, Arthur A., "The Plessy Doctrine: Rise and Demise," Thought 35:138 (Fall 1960). Constitutional history of segregation cases up to the date of writing.

Ogburn, William F., and Charles M. Grigg, "Factors Related to the Virginia Vote on Segregation," Social Forces 34:301-308 (May 1956).

Ohio Civil Rights Commission, Legal Trends in De Facto Segregation: The Meaning to Ohio's Public Schools. Columbus: Civil Rights Commission, 1962.

Palmer, B. W., "Resolving a Dilemma: Congress Should Implement Integration," American Bar Association Journal 45:39 (January 1959).

Palmer, C. L., "The Fourteenth Amendment: Some Reflections on Segregation in Schools," American Bar Association Journal 49:645 (July 1963).

Palmer, R. Roderick, "Colonial Statutes and Present-Day Obstacles Restricting Negro Education," Journal of Negro Education 26:525-529 (Fall 1957).

Papale, A. E., "Judicial Enforcement of Desegregation: Its Problems and Limitations," Northwestern University Law Review 52:301 (July-August 1957). The author, dean of the Law School of Loyola University in New Orleans, concludes that if Southern political leaders would stop leading their constituents to believe that segregation can be preserved, peaceful integration would not be too far off.

Partee, Carter, "Secession--A Century Later," Interracial Review 36:7-9 (January 1963). Legal steps taken to circumvent compliance with 1954 Supreme Court Decision.

Peltason, J. W., Fifty-Eight Lonely Men: Southern Federal Judges and School Desegrega-
    tion. New York: Harcourt, Brace, 1962.
Pollak, Louis H., "Racial Discrimination and Judicial Integrity: A Reply to Professor
    Wechsler," University of Pennsylvania Law Review 108:1 (November 1959).
Pollak, Louis H., "Ten Years After the Decision," Federal Bar Journal 24:123 (Winter 1964).
Popham, John N., "Integration: A Balance Sheet," New York Times, September 30, 1956.
    Report of the Southern Education Reporting Service.
"Presumption of Unconstitutionality Applied to Pupil Placement Plan," Columbia Law
    Review 63:546 (March 1963).
"Private Schools Must Integrate?" Southwestern Law Journal 16:284 (July 1962).
"Public School Segregation: Does the Fourteenth Amendment Require Affirmative Integra-
    tion?" Chicago-Kent Law Review 38:169 (October 1961).
Puryear, Paul L., "Equity Power and the School Desegregation Cases: the Law of Circum-
    vention and Implementation," Harvard Educational Review 33:421-438 (Fall 1963). The
    author, at Tuskegee Institute, examines the nature and current status of the major legal
    defenses against desegregation and discusses issues of judicial interpretation which
    remain unsolved. Tables on progress of desegregation by state and school district.
"Mr. Putnam's Letter to U.S. Attorney General Rogers," Alabama Lawyer 20:276 (July
    1959).
Racial Balance in the Public Schools: The Current Status of Federal and New York Law.
    Albany: New York State Bar Association, October 20, 1964.
"Racial Segregation in the Public Schools," Catholic University Law Review 5:141 (May
    1955).
Record, Wilson, "Human Rights, Law, and Education," Journal of Negro Education 29:453-
    457 (Fall 1960).
"Report of Commission on Public Education," Race Relations Law Reporter 1:241-247
    (February 1956). Report of the "Gray Commission" to the Governor of Virginia recom-
    mending legislation to circumvent the 1954 and 1955 decisions of the Supreme Court.
Rogers, William P., "U.S. Policy on Desegregation," New South 13:3-7 (October 1958).
    Speech to American Bar Association by the then Attorney General.
Rogers, William P., "The Problem of School Segregation: A Serious Challenge to American
    Citizens," American Bar Association Journal 45:33 (January 1959).
Rogers, William P., "Desegregation in the Schools," Cornell Law Quarterly 45:488 (Spring
    1960).
"School Closing Plans," Race Relations Law Reporter 3:807 (August 1958).
Schutter, C. W., "Segregation Cases," South Dakota Law Review 6:31 (Spring 1961).
Sedler, R. A., "School Segregation in the North and West: Legal Aspects," St. Louis Uni-
    versity Law Journal 7:228 (Spring 1963).
"Segregation," Southern California Law Review 36:493-496 (Number 3, 1963). In the case
    of Jackson v. Pasadena City School District, the Court, while acknowledging the school
    board's right of discretion, equated abuse of discretion with the establishment of segre-
    gation.
Selkow, Samuel, "Hawkins, the United States Supreme Court and Justice," Journal of Negro
    Education 31:97-101 (Winter 1962). Attempt of a Negro student to enter University of
    Florida Law School.
Smith, Ralph Lee, "The South's Pupil Placement Laws: Newest Weapon Against Integration,"
    Commentary 30:326-329 (October 1960).
Smith, Robert C., "Breakthrough in Norfolk: After Five Months Without Public Schools,"
    Commentary 27:185-193 (March 1959).
Spicer, G. W., "Supreme Court and Racial Discrimination," Vanderbilt Law Review 11:821
    (June 1958).
Spurlock, Clark, Education and the Supreme Court. Urbana: University of Illinois Press,
    1955. Detailed discussions of constitutional issues involved, not only in Brown v. Board
    of Education, but in other school cases that appeared before the Court.
"State Statute authorizing Grants in Aid to Private Segregated Schools after a Partial
    Closing of Public Schools under 'Local Option' Plan Held Unconstitutional," Fordham
    Law Review 30:510 (Fall 1962).
Stennis, J. C., "Multiplying Evils of Bad Law," Mississippi Law Journal 29:430 (October
    1958).

Sutherland, Arthur E., "Alabama's Placement Law's Test Will Be Application," New South 14:6-7 (January 1959).

Tansill, C. C., "How Long Will Southern Legislatures Continue to Acquiesce in the Alleged Decision of the Supreme Court on May 17, 1954?" Alabama Lawyer 23:364 (October 1962).

Taylor, W. L., "Actions in Equity by the U.S. to Enforce School Desegregation," George Washington Law Review 29:539 (March 1961).

"Unconstitutional Racial Classification and De Facto Segregation," Michigan Law Review 63:913-923 (March 1965).

United States Commission on Civil Rights, Equal Protection of the Laws in Higher Education. Washington, D.C.: GPO, 1961. Study of the impact of various forms of federal subsidy and assistance on racial discrimination in public higher education.

Van den Haag, E., "Social Science Testimony in the Segregation Cases: A Reply to Professor Kenneth Clark," Villanova Law Review 6:69 (Fall 1960).

Waring, Thomas R., "The Southern Case Against Desegregation," Harper's Magazine 212:39-45 (January 1956). Author is editor of the Charleston, S.C., News and Courier.

Wechsler, Herbert, "Toward Neutral Principles of Constitutional Law," Harvard Law Review 73:1-35 (November 1959). The author, professor at Columbia Law School, singles out three crucial instances in which the Supreme Court has found race discrimination incompatible with the Constitution--the white primary, the restrictive covenant, and segregated public schools. He contends none of them is based "on neutral principles" and therefore doubts that they are supportable.

Wilson, P. E., "Brown v. Board of Education Revisited," Kansas Law Review 12:507 (May 1964).

Winter, William F., "Mississippi's Legislative Approach to the School Segregation Problem," Mississippi Law Journal 26:165-172 (March 1955).

Wright, J. S., "Public School Desegregation: Legal Remedies for De Facto Segregation," New York University Law Review 40:285-309 (April 1965).

Ziegler, Benjamin Munn, ed., Desegregation and the Supreme Court. Boston: Heath, 1958. Historical aspects of desegregation and their relation to the Supreme Court.

2. PATTERNS AND CONDITIONS

a. General Surveys

Arnez, Nancy Levi, "A Study of Attitudes of Negro Teachers and Pupils Toward Their School," Journal of Negro Education 32: 289-293 (Summer 1963).

Ashmore, Harry S., The Negro and the Schools. Chapel Hill: University of North Carolina Press, 1954. Summary of the work of 45 scholars on the condition of Negro schools in 1954 on eve of the Supreme Court decision.

Baldwin, James, "A Talk to Teachers," Saturday Review 46:42-44 (December 21, 1963).

Bibbly, Cyril, Race, Prejudice, and Education. New York: Praeger, 1961.

Boucher, Bertrand P., and Hugh C. Brooks, "School Integration and Its Relation to the Distribution of Negroes in U.S. Cities," Educational Forum 24:185-190 (January 1960).

Boykin, Leander L., "An Experiment in Reducing the Number of Over-Age Pupils in Elementary School," Journal of Negro Education 29:30-36 (Winter 1960).

Brameld, Theodore, "Educational Costs in Discrimination and National Welfare," in Robert MacIver, ed., Discrimination and National Welfare: A Series of Addresses and Discussions. New York: Institute for Religious and Social Studies, 1949. Cited in 1954 decision: Brown v. Board of Education.

Brickman, William W., "Silence and Segregation," School and Society 85:360 (November 23, 1957).

Brickman, William W., "Speaking Up Against Segregation," School and Society 86:420 (November 22, 1958).

Brickman, William W., "The NEA and School Racial Segregation," School and Society 87: 356-358 (September 26, 1959).

Brickman, William W., "Segregation: Past and Present," School and Society 88:219-220 (May 7, 1960).

Brickman, William W., "Segregated Education in International Perspective," School and Society 88:253-255 (May 21, 1960).

Brickman, William W., and Stanley Lehrer, eds., The Countdown on Segregated Education. New York: Society for the Advancement of Education, 1960.

Brookover, William B., and Sigmund Nosow, A Sociological Analysis of Vocational Education in the United States. Office of Education Publication No. 80026, Washington, D.C.: GPO, 1963.

Clift, Virgil A., "The History of Racial Segregation in American Education," School and Society 88:220-229 (May 7, 1960).

Clift, Virgil A., Archibald W. Anderson, and H. Gordon Hullfish, Negro Education in America: Its Adequacy, Problems and Needs. New York: Harper, 1962. Authors from different fields present wide range of points of view.

Coombs, Philip, "The Search for Facts," Annals of the American Academy of Political and Social Science 304:26-34 (March 1956). About segregation in schools.

Cozart, L. S., "Education in a Scientific Age--Problems and Responsibilities," Journal of Negro Education 28:173-184 (Spring 1959). Report on conference of Association of Colleges and Secondary Schools.

"Displaced Teachers," Commonweal 82:613 (September 3, 1965).

Dwyer, Robert J., "A Report on Patterns of Interaction in Segregated Schools," Journal of Educational Sociology 31:253-256 (March 1958).

"Education and Civil Rights in 1965," Journal of Negro Education 34:197-379 (Summer 1965). Entire issue. Discussions of scope of issues involved, administrative, community, and psychological aspects of the problems, and methods for equalizing educational opportunities.

Edwards, Esther P., "The Children of Migratory Agricultural Workers in the Public Elementary Schools of the United States: Needs and Proposals in the Area of Curriculum," Harvard Educational Review 30:12-52 (Winter 1960).

Fen, Sing-Nan, "Liberal Education for Negroes: As Viewed in the General Context of American Higher Education," Journal of Negro Education 30:17-24 (Winter 1961).

Ferguson, Harold A., and Richard L. Plaut, "Talent--To Develop or Lose," Educational Record 35:137-140 (April 1954).

Friedenberg, Edgar Z., "An Ideology of School Withdrawal," Commentary 35:492-500 (June 1963).

Ginzberg, Eli, ed., The Nation's Children: Vol. II. Development and Education. New York: Columbia University Press, 1960.

Hechinger, Fred M., "Failure up Front: Rights Issue Points up Lack of Strong Education Leadership," New York Times, February 23, 1964. "The National Education Association could not agree on a resolution urging integration until its convention in 1961."

Humphrey, Hubert H., ed., Integration vs. Segregation: The Crisis in our Schools as Viewed by 17 Outstanding Commentators. New York: Crowell, 1964. A useful collection of material covering the history of litigation on school segregation as well as selections on the complexities of enforcement under varying circumstances and in various regions. Published as textbook under title School Desegregation: Documents and Commentaries.

Juvigny, Pierre, Towards Equality of Education: The Fight Against Discrimination. Paris: UNESCO, 1962. A short book on the international movement against discrimination in education on the basis of race, sex, religion, and origins.

Lee, Frank F., "A Comparative Analysis of Colored Grade School Children: Negroes in the United States and West Indians in Britain," Journal of Educational Sociology 34:127-136 (November 1960).

Lieberman, Myron, "Civil Rights and the N.E.A.," School and Society 85:166-169 (May 11, 1957). On the weak record of the N.E.A. in the area of civil rights.

Lieberman, Myron, "Equality of Educational Opportunity," Harvard Educational Review 29:167-183 (Summer 1959).

Mallery, David, Negro Students in Independent Schools. Boston: National Association of Independent Schools, 1963.

Meyer, Agnes E., "Race and the Schools," Atlantic 201:29-34 (January 1958).

Miller, S. M., "Dropouts: A Political Problem," Integrated Education 1:32-40 (August 1963).

Miller, S. M., Betty Saleem, and Harrington Bryce, School Dropouts: A Commentary and Annotated Bibliography. Syracuse, N.Y.: Syracuse University Youth Development Center, 1963.

Morse, H. T., "White House Meeting on Schools," Integrated Education 1:13-14 (October-November 1963).

"Negro Education in the United States," Harvard Educational Review 30:1+ (Summer 1960). Entire issue; articles listed separately.

Noble, Jeanne L., "Negro Women Today and Their Education," Journal of Negro Education 26:15-21 (Winter 1957).

Parker, Franklin, "Public School Desegregation: A Partial Bibliography of 113 Doctoral Dissertations," Negro History Bulletin 26:288+ (April 1963).

Patterson, Fred D., "Negro Youth on Democracy's Edge," in Reference Papers on Children and Youth, Golden Anniversary White House Conference on Children and Youth. New York: Columbia University Press, 1960.

Plaut, Richard L., "Closing the Educational Gap." Journal of Intergroup Relations, Spring, 1962.

Project: School Dropouts Newsletter. Washington, D.C.: National Education Association, 1963.

Rivlin, Harry N., Teachers for the Schools in our Big Cities. New York: Division of Teacher Education of the City University of New York, 1962.

Schrag, Peter, Voices in the Classroom. Boston: Beacon, 1965. The author studied various school systems throughout the country and discusses both big city and rural Southern situations that compound the educational disabilities of Negro children.

Schreiber, Daniel, ed., The School Dropout. Washington, D.C.: National Education Association, 1964. A symposium in which the problem of the Negro dropout is a recurring topic.

Segregation and Desegregation in American Education. Gainesville, Fla.: Education Library of the College of Education, University of Florida, 1962. Third edition of a brief but useful bibliographical guide.

Sexton, Patricia Cayo, Education and Income: Inequalities in our Public Schools. New York: Viking, 1961; Compass paperback, 1964.

"Textbooks, Civil Rights, and the Education of the American Negro," Publishers' Weekly 187:26-32 (May 10, 1965). Report of conference sponsored by American Textbook Publishers Institute and National Urban League.

Thompson, Charles H., "Some Unfinished Business for the 1960's," Journal of Negro Education 29:1-6 (Winter 1960).

Thurman, Howard, "The New Heaven and the New Faith: An Interpretation of Certain Aspects of the American Negroes' Encounter with Higher Education," Journal of Negro Education 27:115-119 (Spring 1958).

United States Commission on Civil Rights, Equal Protection of the Laws in Public Higher Education 1960. Washington, D.C., 1961.

United States Commission on Civil Rights, Report 1961: Education. Washington, D.C., 1961.

United States Commission on Civil Rights, Third Annual Conference on Problems of Schools in Transition from the Educators' Viewpoint. Washington, D.C.: 1961.

West, Earle H., "Summary of Research During 1963 Related to the Negro and Negro Education," Journal of Negro Education 34:30-38 (Winter 1965). Member of Howard University Department of Education finds that for the most part "we are engaged in refining our understanding of the status quo." The time has come for new directions and new thinking.

Yoshino, I. Roger, "Children, Teachers, and Ethnic Discrimination," Journal of Educational Sociology 34:391-397 (May 1961).

b. North

American Jewish Committee, Philadelphia Chapter, Equal Educational Opportunities and the Philadelphia Public Schools. Philadelphia, 1963.

Bell, Odessa Khaton, "School Segregation in Gary," Integrated Education 1:31-35 (October-November 1963).

Bullock, Paul, and Robert Singleton, "Some Problems of Minority-Group Education in the Los Angeles Public Schools," Journal of Negro Education 32:137-145 (Spring 1963).

Chaffee, John, Jr., Boston Herald, February 24, 25, 26, 1964. "Paradoxically, the Negro seeks both equality and discrimination--the equality of racial balance and the discrimination of special programs for the culturally deprived."

Citizens Commission of the Berkeley Unified School District, De Facto Segregation in Berkeley Public Schools. Berkeley, Calif., 1963.

Clark, Kenneth B., "Segregated Schools in New York City," Journal of Educational Sociology 36:245-250 (February 1963).

Conant, James B., Slums and Schools. New York: McGraw-Hill, 1961. The first two chapters, "City Slums and Negro Education," and "Schools and Jobs in the Big Cities," recommend provision of educational experiences to fit future employment, the continuation of responsibility by guidance officers for post-high-school careers of youth, and improvement of slum area schools in order to counteract unfavorable socioeconomic factors of the environment.

Cowgill, Donald O., "Segregation Scores for Metropolitan Areas," American Sociological Review 27:400-402 (June 1962).

Decter, Midge, "The Negro and the New York Schools," Commentary 38:25-43 (September 1964).

Dodson, Dan W., "Public Education in New York City in the Decade Ahead," Journal of Educational Sociology 34:274-287 (February 1961).

Dunnegan, Marjorie Lord, "Vocational Education at Dunbar," Integrated Education 1:29-35 (June 1963). Dunbar is in Chicago.

Fauman, S. Joseph, "Housing Discrimination, Changing Neighborhoods, and Public Schools," Journal of Social Issues 13:21-30 (Winter 1957). Primarily a set of hypotheses, this paper contends that school quality is a key factor in causing moves from interracial middle-class neighborhoods and that school administrators must act on the belief that standards can be maintained.

"Fifty-eight Boston College Educators Issue School Crisis Statement, Pilot (Boston), November 2, 1963. "When more than ninety percent of the Negro students in public elementary and junior high schools are in schools of predominantly, often almost exclusively Negro enrollment, such extreme racial imbalance is, in its social and psychological results, effective segregation."

Fischer, John H., "De Facto Issue: Notes on the Broader Context," Teachers College Record 65:490-495 (March 1964).

Goldblatt, Harold, and Cyril Tyson, Some Self-Perceptions and Teacher Evaluations of Puerto Rican, Negro, and White Pupils in 4th, 5th and 6th Grades. Research Report No. 12, New York: Commission on Human Rights, October, 1962.

Golightly, Cornelius L., "De Facto Segregation in Milwaukee Schools," Integrated Education 1:27-31 (December 1963-January 1964).

Gross, Calvin E., Report on New York City Public Schools to Dr. James Allen, Jr., State Commissioner of Education, August 1963.

Havighurst, Robert J., The Public Schools of Chicago: A Survey. Chicago: Board of Education, 1964.

Heyman, Ira Michael, Civil Rights U.S.A., Public Schools, Cities in the North and West, 1963; Oakland. Staff Report submitted to the United States Commission on Civil Rights, Washington, D.C., 1963.

Jones, Frederick, and June Shagaloff, "NAACP on New York Situation," Integrated Education 2:33-36 (February-March 1964).

Levey, Robert, "The Dilemma of Boston Schools," Boston Globe, December 13-18, 1964. A rigorously documented scrutiny of the declining state of public education in Boston, including a review of the dispute on racial imbalance in the schools.

Maslow, Will, and Richard Cohen, School Segregation, Northern Style. New York: Public Affairs Committee, 1961.

Mayer, Martin, "The Good Slum Schools," Harper's Magazine 222:46-52 (April 1961). Such projects as New York City's "Higher Horizons" and programs in Detroit, Philadelphia, Kansas City, and Tucson demonstrate value of utilizing special teaching methods.

Meckler, Zane, "De Facto Segregation in California," California Teachers Association Journal, January 1963.

Miller, S. M., Carolyn Comings, and Betty Saleem, The School Dropout Problem: Syracuse. Syracuse, N.Y.: Syracuse University Youth Development Center, 1963).

Poinsett, Alex, "School Segregation up North," Ebony 17:89-90 (June 1962).

Public School Segregation: City of Chicago 1963-1964 and 1964-1965. Chicago Urban League
Research Report, May 12, 1965.
Racial Imbalance in the Boston Public Schools. Report of the Massachusetts State Advisory
Committee to the United States Commission on Civil Rights, January 1965.
Reller, Theodore L., Problems of Public Education in the San Francisco Bay Area.
Berkeley, Calif.: Institute of Governmental Studies, 1963.
Robison, Joseph B., "De Facto Segregation in the Northern Public Schools: Its Anatomy and
Treatment," Journal of Jewish Communal Service 39:98-106 (Fall 1962).
Stetler, Henry G., Comparative Study of Negro and White Dropouts in Selected Connecticut
High Schools. Hartford: State of Connecticut Commission on Civil Rights, 1959.
United States Commission on Civil Rights, Civil Rights U.S.A.--Public Schools North and
West 1962. Washington, D.C., 1962.
Wolff, Max, "Segregation in the Schools of Gary, Indiana," Journal of Educational Sociology
36:251-261 (February 1963).

c. South

Abraham, Henry J., "School Desegregation in the South," Current History 41:94-96 (August
1961).
Allman, Reva White, "An Evaluation of the Goals of Higher Education by 294 College
Seniors of Alabama," Journal of Negro Education 29:198-203 (Spring 1960).
American Association of University Professors, "Council Resolution of October 27, 1962,
on Recent Events at the University of Mississippi and on Racial Discrimination in
Higher Education," School and Society 91:45 (January 26, 1963).
Anderson, C. Arnold, "Inequalities in Schooling in the South," American Journal of
Sociology 60:547-561 (May 1955).
Brown, Aaron, ed., Ladders to Improvement. New York: Phelps-Stokes Fund, 1960.
Report of a five-year study conducted in Alabama, Georgia, Mississippi, and North
Carolina seeking ways to improve the quality of instruction in secondary schools.
Caliver, Ambrose, "Segregation in American Education: An Overview," Annals of the
American Academy of Political and Social Science 304:17-25 (March 1956). Author
suggests that Southern whites deliberately instituted the policy of segregation in order
to condition Negroes to an inferior status.
Campbell, Ernest Q., with the assistance of Charles E. Bowerman and Daniel O. Price,
When a City Closes Its Schools. Chapel Hill: University of North Carolina Press, 1960.
In September 1958 Norfolk, Virginia, "acted out the ritual of resistance" by closing the
public junior and senior high schools rather than to desegregate. In the author's words,
"Norfolk learned the hard way that public schools are a necessity if a city is to remain
a city."
"Deep South Now Facing School Desegregation," New South 16:4-8 (May 1961).
Georgia Conference on Educational Opportunities, "Georgia's Education: Separate and
Unequal," New South 15:9-11 (December 1960).
Goodman, Mary Ellen, "The Future of Private Schools," New South 16:3-6 (April 1961).
Green, Reginald H., ed., The College Student and the Changing South. Philadelphia: U.S.
National Student Association, 1959.
Greene, James E., Sr., "A Comparison of the 'School Morale' of White and Negro Students
in a Large Southeastern School System," Journal of Negro Education 31:132-138 (Spring
1962).
Greene, James E., Sr., "A Comparison of Certain Characteristics of White and Negro
Teachers in a Large Suotheastern School System," Journal of Social Psychology 58:383-
391 (December 1962).
Greene, James E., Sr., "Disciplinary Status of White and Negro High School Students in a
Large Southeastern School System," Journal of Negro Education 31:25-29 (Winter 1962).
Griswold, Nat, "Arkansans Organize for Public Schools," New South 14:3-7 (June 1959).
By the Executive Director of Arkansas Council on Human Relations.
Guzman, Jessie P., ed., The New South and Higher Education. Montgomery, Ala.: Paragon,
1954. Prepared by the Department of Records and Research of Tuskegee Institute.
Harlan, Louis R., Separate and Unequal: Public School Campaigns and Racism in the
Southern Seaboard States, 1901-1915. Chapel Hill: University of North Carolina Press,

1958. A study of the first significant effort by native Southerners to improve schools according to Northern standards and of how this widened the gap between Negro and white education.

Howell, Elva J., "Student Activities in Twenty-five High Schools in Alabama, 1955-56," Journal of Negro Education 27:90-93 (Winter 1958). Negro schools and extracurricular activities.

Jenkins, Iredell, "Segregation and the Professor," Yale Review 46:311-320 (Winter 1957). Views of university professor in the South.

Johnson, Guy B., "A Southern Sociologist Views Segregation," School and Society 86:45 (January 18, 1958).

Johnson, R. O., "Desegregation of Public Education in Georgia--One Year Afterward," Journal of Negro Education 24:228-247 (Summer 1955).

Klausler, Alfred P., "The Shame and the Glory," Christian Century 79:977-979 (August 15, 1962). Prince Edward County, Virginia.

Maclachlan, John M., "Population Factors Affecting Education in the South," Journal of Public Law 3:108-121 (Spring 1954).

Miller, Carroll L., "Educational Opportunities and the Negro Child in the South," Harvard Educational Review 30:195-208 (Summer 1960).

Miller, Helen Hill, "Private Business and Education in the South," Harvard Business Review 38:75-88 (July-August 1960).

Patrick, T. L., "Segregation and the Future of Public Education in the South," School and Society 89:175-177 (April 8, 1961).

Pierce, T. M., J. B. Kincheloe, R. E. Moore, G. N. Drewry, and B. E. Carmichael, White and Negro Schools in the South. Englewood, N.J.: Prentice-Hall, 1955. Still useful for comparative data.

Pettigrew, Thomas F., "De Facto Segregation, Southern Style," Integrated Education 1:15-18 (October-November 1963).

"Private School Plans Facing Many Problems," New South 14:6-7 (October 1959).

Reif, Janet, Crisis in Norfolk. Richmond: Virginia Council on Human Relations, 1960. The closing of public schools to prevent integration.

Rich, John Martin, "Social Pressures and School Segregation in a Southern Town," Journal of Negro Education 29:91-92 (Winter 1960).

Smith, Bob, They Closed Their Schools: Prince Edward County, Virginia, 1951-1964. Chapel Hill: University of North Carolina Press, 1965. The author, an associate editor of the Norfolk Virginian-Pilot, concludes with a description of "The Crippled Generation."

Smith, Stanley H., "Academic Freedom in Higher Education in the Deep South," Journal of Educational Sociology 32:297-308 (February 1959).

Southern Schools: Progress and Problems, Nashville, Tenn.: Benson Printing Co., 1959. Prepared by staff members and associates of the Southern Education Reporting Service.

Stallings, Frank H., "Desegregation and Academic Achievement," Southern Regional Council Report No. L-17, Atlanta, Ga., 1960.

Swanson, Ernst W., and John A. Griffin, eds., Public Education in the South Today and Tomorrow. Chapel Hill: University of North Carolina Press, 1955. Presents comparative data on white and Negro schools, including extensive data on expenditures, costs of desegregation, etc.

Thompson, Lorin A., "Virginia Education Crisis and Its Economic Aspects," New South 14:3-8 (February 1959).

United States Commission on Civil Rights, Civil Rights U.S.A.--Public Schools Southern States 1962. Washington D.C., 1962.

Vander Zanden, James W., "Foundations of the Second Reconstruction," School and Society 88:229-231 (May 7, 1960).

Walker, LeRoy T., "Performance Level of Negro Teachers of Physical Education in North Carolina," Journal of Negro Education 28:76-80 (Winter 1959).

Wilkerson, Doxey A., "Conscious and Impersonal Forces in Recent Trends Toward Negro-White School Equality in Virginia," Journal of Educational Sociology 32:402-408 (April 1959).

d. Negro Colleges and Higher Education

Bakelman, W. Robert, and Louis A. D'Amico, "Changes in Faculty Salaries and Basic Student Charges in Negro Colleges: 1960-61 and 1961-62," Journal of Negro Education 31:507-510 (Fall 1962).

Boykin, Leander L., "Trends in American Higher Education with Implications for the Higher Education of Negroes," Journal of Negro Education 26:193-199 (Spring 1957).

Brazziel, William F., "Curriculum Choice in the Negro College," Journal of Negro Education 29:207-209 (Spring 1960).

Brazziel, William F., "Some Dynamics of Curriculum Choice in the Negro Colleges," Journal of Negro Education 33:436-439 (Fall 1961).

Brown, Aaron, "Graduate and Professional Education in Negro Institutions," Journal of Negro Education 27:233-242 (Summer 1958).

Bryant, Lawrence C., "Graduate Training in Negro Colleges," Journal of Negro Education 30:69-71 (Winter 1961).

Clark, Kenneth B., and Lawrence Plotkin, The Negro Student at Integrated Colleges. New York: National Scholarship Service and Fund for Negro Students, 1964. Based on the analysis of college records of 1,278 Negro students.

Cranford, Clarence W., "The Furnishings of a Healthy Mind," Journal of Negro Education 27:103-106 (Spring 1958). American Baptist Home Missionary Society on the importance of Negro higher education in church-related institutions.

DeCosta, Frank A., "The Tax-Supported College for Negroes," Journal of Educational Sociology 32:260-266 (February 1959).

"Desegregation and the Negro College," Journal of Negro Education 27:209-435 (Summer 1958). Entire issue.

Doddy, Hurley H., "The Status of the Negro Public College: A Statistical Summary," Journal of Negro Education 31:370-385 (Summer 1962).

Doddy, Hurley H., "The Progress of the Negro in Higher Education, 1950-1960," Journal of Negro Education 32:485-492 (Fall 1963).

Eells, Walter Crosby, "The Higher Education of Negroes in the United States," Journal of Negro Education 24:426-434 (Fall 1955).

Foster, Luther H., and Charles E. Prothro, "Minimum Income Necessary to Maintain a Small College Effectively," Journal of Negro Education 29:345-355 (Summer 1960).

Gipson, Theodore H., "Relationship of Teaching Aptitude to Age, Sex and Classification of Students at Southern University," Journal of Negro Education 29:96-99 (Winter 1960).

Goldman, Freda H., ed., Educational Imperative: The Negro in the Changing South. Chicago: Center for Study of Liberal Education for Adults, 1963. Papers presented at a twelve-day institute on "The Negro College in the Changing South," held at Fisk University, Nashville, Tenn., June 9-21, 1962. Reviewed by Charles H. Wesley, Harvard Educational Review, Winter 1964.

Gordon, Vivian Verdell, "A Short History of Storer College, Harpers Ferry, West Virginia," Journal of Negro Education 30:445-449 (Fall 1961).

Grant, George C., "An Approach to Democratizing a Phase of College Education," Journal of Negro Education 27:463-475 (Fall 1958). Curriculum reconsiderations at Morgan State College.

Hargrett, Andrew J., "Feelings of Depression Among Students of Savannah State College, 1957-1958," Journal of Negro Education 27:539-543 (Fall 1958).

Henderson, Thomas H., "The Role of the Negro College in Retrospect and Prospect," Journal of Negro Education 27:136-140 (Spring 1958).

Hope, John, II, "The Negro College, Student Protest and the Future," Journal of Negro Education 30:368-376 (Fall 1961).

McConnell, Roland C., "A Small College and the Archival Record," Journal of Negro Education 32:84-86 (Winter 1963).

McGrath, Earl J., The Predominantly Negro Colleges and Universities in Transition. New York: Bureau of Publications, Teachers College, Columbia University, 1965.

Manley, Albert E., "The Role of the Negro College in Retrospect and Prospect," Journal of Negro Education 27:132-135 (Spring 1958).

Mitchell, James J., "Negro Higher Education--Years of Crisis," Quarterly Review of Higher Education for Negroes 30:18-21 (January 1962). Problems faced by Negro institutions in years of increasing integration.

Miller, K. C., "Take Them Where You Find Them," Journal of Negro Education 26:530-531 (Fall 1957). The role of the Negro colleges.

Moron, Alonzo G., "Maintaining the Solvency of the Private College Through Efficient Management," Journal of Negro Education 27:141-144 (Spring 1958).

"The Negro Private and Church-Related College," Journal of Negro Education 29:211-407 (Summer 1960). Entire issue.

"The Negro Public College," Journal of Negro Education 31:215-428 (Summer 1962). Entire issue.

Oppenheimer, Martin, "Institutions of Higher Learning and the 1960 Sit-Ins: Some Clues for Social Action," Journal of Negro Education 32:286-288 (Summer 1963).

"Outlook for Graduates from Segregated Schools," Negro History Bulletin 18:117+ (February 1955). Negroes represent ten percent of the population but less than one percent of interracial colleges.

Patterson, Fred D., "Colleges for Negro Youth and the Future," Journal of Negro Education 27:107-114 (Spring 1958).

Patterson, Fred D., "Foundation Policies in Regard to Negro Institutions of Higher Learning," Journal of Educational Sociology 32:290-296 (February 1959).

Payne, Joseph Arthur, Jr., "The Role of the Association of Colleges and Secondary Schools for Negroes from 1934-1954," Journal of Negro Education 27:532-536 (Fall 1958).

Rand, E. W., "The Cost of Board, Room and Student Fees in a Selected Group of Negro Publicly Supported Colleges," Journal of Negro Education 26:207-212 (Spring 1957).

Reddick, L. D., "Critical Review: The Politics of Desegregation," Journal of Negro Education 31:414-420 (Summer 1962). Integration of Negro public colleges.

Roth, Robert M., "A Self-Selection Process by Northern Negroes Existing in a Southern Negro College," Journal of Negro Education 28:185-186 (Spring 1959).

Roth, Robert M., "The Adjustment of Negro College Students at Hampton Institute," Journal of Negro Education 30:72-74 (Winter 1961).

Saundle, J. S., "Non-Resident Students and Non-Resident Fees," Journal of Negro Education 27:84-89 (Winter 1958).

Sawyer, Broadus E., "The Baccalaureate Origins of the Faculties of Twenty-One Selected Colleges," Journal of Negro Education 31:83-87 (Winter 1962).

Silard, John, "Federal Aid to Segregated Universities and Colleges: Suggestions for a Remedial Program," Journal of Intergroup Relations 2:115-123 (Spring 1961). Federal aid should be withheld from institutions practicing segregation.

Thompson, Charles H., "The Southern Association and Negro College Membership," Journal of Negro Education 27:1-3 (Winter 1958).

Thompson, Charles H., "The Negro College: In Retrospect and in Prospect," Journal of Negro Education 27:127-131 (Spring 1958).

Thompson, Charles H., "The Prospect of Negro Higher Education," Journal of Educational Sociology 32:309-316 (February 1959).

Thompson, Charles H., "The Southern Association and the Predominantly Negro High School and College," Journal of Negro Education 31:105-107 (Spring 1962).

Trent, William J., Jr., "Solvency of the Private Colleges," Journal of Negro Education 27:145-150 (Spring 1958).

Trent, William J., Jr., "Private Negro Colleges Since the Gaines Decision," Journal of Educational Sociology 32:267-274 (February 1959).

Trent, William J., Jr., "The United Negro College Fund's African Scholarship Program," Journal of Negro Education 31:205-209 (Spring 1962).

Weaver, Robert C., "The Private Negro Colleges and Universities--An Appraisal," Journal of Negro Education 29:113-120 (Spring 1960).

Wright, Stephen J., "The Negro College in America," Harvard Educational Review 30:280-297 (Summer 1960).

e. Achievement and Deprivation

Benson, Arthur L., "Problems of Evaluating Test Scores of White and Negro Teachers," Proceedings of the Fifty-ninth Annual Meeting, Southern Association of Colleges and Secondary Schools, 1954.

Boldon, Wiley S., "Tasks for the Negro Teacher in Improving Academic Achievement of Negro Pupils in the South," Journal of Negro Education 32:173-178 (Spring 1963).

Bond, Horace Mann, "Talents and Toilets," Journal of Negro Education 28:3-14 (Winter 1959). Relation of "talent" to percentage of toilets in census areas, and its relation to educational opportunity.

Boykin, Leander L., "The Adjustment of 2,078 Negro Students," Journal of Negro Education 26:75-79 (Winter 1957). To college

Brazziel, William F., and Mary Terrell, "An Experiment in the Development of Readiness in a Culturally Disadvantaged Group of First Grade Children," Journal of Negro Education 31:4-7 (Winter 1962).

Clift, Virgil A., "Factors Relating to the Education of Culturally Deprived Negro Youth," Educational Theory 14:76-82 (April 1964).

Davis, Allison, "The Future Education of Children from Low Socio-Economic Groups," in T. M. Stinnett, ed., New Dimensions for Educational Progress, Bloomington, Ind.: Phi Delta Kappa, 1963.

Deutsch, Martin, "Minority Group and Class Status as Related to Social and Personality Factors in Scholastic Achievement," in Martin M. Grossack, ed., Mental Health and Segregation. New York: Springer, 1963.

Educational Policies Commission, Education and the Disadvantaged American. Washington, D.C.: National Education Association, 1962.

Freedman, Marcia K., "Part-Time Work Experience and Early School-Leavers," American Journal of Orthopsychiatry 33:509-514 (April 1963).

Green, Gordon G., "Negro Dialect, the Last Barrier to Integration," Journal of Negro Education 32:81-83 (Winter 1963).

Green, Robert L., and Louis J. Hoffman, "A Case Study of the Effects of Educational Deprivation on Southern Rural Negro Children," Journal of Negro Education 34:327-341 (Summer 1965). Effects both on academic achievement and measured intelligence of the Negro children of Prince Edward County, Va., of closing of public schools.

Hansen, Carl F., "The Scholastic Performance of Negro and White Pupils in the Integrated Public Schools of the District of Columbia," Harvard Educational Review 30:216-236 (Summer 1960).

Harrison, E. C., "Working at Improving the Motivational and Achievement Levels of the Deprived," Journal of Negro Education 32:301-307 (Summer 1963).

Haubrich, Vernon, "The Culturally Different: New Context for Teacher Education," Journal of Teacher Education 14:163-167 (June 1963).

Hobart, Charles W., "Underachievement Among Minority Group Students: An Analysis and a Proposal," Phylon 24:184-196 (Summer 1963). Advocates special enrichment programs.

Hurley, Philip S., "Fordham's Tutorial Program: 'Before They Drop Out!'" Interracial Review 36:222-223 (November 1963).

Kornberg, Leonard, "Slum Children and New Teachers," Journal of Negro Education 32:74-80 (Winter 1963).

Newton, Eunice Shaed, "Verbal Destitution: The Pivotal Barrier to Learning," Journal of Negro Education 29:497-499 (Fall 1960).

Newton, Eunice Shaed, "The Culturally Deprived Child in our Verbal Schools," Journal of Negro Education 31:184-187 (Spring 1962). Lack of language fluency a serious bar to the Negro child's educational progress.

Newton, Eunice Shaed and E. H. West, "The Progress of the Negro in Elementary and Secondary Education," Journal of Negro Education 32:465-484 (Fall 1963).

Passow, Harry A., ed., Education in Depressed Areas. New York: Teachers College, Columbia University, 1963. Findings of a work conference on curricula and teaching in depressed urban areas.

Pittman, Joseph A., "A Study of the Academic Achievement of 415 College Students in Relation to Remedial Courses Taken," Journal of Negro Education 29:426-437 (Fall 1960).

Riessman, Frank, The Culturally Deprived Child and His Education. New York: Harper, 1962. Chapters 4 and 11 are particularly concerned with Negro children, although their problems are considered throughout.

Rousseve, Ronald, "Teachers of Culturally Disadvantaged American Youth," Journal of Negro Education 32:114-121 (Spring 1963).

St. John, Nancy, "The Relation of Racial Segregation in Early Schooling to the Level of Aspiration and Acdemic Achievement of Negro Students in a Northern High School," unpub. doc. diss., Harvard University, 1962.

Sand, Mary E., "To Show the Way," New South 17:11-12 (November-December 1962). Program for closing the cultural gap between Negro and white children.

Scales, Eldridge E., "A Study of College Student Retention and Withdrawal," Journal of Negro Education 29:438-444 (Fall 1960).

Southern Regional Council, "Desegregation and Academic Achievement," Council Report No. L-17, March 14, 1960.

Stallings, Frank H., "A Study of the Immediate Effects of Integration on Scholastic Achievement in the Louisville Public Schools," Journal of Negro Education 28:439-444 (Fall 1959).

Stallings, Frank H., "Racial Differences in Academic Achievement," Southern Regional Council Report No. L-16, Atlanta, Ga., 1960.

Weiner, Max, and Walter Murray, "Another Look at the Culturally Deprived and the Levels of Aspirations," Journal of Educational Sociology 36:319-321 (March 1963).

Wolfe, Deborah Partridge, "Curriculum Adaptations for the Culturally Deprived," Journal of Negro Education 31:139-151 (Spring 1962).

Wrightstone, J. Wayne, "Demonstration Guidance Project in New York City," Harvard Educational Review 30:237-251 (Summer 1960). Report of a project which identified and tried to stimulate able but culturally deprived students.

See also Chapter II, section 3b on Intelligence.

f. Guidance and Occupational Choice

Amos, William E., "A Study of the Occupational Awareness of a Selected Group of 9th Grade Negro Students," Journal of Negro Education 29:500-503 (Fall 1960). Students are in acute need of realistic knowledge of what occupational opportunities and requirements they will confront.

Antonovsky, Aaron, and Melvin J. Lerner, "Occupational Aspirations of Lower Class Negro and White Youth," Social Problems 7:132-138 (Fall 1959).

Antonovsky, Aaron, "Looking Ahead at Life: A Study of the Occupational Aspirations of New York City Tenth Graders," New York State Commission Against Discrimination, 1960, mimeo.

Blalock, H. M., Jr., "Educational Achievement and Job Opportunities: A Vicious Circle," Journal of Negro Education 27:544-548 (Fall 1958).

Boykin, Leander L., and William F. Brazziel, Jr., "Occupational Interests of 1741 Teacher Education Students as Revealed on the Lee-Thorpe Inventory," Journal of Negro Education 28:42-48 (Winter 1959).

Brazziel, William F., Jr., "Meeting the Psychological Crises of Negro Youth Through a Coordinated Guidance Service," Journal of Negro Education 27:79-83 (Winter 1958).

Briggs, William A., and Dean L. Hummel, Counseling Minority Group Youth: Developing the Experience of Equality Through Education. Columbus: Ohio Civil Rights Commission, 1962.

Coleman, A. Lee, "Occupational, Educational and Residence Plans of Negro High-School Seniors in Lexington and Fayette County, Kentucky," Journal of Negro Education 29:73-79 (Winter 1960).

Dummett, Clifton O., "The Negro in Dental Education: A Review of Important Occurrences," Phylon 20:439-454 (Winter 1959).

Gellhorn, Walter, "Presidential Address," Proceedings of the Association of American Law Schools 29:33-44 (1964). The shortage of Negro lawyers cited as a major problem for American law schools.

Grier, Eunice S., In Search of a Future: A Pilot Study of Career-Seeking Experiences of Selected High-School Graduates in Washington, D.C. Washington, D.C.: The Washington Center for Metropolitan Studies, 1963.

Guba, E. G., P. W. Jackson, and C. E. Bidwell, "Occupational Choice and the Teaching Career," Educational Research Bulletin 38:1-12, 27-28 (January 14, 1959).

Holloway, Robert G., and Joel V. Berreman, "The Educational and Occupational Aspirations and Plans of Negro and White Male Elementary School Students," Pacific Sociological Review 2:56-60 (Fall 1959). While educational aspirations may be similar, occupational hopes and plans reflect the subculture of the Negro in that he anticipates more limited opportunity.

Landes, Ruth, "Cultural Factors in Counselling," Journal of General Education 15:55-67 (April 1963).

Mose, Ashriel I., A Study of the Nature of Guidance and Counseling Services Among Negro High Schools in South Carolina. Orangeburg, S.C.: School of Education, South Carolina State College, 1962.

Ostlund, Leonard A., "Occupational Choice Patterns of Negro College Women," Journal of Negro Education 26:86-91 (Winter 1957).

Phillips, Waldo B., "Counseling Negro Pupils: An Educational Dilemma," Journal of Negro Education 29:504-507 (Fall 1960).

Plaut, Richard L., "Increasing the Quantity and Quality of Negro Enrollment in College," Harvard Educational Review 30:270-279 (Summer 1960). Project by National Scholarship Services and Fund for Negro Students.

Record, Wilson, "Counseling and Communication," Journal of Negro Education 30:450-454 (Fall 1961).

Rousseve, Ronald, "Updating Guidance and Personnel Practices," Journal of Negro Education 31:182-187 (Spring 1962).

Russell, James W., "Counseling Negro Students," Journal of Negro Education 28:74-75 (Winter 1959).

Sprey, Jetse, "Sex Differences in Occupational Choice Patterns Among Negro Adolescents," Social Problems 10:11-23 (Summer 1962).

Strong, Edward K., Jr., "Are Medical Specialist Interest Scales Applicable to Negroes?" Journal of Applied Psychology 39:62-64 (February 1955). On degree of vocation represented by stated preference by Negroes for medical profession.

Trueblood, Dennis L., "The Role of the Counselor in the Guidance of Negro Students," Harvard Educational Review 30:252-269 (Summer 1960).

See also Chapter VII, section 2 on Employment: Patterns and Conditions.

3. THE DESEGREGATION EFFORT

a. General Surveys

Aber, Elaine M., "A Reverse Pattern of Integration," Journal of Educational Sociology 32: 283-289 (February 1959).

Amos, R. T., "The Dominant Attitudes of Negro Teachers Toward Integration in Education," Journal of Educational Psychology 41:470-476 (December 1955).

Anastasi, Anne, "Psychological Research and Educational Desegregation," Thought 35: 421-429 (Fall 1960).

Anderson, Margaret, "After Integration--Higher Horizons," New York Times Magazine, April 21, 1963.

Armstrong, C. P., et al., "Integrated Schools and Negro Character Development: Some Considerations of the Possible Effects," Psychiatry 27:69-72 (February 1964).

Bradley, Gladyce H., "Teacher Education and Desegregation," Journal of Negro Education 26:200-203 (Spring 1957).

Brain, George B., ed., School Superintendents' Conference on the Practical Problems of Public School Desegregation. Bureau of Publications, Baltimore City Public Schools, 1964.

Carmack, William R., and Theodore Freedman, Factors Affecting School Desegregation. New York: Anti-Defamation League, 1962.

Carter, Barbara, "Integrating the Negro Teacher Out of a Job," Reporter 33:31-33 (August 12, 1965).

Clark, Dennis, "Color and Catholic Classrooms," Integrated Education 1:9-15 (June 1963).

Clark, Kenneth B., "The Most Valuable Hidden Resource," College Board Review No. 29 (1956), pp. 23-26.

Clark, Kenneth B., "Desegregation: An Evaluation of Social Science Predictions," Teachers College Record 62:1-17 (October 1960). In addition to his own article, Professor Clark served as general editor of a special section in this issue on "Segregation: Six-Year Perspective." Other articles listed separately.

Clark, Kenneth B., "Clash of Cultures in the Classroom," Integrated Education 1:7-14 (August, 1963). American use of education as an instrument for socioeconomic mobility.

Clift, Virgil A., "Does the Dewey Philosophy Have Implications for Desegregating the Schools?" Journal of Negro Education 29:145-154 (Spring 1960).

Coles, Robert, The Desegregation of Public Schools. New York: Anti-Defamation League, 1963.

Daniel, Walter G., "New Perspectives on School Desegregation," Journal of Negro Education 28:480-483 (Fall 1959).

"The Desegregation Decision--One Year Afterward," Journal of Negro Education 24:161-404 (Summer 1955). Entire issue. State by state survey of action taken--or not taken.

"Desegregation in Higher Education," Interracial Review 36:104-108 (May 1963). List of formerly all-white colleges and universities now desegregated.

Dodson, Dan, "The School and the Civil Rights Revolution," Integrated Education 3:20-29 (August-November 1965).

Fischer, John H., "Race and Reconciliation: The Role of the Schools," Daedalus 95: 24-44 (Winter 1966). Proceeding from the 1954 decision that "separate schools are inherently unequal," the author examines various plans for urban school integration, including compensatory and remedial programs.

Giles, H. Harry, The Integrated Classroom. New York: Basic Books, 1959.

Giles, H. Harry, "Using the Integrated Classroom," Journal of Intergroup Relations, Summer 1962.

Gregory, Francis A., Carl F. Hansen, and Irene C. Hypps, "From Desegregation to Integration in Education," Journal of Intergroup Relations, Winter 1962-1963.

Groff, Patrick J., "The NEA and School Desegregation," Journal of Negro Education 29: 181-186 (Spring 1960).

Groff, Patrick J., "Teacher Organizations and School Desegregation," School and Society 90:441-443 (December 15, 1962).

Group for the Advancement of Psychiatry, Psychiatric Aspects of School Desegregation. Report No. 37, 1957.

Hager, Don J., "Social and Psychological Factors in Integration," Journal of Educational Sociology 31:57-63 (October 1957). A study of variations in response to integration which emphasizes the need for preparation.

Havighurst, Robert J., "The Bearing of Integration on Educational Problems," American Journal of Orthopsychiatry 34:217-218 (March 1964).

Hilliard, Robert L., "Desegregation in Educational Theatre," Journal of Negro Education 26:509-513 (Fall 1957).

How the Curriculum Can Promote Integration. New York: Board of Education, 1964. Report of 16th annual curriculum conference.

"Integration in Public Education Programs," Hearings before the Subcommittee on Integration in Federally Assisted Education of the Committee on Education and Labor, March 1, 1962-June 15, 1962. U.S. House of Representatives, 87th Congress, 2nd Session, 1962.

Johnson, Guy B., "Progress in the Desegregation of Higher Education," Journal of Educational Sociology 32:254-259 (February 1959).

Kenealy, William J., "Desegregation," Social Order 12:249-256 (June 1962). In a debate with William F. Buckley, Jr., editor of National Review, Father Kenealy advocates use of federal power to combat segregation.

Keppel, Francis H., "In the Battle for Desegregation: What Are the Flanking Skirmishes? What is the Fundamental Struggle?" Phi Delta Kappan 46:3-5 (September 1964).

Keppel, Francis H., "Segregation and the Schools," National Education Association Proceedings 102:36-40 (1964).

Klopf, Gordon J., and Israel A. Laster, Integrating the Urban School. New York: Teachers College, Columbia University, 1963. An introduction to problems of de facto segregation. Selective bibliography.

Kupferer, Harriet J., "An Evaluation of the Integration Potential of a Physical Education Program," Journal of Educational Sociology 28:89-96 (September 1954).

Levine, Naomi, and Will Maslow, "An Integration Program," Integrated Education 2:37-40 (February-March, 1964).

Lloyd, J., "Washington Report: Project to Resolve Teacher Displacement Problems," Senior Scholastic 87:sup 4 (September 30, 1965).

McGavern, John, and Douglas K. Stafford, "TN: A Modest Proposal for Educators," Journal of Negro Education 31:511-514 (Fall 1962). The Token Negro in educational institutions.

Martin, William H., "Desegregation in Higher Education," Teachers College Record 62: 36-47 (October 1960).

Mays, N., "Behavioral Expectations of Negro and White Teachers on Recently Desegregated Public School Faculties," Journal of Negro Education 32:218-226 (Summer 1963).

Montserrat, Joseph, "School Integration: A Puerto Rican View," Integrated Education 1:7-12 (October-November 1963).

Moore, William P., "Why Difficult Schools," Integrated Education 1:37-42 (June 1963). Difficult schools and a proposal for change.

Morland, J. Kenneth, Token Desegregation and Beyond. New York: Anti-Defamation League, 1963.

Muse, Benjamin, Ten Years of Prelude: The Story of Integration Since the Supreme Court's 1954 Decision. New York: Viking, 1964. Because of its accuracy, its comprehensiveness, and its thorough documentation, this is a work that should be of lasting value.

Nabrit, James M., Jr., "Desegregation and Reason," Phylon 17:286-290 (Fall 1956).

Parsons, Howard L., "Integration and the Professor," Journal of Negro Education 27:439-450 (Fall 1958).

Pettigrew, Thomas F., "Desegregation and Its Chances for Success: Northern and Southern Views," Social Forces 35:339-344 (May 1957).

Powledge, Fred, "Black Man, Go South," Esquire, August 1965. A comparison of race relations, especially in school segregation, between Atlanta, Ga., and New York City.

"Problems and Responsibilities of Desegregation: A Symposium," Notre Dame Lawyer 34:607+ (No. 5, 1959). Topics discussed: The Role of Public Officials, The Role of the Churches, The Role of Educators, Toward a National Education Policy, The Role of the Negro Community and School Integration, The Problems and Responsibilities of the Negro Community with Regard to Integration, and The Role of the Legal Profession.

"Racial Integration and Academic Freedom," New York University Law Review 34:725-752 (May 1959).

Reid, Ira De A., "Integration Reconsidered," Harvard Educational Review 27:85-91 (Spring 1957). Racial integration in education put into the wider context of goals and community.

Robinson, William H., "Integration's Delay and Frustration Tolerance," Journal of Negro Education 28:472-476 (Fall 1959).

Rogers, William P., "Desegregation in the Schools," Cornell Law Quarterly 45:488 (Spring 1960).

Rosenthal, Jonas O., "Negro Teachers' Attitudes Toward Desegregation," Journal of Negro Education 26:63-71 (Winter 1957). Many fear resultant loss of jobs.

Rosner, Joseph, "When White Children are in the Minority," Journal of Educational Sociology 28:69-72 (October 1954).

Shaffer, Helen B., "School Desegregation: 1954-1964," Editorial Research Reports 1964: 301-320 (April 29, 1964).

Sitton, Claude, "Since the School Decree: Ten Years of Racial Ferment," New York Times, May 18, 1964.

Spruill, Albert W., "The Negro Teacher in the Process of Desegregation of Schools," Journal of Negro Education 29:80-84 (Winter 1960).

Stephan, A. Stephen, "Integration and Sparse Negro Populations," School and Society 81: 133-135 (April 30, 1955). Sparsely populated communities especially suitable for early desegregation, particularly since they are heavily burdened by school costs.

Terte, Robert H., "City School Integration," New York Times, October 22, 1963. Special article addressed to the problem of ways to improve Negro education in city schools.

Thayer, V. T., "Some Significant Aspects of School Desegregation," School and Society 87:469-471 (November 21, 1959). From the author's The Role of the School in American Society. New York: Dodd, Mead, 1960.

Thompson, Charles H., "Desegregation Pushed Off Dead Center," Journal of Negro Education 29:107-111 (Spring 1960).

Thompson, Daniel C., "Social Class Factors in Public School Education as Related to Desegregation," American Journal of Orthopsychiatry 26:449-452 (July 1956).

Tumin, Melvin M., Robert Rotberg, Paul Barton, and Bernie Burrus, "Education, Prejudice and Discrimination: A Study in Readiness for Desegregation," American Sociological Review 23:41-49 (February 1958).

Turman, James A., and Wayne H. Holtzman, "Attitudes of White and Negro Teachers Toward Non-Segregation in the Classroom," Journal of Social Psychology 42:61-70 (August 1955).

Tyson, Cyril, "'Open Enrollment': An Assessment," Journal of Educational Sociology 35:93-96 (October 1961).

Valien, Preston, "Desegregation in Higher Education: A Critical Summary," Journal of Negro Education 27:375-380 (Summer 1958).

Vander Zanden, James W., "Turbulence Accompanying School Desegregation," Journal of Educational Sociology 32:68-75 (October 1958).

Walker, George W., Jr., and David W. Hazel, "Integration in the Junior College," Journal of Negro Education 29:204-206 (Spring 1960).

Weinberg, Meyer, "Chronicle of School Integration: July-August, 1963," Integrated Education 1:4-6 (October-November 1963).

Weinberg, Meyer, "Chronicle of School Integration: September-October, 1963," Integrated Education 1:4-12 (December 1963-January 1964).

Weinberg, Meyer, "School Integration in American History," Integrated Education 1:17-26 (December 1963-January 1964).

Weinberg, Meyer, ed., Learning Together: A Book on Integrated Education. Chicago: Integrated Education Associates, 1964.

Wey, Herbert, Planning and Preparation for Successful School Desegregation: A Guidebook. Bloomington, Ind.: Phi Delta Kappa, 1965.

Wey, Herbert, and John Corey, Action Patterns in School Desegregation. Bloomington, Ind.: Phi Delta Kappa, 1959.

Williams, Robin, Jr., Burton R. Fisher, and Irving L. Janis, "Educational Desegregation as a Context for Basic Social Science Research," American Sociological Review 21:577-583 (October 1956).

Williams, Robin M., Jr., and Margaret W. Ryan, eds., Schools in Transition: Community Experiences in Desegregation. Chapel Hill: University of North Carolina Press, 1954.

"With All Deliberate Speed," Phi Delta Kappan 45:361-425 (May 1964). Entire issue on tenth anniversary of 1954 Supreme Court decision.

Wolff, Max, "The Issues in Integration," Journal of Educational Sociology 36:241-244 (February 1963).

Wolff, Max, "A Plan for Desegregation," Integrated Education 2:43-47 (February-March 1964).

Wright, Charles Allen, "School Integration: An Almost Lost Fight," Progressive 22:7-9 (August 1958).

b. North

Barnes, William W., "Eliminating Segregation in New Jersey Public Schools: A Review of Methods Employed by Local Boards of Education," Report to Division Against Discrimination, New Jersey Department of Education (no date).

Baron, W., "Samuel Shepard and the Banneker Project," Integrated Education 1:25-27
    (April 1963). Shepard is director of the Banneker Elementary School District in St.
    Louis, where 95 percent of the school children are Negro. Purpose of the project: to
    bring the achievement of the culturally deprived Negro children up to national standards.
Because It Is Right--Educationally: Report of the Advisory Committee on Racial Imbalance
    and Education. Boston: Massachusetts State Board of Education, April 1965. Kiernan
    Report on Massachusetts public schools. In March 1964 the State Board of Education and
    Dr. Owen Kiernan, State Commissioner of Education, appointed an advisory committee
    to determine whether racial imbalance existed in the public schools, whether, if so, it
    was educationally harmful, and what steps should be taken to eliminate it. With affirma-
    tive findings in the first two cases, the committee made recomendations for remedial
    action.
Buder, Leonard, "City Considers Shifting Classes for Integration," New York Times, May
    23, 1964. Details of plan for shifting 6th graders to junior high, 9th graders to senior
    high, in order to release space for expanded preschool and kindergarten classes.
Coles, Robert, "Bussing in Boston," New Republic 153:12-15 (October 2, 1965).
Crockett, Harry J., Jr., "A Study of Some Factors Affecting the Decision of Negro High
    School Students to Enroll in Previously All-White High Schools, St. Louis, 1955," Social
    Forces 35:351-356 (May 1957).
Dentler, Robert A., "Barriers to Northern School Desegregation," Daedalus 95:45-63
    (Winter 1966). While school desegregation in smaller cities can be accomplished
    relatively easily, in the very largest Northern cities, racial imbalance will continue to
    be an intractable problem.
Desegregating the Schools of New York City. Albany: New York State Department of
    Education, May 1964. Report of the state advisory committee (Allen Report).
Donavan, James B., "We Are the Leaders," Integrated Education 2:29-33 (February-March
    1964).
Gibel, Inge Lederer, "How Not to Integrate the Schools," Harper's Magazine 227:57-60
    (November 1963). White wife of a Negro, with two children in New York schools. "Their
    increasingly orthodox slogans are blinding some civil-rights leaders to the real needs
    of most Negro--and white--children."
Glazer, Nathan, "Is Integration Possible in New York Schools?" Commentary 30:185-193
    (September 1960).
Glazer, Nathan, "School Integration Policies in Northern Cities," Journal of the American
    Institute of Planners 30:178-188 (August 1964).
Gross, Calvin E., "Progress Toward Integration," Integrated Education 2:12-21 (February-
    March 1964). By the head of the New York City public schools.
Hickey, Philip J., Replies to 136 Statements, Accusations, and Criticisms of Desegregation
    Policies and Practices of the St. Louis Board of Education and School Administration.
    St. Louis, 1963.
Klaw, Spencer, "Englewood, New Jersey: Visitors in the Classroom," Reporter 19:14-17
    (July 4, 1963).
Landry, Lawrence, "The Chicago School Boycott," New University Thought 3:21-29
    (December 1963-January 1964).
Lasch, Robert, "Surprise in St. Louis," Progressive 21:14-16 (January 1957).
Lurie, Ellen, "School Integration in New York City," Integrated Education 2:3-11 (February-
    March 1964).
New York City Board of Education, "Plan for Better Education Through Integration," New
    York Times, January 30, 1964.
"The Open Enrollment Program in the Elementary Schools, Progress Report, School Year
    1960-1961," Board of Education of the City of New York, 1961.
Proceedings of the Invitational Conference on Northern School Desegregation: Progress
    and Problems, April 29, 1962. New York: Graduate School of Education, Yeshiva Uni-
    versity, 1962.
A Proposal for Integrating Philadelphia Public Schools. Philadelphia: Urban League, 1964.
Raubinger, Frederick M., "The New Jersey Doctrine," Integrated Education 1:14-17
    (August 1963). Extracts from statement by the New Jersey State Commissioner of
    Education on integration.
Ravitz, Mel, "Unequal School Progress in Detroit," Integrated Education 1:3-9 (June 1963).

Record, Wilson, "Racial Integration in California Schools," Journal of Negro Education 27:17-23 (Winter 1958).

Record, Wilson, "Racial Diversity in California Public Schools," Journal of Negro Education 29:15-25 (Winter 1960).

Reedy, Sidney J., "Higher Education and Desegregation in Missouri," Journal of Negro Education 27:284-294 (Summer 1958).

Report to the Board of Education of Chicago by the Advisory Panel on Integration of the Public Schools. Chicago: Board of Education, March 31, 1964.

Rooney, Isabel W., "Integration of Parochial School in New York," Interracial Review, February 1964.

Schickel, Richard, "P.S. 165," Commentary 27:43-51 (January 1964). On a New York elementary school, a program of cultural enrichment, and the relations between Negroes and the white middle class.

Schools for Hartford. Cambridge: Center for Field Studies, Harvard Graduate School of Education, 1965. The proposal of a "metropolitan plan" for Hartford, Conn., which recommends that surrounding suburban communities assume part of the burden of educating children from the city's poverty areas.

Sexton, Patricia Cayo, "Comments on Three Cities," Integrated Education 1:27-32 (August 1963). New York, Chicago, Detroit and their schools.

Shagaloff, June, "A Review of Public School Desegregation in the North and West," Journal of Educational Sociology 36:292-294 (February 1963).

Solomon, Benjamin, "Integration and the Educators," Integrated Education 1:18-26 (August 1963). Tactics, strategies, and goals of Northern and Western school integration movements.

"State Calling on Schools to End Racial Imbalance," New York Times, June 19, 1963. News story on request by James Allen, New York State Commissioner of Education, that all school district boards report on imbalance in schools. Text of message on page 21.

Study of the Effect of the 1964-1970 School Building Program on Segregation in New York City's Public Schools. New York: New York City Commission on Human Rights, 1964.

Tillman, James A., Jr., Segregation and the Minneapolis Public Schools: An Overview with Recommendations for its Arrest and Reversal. Minneapolis: Greater Minneapolis Inter-faith Fair Housing Program, 1962.

Tillman, James A., Jr., "Minneapolis: Chronology of Success," Integrated Education 1:41-44 (August 1963). Problem of de facto segregation.

Turner, Francis A., "Integration in the New York City Schools," Journal of Human Relations 7:491-503 (Summer 1959).

Vespa, Marcia Lane, "Chicago's Regional School Plans," Integrated Education 1:24-31 (October-November 1963).

Vincent, William S., and Maurice A. Lohman, Meeting the Needs of New York City's Schools. New York: Public Education Association, United Federation of Teachers, and United Parents Association, 1965.

Walker, Gerald, "Englewood and the Northern Dilemma," Nation 197:7-10 (July 6, 1963).

Wennerberg, C. H., Desegregation of the Berkeley Public Schools: Its Feasibility and Implementation. Berkeley, Calif.: Berkeley Unified School District, 1964.

Wolff, Max, "Racial Imbalance in Plainfield Public Schools," Journal of Educational Sociology 36:275-286 (February 1963).

Wolff, Max, ed., "Toward Integration of Northern Schools," Journal of Educational Sociology 36:1-296 (February 1963). Entire issue.

c. South

Barrett, Russell, Integration at Ole Miss. Chicago: Quandrangle, 1965. The author, professor of political science at the University of Mississippi, covers much the same material as James Silver in The Closed Society.

Bates, Daisy, The Long Shadow of Little Rock. New York: McKay, 1962. The author was engaged in every stage of the effort to enroll the Negro children in the high school.

Bittle, William E., "The Desegregated All-White Institution . . . The University of Oklahoma," Journal of Educational Sociology 32:275-282 (February 1959).

Blossom, Virgil T., It Has Happened Here. New York: Harper, 1959. This is the personal account, by the Little Rock Superintendent of Schools, of the sequence of events from early preparations for compliance down to the climax in the fall of 1957.

Bower, R. J., and H. Walker, "Early Impact of Desegregation in D.C.," Bureau of Social Science Research, American University, Washington, D.C., mimeo., no date. Just before the successful desegregation of Washington's schools, 52 percent of all citizens disapproved of the Brown v. Board of Education decision. A short time later, most of them found no fault with the desegregation process.

Brazeal, B. R., "Some Problems in the Desegregation of Higher Education in the 'Hard Core' States," Journal of Negro Education 27:352-372 (Summer 1958).

Brazziel, William F., and Margaret Gordon, "Replications of Some Aspects of the Higher Horizons Program in a Southern Junior High School," Journal of Negro Education 32: 107-113 (Spring 1963).

Breed, Warren, Beaumont, Texas: College Desegregation Without Popular Support. New York: Anti-Defamation League, 1957.

Brooks, Albert N. D., "Public Education in Washington [D.C.]," Negro History Bulletin 26: 196-197 (March 1963).

Clark, Kenneth B., "Observations on Little Rock," New South 13:3-8 (June 1958).

Coles, Robert, "Separate but Equal Lives," New South 17:3-8 (September 1962). Case study of a Negro student "integrated" into white school.

Coles, Robert, "Southern Children under Desegregation," American Journal of Psychiatry 120:332-344 (October 1962).

Coles, Robert, The Desegregation of Southern Schools. New York: Anti-Defamation League, no date.

Cooke, Paul, "Desegregated Higher Education in the District of Columbia," Journal of Negro Education 27:342-351 (Summer 1958).

Cooke, Paul, "Desegregated Education in the Middle-South Region: Problems and Issues," Journal of Negro Education 30:75-79 (Winter 1961).

Cramer, M. Richard, "School Desegregation and New Industry: The Southern Community Leaders' Viewpoint," Social Forces 41:384-389 (May 1963).

Cuninggim, Merrimon, "Integration in Professional Education: The Story of Perkins, Southern Methodist University," Annals of the American Academy of Political and Social Science 304:109-115 (March 1956).

Demerath, Nick J., "Desegregation, Education, and the South's Future," Phylon 18:43-49 (Spring 1957).

"Desegregation--Or No Public Schools," New South 14:3-6 (March 1959).

Doddy, Hurley H., and G. Franklin Edwards, "Apprehensions of Negro Teachers Concerning Desegregation in South Carolina," Journal of Negro Education 24:26-43 (Winter 1955).

Donahue, John W., "Biracial Public School Education in the South," Thought 35:393-420 (Fall 1960). Historical and philosophical background of biracial education.

Dunne, George H., "Footnote on Gradualism," Interracial Review 35:273 (December, 1962).

Eight Years of Desegregation in the Baltimore Public Schools: Fact and Law. Baltimore: Baltimore Neighborhoods, Inc., 1963.

Fleming, G. J., "Desegregation in Higher Education in Maryland," Journal of Negro Education 27:275-283 (Summer 1958).

Friedman, Murray, "Virginia Jewry in the School Crisis: Anti-Semitism and Desegregation," Commentary 27:17-22 (January 1959).

Gandy, Samuel L., "Desegregation of Higher Education in Louisiana," Journal of Negro Education 27:269-274 (Summer 1958).

Gandy, Willard E., "Implications of Integration for Southern Teachers," Journal of Negro Education 31:191-197 (Spring 1962).

"Georgia Abandons Laws of Massive Resistance," New South 16:3-6 (February 1961). A report on the desegregation of the University of Georgia.

Gessell, John M., "Test at Sewanee," Christian Century 79:626-627 (May 16, 1962). University of the South and integration.

Goodall, Merrill R., "Southern Politics and School Integration," Journal of Educational Sociology 32:62-67 (October 1958).

Griffin, John Howard, and Theodore Freedman, Mansfield, Texas: A Report of the Crisis Situation Resulting from Efforts to Desegregate the School System. New York: Anti-Defamation League, 1957.

Griffin, Roscoe, Sturgis, Kentucky: A Tentative Description and Analysis of the School
    Desegregation Crisis. New York: Anti-Defamation League, 1958.

Hansen, Carl F., Miracle of Social Adjustment: Desegregation in the Washington, D.C.
    Schools. New York: Anti-Defamation League, 1957.

Hansen, Carl. F., "Desegregation in the District of Columbia: A Developmental Process,"
    School and Society 88:239-241 (May 7, 1960).

Hansen, Carl F., "Six Years of Integration in the District of Columbia," Teachers College
    Record 62:27-35 (October 1960).

Hansen, Carl F., Addendum: A Five-Year Report on Desegregation in the Washington, D.C.,
    Schools. New York: Anti-Defamation League, 1960.

Harris, Nelson H., "Desegregation in North Carolina Institutions of Higher Learning,"
    Journal of Negro Education 27:295-299 (Summer 1958).

"Higher Education Desegregation Slowly Gaining Ground in South: Report on 17 States and
    District of Columbia," New South 16:8-12 (February 1961).

Holden, Anna, Bonita Valien, Preston Valien, and Francis Manis, Clinton, Tennessee:
    A Tentative Description and Analysis of the School Desegregation Crisis. New York:
    Anti-Defamation League, no date.

Hronek, Mary Linda, "A Catholic High School Integrates," Interracial Review 36:238-241
    (December 1963). A day-to-day account of the desegregation of a school in New Orleans.

Johnson, Guy B., "Racial Integration in Southern Higher Education," Social Forces 34:309-
    312 (May 1956).

Jordan, Lawrence V., "Desegregation of Higher Education in West Virginia," Journal of
    Negro Education 27:332-341 (Summer 1958).

Kentucky Council on Human Relations, "Kentucky Is Successfully Integrating Its Teachers,"
    New South 12:7-12 (April 1957).

Kentucky Department of Education, Report, "Kentucky Desegregation Proceeds At All
    Levels," New South 14:9-10 (February 1959).

Kirk, W. Astor, and John Q. Taylor King, "Desegregation of Higher Education in Texas,"
    Journal of Negro Education 27:318-323 (Summer 1958).

Knoll, Erwin, "Washington: Showcase of Integration: A Progress Report," Commentary
    27:194-202 (March 1959).

Knoll, Erwin, "The Truth About Desegregation in the Washington, D.C., Public Schools,"
    Journal of Negro Education 28:92-113 (Spring 1959).

Korey, William, and Charlotte Lubin, "Arlington--Another Little Rock: School Integration
    Fight on Washington's Doorstep," Commentary 26:201-209 (September 1958).

Long, Herman H., "The Status of Desegregated Higher Education in Tennessee," Journal of
    Negro Education 27:311-317 (Summer 1958).

Lord, Walter, The Past That Would Not Die. New York: Harper, 1965. Account of Missis-
    sippi's defiance of federal authority as triggered by the 1962 Meredith Case at the
    University of Mississippi.

McCauley, Patrick, and Edward D. Ball, eds., Southern Schools: Progress and Problems.
    Nashville, Tenn.: Southern Education Reporting Service, 1959.

Miller, Arthur S., Racial Discrimination and Private Education. Chapel Hill: University of
    North Carolina Press, 1957. The author believes success in integrating private education
    might ease Southern doubts about public facilities.

Moon, F. D., "Higher Education and Desegregation in Oklahoma," Journal of Negro Educa-
    tion 27:300-310 (Summer 1958).

Nelson, J. Robert, "Vanderbilt's Time of Testing," Christian Century 77:921-925 (August
    10, 1960). Former dean comments on dismissal of James Lawson.

"New Orleans Experience Is New Lesson for South: An Analysis of New Orleans Crisis,"
    New South 16:3-8 (March 1961). The strife over desegregation of both public and paro-
    chial schools.

Osborne, Irene, and Richard J. Bennett, "Eliminating Educational Segregation in the
    Nation's Capital, 1951-1955," Annals of the American Academy of Political and Social
    Science 304:98-108 (March 1956).

Parrish, Charles H., "Desegregated Higher Education in Kentucky," Journal of Negro
    Education 27:260-268 (Summer 1958).

Picott, J. Rupert, "Desegregation of Higher Education in Virginia," Journal of Negro
    Education 27:324-331 (Summer 1958).

Powledge, Fred, "The Summer Institutes," New South 18:11-12 (April 1963). Integration of federally sponsored summer institutes in the South.

Record, Wilson, and Jane Cassels Record, eds., Little Rock, U.S.A.: Materials for Analysis. San Francisco: Chandler, 1960.

Redding, Louis L., "Desegregation of Higher Education in Delaware," Journal of Negro Education 27:253-259 (Summer 1958).

"Report: Desegregation of Southern Parochial Schools," Interracial Review 36:218-219 (November 1963). Prepared by the Southern Regional Council.

Robinson, William H., "Desegregation in Higher Education in the South," School and Society 88:234-239 (May 7, 1960).

Rosenbaum, J. B., "The Integration of 'Ole Miss,'" Bulletin of the Philadelphia Association of Psychoanalysis 13:25-27 (March 1963).

Samuels, Gertrude, "Little Rock Revisited--Tokenism Plus," New York Times Magazine, June 2, 1963.

"School Desegregation is Entering New Phase: Analysis of Houston and New Orleans," New South 15:3-7 (October 1960).

Shoemaker, Don, ed., With All Deliberate Speed. New York: Harper, 1959. A collection of essays about the progress--or lack of progress--in public school desegregation in the South, prepared by the Southern Educational Reporting Service. Bibliography.

Stephan, A. Stephen, "Desegregation of Higher Education in Arkansas," Journal of Negro Education 27:243-252 (Summer 1958).

Sullivan, Neil V., with Thomas LaSalle and Carol Lynn Yellin, Bound for Freedom: An Educator's Adventures in Prince Edward County, Virginia. Boston: Little, Brown, 1965. Account of the author's experience in setting up the Free Schools in that county, and of who did, and who did not, help in the task.

Trillin, Calvin, An Education in Georgia: The Integration of Charlayne Hunter and Hamilton Holmes. New York: Viking, 1963. Recounts the day-to-day experiences of first two Negro students to attend the University of Georgia, and the coldness, hostility, and only occasional understanding they encountered.

Tumin, Melvin M., "Imaginary vs. Real Children: Some Southern Views on Desegregation," School and Society 86:375-360 (October 11, 1958).

Vander Zanden, James W., "The Impact of Little Rock," Journal of Educational Sociology 35:381-384 (April 1962).

Wall, Marvin, "Events in Southern Education Since 1954," Harvard Educational Review 30:209-215 (Summer 1960). Good tables of statistics.

Wilkerson, Doxey A., "The Negro School Movement in Virginia: From 'Equalization' to 'Integration,'" Journal of Negro Education 29:17-29 (Winter 1960).

X. PUBLIC ACCOMMODATIONS

On Monday, February 1, 1960, four Negro students of Greensboro, North Carolina, sat down at the lunch counter in the F. W. Woolworth store. It was the beginning of the sit-ins, the inauguration of a new tactic in the Freedom Revolution. Other sit-ins followed, and then the Freedom Rides. In large measure it was young Negroes who engaged in the sit-ins, students who found a new self-confidence and strength and pride in these modes of resistance to discrimination. At once the legal implications of the new tactics multiplied. Cases that involved interstate transportation were resolved in favor of the sit-ins, as were others involving public accommodations adjudged basic rights. So long as the demonstrations were directed against particular discriminations which could be solidly termed unconstitutional, they met with both popular support and legal victories. Subsequent extension of the device to acts of public dislocation as a means of generalized protest has both generated greater resistance and raised difficult questions for the law concerning the precise point at which the right of public petitioning for redress of grievances and civil disobedience. no matter how nonviolent, meet in collision.

Access to Public Libraries. Chicago: American Library Association, 1963. A research project for the Library Administration Division of the American Library Association.

"Arts and Entertainment for Southern Negroes," New South 17:10-14 (September 1962). What types of entertainment are available to Negroes: statistics and examples.

Babow, Irving, "Discrimination in Places of Public Accommodation: Findings of the San Francisco Civil Rights Inventory," Journal of Intergroup Relations 2:332-341 (Fall 1961).

Babow, Irving, "Restrictive Practices in Public Accommodations in a Northern Community," Phylon 24:5-12 (Spring 1963).

"Biracial Conventions Pose Added Problems for South," New South 15:3-10 (September 1960). State by state review of convention facilities available to groups including Negroes, a report prepared by the Southern Regional Council.

Carl, E. L., "Reflections on the 'Sit-ins,'" Cornell Law Quarterly 46:444-457 (Spring 1961).

"The Common-Law and Constitutional Status of Anti-Discrimination Boycotts," Yale Law Journal 66:397-412 (January 1957).

"Conviction for Disturbing the Peace in Lunch-Counter Sit-in Held to Violate Due Process for Lack of Evidence," Vanderbilt Law Review 15:1325-1329 (October 1962).

DeLacy, G. L., " 'Segregation Cases' Supreme Court," Nebraska Law Review 38:1017-1038 (June 1959).

Dixon, R. G., Jr., "Civil Rights in Transportation and the I.C.C.," George Washington Law Review 31:198-241 (October 1962).

Dixon, R. G., Jr., "Civil Rights in Air Transportation and Government Initiative," Virginia Law Review 49:205-231 (March 1963).

Drinan, Robert F., "Will Public Accommodations Be Desegregated in 1963?" Interracial Review 36:188-190 (October 1963).

Ervin, R. W., and B. R. Jacob, "'Sit-in' Demonstrations: Are They Punishable in Florida?" University of Miami Law Review 15:123-137 (Winter 1960).

Feagans, Janet, "Atlanta Theatre Segregation: A Case of Prolonged Avoidance," Journal of Human Relations 13:208-218 (Winter 1965).

Ferguson, Clarence Clyde, Jr., "Civil Rights Legislation, 1964: A Study of Constitutional Resources," Federal Bar Journal 24:102 (Winter 1964). The author deals in detail with constitutional issues of the public accommodations section.

Gremley, William H., "A Survey of Eating Places," Journal of Intergroup Relations 1:53-58 (Autumn 1960).

"Innkeeper's 'Right' to Discriminate," University of Florida Law Review 15:109-128 (Summer 1962).

Jones, Charles, "Outcome Up to Conscience and to Sense of Fair Play," New South 15:14 (March 1960). By a student sit-in.

Karst, K. L., and W. W. Van Alstyne, "Comment: Sit-ins and State Action--Mr. Justice Douglas, Concurring," Stanford Law Review 14:762-776 (July 1962).

Kenealy, William, "The Legality of the Sit-Ins," in Mathew Ahmann, ed., The New Negro, Notre Dame, Ind.: Fides Press, 1962. The author, former dean of Boston College Law School, argues that the Supreme Court should reverse convictions of Louisiana sit-ins.

Knoxville Area Human Relations Council, A Chronology of Negotiations Leading to Lunch Counter Desegregation in Knoxville, Tennessee. Knoxville, Tenn., no date.

"Lunch Counter Demonstrations: State Action and the Fourteenth Amendment," Virginia Law Review 47:105-121 (January 1961).

McKay, Robert B., "Segregation and Public Recreation," Virginia Law Review 40:697-717 (October 1954).

McKinney, Theophilus E., Jr., "United States Transportation Segregation, 1865-1954," Quarterly Review of Higher Education Among Negroes 22:101-149 (July 1954).

Morland, Kenneth, Lunch-Counter Desegregation in Corpus Christi, Galveston, and San Antonio, Texas. Atlanta, Ga.: Southern Regional Council, May 1960.

Pollitt, Daniel H., "Dime Store Demonstrations: Events and Legal Problems of the First Sixty Days," Duke Law Journal 1960:315 (Summer 1960).

"Racial Discrimination by Restaurant Serving Interstate Travelers," Virginia Law Review 46:123-131 (January 1960).

"Racial Integration of Public Libraries," School and Society 91:345-347 (November 16, 1963).

"Racial Segregation of Spectator Seating in Courtroom," Michigan Law Review 60:503-506 (Fall 1962).

Rudman, W. G., "Sitting-in on the Omnibus--The 1961 Segregation Cases," Law in Transition 22:206-221 (Winter 1963).

Schwelb, F. E., "The Sit-in Demonstration: Criminal Trespass or Constitutional Right?" New York University Law Review 36:779-809 (April 1961).

"Sit-ins and the Civil Rights Act," Tennessee Law Review 32:183 (Winter 1965).

"State Anti-Discrimination Act and Interstate Commerce," University of Cincinnati Law Review 32:313-323 (Summer 1963).

"Survey of Waiting Rooms in 21 Southern Cities," New South 14:11-12 (September 1959).

"Theories of State Action as Applied to the 'Sit-in' Cases," Arkansas Law Review 17:147-162 (Summer 1963).

"Threat of Mob Violence as Justification for Restraint on Exercise of Right to Travel in Interstate Commerce," Michigan Law Review 60:802-805 (April 1962).

Van Alstyne, W. W., "Civil Rights: A New Public Accommodations Law for Ohio," Ohio State Law Journal 22:683-690 (Fall 1961).

Verst, Edward C., "State Anti-Discrimination Acts and Interstate Commerce," University of Cincinnati Law Review 32:313-323 (Summer 1963).

Wright, M. A., "Sit-in Movement: Progress Report and Prognosis," Wayne Law Review 9:445-457 (Spring 1963).

See also Chapter XII on The Freedom Revolution, section 1: Civil Rights and Wrongs, and section 2: Protest: Theory and Practice.

XI. POLITICAL RIGHTS AND SUFFRAGE

As has been seen, one of the principal techniques of Negro protest has been the voter registration drive, in the North as well as in the South. During the past ten years the Courts and the Congress have progressively struck down a variety of Southern legal dodges for denying the ballot to the Negroes--the white primary, the poll tax in federal elections, the redrawing of municipal boundaries to exclude Negroes. At the beginning of his administration, President Kennedy, for whom the Negro vote may well have been the margin of victory, placed major emphasis on insuring that the Negro masses of the South might move freely to the polls, and civil rights legislation safeguarding voting rights has finally survived Southern battle in Congress. On August 6, 1965, President Johnson signed the Voting Rights Act which affirmatively provides direct federal action to guarantee Negro voting rights.

A number of years ago Professor V. O. Key presented a brilliant analysis of the one-party political system in the South, and a description of how the institution of white supremacy maintained itself by means of ingeniously devised limitations on Negro voting rights. That the situation is changing is clearly demonstrated by the results of the elections of November 1964. While it is early to assess gains and predicate voting patterns, these elections returned a record 280 Negroes to elective jobs (see the New York Times, December 23, 1964), all but 10 of whom are Democrats. They include 6 congressmen (a gain of one); 90 members of state legislatures (a gain of 33); 184 in state and local offices (a gain of 27). Among these were two justices of the peace, a member of the county board of revenue, and a member of the county board of education in Macon County, Alabama; two state senators in Georgia; one member of the legislature in Tennessee; in Texas, two members of the school board; in Oklahoma, four members of the legislature.

The extent to which the Negro problem has become nationalized was evidenced by the fact that the six members of the Congress are from New York, Chicago, Detroit (2), Los Angeles, Philadelphia, all non-Southern urban centers with great Negro concentrations that have been growing ever since the surge of migrations began about 1915. Since writer after writer testifies to the Negro's increasing tendency to vote "race" first and foremost, it clearly behooves both the politician and political scientist to take careful cognizance of this growing power of a Negro electorate to challenge the "white power structure." Recently John H. Johnson, founder and publisher of Ebony, predicted, "By 1985 we will probably have Negro mayors in two or three of our ten largest cities, Negro congressmen from the South, and perhaps even a Negro vice president."

1. THE LAW, THE COURTS, AND REGULATORY ACTION

"Abolition of Poll Tax in Federal Elections," Hearings before Subcommittee No. 5 of the Committee on the Judiciary, March 12-May 14, 1962. U.S. House of Representatives, 87th Congress, 2nd Session, 1962.

Aikin, Charles, ed., The Negro Votes. San Francisco: Chandler, 1962. A compilation of leading cases dealing with Negro voting rights, including cases involving the "grandfather clause," the white primary, and the use of the gerrymander.

"Alteration of Municipality's Boundary to Exclude Almost All Negro Voters Presents No Justiciable Issue," Virginia Law Review 46:132-134 (January 1960).

"Attorney-General Authorized to Seek Injunctive Relief Against Interference with Right to Vote: The Civil Rights Act of 1957," Harvard Law Review 71:573-575 (January 1958).

Bernd, Joseph L., and Lynwood M. Holland, "Recent Restrictions upon Negro Suffrage: The Case of Georgia," Journal of Politics 21:487-513 (August 1959).

Bernhard, B. I., "The Federal Fact-Finding Experience--A Guide to Negro Enfranchisement," Law and Contemporary Problems 27:468-480 (Summer 1962).

Beth, L. P., "The White Primary and the Judicial Function in the United States," Political Quarterly 29:366-377 (October-December 1958).

Bickel, Alexander M., "Voting Rights Bill is Tough," New Republic 152:16-18 (April 3, 1965).

Blackford Staige, "The Twenty-Fourth Amendment," New South 19:13-15 (February 1964). Passage of the poll tax amendment.

Bonfield, A. E., "The Right to Vote and Judicial Enforcement of Section Two of the Fourteenth Amendment," Cornell Law Quarterly 46:108-137 (Fall 1960).

Brittain, Joseph M., "Some Reflections on Negro Suffrage in Alabama--Past and Present," Journal of Negro History 47:127-138 (April 1962).

Bullock, Henry Allen, "Expansion of Negro Suffrage in Texas," Journal of Negro Education 26:369-377 (Summer 1957).

Carter, Barbara, "The Fifteenth Amendment Comes to Mississippi," Reporter 28:20-24 (January 17, 1963).

Commission on American Citizenship of the Catholic University of America, The American Negro. Washington, D.C.: Catholic University Press, 1962.

"Congressional Authority to Restrict the Use of Literacy Tests," California Law Review 50:265-282 (May 1962).

"The Constitutionality of an Alabama Statute Re-defining Municipal Boundaries is not a 'Political Question' if it Effects a Deprivation of a Negro's Right to Vote," Temple Law Quarterly 34:326-331 (Spring 1961).

De Grazia, Alfred, "A New Way Toward Equal Suffrage," New York University Law Review 34:716-724 (April 1959).

Douglas, Paul H., "Trends and Developments: The 1960 Voting Rights Bill: The Struggle, the Final Results and the Reason," Journal of Intergroup Relations 1:82-86 (Summer 1960).

Ervin, Sam J., "Political Rights as Abridged by Pending Legislative Proposals," Federal Bar Journal 24:4-17 (Winter 1964). U.S. Senator from North Carolina denounces provision for federal protection of voter registration in Civil Rights Act of 1964 as unconstitutional. He also considers Title VI unconstitutional, and the Court's protection of demonstrators guilty of "civil disobedience" indefensible.

"Exclusion of Negro Voters by Alteration of Municipality's Boundary Held Unconstitutional," Ohio State Law Journal 22:213-219 (Winter 1961).

Farris, Charles D., "The Re-Enfranchisement of Negroes in Florida," Journal of Negro History 39:259-283 (October 1954). The author suggests that among reasons for defeat of white primary was the conviction among whites that political apathy among Negroes and an absence of vigorous Negro leadership would inhibit any great increase in registration.

Franklin, John Hope, " 'Legal' Disfranchisement of the Negro," Journal of Negro Education 26:241-248 (Summer 1957). A review of the period around the turn of the century.

Hamilton, Charles V., "Race, Morality and Political Solutions," Phylon 20:242-247 (September 1959).

Hamilton, Charles V., "Southern Judges and Negro Voting Rights: The Judicial Approach to the Solution of Controversial Social Problems," Wisconsin Law Review 1965:72-102 (Winter 1965).

Havens, Charles W., III, "Federal Legislation to Safeguard Voting Rights: The Civil Rights Act of 1960," Virginia Law Review 46:945-975 (June 1960).

Heyman, Ira M., "Federal Remedies for Voteless Negroes," California Law Review 48:190-215 (May 1960).

Horsky, C. A., "The Supreme Court, Congress, and the Right to Vote," Ohio State Law Journal 20:549-556 (Summer 1959).

Jones, Lewis W., "Struggle in the Vote at Tuskegee," in Jitsuichi Masuoka and Preston Valien, eds., Race Relations: Problems and Theory, Chapel Hill: University of North Carolina Press, 1961.

Jones, Lewis W., and Stanley Smith, Tuskegee, Alabama: Voting Rights and Economic Pressure. New York: Anti-Defamation League, 1958.

Katzenbach, Nicholas de B., "The Protection of 'Political Rights,'" Federal Bar Journal 24:18-30 (Winter 1964). Pointing to congressional tardiness in implementing the 15th Amendment, the author urges passage of civil rights bill in order to prevent continuation of traditional evasions of Negro right to register.

Kyle, Keith, "Desegregation and the Negro Right to Vote," Commentary 24:15-19 (July 1957).

Lewis, Anthony, "Negro Vote Curbs Exposed by F.B.I.," New York Times, August 4, 1957.

"Literacy Tests and Voter Requirements in Federal and State Elections," Hearings before the Subcommittee on Constitutional Rights of the Committee on the Judiciary, March 27-April 12, 1962. U.S. Senate, 87th Congress, 2nd Session, 1962.

McIntyre, William R., "Right to Vote," Editorial Research Reports 1958:201-219 (March 19, 1958). An examination of the prospects for effective implementation of the Civil Rights Bill of 1957.

Marshall, Thurgood, "The Rise and Collapse of 'White Democratic Primary,'" Journal of Negro Education 26:249-254 (Summer 1957). The author, United States Solicitor General and for many years special counsel of the NAACP Legal Fund, in 1944 argued the Texas Primary Case before the Supreme Court.

Ogden, Frederick D., The Poll Tax in the South. University, Ala.: University of Alabama Press, 1958.

"Poll Tax and Enfranchisement of District of Columbia," Hearings before the Subcommittee on Constitutional Amendments of the Committee on the Judiciary, August 17 and 27, 1959. U.S. Senate, 86th Congress, 1st Session, 1959.

"Power of a State to Alter or Destroy the Corporate Boundaries of a City, Extensive Though it is, is Met and Overcome by the 15th Amendment to the Federal Constitution," University of Pittsburgh Law Review 22:773-776 (June 1961).

"Preservation of Evidence in Federal Elections," Hearings before the Subcommittee on Rules and Administration, July 13, 1961. U.S. Senate, 87th Congress, 1st Session, 1961.

Spicer, George W., "The Federal Judiciary and Political Change in the South," Journal of Politics 26:154-176 (February 1964).

"State Statute Altering Municipal Boundaries with Effect of Excluding Negro Voters Held Invalid," Villanova Law Review 6:411-415 (Spring 1961).

Steinberg, C., "The Southern Negro's Right to Vote," American Federationist 69:1-6 (July 1962).

Taper, Bernard, Gomillion versus Lightfoot: The Tuskegee Gerrymander Case. New York: McGraw-Hill, 1962. At issue in the Tuskegee Case was whether districting was a political or a constitutional question. The Supreme Court held it to be constitutional. The decision had relevance for subsequent decisions on reapportionment of districts for Congressional and Senatorial elections.

"Tuskegee Case and the Political Question Dilemma," Georgia Bar Journal 23:545-548 (May 1961).

"Unconstrued State Registration Statute Basis for Court Abstention where Federal Jurisdiction Invoked under Civil Rights Acts," Rutgers Law Review 14:185-192 (Fall 1959).

U.S. Commission on Civil Rights, Report 1959. Washington, D.C.: GPO, 1959.

U.S. Commission on Civil Rights, Report 1961, Book I, Voting. Washington, D.C.: GPO, 1962.

"Voting," Hearings before the U.S. Commission on Civil Rights, Montgomery, Ala., December 8, 1958-January 9, 1959; New Orleans, September 27, 1960-May 6, 1961. Washington, D.C.: GPO, 1961.

"Voting Rights," Hearings before the Committee on the Judiciary, February 9 and 16, 1960. U.S. House of Representatives, 86th Congress, 1st Session, 1960.

Weaver, Robert C., and Hortense W. Gabel, "Some Legislative Consequences of Negro
  Disfranchisement," Journal of Negro Education 26:255-261 (Summer 1957). Analysis of
  Southern congressmen and their effectiveness as impediments to liberal legislation.
Werdegar, Kathryn Mickle, "The Constitutionality of Federal Legislation to Abolish
  Literacy Tests," George Washington Law Review 30:723-743 (April 1962).
Worsnop, Richard L., "Protection of Voting Rights," Editorial Research Reports 1962:277-
  296 (April 18, 1962).

2. PATTERNS AND CONDITIONS

Aikin, Charles, ed., The Negro Votes. San Francisco: Chandler, 1962.
Bacote, C. A., "The Negro in Atlanta Politics," Phylon 16:333-350 (Winter 1955).
Bacote, C. A., "The Negro Voter in Georgia Politics Today," Journal of Negro Education
  26:307-318 (Summer 1957).
Banfield, Edward C., Political Influence. Glencoe, Ill.: Free Press, 1961. Drawing on six
  case studies of Chicago politics, the author analyzes the way influence works in a large
  American city, pointing out that in Chicago Negro political leadership is more apt to
  operate through the machine than in New York, with consequent greater indifference to
  issues.
Banfield, Edward C., ed., Urban Government: A Reader. New York: Free Press, 1961.
Banfield, Edward C., and Martha Derthick, eds., "A Report on the Politics of Boston."
  Cambridge: Joint Center for Urban Studies, 1960, mimeo. The role of the Negro is not
  only integrated with the study as a whole, but is the subject of a chapter by Ralph Otwell.
Banfield, Edward C., and James Q. Wilson, City Politics. Cambridge: Harvard University
  Press and MIT Press, 1963. While the authors consider the role of the Negro throughout,
  Chapter 20 specifically analyzes "the anomaly of the Negro's numerical strength and
  political weakness," with the result that much of the Negro's civic action takes place in
  the courts or in the streets.
Brazeal, Brailsford R., "A Blackbelt County: Total Disfranchisement," in Margaret Price,
  The Negro and the Ballot in the South, Atlanta, Ga.: Southern Regional Council, 1959. A
  pessimistic in-depth report on one rural county in the Deep South by the dean of Morehouse College. Whites control all power, and though there are 60 percent Negro inhabitants in the county, there is no prospect today for equal Negro civil rights in any
  area.
Broder, David S., "Negro Vote Upset Off-Year Pattern," New York Times, November 4,
  1965. Republican reform candidates, with Negro support, elected to office in New York,
  Philadelphia, Cleveland, and Louisville, thus challenging Democratic control of large
  urban centers.
Brogan, Dennis W., Politics in America. New York: Harper, 1954. Chapter 3, "Race and
  Politics."
Brooks, Maxwell R., The Negro Press Re-examined: Political Content of Leading Negro
  Newspapers. Boston: Christopher, 1959.
Carleton, W. G., and H. D. Price, "America's Newest Voter: A Florida Case Study,"
  Antioch Review 14:441-457 (Winter 1954).
Clayton, Edward T., The Negro Politician: His Success and Failure. Chicago: Johnson,
  1964.
Clubok, Alfred B., John M. Degrove, and Charles D. Farris, "The Manipulated Negro Vote:
  Some Pre-Conditions and Consequences," Journal of Politics 26:112-129 (February
  1964).
Cornwell, Elmer E., "Bosses, Machines, and Ethnic Groups," Annals of the American
  Academy of Political and Social Science 353:27-39 (May 1964).
Cothran, Tilman C., and William M. Phillips, Jr., "Expansion of Negro Suffrage in
  Arkansas," Journal of Negro Education 26:287-296 (Summer 1957).
"Deluge: Negro Registration in the South," Newsweek 66:17-18 (August 23, 1965). As
  immediate consequence of passage of Voting Rights Act of July 1965.
"Desegregation Resistance Slows Negro Registration," New South 14:3-5 (October 1959).
Dowd, Douglas F., "The Campaign in Fayette County," Monthly Review 15:675-679 (April
  1964). Tennessee vote drive.

Fenton, John H., "The Negro Voter in Louisiana," Journal of Negro Education 26:319-328 (Summer 1957).

Fenton, John H., and Kenneth N. Vines, "Negro Registration in Louisiana," American Political Science Review 51:704-713 (September 1957). How Catholic culture creates a permissive climate for Negro registration and weakens white segregationists' effectiveness.

Fleming, G. James, An All-Negro Ticket in Baltimore. New York: Holt, 1960. A case study in local politics issued by the Eagleton Institute of Politics: In 1958 congressional and state elections in the 4th district in Baltimore, an all-Negro coalition (bipartisan) ticket challenged the Democratic machine for seven seats in the state legislature--and lost.

Gamarckian, Edward, "A Report from the South on the Negro Voter," Reporter 20:9-10 (June 27, 1957).

Gauntlett, John, and John B. McConaughy, "Some Observations on the Influence of the Income Factor on Urban Negro Voting in South Carolina," Journal of Negro Education 31:78-82 (Winter 1962).

Gauntlett, John, and John B. McConaughy, "Survey of Urban Negro Voting Behavior in South Carolina," South Carolina Law Quarterly 13:365 (Spring 1962).

Glantz, Oscar, "Recent Negro Ballots in Philadelphia," Journal of Negro Education 28:430-438 (Fall 1959). Includes presidential elections of 1944-1956. Author foresees Negroes exercising balance of power in the future. In November 1965, reform Republican Arlen Specter, with Negro support, became first Republican elected District Attorney in Philadelphia since 1953.

Glantz, Oscar, "The Negro Voter in Northern Industrial Cities," Western Political Quarterly 13:999-1010 (December 1960).

Gomillion, Charles G., "The Negro Voter in Alabama," Journal of Negro Education 26:281-286 (Summer 1957).

Gomillion, Charles G., "Civic Democracy and the Problems of Registration and Voting of Negroes in the South," Lawyers Guild Review 18:149-151 (Winter 1958). It was in the name of Professor Gomillion of Tuskegee Institute that litigation was entered against the gerrymandering of Tuskegee municipal boundaries to exclude Negro voters (see above Bernard Taper, Gomillion versus Lightfoot). In November, 1964, he was elected to the Macon County Board of Education, one of the first three Negroes ever to obtain elective office in that county.

Gosnell, Harold F., and R. E. Martin, "The Negro as Voter and Office Holder," Journal of Negro Education 32:415-425 (Fall, 1963).

Gray, Kenneth, "A Report on City Politics in Cincinnati," Cambridge, Mass: Joint Center for Urban Studies, 1959, mimeo. An examination of the circumstances under which PR was abandoned, which took the form of a struggle between two coalitions, each of which had its Negro bosses or leaders.

Greenstone, David, "A Report on the Politics of Detroit." Cambridge, Mass.: Joint Center for Urban Studies, 1961, mimeo.

Halberstam, David, "'Good Jelly's' Last Stand," Reporter 24:40-41 (January 19, 1961). "Good Jelly" Jones, a Negro restaurant owner and bootlegger, runs a one-precinct machine in Nashville.

Holloway, Harry, "The Negro and the Vote: The Case of Texas," Journal of Politics 23:526-556 (August 1961). Negro voters often manipulated by landowners and white conservatives.

Holloway, Harry, "The Texas Negro as a Voter," Phylon 24:135-145 (Summer 1963).

Hunter, Floyd, Community Power Structures. Chapel Hill: University of North Carolina Press, 1953. Useful for observations on Negro politics in the South and on the class status of the Negro leaders.

Jennings, M. Kent, and L. Harmon Zeigler, "A Moderate's Victory in a Southern Congressional District," Political Opinion Quarterly 28:595-603 (Winter 1964). In a district with 33.3 percent Negro population, Negroes support moderate Democrat.

Jewell, Malcolm, "State Legislatures in Southern Politics," Journal of Politics 26:177-196 (February 1964).

Jones, Lewis, and Stanley Smith, Voting Rights and Economic Pressure. New York: Anti-Defamation League, 1958. Prepared at Tuskegee in cooperation with the National Council of Churches. Reports on Mansfield, Tex., Clinton, Tenn., Sturgis, Ky., and Tallahassee, Fla.

Kesselman, Louis C., "Negro Voting in a Border Community: Louisville, Kentucky," Journal of Negro Education 26:273-280 (Summer 1957).

Key, V. O., Jr., Southern Politics in State and Nation. New York: Knopf, 1949; reissued, Vintage Caravelle, 1963. A classic study which underlines the historical and contemporary importance of the Negro in Southern politics. While all the data are from the period before 1949, the comprehensiveness of the analysis of the one-party system and of a Southern unity based on the maintenance of white supremacy and the willingness to subordinate all other issues makes this an indispensable work for the understanding of present developments.

Lane, Robert E., Political Life. Glencoe, Ill.: Free Press, 1959. Includes an analysis of Negro politics as a form of ethnic behavior.

Leggett, John C., "Working-Class Consciousness, Race, and Political Choice," American Journal of Sociology 69:171-176 (September 1963). Among 375 Detroit blue-collar workers, race was found to be the decisive factor in political choice.

Lewinson, Paul, Race, Class, and Party: A History of Negro Suffrage and White Politics in the South. New York: Grosset & Dunlap, 1965; 1st ed. 1932. Reissued with a new foreword, "Postscript, 1964," which reviews briefly Negro suffrage gains of the past thirty years and speculates concerning the future political alignments of both Negro and white Southerners. Bibliography.

Lewis, Earl M., "The Negro Voter in Mississippi," Journal of Negro Education 26:329-350 (Summer 1957).

Lipsky, Roma, "Electioneering Among the Minorities," Commentary 31:428-432 (May 1961).

Lubell, Samuel, The Future of American Politics. New York: Harper, 1952. Two chapters on the Negro: 5, "Civil Rights Melting Pot," deals with problems of Negro migrants to Northern cities, the Negro slums as seedbeds of violence and protest, and possible balance of political power; 6, "The Conservative Revolution," focuses on the South, the hardening of white supremacism, and the expansion of the Negro franchise.

Lubell, Samuel, "The Negro and the Democratic Coalition," Commentary 38:19-27 (August 1964). Contends that Negroes will continue to pull Democrat levers, but that Democrats must "unify the nation racially."

McCain, James T., "The Negro Voter in South Caroline," Journal of Negro Education 26: 359-366 (Summer 1957).

McGill, Ralph, "If the Southern Negro Got the Vote," New York Times Magazine, June 21, 1959.

McGuinn, Henry J., and Tinsley Lee Spraggins, "Negro Politics in Virginia," Journal of Negro Education 26:378-389 (Summer 1957).

Matthews, Donald R., and James W. Prothro, "Social and Economic Factors and Negro Voter Registration in the South," American Political Science Review 57:24-44 (March 1963).

Matthews, Donald R., and James W. Prothro, "Political Factors and Negro Voter Registration in the South," American Political Science Review 57:355-367 (June 1963).

Matthews, Donald R., and James W. Prothro, "Southern Images of Political Parties: An Analysis of White and Negro Attitudes," Journal of Politics 26:82-111 (February 1964).

Maxwell, Neil, "Voting Strength Wins City Jobs, Projects for Tuskegee Negroes, Wall Street Journal, March 16, 1965. Not only have two Negroes been elected to City Council, but a general improvement in business has taken place, streets have been paved in all poor sections, garbage collection and other city services improved.

Middleton, Russell, "The Civil Rights Issue and Presidential Voting Among Southern Negroes and Whites," Social Forces 40:209-215 (March 1962). Analysis of the 1960 election.

Miller, Loren, "The Negro Voter in the Far West," Journal of Negro Education 26:262-272 (Summer 1957).

Minnis, Jack, "The Mississippi Freedom Democratic Party: A New Declaration of Independence," Freedomways, Spring 1965.

Mitchell, George S., "The Extension of Citizenship," in Jessie P. Guzman, ed., The New South and Higher Education, Tuskegee: Tuskegee Institute, 1954.

"The Mississippi Freedom Vote," New South 18:10-13 (December 1963).

Moon, Henry Lee, "The Southern Scene," Phylon 16:351-358 (Winter 1955). Gains in the franchise since the banning of the white primary.

Moon, Henry Lee, "The Negro Vote in the Presidential Election of 1956," Journal of Negr
    Education 26:219-230 (Summer 1957).
Morrison, Allan, "Negro Political Progress in New England," Ebony 18:25-28+ (October
    1963). Chiefly on Edward W. Brooke, Attorney General of Massachusetts.
"The Negro Voter in the South," Journal of Negro Education 26:213-431 (Summer 1957).
    Entire issue.
"Negro Voter Registration Remains Constant in South," New South 14:8-9 (January 1959).
Newton, I. G., "Expansion of Negro Suffrage in North Carolina," Journal of Negro Education
    26:351-358 (Summer 1957).
Price, Hugh D., The Negro and Southern Politics: A Chapter of Florida History. New York:
    New York University Press, 1957. A detailed study of the actual voting behavior of
    Negro voters in Florida, including Negro registration, the Negro Political League, the
    Negro as candidate, and campaign tactics.
Price, Margaret, The Negro Voter in the South. Atlanta, Ga.: Southern Regional Council,
    1957. A report on Negro registration, political consciousness, political organization, and
    leadership. Also included are data on Negro voting performance in 10 Southern states as
    of 1956. Brief but useful.
Price, Margaret, ed., "The Negro Voter in the South," New South 12:1-55 (September 1957).
    Entire issue. Based on voting surveys by state consultants of Southern Regional Council.
    Includes sections on voter registration, legal determinants, discrimination and intimida-
    tion, socioeconomic factors, organization and leadership, and future patterns.
Sigel, Roberta S., "Race and Religion as Factors in the Kennedy Victory in Detroit, 1960,"
    Journal of Negro Education 31:436-447 (Fall 1962).
Ranney, Austin, Illinois Politics. New York: New York University Press, 1960. A short,
    well-executed analysis of contemporary politics in Illinois. Treatment of Negro partici-
    pation is brief, limited to statistical data and comments on leadership.
Roady, Elston E., "The Expansion of Negro Suffrage in Florida," Journal of Negro
    Education 26:297-306 (Summer 1957).
Roady, Elston E., The Negro's Role in American Society. Tallahassee: Florida State
    University, 1958. Extension of Negro participation in politics now demands greater
    efforts by Negro citizens themselves.
Seasholes, Bradbury, and Frederic W. Cleaveland, "Negro Political Participation in Two
    Piedmont Crescent Cities," in F. Stuart Chapin and Shirley F. Weiss, eds., Urban
    Growth Dynamics, New York: Wiley, 1962.
"Socialism and the Negro Movement," Monthly Review, September 1963.
Straetz, Ralph A., PR Politics in Cincinnati. New York: New York University Press, 1958.
    For the effect of proportional representation on Negro politics in that city, see
    especially Chapter 8.
Stroud, Virgil C., "Voter Registration in North Carolina," Journal of Negro Education 30:
    153-155 (Spring 1961).
Taper, Bernard, "A Break With Tradition," New Yorker, June 24, 1965, pp. 58+. Changes
    that have occurred in Tuskegee and in Macon County since most of the obstacles to
    Negro registration have been removed in that voting district.
Travis, Fred, "The Evicted," Progressive 25:10-13 (February 1961). An account of
    pressure by landlords to prevent Negroes of Fayette and Haywood counties in Tennessee
    from voting.
Valien, Preston, "Expansion of Negro Suffrage in Tennessee," Journal of Negro Education
    26:362-368 (Summer 1957).
Vines, Kenneth N., "A Louisiana Parish: Wholesale Purge," in Margaret Price, The Negro
    and the Ballot in the South, Atlanta, Ga.: Southern Regional Council, 1959.
Walker, Jack, "Negro Voting in Atlanta: 1953-1961," Phylon 24:379-387 (Winter 1963).
Wilson, James Q., "How the Northern Negro Uses His Vote," Reporter 22:20-22 (March 31,
    1960).
Wilson, James Q., "Two Negro Politicians: An Interpretation," Midwest Journal of
    Political Science 4:346-369 (November 1960). Congressmen Adam Clayton Powell and
    William L. Dawson.
Wilson, James Q., Negro Politics: The Search for Leadership. Glencoe, Ill.: Free Press,
    1960. A valuable study of contemporary Negro politics in Northern cities, this volume is
    an examination of Negro public life at leadership level, with the main emphasis on
    Chicago. The author comments on the greater aggressiveness of Negroes in New York

than in Chicago, and on the fact that New York Negroes in public office are apt to take stronger stands on race issues.

Wilson, James Q., The Amateur Democrat. Chicago: University of Chicago Press, 1962. Chapter 9 contains discussion of reform-Negro relations.

Wilson, James Q., "The Negro in Politics," Daedalus 94:949-973 (Fall 1965). To the author the possibility of an "effective radical political strategy seems remote"; Negro alliances with labor or white liberals will continue to be ad hoc; Negro politics, qua politics, will achieve limited objectives.

Wilson, James Q., "The Flamboyant Mr. Powell," Commentary 41:31-35 (January 1966).

Wilson, James Q., and Edward C. Banfield, "Public-Regardingness as a Value Premise in Voting," American Political Science Review 58:876-887 (December 1964).

Wood, Robert C., Suburbia. Boston: Houghton Mifflin, 1959. The leading work on suburban politics, it points out the widely varying character of the suburbs and their populations.

Woodward, C. Vann, "The Political Legacy of Reconstruction," Journal of Negro Education 26:231-240 (Summer 1957).

Zinn, Howard, "Registration in Alabama," New Republic 149:11-12 (October 26, 1963).

XII. THE FREEDOM REVOLUTION

In the epilogue to his The Negro Revolt Louis Lomax writes: "Whatever else the Negro is, he is American. Whatever he is to become--integrated, unintegrated, or disintegrated--he will become it in America . . . and whatever future awaits America awaits the Negro; whatever future awaits the Negro, awaits America." It is not only the identification with America that merits attention to these words, but the confrontation of the future. Not a distant future. The cry is "Freedom Now." Martin Luther King, Jr., explains "Why We Cannot Wait."

The literature of protest during the past decade follows certain well-defined themes. There are the polemic and the jeremiad, the tocsin and the challenge. There is the tale of what happened, how it actually was-- the Montgomery story, the diary of a sit-in, the freedom ride, the March on Washington. Then there is the theme of what happens to the people who act, the theme of the new Negro, his sources of strength, his pride, his sense of power, as individual and in community, how the fact of protest molds identity. And as a thread linking all aspects of the Freedom Movement, the question of leaders--who are the leaders, what is the Negro Establishment, how well do the leaders serve their fellows, in the streets, in the courts, in the schools and pulpits, who are to be the leaders in succeeding phases of the struggle. The theme of what the Negro wants perhaps most clearly reflects the revolutionary dynamics of the movement. With each success, sights are raised, with each frustration, determination hardens. Thus the final theme is what next, what the strategy, what the tactics, where the targets. Selma was one portent, Los Angeles another--and quite different--omen.

So far as public utterance is concerned, the federal government is now fully committed to the cause of civil rights, and Negro leaders from all groups are unrelentingly disposed to weigh this commitment on the scales of performance. Thus far the conviction that nonviolent methods are the best methods has been preponderant. The techniques of protest have moved from litigation, through boycotts, sit-ins, freedom rides, voter registration drives, to public dislocation. The goal is equality of opportunity, at every level of American life. At the moment many of the Negro leaders are moving toward involvement in the federal poverty program, and are seeking to capitalize on the Negro's pride in what has been achieved to stimulate programs of self-help, self-improvement, Negro community responsibility. The country has been fortunate that so many Negroes continue to say, with the playwright Ossie Davis, "You can't cut yourself off from the mainstream of American life."

The questions arise as to how the goal is to be achieved, and just what, indeed, it actually means. It has been argued that the emphasis on integration has clouded the true issue of equality, and there are many Negro groups who view any really extensive assimilation into American life with apprehension. James Baldwin has said that what most young Negro intellectuals want is not integration--"It's like being asked to take up residence in a burning building"--but "having society transformed so it's a better thing."

If it is difficult to measure the extent of deep-down Negro racism in America, it is equally difficult to predict to what lengths white resistance may go. On the same day on which Dr. Martin Luther King received the Nobel Peace Prize in Oslo, Norway, United States Commissioner Esther Carter in Meridian, Mississippi, dismissed the charges against nineteen white men accused of conspiracy to murder three civil rights workers in the summer of 1964. Whoever essays to write The Mind of the South for the past decade will find much of his most precise documentation in this and like court actions, in acts of state legislatures, in the accounts in daily newspapers, and in such a volume as Anthony Lewis's Portrait of a Decade.

In the light of such evidence, those Southerners who counsel moderation, acceptance of change, respect for law even when distasteful, loom as heroes. Several of those who have most courageously challenged their Southern neighbors no longer live there. The young lawyer, Charles Morgan, Jr., who arraigned his fellow citizens of Birmingham after the bombing of little Negro girls in Sunday School, has found it advisable to practice his profession elsewhere. Harry Ashmore, the crusading editor of the Greenville, South Carolina, News, and later of the Little Rock, Arkansas, Gazette, has withdrawn to California. Professor James W. Silver whose Mississippi: The Closed Society documents the totalitarian tyranny of that state, subsequently took leave from the University of Mississippi.

Until comparatively recently, the white churches were not notably forward in the support of the Negro drive for equality. Segregated church-affiliated schools, segregated congregations, segregated parishes continued to be the rule--and not only in the South. In his Race and the Renewal of the Church, the Reverend Will D. Campbell charges that by refraining from joining the Negroes' struggle, the Church "has waited too long to carry out its mandate, and to a large part of the world, what we Christians do from here on out really does not matter very much." Clearly much of the response of white religious groups is sparked by a sense of guilt, but the involvement is growing, as reflected not only in increased self-examination but in active participation in the Negroes' cause. To date the large numbers of the clergy and laity of all faiths who took part in the Selma, Alabama, protest march has been the most striking demonstration of this commitment of the churches to the Freedom Revolution.

1. CIVIL RIGHTS AND WRONGS

Abrams, Charles, "Civil Rights in 1956," Commentary 22:101-109 (August 1956). A survey by the then chairman (1955-1959) of the New York State Commission Against Discrimination.

Alfange, Dean, Jr., "'Under Color of Law': Classic and Screws Revisited," Cornell Law Quarterly 47:395 (Spring 1962). The problem of state officers who, in the course of their duties but in violation of state law, deprive others of federal rights.

Anderson, John Weir, Eisenhower, Brownell and the Congress: The Tangled Origin of the Civil Rights Bill of 1956-57. University, Ala.: University of Alabama Pres, 1964. A detailed account of all stages leading up to passage of the Civil Rights Bill of 1957, especially of Brownell's achievement of inclusion of the right of the Justice Department to bring suit on behalf of Negroes denied voting rights.

"Anti-Discrimination Commissions," Race Relations Law Reporter 3:1085 (October 1958).

"Application of Exhaustion of State Remedies to Anti-NAACP Legislation," Southern California Law Review 33:82 (Fall 1959).

Aptheker, Herbert, Soul of the Republic: The Negro Today. New York: Marzani and Munsell, 1964. After attacking racist mythology, the author examines the data on which the 1963 reports of the U.S. Commission on Civil Rights were based.

Avins, Alfred, "Weapons against Discrimination in Public Office," Syracuse Law Review 14:24 (Fall 1962).

Barnett, Richard, and Joseph Garai, Where the States Stand on Civil Rights. New York: Sterling, 1962.

Berger, Morroe, Equality by Statute: Legal Controls over Group Discrimination. New York: Columbia University Press, 1952. An important study based on the New York State Law Against Discrimination. Bibliography.

Berman, Daniel M., A Bill Becomes a Law: The Civil Rights Act of 1960. New York: Macmillan, 1962.

Bickel, Alexander M., "Civil Rights: The Kennedy Record," New Republic 147:11-16 (December 15, 1962).

Bickel, Alexander M., "The Civil Rights Act of 1964," Commentary 38:33-39 (August 1964). A survey of the genesis and final form of the 1964 Act. Anticipating substantial compliance, the author considers Act soundly constitutional, while pointing out certain questions for judicial definition.

Bickel, Alexander M., Politics and the Warren Court. New York: Harper, 1965.

Bloch, Charles P., States Rights: The Law of the Land. Atlanta, Ga.: Harrison, 1958. A Southern view of the legal aspects of the Negro problem.

Bloch, Charles P., "Civil Rights--or Civil Wrongs?" Georgia Bar Journal 22:127 (November 1959).

Bonfield, A. E., "State Civil Rights Statutes: Some Proposals," Iowa Law Review 49:1067 (Summer 1964).

Borinski, Ernst, "The Litigation Curve and the Litigation Filibuster in Civil Rights Cases: A Study of Conflict Between Legally Commanded and Socio-Culturally Accepted Changes in the Negro-White Caste Order in the Southern Community," Social Forces 37:142-147 (December 1958).

Carter, Elmer, "Policies and Practices of Discrimination Commissions," Annals of the American Academy of Political and Social Science 304:62-77 (March 1956).

"A Chronology of Principal Cases on Segregation, 1878-1959," New South 14:8-13 (October 1959). Listed according to type (school, housing, transportation, etc.), together with legal references.

"Civil Disobedience and the Law: A Symposium," American Criminal Law Quarterly 3:11 (Fall 1964). Contributors include J. W. Riehm, M. L. Ernst, H. Brownell.

"Civil Rights," Hearings before the Committee on the Judiciary, July 13-27, 1955. U.S. House of Representatives, 84th Congress, 1st Session, 1955.

"Civil Rights Proposals," Hearings before the Committee on the Judiciary, April 24, July 13, 1956. U.S. Senate, 84th Congress, 2nd Session, 1956.

"Civil Rights," Hearings before Subcommittee No. 5 of the Committee on the Judiciary, February 4-26, 1957. U.S. House of Representatives, 85th Congress, 1st Session, 1957.

"Civil Rights," Hearings before the Committee on Rules, June 20-27, 1956, and May 2-17,

1957. U.S. House of Representatives, 84th Congress, 2nd Session, 1956, and 85th Congress, 1st Session, 1957.

"Civil Rights," Baylor Law Review 13:97 (Winter 1961).

"Civil Rights Act of 1960," Hearings before the Committee on the Judiciary, March 28 and 29, 1960. U.S. Senate, 86th Congress, 2nd Session, 1960.

"Civil Rights Act of 1964," Harvard Law Review 78:684 (January 1963).

The Civil Rights Act of 1964: Operations Manual. Washington, D.C.: Bureau of National Affairs, 1964. Text, analysis, legal history: the definitive text.

"Civil Rights Bill: Pro and Con," Gavel 25:8 (June 1964).

Civil Rights in the Nation's Capital: A Report on a Decade of Progress, New York: National Association of Intergroup Relations Officials, 1959. Pamphlet.

Commission on Law and Social Action of the American Jewish Congress, Assault Upon Freedom of Association. New York: American Jewish Congress, 1957. A study of the Southern attack on the NAACP.

Commission on Law and Social Action of the American Jewish Congress, The Civil Rights and Civil Liberties Decisions of the U.S. Supreme Court: A Summary and Analysis. New York: American Jewish Congress. Published annually.

Countryman, Vern, ed., Discrimination and the Law. Chicago: University of Chicago Press, 1965. What the due processes of the law have achieved in four areas: employment, education, public accommodation, and housing. Discussions of specific cases and general principles in relation to constitutional law against race discrimination.

Cushman, Robert E., Civil Liberties in the United States: A Guide to Current Problems and Experience. Ithaca, N.Y.: Cornell University Press, 1956. Chapter 9 deals with racial discrimination.

"Custom as Law Within the Meaning of the Equal Protection Clause--An Approach to Problems of Racial Discrimination," Rutgers Law Review 17:563 (Spring 1963).

Duplantier, Adrian G., "Matter of Racial Differences and Local Police Legislation," Loyola Law Review 5:1:73-81 (1949). A review of those areas in which police are legally enjoined to enforce segregation.

"Emancipation Proclamation Centennial Symposium," Wayne Law Review 9:401+ (Spring 1963).

"Enforcing Civil Rights," New Republic 149:3-4 (October 26, 1963).

"Equal Protection and the Race Problem," West Virginia Law Review 63:171 (Fall 1960).

"Equality Before the Law: A Symposium on Civil Rights," Northwestern University Law Review 54:330+ (July-August 1959).

Ervin, R. W., "Freedom of Assembly and Racial Demonstrations," Cleveland and Marshall Law Review 10:88 (January 1961).

"The Federal Executive and Civil Rights," New South 16:11-14 (March 1961). Summary of report submitted to President Kennedy by the Southern Regional Council.

Ferguson, Clarence Clyde, Jr., "Civil Rights Legislation, 1964: A Study of Constitutional Resources," Federal Bar Journal 24:102 (Winter 1964). The ultimate test of the Civil Rights Bill is not its strength or weakness but "the completeness of the constitutional response to the present social crisis in America."

Fleming, Harold C., "The Federal Executive and Civil Rights," Daedalus 94:921-948 (Fall 1965).

Franklin, M., "Relation of 5th, 9th and 14th Amendments to the Third Constitution," Howard Law Journal 4:170 (June 1958).

Freund, Paul A., "Civil Rights and the Limits of Law," Buffalo Law Review 14:199 (Winter 1964).

Friedman, Leon, ed., Southern Justice. New York: Pantheon, 1965. Reports of the practices of local police, sheriffs, prosecuting attorneys, trial courts, and juries in the South, as well as of the Federal courts and the F.B.I., all of which demonstrate that the law is made to work against individuals who seek its protection.

Gill, Robert L., "The Role of Five Negro Lawyers in the Civil Rights Struggle," Quarterly Review of Higher Education Among Negroes 31:31-58 (April 1963). Description of general professional position of Negro lawyers and a brief resume of cases in which they were involved.

Greenberg, Jack, "Race Relations and Group Interests in the Law," Rutgers Law Review 13:503 (Spring 1959).

Greenberg, Jack, Race Relations and American Law. New York: Columbia University Press, 1959. The author is special counsel of NAACP Legal and Educational Fund. After chapters on the capacity of law to affect race relations and on leading legal issues (i.e., equal protection of law and due process), he analyzes the basic law dealing with race relations in institutional fields, education, employment, travel, armed forces, etc. Full bibliographical data in appendices.

Griswold, Erwin N., Law and Lawyers in the United States: The Common Law Under Stress. Cambridge: Harvard University Press, 1964. Four lectures, of which the fourth is on "The Problem of Civil Rights--Its Legal Aspects."

Handlin, Oscar, "Civil Rights After Little Rock," Commentary 24:392-396 (November 1957).

Handlin, Oscar, Fire-Bell in the Night: The Crisis in Civil Rights. Boston: Atlantic-Little, Brown, 1964. Assessing, after ten years, the consequences of the 1954 Court decision, the author believes that concentration on segregation as the evil and integration as the good has obscured the real issue, the complex problem of achieving equality under present urban and technological circumstances.

Hannah, J. A., "Civil Rights--A National Challenge," South Dakota Law Review 6:1+ (Spring 1961).

Harris, Robert J., The Quest for Equality: The Constitution, Congress and the Supreme Court. Baton Rouge: Louisiana State University Press, 1960. A history of judicial interpretations of the Fourteenth Amendment. Last two chapters, "The Court Returns to the Constitution" and "The Judicial Burial of Jim Crow," cover period of public school and other segregation cases.

Hartman, Paul, Civil Rights and Minorities. 5th ed. rev., New York: Anti-Defamation League, 1962.

Henderson, George, "Legal Aspirations and Successes in the American Negro Revolution," Journal of Human Relations 13:185-196 (Winter 1965).

Henderson, Thelton, "The Law and Civil Rights: The Justice Department in the South," New University Thought 3:36-45 (February 1964).

Hill, Herbert, and Jack Greenberg, Citizen's Guide to Desegregation. Boston: Beacon, 1955. A study of social and legal change in the United States.

Holzer, Phyllis Tate, and Henry Mark Holzer, "Liberty of Equality," Modern Age 8:134-142 (Spring 1964). "How the Court chose equality" in civil rights cases instead of supporting liberty.

Hopkins, L. L., and J. V. Hopkins, "How Some States Combat Bigotry," Progressive 22:33-35 (February 1958). State commissions on civil rights.

Howe, Mark DeWolfe, "Religion and Race in Public Relations," Buffalo Law Review 8:242 (Winter 1959).

"J. Edgar Hoover and the F.B.I.," Progressive 24:24-30 (February 1960). An Attack on erratic enforcement of civil rights by F.B.I.

Konvitz, Milton R., and Theodore Leskes, A Century of Civil Rights: With a Study of State Law Against Discrimination. New York: Columbia University Press, 1961. Legislation and judicial decisions on the federal level from the Civil War to the present, and the history of state laws and decisions with reference to public accommodations, employment, education, housing, etc.

Leskes, Theodore, "State Segregation Laws," Journal of Intergroup Relations 2:243-251 (Summer 1961).

Leskes, Theodore, "The Federal Executive and Civil Rights," Journal of Intergroup Relations 3:171-178 (Spring 1962).

Leskes, Theodore, "Civil Rights Story: A Year's Review," Wayne Law Review 9:484 (Spring 1963).

Losos, J., "Impact of the 14th Amendment upon Private Law," St. Louis University Law Journal 6:368 (Spring 1961).

Lusky, Louis, "Justice with a Southern Accent: Do Our Federal Courts Need Emancipating?" Harper's Magazine 228:69-70, 73-77 (March 1964).

McCloskey, R. G., "Deeds without Doctrines: Civil Rights in the 1960 Term of the Supreme Court," American Political Science Review 56:71-89 (March 1962). Deals with all civil rights issues as well as with Negro rights.

McKay, Robert B., "The Repression of Civil Rights as an Aftermath of the School Segregation Decision," Howard Law Journal 4:9 (January 1958).

Marshall, Burke, Federalism and Civil Rights. New York: Columbia University Press, 1964. A penetrating, deeply informed examination by the former Assistant Attorney General of efforts of the federal government to secure full civil rights and equality of opportunities for Negroes, together with an appraisal of problems likely to be caused by Southern maladministration of justice.

Miller, Loren, The Petitioners: The Story of the Supreme Court of the United States and the Negro. New York: Pantheon, 1966. Judge Miller analyzes the reversal of the Court's position from the time of its declaring the 1875 Civil Rights Act unconstitutional to its decision affirming the constitutionality of 1964 Civil Rights Act.

Murphy, Walter F., "The Southern Counterattacks: The Anti-NAACP Laws," Western Political Quarterly 12:371-390 (June 1959).

"Negro Defendants and Southern Lawyers: Review in Federal Habeas corpus of Systematic Exclusion of Negroes from Juries," Yale Law Journal 72:559 (January 1963).

Nelson, Gaylord, "The Conservative Compromise," Gavel 25:8 (June 1964). On the Civil Rights Bill of 1964.

"Notre Dame Conference on Civil Rights," Notre Dame Lawyer 35:328-367 (May 1960).

"Notre Dame Conference on Congressional Civil Rights Legislation--A Report," Notre Dame Lawyer 38:430+ (June 1963).

"Permissive Area of State Anti-discrimination Acts," Duquesne University Law Review 1: 231 (Spring 1963).

Pittman, R. C., "Equality Versus Liberty, the Eternal Conflict," American Bar Association Journal 46:873 (August 1960).

Pollak, Louis H., "Ten Years After the Decision," Federal Bar Journal 24:123 (Winter 1964). The author traces the major types of civil rights action covered by Supreme Court decisions and speculates that the Court may, in the future, begin to "probe the constitutional dimensions" of economic discrimination.

Pollitt, Daniel H., "The President's Powers in Areas of Race Relations: An Exploration," North Carolina Law Review 39:238 (April 1961).

"Power of State Legislature to Exclude Negroes from Municipal Corporations," Mississippi Law Journal 31:173 (March 1960).

Rabkin, Sol, "Administrative Rulings on Civil Rights," Journal of Intergroup Relations 2:82-84 (Winter 1960-1961).

"Racial Discrimination and the Role of the State," Michigan Law Review 59:1054 (May 1961).

"Racial Discrimination and State Action under the Fourteenth Amendment," Georgia Bar Journal 25:333 (Fall 1963).

"The Right to Equal Treatment: Administrative Enforcement of Anti-discrimination Legislation," Harvard Law Review 74:526 (January 1961).

Robison, Joseph B., "Protection of Associations from Compulsory Disclosure of Membership," Columbia Law Review 58:614 (May 1958).

Robison, Joseph B., "The Supreme Court and Civil Rights in the 1959-1960 Term," Journal of Intergroup Relations 1:64-70 (Fall 1960).

St. Antoine, T. J., "Color Blindness but not Myopia: A New Look at State Action, Equal Protection, and 'Private' Racial Discrimination," Michigan Law Review 59:993-1016 (May 1961). The question of when private action is state action hinges on "whether a private activity was so invested with the public interest, and so subject to the control of powerful private forces, that effective impairment of fourteenth amendment rights could result."

Shapiro, Harry H., "Limitations in Prosecuting Civil Rights Violations," Cornell Law Quarterly 46:532 (Summer 1961).

Shurman, Howard E., "Senate Rules and the Civil Rights Bill," American Political Science Review 51:955-975 (December 1957). Survey and analysis of role of the filibuster in retarding Civil Rights Bill of 1957.

Silard, John, and Harold Galloway, State Executive Authority to Promote Civil Rights. Washington, D.C.: Potomac Institute, 1963. Study of civil rights measures promulgated by executive branch of state governments.

Sitton, Claude, "When a Southern Negro Goes to Court," New York Times Magazine, January 7, 1962.

"State Involvement in Private Discrimination under the Fourteenth Amendment," Louisiana Law Review 21:433 (February 1961).

"State Universities and the Discriminatory Fraternity: A Constitutional Analysis," UCLA Law Review 8:169 (January 1961).

"Symposium on Civil Rights," Federal Bar Journal 24:1+ (Winter 1964). Three main areas explored: political rights, property rights, employment rights.

Thompson, Daniel C., "The Role of the Federal Courts in the Changing Status of Negroes Since World War II," Journal of Negro Education 30:94-101 (Spring 1961).

To Secure These Rights. Washington, D.C.: GPO, 1947. Report of President's Committee on Civil Rights.

Ulmer, S. S., "Supreme Court Behavior in Racial Exclusion Cases: 1935-1960," American Political Science Review 56:325-330 (June 1962). Chiefly Negro exclusion from state jury systems.

United States Commission on Civil Rights, Law Enforcement: A Report on Equal Protection in the South. Washington, D.C.: GPO, 1965. Three main sections consider Denials of Constitutional Rights, Remedies, and a Conclusion, with recommendations for criminal remedies, civil remedies, and executive action. In a separate statement Dean Erwin N. Griswold of the Harvard Law School points out that the need for federal action is caused by the South's flagrant flouting of justice, and that the Negro has taken to protest in the streets because he knows any appeal to the courts and to officers of the law would be fruitless. A damning indictment of a whole society.

United States Commission on Civil Rights, Report, 1959. Washington, D.C.: GPO, 1959.

United States Commission on Civil Rights, Report, 1961. Washington, D.C.: GPO, 1961.

United States Commission on Civil Rights, The 50 States Report. Washington, D.C.: GPO, 1961. Cites the "condonation of or connivance in private violence" on the part of Southern police officers.

United States Commission on Civil Rights, Report, 1963. Washington, D.C.: GPO, 1963.

Van Alstyne, W. W., and K. L. Karst, "State Action," Stanford Law Review 14:3 (December 1961). Examination of the relation between state action and the national interest in racial equality in all areas, education, employment, suffrage, freedom from brutality.

Vines, K. N., "Southern State Supreme Courts and Race Relations," Western Political Quarterly 18:5-18 (March 1965).

Warren, Earl, "The Law and the Future," Fortune 52:106-107+ (November 1955).

Williams, Franklin H., "California's New Civil Rights Tool," Christian Century 77:720-721 (June 15, 1960). Constitutional rights section in State Justice Department.

Wilson, R. B., "Massive Insistence or Massive Resistance? The Judicial Administration of the Civil Rights Revolution," George Washington Law Review 33:827 (April 1965).

Wollett, Donald H., "Race Relations," Louisiana Law Review 21:85-108 (December 1960). A survey of action on interracial relations taken by Louisiana legislature during 1960, namely, 35 acts and 4 resolutions for constitutional amendments, covering everything from cohabitation to public welfare.

Woodward, C. Vann, "The Great Civil Rights Debate," Commentary 24:283-291 (October 1957). Civil Rights Act of 1957.

2. PROTEST: THEORY AND PRACTICE

Ahmann, Mathew, ed., The New Negro: A Symposium. Notre Dame, Ind.: Fides Press, 1962.

Aptheker, Herbert, Toward Negro Freedom. New York: New Century, 1956.

Baldwin, James, "The Dangerous Road Before Martin Luther King," Harper's Magazine 222:33-42 (February 1961). Baldwin doubts that Dr. King's role in the Negro movement of protest will continue to be of as great importance as in the past.

Baldwin, James, "A Negro Assays the Negro Mood," New York Times Magazine, March 12, 1961.

Baldwin, James, The Fire Next Time. New York: Dial, 1963; New York: Dell, Delta paperbacks. Powerful jeremiad, apocalyptic warning, and call to repentance, this volume consists of a "Letter to My Nephew on the One Hundredth Anniversary of the Emancipation," and "Letter from a Region of My Mind," including an examination of the Black Muslims.

Belfrage, Sally, "Danville on Trial," New Republic 149:11-12 (November 2, 1963). Report on racial conflict in Danville, Virginia.

Belfrage, Sally, Freedom Summer. New York: Viking, 1965. The author's experience as a
    SNCC worker with the summer project in Greenwood, Mississippi.
Bell, Daniel, "Plea for a 'New Phase in Negro Leadership,'" New York Times Magazine,
    May 31, 1964.
Bennett, Lerone, Jr., "What Sit-Downs Mean to America," Ebony 15:35-38+ (June 1960).
Bennett, Lerone, Jr., The Negro Mood. Chicago: Johnson, 1964; Ballantine paperback, 1965.
    Five essays by the senior editor of Ebony which examine the "mood" of the Negro revolt
    both on the streets and in the mind. The author's analysis of the Black Establishment and
    its responses to the world of white power is especially penetrating.
Bennett, Lerone, Jr., Confrontation: Black and White. Chicago: Johnson, 1965. An account of
    the steadily growing intensity of the Negro-white confrontation, both during America's
    past and in the present Freedom Revolution.
Boggs, James, "The Black Revolt," Monthly Review 15:504-510 (January 1964).
Boggs, James, The American Revolution. New York: Monthly Review Press, 1964. The
    author, a Negro radical, starts with the premise that the American power elite is evil,
    that the Negro has nothing to hope for from the CIO-AFL or the NAACP, and that the
    Negro must proceed by means of economic and political power.
Booker, Simeon, Black Man's America. Englewood Cliffs, N.J.: Prentice-Hall, 1964. The
    author is a newspaperman of wide experience whose account of observed facts is lively
    and interesting.
Braden, Anne, ed., "The Southern Freedom Movement in Perspective," Monthly Review,
    July-August 1965. Entire issue.
Brink, William, and Louis Harris, The Negro Revolution in America. New York: Simon &
    Schuster, 1964. Based on surveys made by Newsweek in 1963 for special reports in that
    magazine on July 29, 1963, and October 21, 1963. Expanded to book form, the present
    volume analyzes the two surveys, the first of the Negro's opinions and attitudes, and
    second of what whites think of Negroes.
Bunche, Ralph, "A Critical Analysis of the Tactics and Programs of Minority Groups,"
    Journal of Negro Education 4:308-320 (July 1953). Thesis: the only hope for the better-
    ment of a minority group is their joining with the underprivileged masses of the domi-
    nant group. "Their basic interests are identical and so must be their programs and
    tactics."
Burns, W. Haywood, The Voices of Negro Protest in America. New York: Oxford Uni-
    versity Press, 1963. The nature of the relationship among legal-judicial, nonviolent, and
    radical-separatist forms of Negro protest in the United States.
Bushnell, Paul E., "Passive Insistence--It's Principles and Procedures, It's Promise and
    Peril," Chapel and College, Fall 1960, pp. 4-12.
Carawan, Guy, and Candie Carawan, We Shall Overcome: Songs of the Southern Freedom
    Movement. New York: Oak, 1963.
Carter, Hodding, III, "The Young Negro is a New Negro," New York Times Magazine, May
    1, 1960. On the militancy of the new generation of Negroes.
"Citizens in Protest," Howard Law Journal 6:187 (June 1960).
Clark, Kenneth B., "The New Negro in the North," in Mathew Ahmann, ed., The New Negro,
    Notre Dame, Ind.: Fides Press, 1962. The author discusses the ways in which the
    Northern Negro has used his political power to exert pressure on the white South and the
    reasons that tend to lead Northern Negroes to reject the nonviolent approach in favor of
    more extreme philosophies.
Clark, Kenneth B., The Negro Protest. Boston: Beacon, 1963. Conversations conducted by
    Dr. Clark with James Baldwin, Malcolm X, and Martin Luther King on Boston's WGBH-
    TV station for National Educational Television.
Clark, Kenneth B., "The Civil Rights Movement: Momentum and Organization," Daedalus
    95:239-267 (Winter 1966).
Clarke, Jacquelyne, "Standard Operational Procedures in Tragic Situations," Phylon 22:
    318-328 (Winter 1961). A Study of procedures followed by civil rights organizations in
    Alabama in 1959. The techniques in order of preference were nonviolent protest, mass
    demonstrations, boycotting, legal-judicial measures.
Clarke, Jacquelyne, These Rights They Seek: A Comparison of Goals and Techniques of
    Local Civil Rights Organizations. Washington, D.C.: Public Affairs Press, 1962. A study
    of three civil rights groups in Alabama.

Clayton, Edward T., ed., The SCLC Story. Atlanta, Ga.: Southern Christian Leadership
    Conference, 1964. Historical and descriptive story told in words and pictures.
Coles, Robert, "The Impact of Project Freedom on Mississippi," Boston Sunday Herald,
    September 6, 1964.
Coles, Robert, "Children and Racial Demonstrations," American Scholar 34:78-92 (Winter
    1964-1965).
Constable, John, "Negro Student Protests Challenge N [orth] C [arolina] Leaders," New
    South 15:3-10 (March 1960).
Cook, Samuel DuBois, "Revolution and Responsibility," New South 19:8-12 (February 1964).
    On the responsibility of the Negro revolution to follow a nonviolent, nonracist course.
Cothran, Tilman C., "Potential and Responsibility for National, World Leadership," New
    South 15:3-8 (June 1960).
Daniel, Bradford, ed., Black, White, and Gray: Twenty-one Points of View on the Race
    Question. New York: Sheed and Ward, 1964. Views of a wide range of figures from Orval
    Faubus to Roy Wilkins.
Danzig, David, "The Meaning of Negro Strategy," Commentary 37:41-46 (February 1964).
    Remarking on the emergence of an organized Negro community in a number of cities who
    represent and negotiate Negro interests, the author sees rights of individuals coming to
    rest on the status of the group, with the possibility that group self-interest and Negro
    solidarity may contribute to reshaping goals.
The Day They Changed their Minds. New York: NAACP, 1960. Account of how demonstra-
    tions developed in 1960.
Delavan, V., et al., "Why They Sat In," Social Progress 51:3-46 (February 1961). Entire
    issue.
"The Demonstrations in the South," New University Thought 1:21-27 (Spring 1960). A
    catalogue of places and dates.
DeVree, Charlotte, "The Young Negro Rebels," Harper's Magazine 222:133-138 (October
    1961).
Dienstfrey, Ted, "A Conference on the Sit-Ins," Commentary 29:524-528 (June 1960).
"Direct Action in the South," New South 18: 1-32 (October-November 1963). Entire issue.
    Covers such topics as sit-ins, freedom riders, the ballot, civil disobedience, and events
    in Albany, Ga., and Birmingham, Ala. A Southern Regional Council report.
Doddy, Hurley, "The 'Sit-In' Demonstration and the Dilemma of the Negro College Presi-
    dent," Journal of Negro Education 30:1-3 (Winter 1961).
Dorman, Michael, We Shall Overcome: A Reporter's Eyewitness Account of the Year of
    Racial Strife and Triumph. New York: Delacorte, 1964. A Scripps-Howard reporter
    writes of 1962-1963.
Doss, George A., Jr., "Homegrown Movement in Macon," New South 18:3-10 (April 1963).
Dunbar, Ernest, "The Negro in America Today," Look 26:25-36 (April 10, 1962).
Dunbar, Leslie W., "Reflections on the Latest Reform of the South," Phylon 22:249-257
    (Fall 1961). Sit-ins as a social movement.
Dykeman, Wilma, and James Stokely, "'Sit Down Chillun, Sit Down!'" Progressive 24:8-13
    (June 1960). The Authors assert that the "deeper meaning of the 'sit-in' demonstrations
    is to show that segregation cannot be maintained in the South short of continuous coertion."
Ehle, John, The Free Men. New York: Harper, 1965. Account of attempts to integrate
    Chapel Hill, N.C., in 1963 and 1964, which vividly reveals the strains within the
    community and the failures of leadership.
Farmer, James, "'I Will Keep My Soul,'" Progressive 25:21-22 (November 1961). On the
    first Freedom Ride.
Farmer, James, Freedom--When? New York: Random House, 1966. About the role of
    CORE in the civil rights movement.
Feagans, Janet, "Voting, Violence and Walkout in McComb, Mississippi," New South 16:3-4+
    (October 1961). On the SNCC voter registration drive in McComb County.
Feinstein, Otto, and Gabriel Breton, "Civil Rights: An Analysis," New University Thought
    3:3-7 (September-October 1963). The current status of Negro civil rights.
Feinstein, Otto, and Gabriel Breton, "Civil Rights: A Political Strategy," New University
    Thought 3:3-6 (December 1963-January 1964).
Fey, Harold E., "Revolution Without Hatred," Christian Century 80:1094-1095 (September
    11, 1963). March on Washington.

Fields, Uriah J., The Montgomery Story: The Unhappy Effects of the Montgomery Bus Boycott. New York: Exposition Press, 1959. According to the minister of the Bell Street Baptist Church, the bus boycott in Montgomery, Ala., did more harm than good, the people were betrayed by their leaders (Martin Luther King), and R. D. Abernathy, of the First Baptist Church, got more than his share of funds raised to repair bombed-out churches.

Fischer, John, "What the Negro Needs Most: A First Class Citizens' Council," Harper's Magazine 225:12+ (July 1962).

Fischer, John, "A Small Band of Practical Heroes," Harper's Magazine 227:16+ (October 1963). Account of the work of SNCC in Mississippi, especially in voter registration.

Fleming, Harold C., "The Changing South and Sit-Ins," Journal of Intergroup Relations 2: 56-60 (Winter 1960-1961).

"For Jobs and Freedom: Three Views of the Washington March," Midwest Quarterly 5:99-116 (Winter 1964).

Friedman, Murray, "The White Liberal Retreat," Atlantic 211:42-46 (January 1963). The diminution of the role of the white liberal, whether because of his recoiling from increased Negro militancy or because of aggressive Negro assumption of leadership.

Fuller, H. W., "Rise of the Negro Militant," Nation 197:138-140 (September 14, 1963).

Garfinkel, Herbert, When Negroes March: The March on Washington Movement in the Organizational Politics for FEPC. Glencoe, Ill.: Free Press, 1959.

Goodman, Paul, "The Children of Birmingham," Commentary 36:242-244 (September 1963).

Graham, Frank, "Students 'Standing Up' For the American Dream," New South 15:7-8 (July-August 1960).

Gurin, David, "The Winter Revolution," The Second Coming 1:12-15 (January 1965). On the Harlem rent strike.

Handlin, Oscar, "Is Integration the Answer?" Atlantic 213:49-54 (March 1964).

Handlin, Oscar, "The Goals of Integration," Daedalus 95:268-286 (Winter 1966). An examination and critique of long-term goals of the Negro freedom movement.

Hansberry, Lorraine, The Movement: Documentary of a Struggle for Equality. New York: Simon & Schuster, 1964.

Hardwick, Elizabeth, "Selma, Alabama: The Charms of Goodness," New York Review, April 22, 1965. The author describes the "moral justice of the Civil Rights movement, the responsible program of the leaders, the tragic murderous rage of the white people."

Hare, Nathan, "Integrated Southern Town: How a Small Southern Town Made Integration Work," Phylon 22:180-187 (Summer 1961).

Hare, Nathan, "Rebels Without a Name," Phylon 23:271-277 (Fall 1962). On the terms "colored" and "Negro."

Haselden, Kyle, and Whitney M. Young, Jr., "Should There be 'Compensation' for Negroes?" New York Times Magazine, October 6, 1963. Mr. Young, executive secretary of the Urban League, and Dr. Haselden, managing editor of the Christian Century, present arguments for and against a program of "compensation."

Hayes, Charles L., "The Sit-In Demonstrations--In Retrospect," Interracial Review 35:147-148 (June 1962).

Henry, Anthony, "This Is How We Did It or Profile of a Successful Sit-In," The Intercollegian, October 1960. Account of a student sit-in in Austin, Texas.

Hentoff, Nat, The New Equality. New York: Viking, 1964; rev. with new material, Compass, 1965. Firm, factual, sober of tone and objectively detached in manner, the author's program calls for a revolutionary reordering of society in the areas of unemployment, education, and housing.

Hines, Ralph H., and James E. Pierce, "Negro Leadership After the Social Crisis: An Analysis of Leadership Changes in Montgomery, Alabama," Phylon 26:162-172 (Spring 1965).

Holt, Len, An Act of Conscience. Boston: Beacon, 1965. Account of Danville, Virginia's, "Summer of Protest."

Holt, Len, The Summer That Didn't End. New York: Morrow, 1965. How the summer project continued to operate in Mississippi.

Howe, Florence, "Mississippi's Freedom Schools: The Politics of Education," Harvard Educational Review 35:141-160 (Spring 1965).

Hughes, Langston, Fight for Freedom: The Story of the NAACP. New York: Norton, 1962.

Huie, William Bradford, Three Lives for Mississippi. New York: Trident Press, 1965.
About the murder of the civil rights workers, Michael Schwerner, James Chaney, and
Andy Goodman.

Isaacs, Harold R., "Integration and the Negro Mood," Commentary 34:487-497 (December
1962).

James, Beauregard, The Road to Birmingham. New York: Book Awards, 1964.

Johnson, Haynes, Dusk at the Mountain: The Negro, the Nation, and the Capital; A Report on
Problems and Progress. Garden City, N.Y.: Doubleday, 1963. Developed from a series of
prizewinning articles on the Negro by a Washington, D.C. newspaperman.

Johnson, John H., "A Challenge to Negro Leadership," address to the National Urban
League, New York, September 7, 1960. By the president of the Johnson Publishing
Company of Chicago.

Jones, Charles, "SNCC: Non-violence and Revolution," New University Thought 3:8-19
(September-October 1963).

Jones, Hubert E., "STOP--A Method of Protest," Industry (Massachusetts) 28:14+ (July
1963).

Kahn, Tom, "The 'New Negro' and the New Moderation," New Politics 1:61-76 (Fall 1961).

Kahn, Tom, "Problems of the Negro Movement: A Special Report," Dissent 11:108-138
(Winter 1964). Thorough review of the civil rights movement as of date, and of the
problem it faces in developing new tactics and fresh approaches.

Kempton, Murray, "A. Philip Randolph," New Republic 149:15-17 (July 6, 1963).

Killens, John Oliver, Black Man's Burden. New York: Trident, 1966. The burden is the
prejudiced white man.

King, Marion, "Reflection on the Death of a Child," New South 18:9-10 (February 1963).
Mrs. Slater King, of Albany, Ga., on the loss of a child through miscarriage resulting
from police treatment during a racial incident.

King, Martin Luther, Jr., "Facing the Challenge of a New Age," Phylon 18:25-34 (Spring
1957).

King, Martin Luther, Jr., "The Current Crisis in Race Relations," New South 13:8-12
(March 1958).

King, Martin Luther, Jr., Stride Toward Freedom: The Montgomery Story. New York:
Harper, 1958. The impressive account of the Montgomery bus boycott, which catapulted
Dr. King into leadership of Negro protest.

King, Martin Luther, Jr., "The Burning Truth in the South," Progressive 24:8-10 (May
1960). The sit-ins as a "demand for respect," combining direct action with nonviolence.

King, Martin Luther, Jr., "The Time for Freedom Has Come," New York Times Magazine,
September 10, 1961.

King, Martin Luther, Jr., "Love, Law and Civil Disobedience," New South 16:3-11
(December 1961).

King, Martin Luther, Jr., "The Luminous Promise," Progressive 26:34-37 (December
1962). Reflections on the 100th anniversary of the Emancipation Proclamation.

King, Martin Luther, Jr., "Letter from Birmingham Jail," Christian Century 80:767-773
(June 12, 1963). Dr. King's widely published answer to 8 Alabama clergymen who called
for an end of Negro demonstrations. He directly challenged the churchmen to act by
Christian principles.

King, Martin Luther, Jr., Strength to Love. New York: Harper, 1963.

King, Martin Luther, Jr., Why We Can't Wait. New York: Harper, 1964. This work is among
the most vigorous and cogent statements of Dr. King's philosophy of nonviolence. He
stresses the important gains Negroes have made by nonviolent demonstrations, the most
significant being their new sense of dignity and of power.

King, Martin Luther, Jr., "Let Justice Roll Down," Nation 200:269-273 (March 15, 1965).

Kotler, Neil, "SNCC Strikes the Landlords: A Report from Washington, D,C.," Dissent 11:
328-332 (Summer 1964).

Ladd, Everett C., Jr., "Agony of the Negro Leader," Nation 198:88-91 (September 7, 1964).
"Negro leadership in the United States has been, and remains, issue leadership, and the
one issue that matters is race advancement." The author has in preparation Negro
Political Leadership in the South, to be published by the Cornell University Press.

Lees, Hannah, "The Not-Buying Power of Philadelphia's Negroes," Reporter 24:33-35 (May
11, 1961). A description of the "selective patronage program" organized and run by 400
ministers.

Lewis, Anthony, and The New York Times, Portrait of a Decade: The Second American Revolution. New York: Random House, 1964. A superb portrait of the decade 1954-1964. The author intersperses his narrative with excerpts from articles and news stories from the Times to give a remarkably complete account of all aspects of the struggle. Especially forceful in its impact is the presentation in the last chapter of the corruption of justice and cynical disregard of law in certain areas of the South.

Lincoln, C. Eric, "Anxiety, Fear, and Integration," Phylon 21:278-285 (Fall 1960). Develops theme that "Ours is an era characterized by fear and tension, loneliness and anxiety," and compares events in Birmingham, Ala., and Budapest at time of Hungarian revolt.

Lincoln, C. Eric, "The Strategy of a Sit-In," Reporter 24:20-23 (January 5, 1961).

Lissovoy, Peter de, "Freedom Wars in Georgia," Dissent 11:296-302 (Summer 1964). Author is a full-time worker (white) in the freedom movement out of Albany, Ga.

Lomax, Louis E., "The Negro Revolt Against 'The Negro Leaders,'" Harper's Magazine 220:41-48 (June 1960).

Lomax, Louis E., The Reluctant African. New York: Harper, 1960. Deeply sympathetic with African impatience to be free, Lomax's personal reaction to the racial violence encountered there was that it was the most dangerous way of spreading hate, that even African freedom is not worth the price of continued racist violence. It is in this sense that he calls himself "the reluctant African."

Lomax, Louis E., "The Unpredictable Negro," New Leader 44:3-4 (June 5, 1961).

Lomax, Louis E., The Negro Revolt. New York: Harper, 1962; Signet, 1963. An important statement concerning the background, the forces, and the events that have shaped the Negro revolt.

Long, Herman H., "The Challenge to Negro Leadership," Journal of Intergroup Relations 1: 75-79 (Spring 1960).

Long, Herman H., "Marginal Man and New Negro Identity," New South 17:6-12 (April 1962). On the need for a new Negro leadership that will understand how to use Negro power in new tasks.

Long, Margaret, "March on Washington," New South 18:3-17 (September 1963).

Lubell, Samuel, "Racial War in the South," Commentary 24:113-118 (August 1957).

Lubell, Samuel, White and Black: Test of a Nation. New York: Harper, 1964. As always astute and hardheaded, Lubell proceeds from the contention that "A totally unrealistic, nightmarish concept has been built up by both Negroes and Whites about what can be accomplished through desegregation." He discusses residential mobility, education, crime, job restrictions, political action.

Lynd, Staughton, "Fredom Riders to the Polls," Nation 195:29-32 (July 28, 1962).

Lynd, Staughton, and Roberta Yancy, "Southern Negro Students: The College and the Movement," Dissent 11:39-45 (Winter 1964). The paternalism and restrictive regulations of most Negro colleges are contrasted with the stimulation and liberation of spirit and responsibility generated by "the movement."

McCord, Charles, "The Anatomy of a Registration Drive: A Success Story from New Orleans," Interracial Review 35:122-125 (May 1962).

McCord, William, Mississippi: The Long Hot Summer. New York: Norton, 1965. Probably the best treatment of the summer project, particularly in its realistic appraisal of future prospects.

McDermott, John, "Wade-In Witness at Rainbow Beach," Interracial Review 35:146-147 (June 1962). In Chicago.

Mabee, Carleton, "Prepared for Arrest," Christian Century 78:52-53 (January 11, 1961). Howard University students demonstrate.

Mabee, Carleton, "Evolution of Non-violence: Two Decades of Sit-ins," Nation 193:78-81 (August 12, 1961).

Mabee, Carleton, "Freedom Schools, North and South," Reporter 31:30-32 (September 10, 1964).

Margolis, Joseph, "The American Negro and the Issue of Segregation," American Scholar 28:73-79 (Winter 1958-1959).

"Martin Luther King, Jr., Man of the Year," Time, January 3, 1964.

Mayer, Milton, "The Last Time I Saw Selma," Progressive 29:18-21 (May 1965).

Mayfield, Julian, "Challenge to Negro Leadership: The Case of Robert Williams," Commentary 31:297-305 (April 1961). Cf. Robert Williams, Negroes with Guns.

Meier, August, "Boycotts of Segregated Street Cars, 1894-1909--A Research Note," Phylon 18:296-297 (Fall 1957).

Meier, August, "The Successful Sit-Ins in a Border City: A Study in Social Causation," Journal of Intergroup Relations 2:230-237 (Summer 1961).

Meier, August, "New Currents in the Civil Rights Movement," New Politics 2:7-32 (Summer 1963).

Meier, August, "Negro Protest Movements and Organizations," Journal of Negro Education 32:437-450 (Fall 1963).

Millard, Thomas L., "The Negro and Social Protest," Journal of Negro Education 32:92-98 (Winter 1963).

Miller, Loren, "Freedom Now--But What Then?" Nation 196:539-542 (June 29, 1963).

Miller, Robert William, Nonviolence. New York: Association Press, 1964. Background and ideology of the nonviolent Negro movement.

Mississippi Black Paper: Statements and Notarized Affidavits. New York: Random House, 1965. Collection of affidavits assembled as evidence for a suit against Sheriff Rainey and other state officials.

Nash, Diane, "Inside the Sit-Ins and Freedom Rides," in Mathew Ahmann, ed., The New Negro, Notre Dame, Ind.: Fides Press, 1962. Personal experience of a participant, together with affirmation of her belief in nonviolence.

"The Negro Movement: Where Shall It Go Now?" Dissent 11:279-295 (Summer 1964). Jobs and political action stressed as objectives, acts of social dislocation considered useful only when directed to specific ends.

Nelson, William Stuart, "Do We Dare to Break the Law?" Interracial Review 35:150-151 (June 1962).

New South 17:1-18 (July-August, 1961). Issue on Freedom Rides.

Newfield, Jack, "The Question of SNCC," Nation 201:38-40 (July 19, 1965). Description and prognosis, with discussion of SNCC prospects in urban centers.

Oppenheimer, Martin, "Current Negro Protest Activities and the Concept of Social Movement," Phylon 24:154-159 (Summer 1963).

Parenti, Michael, "White Anxiety and the Negro Revolt," New Politics 3:35-39 (Winter 1964).

Peck, James, Cracking the Color Line: Non-Violent Direct Action Methods of Eliminating Racial Discrimination. New York: CORE, 1960.

Peck, James, Freedom Ride. New York: Simon & Schuster, 1962. By the editor of Corelator, publication of CORE, who participated in the ride from Washington to New Orleans.

Petrof, John V., "The Effect of Student Boycotts Upon the Purchasing Habits of Negro Families in Atlanta, Georgia," Phylon 24:266-270 (Fall 1963).

Phillips, W. M., Jr., "The Boycott: A Negro Community in Conflict," Phylon 22:24-30 (Spring 1961).

Price, Margaret, Toward a Solution of the Sit-In Controversy. Atlanta, Ga.: Southern Regional Council, 1960, mimeo. Analysis of methods used to solve sit-in problems in several cities.

Proudfoot, Merrill, Diary of a Sit-In. Chapel Hill: University of North Carolina Press, 1962.

Record, Wilson, "Intellectuals in Social and Racial Movements," Phylon 15:231-242 (Fall 1954). Negro intellectuals have a specific, obvious, and constant grievance, whereas white intellectuals are only occasionally involved with concrete, well-defined grievances. Whites can choose whether to become involved, Negroes cannot.

Reed, Roy, "The Deacons, Too, Ride by Night," New York Times Magazine August 15, 1965. On the Deacons for Defense and Justice, organized in Jonesboro, La., in 1964.

"The Revolt of Negro Youth," Ebony 15:36+ (May 1960). The Negro student movement as a new force in the civil rights struggle.

Rodell, Fred, "Our Languid Liberals," Progressive 21:5-7 (March 1957). The Democratic party and the Negro.

Rose, Stephen C., "Test for Nonviolence," Christian Century 80:714-716 (May 29, 1963). Martin Luther King and Birmingham.

Rostow, Eugene, "The Freedom Riders and the Future," Reporter 24:18-21 (June 22, 1961).

Rovere, Richard, "Negro Crisis, Letter from the American Kitchen," Encounter 31:3-7 (August 1963).

Rowan, Carl T., "Are Negroes Ready for Equality?" Saturday Evening Post 233:21+ (October 22, 1960).

Rustin, Bayard, "From Protest to Politics: The Future of the Civil Rights Movement," Commentary 39:25-31 (February 1965).

St. James, Warren D., The National Association for the Advancement of Colored People: A Case Study in Pressure Groups. New York: Exposition Press, 1958. Most useful portions are the addenda: NAACP constitutions, bibliography, and summary of cases.

Samuels, Gertrude, "Five Angry Men Speak Their Minds," New York Times Magazine, May 17, 1964. Negro leaders warn that, even after the Civil Rights Bill passes, the Negro will still be a long way from equality and that he intends to attain it: Roy Wilkins, Adam Clayton Powell, James Farmer, Bayard Rustin, Milton Galamison.

Saunders, Doris E., The Day They Marched. Chicago: Johnson, 1963. March on Washington, briefly described, with illustrations.

Searles, Ruth, and J. Allen Williams, Jr., "Negro College Students' Participation in Sit-Ins," Social Forces 40:215-220 (March 1962).

Sibley, Mulford Q., ed., The Quiet Battle: Writings on the Theory and Practice of Non-violent Resistance. Garden City, N.Y.: Doubleday, 1963.

Silberman, Charles E., Crisis in Black and White. New York: Random House, 1964. The problem of acting with justice toward the Negro is "the greatest moral imperative of our time," and "the question. . .is no longer what to do, but whether there is still time in which to do it."

Simpson, George E., "Recent Political Developments in Race Relations," Phylon 19:208-221 (Summer 1958). As a result of the growing impact of Negro protest action in areas of housing, education, public accommodations.

"Sit-In, Other Techniques Are Likely to Continue," New South 16:3-5 (June 1961).

Sit-Ins, the Students Report. New York: CORE, 1960.

Smith, Charles U., "The Sit-Ins and the New Negro Student," Journal of Intergroup Relations 2:223-229 (Summer 1961). An account of civil rights movements at Florida Agriculture and Mechanical University, Tallahassee, by the chairman of the Department of Sociology.

Smith, Charles U., and Lewis M. Killian, Tallahasee, Florida: The Tallahassee Bus Protest. New York: Anti-Defamation League, 1958.

Smith, Howard K., "Luxury We Cannot Afford," New South 12:6-9 (October 1957). That is, another Little Rock. CBS broadcast of September 29, 1957.

Smith, Lillian, "The Winner Names the Age," Progressive 21:6-10 (August 1957). The need for individual commitment and the Negro revolution.

Sullivan, Terry, "What is it Like to be a Freedom Rider?" Interracial Review 35:143-145 (June 1962).

Sutherland, Elizabeth, ed., Letters From Mississippi. New York: McGraw-Hill, 1965. By white "visitors" to Mississippi in 1964 summer project.

Taper, Bernard, "A Reporter at Large: A Break with Tradition," New Yorker July 24, 1965. A report of the advances made in voter registration and in school desegregation in Macon County, Alabama, since the Supreme Court decision in Gomillion vs. Lightfoot.

Thompson, Daniel C., The Case for Integration. Atlanta, Ga.: Southern Regional Council, 1961.

Thompson, Era Bell, and Herbert Nipson, White on Black. Chicago: Johnson, 1963. Twenty-two pieces from Ebony by a variety of white figures, from Bishop Oxnam to Mike Jacobs.

Thurman, Howard, Disciplines of the Spirit. New York: Harper, 1963. The technique of nonviolence in the revolutionary struggle of the Negro.

Toby, Jackson, "Bombing in Nashville: A Jewish Center and the Desegregation Struggle," Commentary 25:385-389 (May 1958).

Turner, John B., and Whitney M. Young, Jr., "Who Has the Revolution or Thoughts on the Second Reconstruction," Daedalus 94:1148-1163 (Fall 1965).

Valien, Preston, "The Montgomery Bus Protest as a Social Movement," in Jitsuichi Masuoka and Preston Valien, eds., Race Relations: Problems and Theory, Chapel Hill: University of North Carolina Press, 1961.

Vanderburgh, Charles, "A Draftee's Diary from the Mississippi Front," Harper's Magazine 228:37-45 (February 1964).

Vander Zanden, James W., "The Non-Violent Movement Against Segregation," American Journal of Sociology 68:544-550 (March 1963).

Vose, Clement E., "Litigation as a Form of Pressure Group Politics," Annals of the American Academy of Political and Social Science 319:20-31 (September 1958).

Wakefield, Dan, Revolt in the South. New York: Grove—Evergreen, 1960.

Walker, Wyatt Tee, "Albany, Failure or First Step," New South 18:3-8 (June 1963).

Walter, Norman W., "The Walking City: A History of the Montgomery Boycott," Negro History Bulletin vol. 20, October, November 1956; February, April 1957. The continued story of the Montgomery bus boycott.

Warren, Richard L., "Birmingham: Brinkmanship in Race Relations," Christian Century 79: 689-690 (May 30, 1962).

Warren, Robert Penn, Who Speaks for the Negro. New York: Random House, 1965. Based on interviews with Negroes of every social status and from many regions of the country, most effective in its refraction of images and impressions as they presented themselves to the novelist's eye and ear.

"Washington March Is 'Played By Ear,'" Editor and Publisher 96:11 (August 24, 1963). Press coverage for the March on Washington.

Watts, Marzette, "Sit-ins and Pickets: The Students Move in Montgomery," New University Thought 1:16-20 (Spring 1960).

Weaver, Robert C., "The NAACP Today," Journal of Negro Education 29:421-425 (Fall 1960).

Westfeldt, Wallace, Settling a Sit-In. Nashville, Tenn.: Nashville Community Relations Conference, 1960.

Westin, Alan F., ed., Freedom Now! The Civil Rights Struggle in America. New York: Basic Books, 1964. An anthology of 51 brief articles on "the moral dimension of the civil rights struggle." The volume constitutes a sustained dialogue on the management and methods of the civil rights struggle.

White, Lewis W., "A Current Lament," New South 18:12-13 (May 1963). Reflections of a Negro teacher in Birmingham on the need for more forceful and realistic leadership.

Wilkins, Roy, "Freedom Tactics for 18,000,000," New South 19:3-7 (February 1964).

Williams, Robert, Negroes with Guns. New York: Marzani & Munsell, 1964. The author, a Negro radical now in Cuba, returned to Monroe, N.C., from Marine Corps in 1955. He attempted to organize the Negroes, and came to the conclusion that Negroes should meet violence with violence. He insists, however, that he favors nonviolence when it works.

Wilson, C. E., "The Pilgrimage: A Reappraisal of August 28," Liberator 3:4-7 (October 1963).

Wright, Marion A., "The Right to Protest," New South 17:6-13 (February 1962).

Wright, Stephen, "The New Negro in the South," in Mathew Ahmann, ed., The New Negro, Notre Dame, Ind.: Fides Press, 1962. The author, president of Fisk University, characterizes the "new" Negro as increasingly aggressive, self-sacrificing, and aware that left to themselves, whites will be slow to change the status of the Negro.

Young, Whitney M., Jr., To Be Equal. New York: McGraw-Hill, 1964. A stern, factual presentation of why Negroes demand, in simple justice, the opportunity "to be equal," and a persuasive argument for a special program for the Negro on the grounds that he has the right to equality of opportunity, and that as things now stand, that equality is not available to him.

Zietlow, Carl P., "Race, Students, and Non-Violence," Religious Education 59:116-120 (January-February 1964).

Zinn, Howard, "A Fate Worse Than Integration," Harper's Magazine 219:53-56 (August 1959).

Zinn, Howard, "The Battle-Scarred Youngsters," Nation 197:193-197 (October 5, 1963).

Zinn, Howard, "The Double Job in Civil Rights," New Politics 3:29-34 (Winter 1964). Discussion of strategies to be pursued: civil rights and the more general social revolution.

Zinn, Howard, SNCC: The New Abolitionists. Boston: Beacon, 1964. Through accounts of the many protest campaigns SNCC has engaged in, the author illustrates the spirit of revolution in this youth organization.

3. RESPONSE AND RESISTANCE

Alexander, Charles C., The Ku Klux Klan in the Southwest. Lexington: University of Kentucky Press, 1965. The author contends that the "distinctive quality of the Klan. . .

lay not so much in racism and nativism as in moral authoritarianism," a thesis hardly
borne out by facts he himself brings forth.

American Friends Service Committee of the Society of American Friends, Southern Office,
    Intimidation, Reprisal, and Violence in the South's Racial Crisis. Atlanta, Ga.: Southern
    Regional Council, 1959. 530 cases between January 1, 1955, and January 1, 1959.
Ashmore, Harry S., The Other Side of Jordan. New York: Norton, 1960.
Bachrach, Arthur J., and Gordon W. Blackwell, eds., "Human Problems in the Changing
    South," Journal of Social Issues 10:1-43 (January 1954). Entire issue.
Beach, Waldo, "The Changing Mind of the South," Christianity and Crisis 22:119-122 (July
    9, 1962).
Benedict, Roger W., "Civil Rights Test: Federal Move to Cut Funds for Segregated Facilities
    Hits Snag," Wall Street Journal, March 12, 1965. Many schools, hospitals, other facilities,
    after signing commitments to desegregate, simply do not do so.
Bernard, Raymond, "Calm Voices in the South," Social Order 8:74-84 (February 1958).
    Summaries of works on segregation and integration in the South as evidence that
    Southern writers are speaking out.
Boyle, Sarah Patton, The Desegregated Heart. New York: Morrow, 1962. Account by a
    Southern woman of what it means actively to work for desegregation in the South.
Boyle, Sarah Patton, For Human Beings Only: A Primer of Human Understanding. New
    York: Seabury Press, 1964.
Cahill, Edward, "The Changing South: Revolution or Reconciliation," Phylon 19:199-207
    (Summer 1958).
Caldwell, Erskine, "The Deep South's Other Venerable Tradition," New York Times
    Magazine, July 11, 1965. On the extent to which cruelty and violence are indigenous
    characteristics of the Deep South.
Canzoneri, Robert, "I Do So Politely": A Voice From the South. Boston: Houghton Mifflin,
    1965. A Mississippian, cousin of Ross Barnett, attacks the closed society.
Carter, Hodding, III, Southern Legacy. Baton Rouge: Louisiana State University Press,
    1950; Garden City, N.Y.: Doubleday paperback, 1965.
Carter, Hodding, III, "A Wave of Terror Threatens the South," Look 19:32-36 (March 22,
    1955). Abetted by the White Citizens' Councils.
Carter, Hodding, III, The South Strikes Back: Garden City, N.Y.: Doubleday, 1959. Through
    the White Citizens' Councils.
Carter, Hodding, III, First Person Plural. Garden City, N.Y.: Doubleday, 1963. Author,
    editor-publisher of the Delta Democrat-Times, Greenville, Miss., is saddened by the
    path the South has taken.
Carter, Hodding, III, So the Heffners Left McComb. Garden City, N.Y.: Doubleday, 1965.
Chalmers, David M., Hooded Americanism: The First Century of the Ku Klux Klan 1865 to
    the Present. Garden City, N.Y.: Doubleday, 1965.
Cook, James Graham, The Segregationists. New York: Appleton, 1962. Impressionistic
    interviews with a variety of Southern segregationists, white and Negro, and descriptions
    of various organizations combating integration.
Cook, Samuel DuBois, "Political Movements and Organizations," Journal of Politics 26:
    130-153 (February 1964). The 1950's and the organization of support for the status quo.
Cramer, M. Richard, "School Desegregation and New Industry: The Southern Community
    Leaders' Viewpoint," Social Forces 41:384-389 (May 1963).
Dabbs, James McBride, The Southern Heritage. New York: Knopf, 1958. The author
    examines the roots of segregation in the past and the present, the fears and the economic
    and political reasons for the persistence of white supremacy.
Dabbs, James McBride, "Who Speaks for the South?" New South 16:4-11 (November 1961).
    Presidential address to the Southern Regional Council.
Dabbs, James McBride, "To Define Our Love," New South 17:3-9 (November-December
    1962). Presidential address to Southern Regional Council.
Dabbs, James McBride, "The Myth, the Movement, and the American Dream," New South
    18:3-9 (December 1963). Presidential Address to Southern Regional Council.
Dabbs, James McBride, Who Speaks for the South? New York: Funk & Wagnalls, 1964. The
    author's purpose: to discover and explain the "Southern type." While the Negro does not
    enter the story prominently until toward the end, Mr. Dabbs calls on the white South to
    recognize and accept the Negro in his new role.

Daniels, Frank, "Speak Out Strongly," New South 13:3-10 (January 1958). The vice-president of the Charlottesville, Va., Council on Human Relations himself speaks out at Sweet Briar College against economic discrimination, irrational fear, and hysterical notions about miscegenation and intermarriage.

Danzig, David, "Rightists, Racists, and Separatists: A White Bloc in the Making?" Commentary 38:28-32 (August 1964).

Deutsch, Martin, and Kay Steele, "Attitude Dissonances Among Southville's Influentials," Journal of Social Issues 15:44-52 (October 1959). A secondary study based on the Southville investigations (see Johann Galtung), the "influentials" being upper-and middle-class individuals, spokesmen for the community and leaders in organizing private schools. Some cracks in the segregationists' armor are perceived.

Dugger, Ronnie, "Filibusters and Majority Rule," Progressive 21:21-22 (August 1957). In Texas, liberals use filibuster to aid Negro.

Dunbar, Leslie W., "The Changing Mind of the South: The Exposed Nerve," Journal of Politics 26:3-21 (February 1964).

Dykeman, Wilma, "Two Faces of the South," Current History 35:257-261 (November 1958).

Dykeman, Wilma, and James Stokely, Neither Black Nor White. New York: Rinehart, 1957. Account of a trip taken after 1954 through the South by two former Southerners.

Dykeman, Wilma, and James Stokely, "McCarthyism Under the Magnolias," Progressive 23:6-10 (July 1959).

Dykeman, Wilma, and James Stokely, "The Klan Tries a Comeback: In the Wake of Desegregation," Commentary 29:45-51 (January 1960).

Dykeman, Wilma, and James Stokely, with foreword by Alexander Heard, Seeds of Southern Change: The Life of Will Alexander. Chicago: University of Chicago Press, 1962. The career and influence of a white champion of the Negro cause in the South from 1915 to 1954.

East, P. D., The Magnolia Jungle. New York: Simon & Schuster, 1960. A well-written autobiographical sketch by a Mississippi newspaper editor who, aroused by the injustices around him, became an ardent anti-segregationist and critic of Southern bigotry.

Eddy, Mrs. George A., "Alexandria, Va., Council on Human Relations Seeks Improved Race Relations," New South 16:6-12 (June 1961).

Ernst, Harry W., "West Virginia Press Sets Good Example," New South 13:3-8 (September 1958). Responsibility of mass media in freeing American psyche from prejudice, and what some editors have already done.

Faulkner, William, "American Segregation and the World Crisis," in Three Views of the Segregation Decisions. Atlanta, Ga.: Southern Regional Council, 1956.

Fishman, Joshua A., "Southern City," Midstream 7:39-63 (Summer 1961). Jews and civil rights in Montgomery, Alabama.

Fleming, Harold C., "Resistance Movements and Racial Desegregation," Annals of the American Academy of Political and Social Science 304:44-52 (March 1956).

Fleming, Harold C., "The South and Segregation: Where Do We Stant?" Progressive 22:12-14 (February 1958).

Fowler, Grady, "Southern White Citizens and the Supreme Court," Phylon 18:59-68 (Spring 1957).

Galtung, Johann, "A Model for Studying Images of Participants in a Conflict: Southville," Journal of Social Issues 15:38-43 (October 1959). Study of a typical Southern community which actively resisted 1954 Supreme Court decision, designed to determine what kinds of images each of three groups (segregationists, integrationists, Negroes) has of the other groups.

Gilbert, Arthur, "Violence and Intimidation in the South," Social Order 10:450-456 (December 1960). Relationship between prejudice against Negroes and anti-Semitism.

Glenn, Norval D., "The Role of White Resistance and Facilitation in the Negro Struggle for Equality," Phylon 26:105-116 (Spring 1965).

Good, Paul, "Klan Town, U.S.A.," Nation 200:110-112 (February 1, 1965). On Bogalusa, Louisiana.

Good, Paul, "Birmingham Two Years Later," Reporter 33:21-27 (December 2, 1965).

Goodwyn, Larry, "Anarchy in St. Augustine," Harper's Magazine 230:74-81 (January 1965).

Hayden, Tom, "The Power of Dixiecrats," New University Thought 3:6-16 (December 1963-January 1964).

Hays, Brooks, A Southern Moderate Speaks. Chapel Hill: University of North Carolina

Press, 1959. By a moderate Arkansas Congressman who was defeated by an extreme segregationist in the wake of Little Rock.

Heard, Eliza (pseudo.), "In the Name of Southern Womanhood," New South 17:16-18 (November-December 1962). By a white woman ashamed of what has been done in her name.

Heer, David M., "The Sentiment of White Supremacy: An Ecological Study," American Journal of Sociology 64:592-598 (May 1959).

Heller, Ben I., "My Brother's Brother," New South 15:9-11 (July-August 1960).

Hill, Haywood N., "This I Believe," New South 16:7-10 (April 1961). White Southerner who feels that he must live by his conviction and conscience (Christian and scientific) rather than by his preferences and prejudices.

Hyman, Herbert H., and P. B. Sheatsley, "Attitudes Toward Desegregation," Scientific American 195:35-39 (December 1956). Attitudes of white Southerners, and degree to which change has taken place.

Intimidation, Reprisal, and Violence in the South's Racial Crisis. Atlanta, Ga., 1960. Published jointly by the American Friends Service Committee, the National Council of Churches of Christ in America, and the Southern Regional Council.

Jennings, M. Kent, Community Influentials: The Elites of Atlanta. New York: Free Press, 1964. A study seeking to discover patterns of political influence in what is regarded as a progressive Southern community.

Jewell, Malcolm, "State Legislatures in Southern Politics," Journal of Politics 26:177-196 (February 1964).

Johnson, Haynes, "Money and Mississippi," Progressive 29:21-23 (May 1965). Economic interests and the impact of U.S. Civil Rights Commission hearings as instruments of change.

Johnson, Manning, Color, Communism and Common Sense. New York: Alliance, 1958. With a foreword by Archibald B. Roosevelt. A representative example of right-wing extremist, states-rights indictments of the "communist" inspiration of the Negro drive to obtain the franchise.

Jones, Lewis W., Cold Rebellion: The South's Oligarchy in Revolt. London: MacGibbon and Kee, 1962. On Southern rebels who participate in the federal government "while ruling their domain as an oligarchy--irresponsible to federal authority and contemptuous of federal law."

Killian, Lewis M., "Consensus in the Changing South," Phylon 18:107-117 (Summer 1957).

Killian, Lewis M., and Charles M. Grigg, "The Bi-Racial Committee as a Response to Racial Tensions in Southern Cities," Phylon 23:379-382 (Winter 1962).

Kilpatrick, James Jackson, The Soverign States: Notes of a Citizen of Virginia. Chicago: Regnery, 1957. A Southern view, by the editor of the Richmond News Leader.

Laue, James H., "The Movement, Negro Challenge to the Myth," New South 18:9-17 (July-August 1963). The myth being that of a benevolent South.

Lerche, Charles O., Jr., The Uncertain South: Its Changing Patterns of Politics in Foreign Policy. Chicago: Quadrangle, 1964. See especially chapters 5, 7, and 8 for exposition of ways in which political demagogues have exploited poor whites' hatred of Negroes as growing urbanization has exacerbated racial animosities and heightened competition for jobs.

Levy, Charles J., "Deterrents to Militancy," Race 5:20-29 (January 1964). A study of a segregationist militant in Virginia.

Long, Margaret, "A Southern Teen-Ager Speaks His Mind," New York Times Magazine, November 10, 1963. Extreme white-supremacist attitude of young white student.

Long, N. E., "Local Leadership and the Crisis in Race Relations," Public Management 46: 2-6 (January 1964).

Lustig, Norman I., "The Relationships Between Demographic Characteristics and Pro-Integration Vote of White Precincts in a Metropolitan Southern Community," Social Forces 40:205-208 (March 1962).

McGill, Ralph, The South and the Southerner. Boston: Little, Brown, 1963. Closes with plea for compliance with Supreme Court decisions.

McIntyre, Thomas J., "My Mission to Alabama," Boston Sunday Herald, November 7, 1965. Account of trip to Alabama by the New Hampshire senator to investigate the murder of civil rights worker Jonathan Daniels and the flouting of justice in that state.

McIntyre, William R., "Spread of Terrorism and Hatemongering," Editorial Research Reports 1958:893-911 (December 3, 1958).

McMillan, George, Racial Violence and Law Enforcement. Atlanta, Ga.: Southern Regional Council, November 1960. Pamphlet on violence in Chattanooga, Montgomery, and Little Rock.

Malev, William S., "The Jew of the South in Conflict on Segregation," Conservative Judaism 13:33-46 (Fall 1958). Strategy considerations for Jewish community.

Manderson, Marge, "A Solid South. . . Or Else," New South 15:3-11 (April 1960). The aims of Southern segregationists.

Margolis, Joseph, "The Role of the Segregationist," New South 13:7-11 (February 1958). He plays many roles, among them the military hero, the knightly crusader, the martyr, but he always casts the Negro in the same role.

Marion, John H., "Behind Dixie's Gentler Standpatters," Christian Century 79:1288-1290 (October 24, 1962). Southern gentry at bay.

Martin, John Bartlow, The Deep South Says "Never," New York: Ballantine, 1957.

Matthews, Donald R., and James W. Prothro, "Southern Racial Attitudes: Conflict, Aware-ness, and Political Change," Annals of the American Academy of Political and Social Science 344:108-121 (November 1962).

Mayer, Milton, "Deep in the Heart," Progressive 21:12-14 (July 1957). Story of confronta-tion with White Citizens' Council in Texas.

"Mississippi," New South 17:3+ (October 1962). Entire issue.

"Mississippi Eyewitness," Ramparts Magazine, Special Issue, 1964. On the three civil rights workers, Andrew Goodman, James Chaney, and Michael Schwerner, and how they were murdered.

Morgan, Charles, Jr., "Who is Guilty in Birmingham," Christian Century 80:1195-1196 (October 2, 1963). Local lawyer's speech at Young Men's Business Club after bombing of little girls in Sunday School.

Morgan, Charles, Jr., A Time to Speak. New York: Harper, 1964. The author indicts all the good, respectable white citizens of Birmingham, Alabama, who bear, he says, the responsibility for the acts of violent men, and in particular for the bombing of Negro children in church.

Morsell, John A., "Legal Opposition to Desegregation: Its Significance for Intergroup Agencies in the Years Ahead," Journal of Intergroup Relations 1:68-75 (Winter 1959-1960).

Muse, Benjamin, "A Virginia View of 'Race and Reason,'" New South 16:12-16 (December 1961).

Muse, Benjamin, Virginia's Massive Resistance. Bloomington: Indiana University Press, 1961. State legislative and executive action to preserve segregated schools.

New South. Issue of July-August, 1962, on "A Hundred Years Later," with articles by James McBride Dabbs, Frank P. Graham, Paul Green, Benjamin E. Mays, James Stokely, Marion A. Wright.

"'No Shoving Reporters'—It's an Order in Tuscaloosa," Editor and Publisher 96:24 (June 15, 1963). Reflects concern with the "image."

Norris, Hoke, ed., We Dissent. New York: St. Martin's, 1962. Articles by white Protestant Southerners designed "to give voice to the opposition in the South" and to restore a balance in the nation's onesided view of the South.

Opotowsky, Stan, "Silence in the South," Progressive 21:10-12 (August 1957). No word from the moderates.

Perlmutter, Nathan, "Bombing in Miami: Anti-Semitism and the Segregationists," Commentary 25:498-503 (June 1958).

Peters, William, The Southern Temper. Garden City, N.Y.: Doubleday, 1959. A study of the "second South"--the people who are either indifferent to integration or who are actively trying to bring it about.

Polk, William Tarnahill, Southern Accent: From Uncle Remus to Oak Ridge. New York: Morrow, 1953. A Southerner's attempt to describe the modern South, compounded of the "surviving South" and the industrialized South, and its dilemma as between the ideal of equality and the ideal of excellence.

Prothro, Edwin Terry, "Social Psychology of the South, Challenge Without Response," Journal of Social Issues 10:36-43 (January 1954).

Quint, Howard H., Profile in Black and White: A Frank Portrait of South Carolina.
    Washington, D.C.: Public Affairs Press, 1959. White Southerners were permitted, by the
    year's delay in implementation order for 1954 decision, to gather their forces to fight
    integration.
Randel, William Peirce, The Ku Klux Klan: A Century of Infamy. New York: Chilton, 1965.
Ransome, Coleman B., Jr., "Political Leadership in the Governor's Office," Journal of
    Politics 26:197-220 (February 1964). In the Southern states.
Record, Jane Cassels, "The Red-Tagging of Negro Protest," American Scholar 26:325-333
    (Summer 1957).
Rice, Arnold S., The Ku Klux Klan in American Politics. Washington, D.C.: Public Affairs
    Press, 1962.
Rose, Arnold M., "The Course of the South: Descent into Barbarism?" Commentary 27:
    495-499 (June 1959).
Rubin, Louis D., Jr., and James Jackson Kilpatrick, The Lasting South. Chicago: Regnery,
    1957.
Samet, Elaine R., "Quiet Revolution in Miami," Progressive 29:34-37 (April 1965).
Sass, Herbert Ravenal, "Mixed Schools and Mixed Blood," Greenwood, Miss.: Publications
    of Association of Citizens' Councils of Mississippi, no date.
Secrest, A. M., "Moderation Is Key to South's Dilemma," New South 15:3-8 (February
    1960).
Shaffer, Helen B., "Changing South," Editorial Research Reports 1959:423-440 (June 10,
    1959). Economic and population changes and the South's resistance.
Shaffer, Helen B., "Violence and Non-Violence in American Race Relations," Editorial
    Research Reports 1960: 221-238 (March 25, 1960).
Sherrill, Robert, "Portrait of a 'Southern Liberal' in Trouble," New York Times Magazine,
    November 7, 1965. On Senator John Sparkman of Alabama, his 'liberal' record in
    Congress, and what his chances would be were Governor George C. Wallace to contest
    his reelection to the Senate.
Silver, James W., Mississippi: The Closed Society. New York: Harcourt, Brace, 1964. The
    author carefully, doggedly documents the way the "closed society" lets "no scruple,
    legal or ethical, stand in the way of the enforcement of the orthodoxy." He foresees that
    it will be necessary for the federal government to "put an end to the closed society in
    Mississippi."
Simkins, Francis Butler, The Everlasting South. Baton Rouge: Louisiana State University
    Press, 1963. Five essays on the position of the Southern states.
Sisson, John P., "A Southern City Changes Gracefully: Pensacola Pattern," Interracial
    Review 36:98-100 (May 1963). The moral being that if local leaders take realistic steps
    toward granting Negro demands, there will be no crisis.
Smith, Frank E., Congressman from Mississippi. New York: Pantheon, 1964. Autobiography
    of a "moderate" Congressman defeated after 12 years by a fanatical white-supremacist.
    He rather disingenuously justifies his own earlier failure to speak out on the grounds
    that "as a condition of holding my office, I made obeisance to the Southern way of life."
Smith, Frank E., "Valor's Second Prize: Southern Racism and Internationalism," South
    Atlantic Quarterly 64:296-303 (Summer 1965).
Smith, Frank E., Look Away from Dixie. Baton Rouge: Louisiana State University Press,
    1965. Describes the corrosive effect of racism on Southern life.
Smith, Lillian, Killers of the Dream. New York: Norton, 1949; Anchor paperback. Author
    shows, with great insight, the costs to both white and Negro Southerners of the pattern
    of segregation, deprivation, guilt and fear, especially in the stultification of white lives.
Smith, Lillian, "The South's Moment of Truth," Progressive 24:32-35 (September 1960).
Smith, Lillian, "Words That Chain Us and Words That Set Us Free," New South 17:3-12
    (March 1962). Semantic journey in the South.
"South Increases Propaganda," New South 14:3-7 (May 1959). The propaganda campaign
    being waged by white supremacists.
"Southern Bombings," New South 18:8-11 (May 1963). Tabulation of bombings from January
    1, 1956, to June 1, 1963.
"The Southern Regional Council, 1944-1964," New South 19:1-22 (January 1964). Review of
    twenty years' work.
"Southerners Look at Desegregation," Antioch Review 14:387-557 (Winter 1954). Entire
    issue.

Spearman, Walter, and Sylvan Myer, Racial Crisis and the Press. Atlanta, Ga.: Southern
  Regional Council, 1960. Analysis of treatment of racial news by the press.

Three Views of the Segregation Decisions. Atlanta, Ga,: Southern Regional Council, 1956.

Tindall, George B., "The Benighted South: Origins of a Modern Myth," Virginia Quarterly
  40:281-294 (Spring 1964).

Tucker, Shirley, Mississippi from Within. New York: Arco, 1965. An analysis of 5,000
  issues of 20 Mississippi newspapers between July 2, 1964, and May 1965, to show local
  response to Civil Rights Act of 1964.

Tyre, Nedra, "The Diligent Knitters of Southern Sanity," New South 17:3-5+ (February
  1962). How Southerners of good will can become "knitters" of accord.

Vander Zanden, James W., "Desegregation and Social Strains in the South," Journal of
  Social Issues 15:53-60 (October 1959).

Vander Zanden, James W., "The Klan Revival," American Journal of Sociology 65:456-462
  (March 1960).

Vander Zanden, James W., "Turmoil in the South," Journal of Negro Education 29:445-452
  (Fall 1960).

Vander Zanden, James W., "Voting on Segregationist Referenda," Public Opinion Quarterly
  25:92-105 (Spring 1961). Analysis of voting in 15 Southern communities: points to lack of
  simple evidence of correlation of class and attitudes, and presents evidence contradictory to the usual hypothesis that there is an inverse relation between socioeconomic
  class and affirmation of segregationism.

Vander Zanden, James W., "Accommodations to Undesired Change: The Case of the South,"
  Journal of Negro Education 31:30-35 (Winter 1962).

Vandiver, Frank E., ed., The Idea of the South: Pursuit of a Central Theme. Chicago: University of Chicago Press, 1964. In his own essay, "The Southerner as Extremist," the
  editor explains the South's reaction to the 1954 Supreme Court decision as "defensive."
  Northerners can help by not openly provoking Southern resentments and "defenses."

"The Voices of the White South, Divergent Views of Public Men," Life 41:104-117, 119-120
  (September 17, 1956).

Waring, Thomas R., "The Southern Case Against Desegregation," Harper's Magazine 212:
  39-45 (January 1956).

Warner, Bob, "Reporting Racial Strife in the South: Camera is Red Flag to Mob," Editor
  and Publisher 94:23 (June 10, 1961).

Warner, Bob, "The Southern Story: Omens in Alabama: Editors Resentful of Northern
  Attention," Editor and Publisher 94:24 (June 17, 1961).

Warner, Bob, "The Southern Press: Violence and the News," Editor and Publisher 94:25
  (June 24, 1961).

Warren, Robert Penn, Segregation: The Inner Conflict in the South. New York: Random
  House, 1956. The conflict is brilliantly presented through conversations with both
  Negroes and whites.

Weeks, O. Douglas, "The South in National Politics," Journal of Politics 26:221-240
  (February 1964).

"White Americans and Civil Rights," Political Affairs 43:1-6 (May 1964).

Williams, H. Franklin, "The Moderate," New South 13:8-10 (October 1958). Calling on
  Southern moderates to assume responsibility for curbing race conflict.

Woodward, C. Vann, "The South and the Law of the Land: The Present Resistance and Its
  Prospects," Commentary 26:369-374 (November 1958).

Woodward, C. Vann, "The South in Perspective," Progressive 26:12-17 (December 1962).

Woofter, Thomas J., Southern Race Progress: The Wavering Color Line. Washington, D.C.:
  Public Affairs Press, 1957. Substantively a plea for good will and cooperation.

Workman, William D., The Case for the South. New York: Devin-Adair, 1960. A white
  Southerner presents his case for "separate but equal" based on the "unique character"
  of the South. See review by T. F. Pettigrew in Harvard Educational Review Summer 1960,
  who described it as "further evidence of the madness" in the South.

Wright, Marion A., "Integration and Public Morals," New South 12:7-14 (November 1957).
  On author's retirement as president of Southern Regional Council.

Zinn, Howard, The Southern Mystique. New York: Knopf, 1964. After presenting the linea-
  ments of the white Southerners, with every trait of prejudice, violence, racial intolerance,
  the author reminds the reader these traits are also present in the North, that they are
  not instinctive and unchangeable, but not only can be changed but have been changing.

4. THE ROLE OF THE CHURCHES

Abbott, Walter M., "The Bible Abused," Interracial Review 36:26-27+ (February 1963). By white Catholics who resisted school desegregation.

Ahmann, Mathew, ed., Race: Challenge to Religion. Chicago: Regnery, 1963. Essays deriving from a meeting of the National Conference on Religion and Race.

Alexander, W. W., Racial Segregation in theAmerican Protestant Church. New York: Friendship, 1946.

American Friends Service Committee of the Society of American Friends, Race and Conscience in America. Norman: University of Oklahoma Press, 1959.

Bailey, Kenneth K., Southern White Protestantism in the Twentieth Century. New York: Harper, 1964.

Ball, William B., "New Frontiers of Catholic Community Action," Interracial Review 35: 49-51 (February 1962).

Bell, John L., "The Presbyterian Church and the Negro in North Carolina," North Carolina Historical Review 40:15-36 (January 1963). A study of how racial segregation was established in the Presbyterian churches in North Carolina.

Bennett, John C., "Faith and Responsibility," Christian Century 75:1394-1397 (December 3, 1958).

Bennett, John C., "The Demand for Freedom and Justice in the Contemporary World Revolutions," in Walter Leibrecht, ed., Religion and Culture: Essays in Honor of Paul Tillich, New York: Harper, 1959. A thoughtful essay on the relationship between Christianity and social ideals in a changing world.

Bernard, Raymond, "The Negro Prospect," Social Order 7:135-136 (March 1957). Review of The Negro Potential by Eli Ginzberg, and statement of the responsibility of Southern Catholics.

Bernard, Raymond, "Some Anthropological Implications of the Racial Admission Policy of the U.S. Sisterhoods," American Catholic Sociological Review 19:124-135 (June 1958).

Boggs, Marion, "The Crucial Test of Christian Citizenship," New South 12:7-8 (July-August 1957). Little Rock pastor's sermon denouncing legal hindrances in the way of the Negro.

"Bonds of Union," New York Times, November 17, 1963. Statement by U.S. Catholic bishops urging full recognition of Negroes' rights.

Bouton, Ellen Naylor, and Thomas F. Pettigrew, "When a Priest Made a Pilgrimage," Christian Century 80:863-865 (March 20, 1963).

Boyd, Malcolm, ed., On the Battle Lines. New York: Morehouse-Barlow, 1964. A challenge to Christians by 27 clergymen.

Britts, Maurice W., "Interracial Justice: An Issue for Youth," Interracial Review 35:220-221 (October 1962).

Brown, Aubrey N., Jr., "Presbyterians, U.S.: En Route to Broader Concerns," Christian Century 80:1577-1580 (December 18, 1963).

Brown, Robert R., Bigger Than Little Rock. Greenwich, Conn.: Seabury, 1958. Episcopal Bishop in Little Rock since 1955 discusses dilemma of clergymen who favor compliance with Supreme Court ruling, and concludes that the clergy must become involved in the political controversy.

Campbell, Ernest Q., and Thomas F. Pettigrew, "Racial and Moral Crisis: The Role of Little Rock Ministers," American Journal of Sociology 64:509-516 (March 1959).

Campbell, Ernest Q., and Thomas F. Pettigrew, Christians in Racial Crisis: A Study of Little Rock's Ministry, Including Statements on Desegregation and Race Relations by the Leading Religious Denominations of the United States. Washington, D.C.: Public Affairs Press, 1959.

Campbell, Will D., "Perhaps or Maybe," Christian Century 79:1133 (September 19, 1962). Albany, Ga., race incidents, and a minister's protest.

Campbell, Will D., Race and Renewal of the Church. Philadelphia: Westminster, 1962. The author, director of the Committee of Southern Churchmen, charges that the church "has waited too long to carry out its mandate, and to a large part of the world, what we Christians do from here on out really does not matter very much."

"Cardinal McIntyre: A Ramparts Special Report," Ramparts 3:35-44 (November 1964). Three articles on the effect of Cardinal McIntyre's refusal to support racial equality in his southern California jurisdiction.

Carnell, Edward John, "A Christian Social Ethics," Christian Century 80:979-980 (August 7, 1963).

Carr, Warren, "Notes from an Irrelevant Clergyman," Christian Century 80:879-881 (July 10, 1963). In Durham, N.C., laymen are ready to take moral stand on civil rights before the churches are.

Cartwright, Colbert S., "The Southern Minister and the Race Question," New South 13:3-6 (February 1958).

Cartwright, Colbert S., "Band Together for Genuine Unity," New South 16:6-10 (January 1961). Little Rock pastor at Fourth Conference on Community Unity.

Catchings, L. Maynard, "Interracial Activities in Southern Churches," Phylon 13:54-56 (March 1952).

"'Christian Guide' to Race Attitudes," New South 13:3-7 (May 1958). A strong statement by the Gainesville-Hall County Ministerial Association in Georgia.

"A Church Looks at Civil Rights in North Carolina," New South 18:13-15 (April 1963). Statement of Committee on Human Relations of North Carolina Council of Churches.

Clark, Henry, "Churchmen and Residential Segregation," Review of Religious Research 5: 157-164 (Spring 1964).

Cogley, John, "The Clergy Heeds a New Call," New York Times Magazine May 2, 1965. On the Selma, Alabama, march, and its role in the growing involvement of church leaders in the civil rights movement.

Collie, Robert, "A 'Silent Minister' Speaks Up," New York Times Magazine, May 24, 1964. Pastor in a small Louisiana town answers charge that Southern clergy have failed their duty on segregation—a defense and rationalization.

Communism, Christianity and Race Relations. Valparaiso, Ind.: Lutheran Human Relations Association of America, 1960. Report of twelfth annual Valparaiso University Institute on Human Relations.

Congar, Yves M. J., The Catholic Church and the Race Question. Paris: UNESCO, 1953.

Cox, Harvey, "Letter from Williamston," Christian Century 80:1516-1518 (December 4, 1963). North Carolina and protest.

Creger, Ralph, with Erwin McDonald, A Look Down the Lonesome Road. Garden City, N.Y.: Doubleday, 1964. A fundamentalist Baptist attempts to offer a "Christian solution" to the moral problem of integration.

Crook, Roger H., No South or North. St. Louis, Mo.: Bethany, 1959. A Southern white Christian who favors integration raises and answers various arguments used to justify segregation and relates the question of race relations to the demands of Christian faith.

Culver, Dwight W., Negro Segregation in the Methodist Church. New Haven: Yale University Press, 1953.

Cuninggim, Merrimon, "The Southern Temper," New South 13:7-8 (July-August 1958).

Daniels, Jonathan, and Judith Upham, "Report from Selma," Episcopal Theological School Journal 10:2-8 (May 1965). An account written in April 1965 of experiences in Alabama by the young seminarian who was murdered in Hayneville, Alabama, in August 1965.

Davis, Lloyd, "The Religious Dimension of Interracial Justice," Interracial Review 35:46-48 (February 1962).

"Discrimination and the Christian Conscience," Journal of Negro Education 28:66-69 (Winter 1959). Position of Catholic bishops in the United States.

Dunne, George H., "'I Expect More of Christians,'" Interracial Review 35:39-41, 53 (February 1962).

Egan, John J., "Compassion and Community Life," Interracial Review 35:66-69 (March 1962).

Ehle, John, Shepherd of the Streets: The Story of the Reverend James A. Gusweller and His Crusade on the New York West Side. New York: Sloane, 1960.

Elston, Wilbur, "Social, but Little Action," Christian Century 79:106-108 (January 24, 1962). Critique of Christian social action.

Evans, John B., "Alabama," Christian Century 80:188-190 (February 6, 1963). Clergymen and Governor Wallace.

Fey, Harold E., "N.C.C. Acts on Racial Crisis," Christian Century 80:1602-1604 (June 19, 1963). Action taken by General Board of National Council of Churches.

Fey, Harold E., "Uniting and Marching," Christian Century 80:926-927 (July 24, 1963). General Synod of United Church of Christ and race relations.

Fey, Harold E., "Reconciliation in Rochester," Christian Century 80:1125-1127 (September 18, 1963). World Council of Churches meets and discusses racial issues.

Fey, Harold E., "Disciples on Civil Rights," Christian Century 80:1326-1327 (October 30, 1963). Disciples of Christ Convention.

Fey, Harold E., "Churches Meet Racial Crisis," Christian Century 80:1572-1573 (December 18, 1963). Statement of General Assembly of National Council of Churches on civil rights.

Fichter, Joseph H., Social Relations in the Urban Parish. Chicago: University of Chicago Press, 1954. Topics include "A Typology of Parishioners," "Social Correlates of Religious Participation," "Social Relations and Structures," and "Problems of Conceptualization and Research."

Fichter, Joseph, "Negro Spirituals and Catholicism," Interracial Review 35:200-203 (September 1962). "In inquiring thoroughly into the spirituals, we find that both in form and content they can stand comparison with the Hebrew psalms." They have not been put "sufficiently to Catholic use."

Fichter, Joseph H., "The Catholic South and Race," Religious Education 59:30-33 (January-February 1964).

Fichter, Joseph H., "American Religion and the Negro," Daedalus 94:1085-1106 (Fall 1965). The author finds that "this test of America's religious ideology has resulted. . .in the deliberate moral impact of religious leaders on the extra-church institutions of the American culture."

Fichter, Joseph H., and George L. Maddox, "Religion in the South, Old and New," in John McKinney and Edgar Thompson, eds., The South in Continuity and Change. Durham, N.C.: Duke University Press, 1965.

Fitzpatrick, Joseph P., "The Dynamics of Change," Interracial Review 35:7-9 (January 1962). The parish and social change.

Foley, Albert S., God's Men of Color. New York: Farrar, Straus, 1955. Negro priests in the Catholic Church.

Foshey, Gerald, "Divided Flocks in Jackson," Christian Century 80:1469-1471 (November 27, 1963). Church segregation in Jackson, Mississippi.

Fry, John K., "United Presbyterians: Prophecy vs. Tradition," Christian Century 80:1235-1237 (October 9, 1963). Some notes on new tendencies, including those in race relations.

"The Full Catholic Teaching in Racial Justice," Interracial Review 35:224-225 (October 1962). Syllabus prepared by the Diocesan Department of Education, Charleston, S.C.

Gallagher, Buell, Color and Conscience: The Irrepressible Conflict. New York: Harper, 1946. Race relations in terms of the moral dilemma between the "color caste" system and ethical notions of Christianity, brotherhood, and justice.

Gasnick, Roy M., "Franciscan Pledge to Interracial Justice," Social Order 12:173-177 (April 1962). Action for Interracial Understanding, the interracial movement founded by the Third Order of St. Francis.

Geier, Woodrow A., "Tennessee," Christian Century 79:1302 (October 24, 1962).

Geier, Woodrow A., "Tennessee: Students and Race," Christian Century 80:56 (January 9, 1963).

Geier, Woodrow A., "Tennessee," Christian Century 80:1526-1527 (December 4, 1963). Survey of integration in Southern Baptist churches.

"A Ghandi Society?" Christian Century 79:735-736 (June 13, 1962). The Christian Churches and social action: objections to Martin Luther King's proposals.

Gillard, John T., The Catholic Church and the Negro. Baltimore: St. Joseph's Society Press, 1929.

Gillespie, G. T., "A Christian View on Segregation," Greenwood, Miss.: Publications of the Association of Citizens' Councils of Mississippi, no date.

Gleason, Robert W., "Immortality of Segregation," Thought 35:138 (Autumn 1960). Chairman of Departments of Theology and Religious Education, Fordham University, considers the theological aspects of segregation.

Greeley, Andrew M., "White Parish—Refuge or Resource," Interracial Review 35:168-169 (July 1962).

Harbutt, Charles, "The Church and Integration," Jubilee 6:6-15 (February 1959). A survey of Catholics' response to the South's most pressing problem.

Harte, Thomas J., Catholic Organizations Promoting Negro-white Race Relations in the United States. Washington, D.C.: Catholic University Press, 1947. Vol. 24 of Studies in

Sociology published by Catholic University's School of Social Science. An extensive survey of organizations, objectives, and activities of 5 types of voluntary Catholic groups for promoting better race relations.

Hartnett, Robert C., "The 'Divine Doctrine' of Brotherhood," Interracial Review 35:96-97 (April 1962).

Haselden, Kyle, The Racial Problem in Christian Perspective. New York: Harper, 1963. 1st ed., 1959.

Haselden, Kyle, "Too Busy to Hate," Christian Century 80:392-393 (March 27, 1963). Atlanta's motto and the reality.

Haselden, Kyle, "The Birmingham Lull," Christian Century 80:1294-1295 (October 23, 1963).

Haselden, Kyle, "Religion and Race," Christian Century 80:133-135 (January 30, 1963).

Haselden, Kyle, "Eleven A.M. Sunday is Our Most Segregated Hour," New York Times Magazine, August 2, 1964.

Herberg, Will, Protestant, Catholic, Jew. Garden City, N.Y.: Doubleday, 1955. Includes consideration of the Negro problem in Protestant churches in the city.

Hill, Samuel S., Jr., "The South's Culture Protestantism," Christian Century 79:1094-1096 (September 12, 1962).

Hill, Samuel S., Jr., "Southern Protestantism and Racial Integration," Religion in Life 33: 421-429 (Summer 1964).

Holden, Anna, "A Call to Catholics," Interracial Review 35:140-143 (June 1962). To participate in nonviolent direct action movement.

Horchler, Richard, "The Layman's Role in the Changing Community," Interracial Review 35:12-13 (January 1962).

Hurley, Denis E., "Second Vatican and Racism," Interracial Review 36:11 (December 1963).

Hurley, Phillip S., "Role of the Churches in Integration," Journal of Intergroup Relations 1:41-46 (Summer 1960).

Johnson, Benton, "Ascetic Protestantism and Political Preference in the Deep South," American Journal of Sociology 69:359-366 (January 1964). Tie between Republicans and fundamentalists.

Jones, Madison, "On the Neighborhood Level," Interracial Review 35:22-23 (January 1962). Negroes and Catholics.

Kean, Charles D., "For Law and Integration," Christian Century 75:1262-1263 (November 5, 1958). Integration and the Protestant Episcopal Church.

Kean, Charles D., "Pressures on Episcopalians," Christian Century 78:1102-1103 (September 20, 1961).

Kean, Charles D., "District of Columbia," Christian Century 80:725-726 (May 29, 1963). Christians and Negroes in the capital.

Kearney, John, "Interracial Justice and the Indwelling of Christ Among All Men of Earth," Interracial Review 35:263 (December 1962).

Kelsey, George D., Racism and the Christian Understanding of Man. New York: Scribners, 1965.

Kenealy, William J., "Racism Desecrates Liberty, Perverts Justice and Love," Social Order 13:5-20 (May 1963). By professor of law, Loyola University, Chicago.

Kitagawa, Daisuke, Race Relations and Christian Mission. New York: Friendship, 1964.

Kitagawa, Daisuke, The Pastor and the Race Issue. New York: Seabury Press, 1965.

Klausler, Alfred P., "Chicago Area," Christian Century, July 17, 1963.

Kramer, Alfred S., "Patterns of Racial Inclusion Among the Churches of Three Protestant Denominations," Phylon 16:283-294 (Summer 1955).

Kruuse, Elsa, "The Churches Act on Integration," National Council Outlook 7:6-8 (March 1957).

La Farge, John, The Race Question and the Negro. New York: Longmans, Green, 1943.

La Farge, John, The Catholic Viewpoint on Race Relations. Garden City, N.Y.: Doubleday 1956; 2nd ed., Garden City, N.Y.: Hanover House, 1960.

La Farge, John, "American Catholics and the Negro, 1962," Social Order 12:153-161 (April 1962).

La Farge, John, "Why Say 'Interracial'?" Interracial Review 35:44-45 (February 1962).

La Farge, John, "Translating into Action," Interracial Review 35:92-95 (April 1962).

La Farge, John, "Pope John on Racism," Interracial Review 36:110-111+ (June 1963).

La Farge, John, "Direct Action," Interracial Review 36:159+ (September 1963). Admonitions addressed to Catholic employers of labor.

Lally, Francis J., "Needed—A People's Program," Interracial Review 35:2-3 (January 1962).

Lee, J. Oscar, "The Churches and Race Relations—A Survey," Christianity and Crisis 17:4-7 (February 4, 1957).

Lee, Robert, ed., Cities and Churches: Readings on the Urban Church. Philadelphia: Westminster, 1962.

Lenox, G. Merrill, "Michigan," Christian Century, September 11, 1963. The churches and what they have done in civil rights.

Liu, William T., "The Community Reference System, Religiosity, and Race Attitudes," Social Forces 39:324-328 (May 1961).

Loescher, F. S., "Racism in Northern City Churches," Christian Century 73:174-176 (February 8, 1956).

Long, Herman H., "Fellowship for Whom?" Nashville, Tenn.: Race Relations Department, Fisk University, no date. A study of racial inclusiveness in Congregational Christian churches.

McGill, Ralph, "The Agony of the Southern Minister," New York Times Magazine, September 27, 1959.

McManus, Eugene P., Studies in Race Relations. Baltimore: Josephite, 1961. Emphasis is on Christian principles rather than on sociological approaches to the problem.

McMillan, George, "Silent White Ministers of the South," New York Times Magazine, April 5, 1964.

McNeill, Robert, God Wills Us Free: The Ordeal of a Southern Minister. New York: Hill & Wang, 1965. Story of a white clergyman who was dismissed from his pulpit because of his stand on segregation.

McPeak, William, "Social Problems are Human Problems," Interracial Review 35:253-254 (November 1962).

Malev, William S., "The Jew of the South in the Conflict on Segregation," Conservative Judaism 13:35-46 (Fall 1958).

Mantinband, Charles, "From the Diary of a Mississippi Rabbi," American Judaism, Winter 1962-1963.

Maston, T. B., Segregation and Desegregation: A Christian Approach. New York: Macmillan, 1959. Chiefly concerned with school desegregation.

Mather, P. Boyd, "Religion and Race: Local Efforts," Christian Century 80:412-414 (March 27, 1963). Strategy of National Conference on Religion and Race.

Mather, P. Boyd, "Search for Sufficiency," Christian Century 80:1139-1140 (September 18, 1963). Methodist Church and its "Central" (Negro) jurisdiction.

Mays, Benjamin E., Seeking To Be Christian in Race Relations. New York: Friendship, 1957.

Mehan, Joseph, "Catholic Perspectives on Interracialism," Interracial Review 35:222-223 (October 1962).

Meyer, Sylvan, "They Share a Mission," Christian Century 79:1103-1105 (August 22, 1962). Church and press.

Miller, Robert M., American Protestantism and Social Issues. Chapel Hill: University of North Carolina Press, 1958.

Miller, William Robert, Nonviolence: A Christian Interpretation. New York: Association Press, 1965.

"Ministers' Statement of Conviction on Race," New South 12:3-6 (April 1957). By ministers' association of Richmond, Va.

"A Missionary Presence in Mississippi 1964," Social Action 31:1-48 (November 1964). Background information on the role of the NCC and the Mississippi Summer Project.

Mulholland, Joseph A., "The Community and Crime," Interracial Review 35:18-19 (January 1962). Negroes and Catholics.

National Catholic Conference for Interracial Justice, "Statement and Resolutions adopted by Council Delegates in Convention, November 17, 1963, at Washington, D.C.," Interracial Review 37:1+ (January 1964).

National Conference on Religion and Race, "An Appeal to the Conscience of the American People," Christian Century 80:135 (January 30, 1963).

Nelson, J. Robert, "Race and Denomination—One Issue," Christian Century 78:1554-1555 (December 27, 1961).

New South 18:1+ (March, 1963). Issue on "The Other Mississippi," including statements by groups of the state's ministers.

New York Times, February 10, 1957. Survey by Protestant Council of the City of New York of interracial aspects of city's Protestant churches.

Nichols, Lee, and Louis Cassels, "The Churches Repent," Harper's Magazine 211:53-57 (October 1955).

Niebuhr, Reinhold, "The Crisis in American Protestantism," Christian Century 80:1498-1450 (December 4, 1963). Protestant churches must take a stand on issues of justice.

Northwood, Lawrence K., "Ecological and Attitudinal Factors in Church Desegregation," Social Problems 6:150-163 (Fall 1958).

O'Connor, John J., "Catholic Interracial Movement," Social Order 10:290-295 (September 1960).

O'Neill, Joseph E., ed., A Catholic Case Against Segregation. New York: Macmillan, 1961.

Officers of the United Church Board for Homeland Ministries, "Are 'Sanctions' Sub-Christian?" Social Action 30:12-16 (May 1964). End of moral and financial support of work that involves segregation.

"Open or Closed Cities?" Christian Century 78:579-580 (May 10, 1961). Inaugurates controversy on role of the churches in Chicago segregation, continued by "Woodlawn—Open Or Closed," ibid. 78:685-688 (May 31, 1961), and editorial rejoinder ibid. 78:711 (June 7, 1961).

Peerman, Dean, "Death Down a Dark Street," Christian Century 80:166-167 (February 6 1963). Louis Cordell Marsh, a Christian youth worker, killed by a New York gang: an article written by a former classmate at Yale Divinity School.

Pettigrew, Thomas F., "The Myth of the Moderates," Christian Century 78:649-651 (May 24, 1961).

Pettigrew, Thomas F., "Our Caste-Ridden Protestant Campuses," Christianity and Crisis 21:88-91 (May 29, 1961).

Pettigrew, Thomas F., "Wherein the Church has Failed in Race," Religious Education 59:64-73 (January-February 1964).

Pohlhaus, J. Francis, "Catholic Involvement in Civil Rights Legislation," Interracial Review 36:192-195 (October 1963). Report by a NAACP leader.

Pope, Liston, The Kingdom Beyond Caste. New York: Friendship, 1957. A work of scholarship and conviction which examines racial prejudice in general and the forms it may take, particularly in the churches.

Posey, Walter B., "The Protestant Episcopal Church: An American Adaptation," Journal of Southern History 25:3-30 (February 1959).

Presbyterian Outlook 142:3-7 (March 20, 1960). Three brief articles on the sit-ins, the most significant of which is "Protestant-Jewish-Roman Catholic Conversation on the Sit-Ins."

"Race Tension is Costly," Christian Century 78:1068 (September 13, 1961).

Ramsey, Paul, Christian Ethics and the Sit-In. New York: Association, 1961.

Reimers, David M., "The Race Problem and Presbyterian Union," Church History 31:203-215 (June 1962). Bibliography.

Reimers, David M., White Protestantism and the Negro. New York: Oxford University Press, 1965. After an historical retrospect of white Protestantism's relation to the Negro, the author deals with the emergence of changing attitudes and with recent attempts to implement Christian commitments to end segregation.

Religion in Racial Crisis: A Report on the National Conference on Religion and Race and Recommendations. New York: National Conference on Religion and Race, 1963.

Reuter, George S., Jr., August M. Hintz, and Helen H. Reuter, One Blood. New York: Exposition Press, 1964. On the Christian approach to civil rights.

"Revolution--What Kind?" and "Politics--What Kind?" Christian Century, July 18, 1962; and replies: "Inner-City Realities," ibid., August 22, 1962. An interesting controversy over the reaction of the United Presbyterian Church, U.S.A., to a paper on racial problems in the city.

Rose, Stephen C., "Student Interracial Ministry: A Break in the Wall," Christian Century 79:327-328 (March 14, 1962).

Rose, Stephen C., "N.C.C. Visits Clarksdale," Christian Century 80:1104-1106 (September 11, 1963). Delegation from National Council of Churches to a Mississippi town.

Schomer, Howard, "Race and Religion in Albany [Georgia]," Christian Century 79:1155-1156 (September 26, 1962).

Schuyler, Joseph B., Northern Parish: A Sociological and Pastoral Study. Chicago: Loyola University Press, 1961. Survey of a Bronx parish showed majority favoring racial equality.

Schuyler, Joseph B., "Apostolic Opportunity," Interracial Review 35:20-21 (January 1962).

Sellers, James, The South and Christian Ethics. New York: Association Press, 1962. Viewing segregation theologically as a "regional variety of the inevitable fall of man," the author analyzes racial problems in terms of Southern traditions.

Senn, Milton, "Race, Religion and Suburbia," Journal of Intergroup Relations 3:159-170 (Spring 1962).

Senser, Robert, Primer on Interracial Justice. Baltimore: Helicon, 1962. The Roman Catholic position.

Seymour, Robert, "Interracial Ministry in North Carolina," Christian Century 80:109-111 (January 23, 1963).

Shriver, Donald W., Jr., ed., The Unsilent South. Richmond, Va.: John Knox Press, 1965. Sermons delivered by eighteen Presbyterian ministers and one layman in the South, all speaking out on the interracial crisis. Prefatory notes to each detail circumstances of delivery and what later happened to these men who preached equality of all men.

Simms, David McD., "Ethnic Tensions in the 'Inner-City' Church," Journal of Negro Education 31:448-454 (Fall 1962).

Smith, Lauren A., "Saints in the Basement," Christian Century 75:1050-1052 (September 17, 1958). Negroes and clergymen in Arkansas.

Smythe, Lewis S.C., ed., Southern Churches and Race Relations: Report of the Third Interracial Consultation. Lexington, Ky.: College of the Bible, 1961.

Southard, Samuel, "Self-Criticism in the South," Christian Century 79:1488-1490 (December 5, 1962).

Southard, Samuel, "Are Southern Churches Silent?" Christian Century 80:1429-1432 (November 20, 1963).

Spike, Robert W., The Freedom Revolution and the Churches. New York: Association Press, 1965. A manual of recommendations for community action, especially in the North, by the director of The Commission on Religion and Race, National Council of Churches of Christ in the U.S.A.

Stotts, Herbert E., and Paul Deats, Methodism and Society: Guidelines for Strategy. New York: Abingdon, 1962. Vol. 4 of a four-volume survey prepared for the Methodist Board of Social and Economic Relations.

Stringfellow, William, "Race, Religion and Revenge," Christian Century 79:192-194 (February 14, 1962). In Harlem.

Stringfellow, William, My People is the Enemy: An Autobiographical Polemic. New York: Holt, 1964. A passionate indictment of the Christian response to racial crisis by a young white lawyer and Episcopal layman, who lived and worked among Harlem poor.

Tanenbaum, Marc H., "The American Negro: Myths and Realities," Religious Education 59:33-36 (January-February 1964). Christian purpose should be that of "Discovering a relationship between white man and Negro."

Thomas, Mary S., "The Ordeal of Koinonia Farm," Progressive 21:23-25 (January 1957). Account of a Georgia religious and interracial camp and community, and the attacks on it.

Thurman, Howard, Footprints of a Dream: the Story of the Church for the Fellowship of All People. New York: Harper, 1959. A description of the various activities of this "interracial, intercultural, interdenominational" church (35 percent Negro) in San Francisco.

Tilson, Everett, Segregation and the Bible. Nashville, Tenn.: Abingdon, 1958.

Ungar, Andre, "To Birmingham, and Back," Conservative Judaism 18:1-17 (Fall 1963). A trip to the South by 19 rabbis.

"U.S. Bishops on Racial Harmony: Joint Pastoral," Interracial Review 36:182-183 (October 1963). Issued August, 1963.

Visser 't Hooft, W. A., The Ecumenical Movement and the Racial Problem. Paris: UNESCO, 1954

Vorspan, Albert, "Segregation and Social Justice," American Judaism 7:10-11 (January 1958).

Vorspan, Albert, "The Negro Victory—And the Jewish Failure," American Judaism 13:7, 50-52, 54 (Fall 1963).

Walton, O. M., "Presbyterians Aware," Christian Century 77:718-719 (June 15, 1960). Report on General Assembly of United Presbyterian Church, and the choice between a Negro and white integrationist for moderator.

Waltz, Alan K., and Robert L. Wilson, "Ministers' Attitudes Toward Integration," Phylon 19:195-198 (Summer 1958).

Whitman, Frederick L., "Subdimensions of Religiosity and Race Prejudice," Review of Religious Research 3:166-174 (Spring 1962).

Williamson, E. M., "Brownsville Justice," Christian Century, January 3, 1962; also Ernest Bromley, "Another View on Brownsville," ibid., January 31, 1962. Tennessee clergymen and a racial incident.

Wilmore, Gayraud S., Jr., "The New Negro and the Church," Christian Century 80:168-171 (February 6, 1963).

Wilson, Robert L., and James H. Davis, Jr., The Church and the Racially Changing Community. Nashville: Abingdon Press Original, 1966.

Wogaman, Philip, "Focus on Central Jurisdiction," Christian Century 80:1296-1298 (October 23, 1963). Methodist Negro section.

Young, Andrew J., "Demonstrations: A Twentieth Century Christian Witness," Social Action 30:5-12 (May 1964).

Young, Merrill Orne, "For Church's Sake," Christian Century 78:1300-1301 (November 1. 1961). Episcopal pilgrimage in Mississippi.

XIII. BLACK NATIONALISM

In certain respects the Negro protest of the 1950's and 1960's shows striking similarities with what was called the "Negro Renaissance" of the 1920's. Then as now Negro students--initially at Fisk University--became deeply involved in the movement. Then as now there was a literary burgeoning. Then as now there was a black nationalist movement, under the leadership of Marcus Garvey, the "Black Moses" of E. D. Cronon's biography. The mood of black nationalists manifested today, however, displays a strong tendency to stand apart as black men, to reject everything white, everything American, in the case of the Muslims in effect to deny a common humanity, and cannot therefore properly be considered as part of the Freedom Revolution.

Negro leaders are divided as to the true extent of the power of the Black Muslims, the most visible and most influential Negro racist group in America today. Their attraction for the ghetto masses in Northern cities is, however, acknowledged to be strong. Exotic aberration or violent threat, it has been taken seriously enough to be studied and penetratingly analyzed by, most notably, C. Eric Lincoln, Howard Brotz, Louis Lomax, and, in one section of the The Fire Next Time, James Baldwin. Louis Lomax has pointed out in The Negro Revolt that the rise of international racism feeds black chauvinism in the United States, and this, "among other reasons, is why all Americans of good will should be allied with the Negro in his current revolt." Clearly the break between Mr. Muhammad and Malcolm X, with Malcolm's subsequent assassination, are evidence that the Muslim movement is far from monolithic. It would seem that thus far there has been little influence on Negro Americans of the Negritude expounded by certain African and Caribbean writers, although such representatives of the Negro Writers' Group as LeRoi Jones, Ossie Davis, and on occasion James Baldwin, as well as the left-leaning Liberator, frequently enunciate what might be termed an American theory of blackness. It is interesting that Franz Fanon's Les Damnés de la Terre, which has been so profoundly influential in Africa, has finally been published in America (as The Wretched of the Earth, New York: Grove, 1965).

The Autobiography of Malcolm X. New York: Grove, 1965. Prepared with the assistance of
    Alex Haley. An impressive account, beginning with the childhood and youth which in
    effect destined him for conversion to Black Muslimism. His later conversion to Muslim
    in the true sense of the word and subsequent development of his thought suggest he
    might have become a powerful figure in the Negro revolt.
"Baldwin: Gray Flannel Muslim?" Christian Century 80:791 (June 12, 1963). An examination
    of the extent to which Baldwin inclines toward repudiation of the white world.
Berger, Morroe, "The Black Muslims," Horizon 6:48-65 (January 1964). A number of
    slaves brought to America were genuine "black Moslems." Professor Berger's article
    is based on accounts of these groups preserved by nineteenth-century amateur ethnolo-
    gists.
Brown, L. P., "Black Muslims and the Police," Journal of Criminal Law, Criminology and
    Police Science 56:119-126 (March 1965).
Brotz, Howard, "Negro 'Jews' in the United States," Phylon 12:324-337 (Winter 1952).
Brotz, Howard, The Black Jews of Harlem: Negro Nationalism and the Dilemmas of Negro
    Leadership. New York: Free Press, 1964. While the first half of this book deals with the
    "Ethiopian" Jews of Harlem, the second half deals with the problem of Negro leader-
    ship, the total Negro situation in America, and the role that Negro nationalism may play
    in its alleviation.
Burns, W. Haywood, "Black Muslims in America: A Reinterpretation," Race 5:26-37 (July
    1963).
Clark, Michael, "Rise in Racial Extremism," New York Times, January 25, 1960.
"Constitutional Law—Black Muslimism is a Religion Within the Meaning of the First
    Amendment," Georgia Bar Journal 24:519 (May 1962).
Cronon, E. D., Black Moses. Madison, Wis.: University of Wisconsin Press, 1955. Bio-
    graphy of Marcus Garvey and the best study of Garvey's Universal Negro Improvement
    Association, founded in 1918, which appealed to Negro ethnocentrism, and roused
    considerable enthusiasm for his plan to lead American Negroes back to Africa.
Cruse, Harold W., "Revolutionary Nationalism and the Afro-American," Studies on the Left
    2:12-25 (Number 3, 1962); and discussion by Robert Greenleaf, Harold W. Cruse, and
    Clark H. Foreman, ibid. 3:1-8 (Number 1, 1962).
"Discretion of Director of Corrections Not Abused in Refusing to Grant Black Muslim
    Prisoners Rights Afforded Other Religious Groups," UCLA Law Review 9:501 (March
    1962).
Essien-Udom, E. U., Black Nationalism: A Search for an Identity in America. Chicago:
    University of Chicago Press, 1962. Valuable assessment by an African of the Muslim
    movement and the nature of its appeal to lower-class urban Negroes.
Haley, Alex, "Mr. Muhammad Speaks," Reader's Digest 76:100-104 (March 1960).
Hatchett, John F., "The Moslem Influence among American Negroes," Journal of Human
    Relations 10:375-382 (Summer 1962).
Hentoff, Nat, "Elijah in the Wilderness," Reporter 23:37-40 (August 4, 1960).
Hernton, Calvin C., "White Liberals and Black Muslims," Negro Digest 12:3-9 (October
    1963). The failure of the one gave birth to the other.
Kirman, J. M., "Challenge of the Black Muslims," Social Education 27:365-368 (November
    1963).
Krosney, Herbert, "America's Black Supremacists," Nation 192:390-392 (May 6, 1961).
Landry, Lawrence, "Black Muslims and Sit-ins," New University Thought 2:3-7 (Winter
    1962).
Laue, James E., "A Contemporary Revitalization Movement in American Race Relations:
    The 'Black Muslims,'" Social Forces 42:315-323 (March 1964).
Lincoln, C. Eric, The Black Muslims in America. Boston: Beacon, 1961. A full-scale case
    study of the Black Muslim movement. As a Negro the author was able to attend Muslim
    meetings, and he had many interviews with Muhammad and many other Muslim leaders.
    His analysis of both the sociological and psychological context of the movement is
    penetrating and thorough. Bibliography.
Lincoln, C. Eric, "The Black Muslims," Progressive 26:43 (December 1962).
Lincoln, C. Eric, "Extremist Attitudes in the Black Muslim Movement," New South 18:3-10
    (January 1963).
Lincoln, C. Eric, My Face is Black. Boston: Beacon, 1964. The author's thesis is that the
    pauperized Southern Negro masses and the Northern black ghetto masses are being

pushed into acceptance of being black, the "mood ebony" which fosters black chauvinism. The book constitutes a sequel to The Black Muslims in America.

Lomax, Louis E., When the Word is Given: A Report on Elijah Muhammad, Malcolm X, and the Black Muslim World. Cleveland: World, 1963. The history and growing power of the Black Muslim movement and its leaders.

Makdisi, Nadim, "The Moslems of America," Christian Century 76:969-971 (August 26, 1959).

Malcolm X Speaks, ed. George Breitman, New York: Merit Publishers, 1965. Speeches and statements made during the last eight months of his life, edited and published by a group of Trotzkyists.

"Malcolm X Splits with Muhammad," New York Times, March 9, 1964.

Morsell, John A., "Black Nationalism," Journal of Intergroup Relations 3:5-11 (Winter 1961-1962). Black Nationalism as a response to inner tensions and frustrations.

Muhammad, Elijah, The Supreme Wisdom: The Solution to the So-called Negroes' Problem. 2nd ed., Chicago: University of Islam, 1957. The leader's exposition of the basic doctrines of Black Muslimism. See also his column, "Mr Muhammad Speaks," in the Pittsburgh Courier.

Muhammad, Elijah, Message to the Black Man in America. Chicago: Muhammad's Mosque No. 2, 1965.

Record, Wilson, "The Negro Intellectual and Negro Nationalism," Social Forces 32:10-18 (October 1954). The Negro intellectual, even though he may view African nationalist aspirations with sympathy, does not believe solution of Negro problems in America lies in separation from American society.

Record, Wilson, "Extremist Movements Among American Negroes," Phylon 17:17-23 (Spring 1956). Historically Negro extremist movements have been basically urban movements, arising in moments of distress and crisis in Negro life, feeding on the disorganization of migrants.

"The Right to Practice Black Muslim Tenets in State Prisons," Harvard Law Review 75:837 (February 1962).

Snellings, Rolland, "The New Afro-American Writer," Liberator 3:10-11 (October 1963). Concerned with growing militancy of young Negro writers, and their interest in black nationalism.

Spellman, A. B., "Interview with Malcolm X," Monthly Review, May 1964.

Spellman, A. B., "Black Nationalism and Radical Unity," The Second Coming 1:10-12 (January 1965). On the appeal of Malcolm X to Harlem masses who are indifferent to the orthodox Negro leadership

Thorne, Richard, "Integration or Black Nationalism: Which Route Will Negroes Choose?" Negro Digest 12:36-47 (August 1963). A young California intellectual thinks black nationalism the only honorable road to follow.

Samuels, Gertrude, "Two Ways: Black Muslim and NAACP," New York Times Magazine May 12, 1963.

Samuels, Gertrude, "Feud Within the Black Muslims," New York Times Magazine, March 22, 1964. Between Malcolm X and Elijah Muhammad.

Shack, William S., "Black Muslims: A Nativistic Religious Movement Among Negro Americans," Race 3:57-67 (November 1961).

Sherwin, Mark, The Extremists. New York: St. Martin's, 1963. The Black Muslims.

Southwick, Albert B., "Malcolm X: Charismatic Demagogue," Christian Century 80:740-741 (June 5, 1963).

Wallace, Mike, and Louis Lomax, "The Hate That Hate Produced," Newsbeat, New York: WNTA-TV (July 10, 1958).

Worthy, William, "An All Black Party," Liberator, October 1963. Urging support of the all-black Negro Freedom Now party as the only effective instrument of Negro political power.

Young, Harrison, "The Ivy League Negro: Black Nationalist?" Harvard Crimson September 21, 1964. Attitudes of both American and African Negro students.

XIV. TOOLS FOR FURTHER RESEARCH

Events move rapidly in the Negro Freedom Revolution. Scholars hasten into print with their studies of Negro problems. Every day the civil rights movement presents the law with new questions. It would seem, hopefully, that a course is now fairly firmly set toward recognition of the rights to equality of opportunity in the United States. As this is written, an all-white Alabama jury has just convicted a white man of second-degree murder in the slaying of a Negro foundry worker (a verdict of first-degree murder, be it noted, could not have been obtained), and a federal jury in Montgomery, Alabama, has convicted three Ku Klux Klansmen of violating an 1870 civil-rights-conspiracy law in connection with the 1964 killing of Mrs. Viola Liuzzo, a white civil rights worker. Yet granting the encouragement to be derived from entries on the plus side of the ledger, one must foresee tedious impediments set in the way of social change, reversals here, frustrations there.

For the student to keep abreast of the day-to-day events and developments that concern Negro citizens of the United States, conventional sources are not wholly adequate. The daily press is sometimes good, sometimes bad. Scholars will, of course, be aware of the wealth of materials available from the federal government, particularly the publications of the Bureau of Labor Statistics, of the Women's Bureau, as well as the Department of Labor Bulletins; from the Department of Commerce, publications of the Bureau of the Census, the Office of Business Economics, the Small Business Administration are especially useful, as are publications of the Department of Health, Education and Welfare. The Government Printing Office issues current lists as well as its annual catalogue of publications. The Library of Congress issues quarterly lists of additions to the Union Catalogue.

In addition a number of state and municipal commissions against discrimination conduct investigations, issue reports, make recommendations for action, and perform other functions in the area of community relations. Among the more energetic state organizations are the New York State Commission Against Discrimination, the Michigan Fair Employment Practices Commission, the Human Relations Commission of Illinois, the Ohio Civil Rights Commission, the Pennsylvania Human Relations Commission, the Massachusetts Commission Against Discrimination, the California Fair Employment Practices Commission, the Connecticut Commission on Civil Rights. Enquiries of gubernatorial or mayoral offices will elicit information on local agencies.

The following national organizations are most intimately concerned with Negro affairs: The National Association for the Advancement of Colored People (20 West 40th Street, New York City 18), whose official publication is The Crisis; the NAACP also issues an Annual Report, as well as other special reports and releases. The National Urban League (14 East 48th Street, New York City 17) issues Annual Reports, as well as special reports prepared by both national and regional research departments. The Southern Christian Leadership Conference (334 Auburn Avenue, N.E., Atlanta 3, Ga.), founded by Martin Luther King, Jr., publishes a Newsletter. The Congress on Racial Equality, CORE (38 Park Row, New York City 38) publishes CORE-lator. The Student Non-Violent Coordinating Committee (SNCC) publishes the Student Voice (8 1/2 Raymond Street, N.W., Atlanta, Ga., 30314). The Afro-American Research Institute of New York publishes the Liberator. The American Civil Liberties Union (156 Fifth Avenue, New York City 10) publishes an Annual Report. The Center for the Study of Democratic Institutions, Santa Barbara, California, frequently issues publications on the Negro. The specialized by-monthly, Trends in Housing, is published by the National Committee Against Discrimination in Housing (323 Lexington Avenue, New York City) and furnishes up-to-date information on anti-discrimination housing laws and ordinances throughout the nation. The Negro Bibliographic and Research Center, Inc. (117 R Street, N.E., Washington, D.C., 20002), founded in 1965, publishes a quarterly bibliographic survey of information on the Negro.

More specifically Southern-oriented organizations, with their publications, are: The Southern Regional Council (5 Forsyth Street, N.W., Atlanta 3, Ga.), which publishes The New South; the Council also published in May of 1957 a special report, Organizations and Personnel Engaged in Human Relations Activities in the South. The Southern Education Reporting Service (P.O. Box 6156 Nashville, Tenn.) publishes the Southern Education Report, which in September 1965 succeeded the Southern School News; it is a useful reference for desegregation news on the national, state, and local levels. Publications useful for current information on the Freedom Revolution are The Southern Courier, published weekly by the Southern Education Conference, Inc. (Room 622, Frank Leu Building, 79 Commerce Street, Montgomery, Ala.); The Southern Patriot, published by the Southern Conference Educational Fund, Inc. (Nashville, Tenn.); and Freedomways: A Quarterly Review of the Negro Freedom Movement, published by Freedomways Associates (799 Broadway, New York City), each number of which contains a list of recent books.

The popular magazines Ebony, Jet, Tan, and the Negro Digest are published by the Johnson Publishing Company, 1820 South Michigan Avenue, Chicago, Illinois.

The involvement of the churches is expressed in a number of special publications. The Commission on Religion and Race Reports is published by the National Council of the Churches of Christ in the U.S.A. (475 Riverside Drive, New York City 100027). The National Conference on Religion and Race (150 Fifth Avenue, New York City 10011), founded in 1963 by representatives of Protestant, Eastern Orthodox, Roman Catholic, and Jewish churches, issues books, pamphlets, reports, visual aids, and other materials. Renewal, published by the Chicago City Missionary Society (19 South La Salle Street, Chicago 60603) is concerned with urban problems. Church and Race, a monthly bulletin issued by the Department of Christian Social Relations, Episcopal Church Center (815 Second Avenue, New York City 10017), has provided some particularly vivid reporting of crisis situations. The National Catholic Conference for Interracial Justice (21 West Superior, Chicago 60610) publishes Commitment, as well as issues reports, reprints, book lists, and other materials. The American Friends Service Committee (160 North 15th Street, Philadelphia) issues occasional reports on its activities in search of nonviolent resolutions of racial tensions, as on Philadelphia housing. The Anti-Defamation League of B'nai B'rith (515 Madison Avenue, New York City 10022) has made especially useful contributions in the field of race relations. In addition to Rights, in which reports on social, employment, educational, and housing discrimination are published, the League issues an annual Research Bulletin on Intergroup Relations containing research abstracts and reports. The League itself also supports much useful research.

There are other voices as well which should be noted. The Citizens' Councils of America (Jackson, Mississippi) publish The Citizens' Council, as well as reprinting numerous speeches and other documents. The Defender's News and Views is published by the Defenders of State Sovereignty and Individual Liberties, Richmond, Virginia. The Citizen's Press of Birmingham, Alabama, publishes the Dixie American: Voice of the Anglo-Saxon South. The Thunderbolt: The White Man's Viewpoint is published by the National States Rights Party, Augusta, Georgia.

The researcher will discover other materials, often ephemeral, as events occasion response. It is hoped that the sources noted above will suggest the kind of publications for which the student should be on the watch. A list of general bibliographic aids and special collections follows.

American Library Directory. 22nd ed. New York: Bowker, 1960. A number of special
  collections on the Negro are listed herein, the most important of which are to be found
  below. As Paul M. Smith observed in the Journal of Negro Education 30:150-152 (Spring
  1961), the majority of the collections named can be called "special" by courtesy only.
N. W. Ayer & Sons, Directory of Newspapers and Periodicals, Philadelphia, 1965, pp. 1406-
  1407. Published annually.
Brooks, Alexander D., and Virginia H. Ellison, Civil Rights and Liberties in the United
  States: An Annotated Bibliography. New York: Civil Liberties Educational Foundation,
  1962. Section on "Civil Rights and Intergroup Relations," pp. 53-77, contains a selection
  of general and scholarly works on Negro civil rights.
Davis, John P., ed., The American Negro Reference Book. New York: Prentice-Hall, 1966.
  A summary of current information on the main aspects of Negro life in the United States.
Detroit Public Library. Collection on Negro Songs and Music, 849 volumes. Contains music,
  recordings, extensive clipping files pertaining to Negroes and the performing arts.
Dictionary Catalog of the Schomburg Collection of Negro Literature and History, 9 vols.
  Boston: Hall, 1962. The Schomburg Collection, located in a branch of the New York
  Public Library, 103 W. 135th Street, as of 1962 contained more than 36,000 bound
  volumes and 80 drawers of vertical file materials covering every aspect of the
  experience of peoples of African descent, historical and contemporary. The life work of
  a Puerto Rican-born Negro, Arthur A. Schomburg (1874-1938), materials include books,
  periodicals, records, sheet music, objects d'art. Use restricted to premises.
Dumond, Dwight L., A Bibliography of Anti-Slavery in America. Ann Arbor: University of
  Michigan Press, 1961.
Fisk University Library. Special Negro collection contains 10,000 volumes, considerable
  manuscript material. Use restricted to the library premises.
A Guide to Negro Periodical Literature. Published quarterly in Winston Salem, N.C., 1941-
  1946. Superseded in 1950 by Index to Selected Periodicals issued by Ohio Central State
  College Library.
Hampton Institute, Collis P. Huntington Memorial Library, George Foster Peabody
  Collection, 9,289 volumes .
Harvard Journal of Negro Affairs. Published semiannually by the Association of African
  and Afro-American Students at Harvard and Radcliffe.
Homer, Dorothy R., The Negro: A List of Significant Books. 8th rev. ed., New York: New
  York Public Library, 1960; 9th ed., 1965, published under title The Negro in the United
  States: A List of Significant Books. Annotated list of some 300 titles.
Howard University Library. Negro Collection contains 70,000 volumes.
Index to Selected Periodicals. Published since 1950 by Ohio Central State College Library,
  it supersedes A Guide to Negro Periodical Literature.
Integrated Education. Issued bimonthly by Integrated Education Associates, Chicago.
  Contains bibliography and reviews of books and articles on integration and education.
Interracial News Service. A bi-monthly published by the National Council of Churches of
  Christ in America, 475 Riverside Drive, New York 27, N.Y.
Kessler, S. H., "American Negro Literature, A Bibliographic Guide," Bulletin of Biblio-
  graphy 21:181-185 (September 1955). Lists 93 bibliographies dealing with various areas
  of Negro life.
Journal of Intergroup Relations. Quarterly publication of the National Association of Inter -
  group Relations Officials (NAIRO), 55 W. 42nd St., New York 36, N.Y.
Journal of Negro Education. Published quarterly by the Bureau of Educational Research,
  Howard University, Washington, D.C. An extremely useful index to volumes 1-31 (1932-
  1962) was prepared by the staff of the Negro Collection, Howard University Library, and
  published by the Journal in 1963.
Journal of Negro History. Quarterly publication of Association for the Study of Negro Life
  and History.
Journal of Southern History. Quarterly published by Southern Historical Association.
  Annual bibliography contains section on "Slavery and the Southern Negro."
Negro History Bulletin. Monthly publication of the Association for the Study of Negro Life
  and History.
Negro Newspapers on Microfilm: A Selected List. Washington, D.C.: The Library of
  Congress, 1953.

New York Times Index. Published annually by the New York Times Company of New York City.

Phylon. Published quarterly by Atlanta University. Presents annual review, usually in Summer issue, of literary works by or about Negroes.

Quarterly Review of Higher Education Among Negroes. Published at Johnson C. Smith University, Charlotte, N.C. Each issue carries section of "News Items" or a "News Release" useful for information on occupations of college graduates and honors to individual Negroes.

Race Relations Law Reporter. Published quarterly by Vanderbilt University School of Law, Nashville, Tennessee. Presents court cases, legislation, orders, and regulations on all aspects of race relations.

Redden, C. L., "The American Negro: An Annotated List of Educational Films and Film-strips," Journal of Negro Education 33:79-82 (Winter 1964).

Selected Bibliography on the Negro. 4th ed., New York: National Urban League Department of Research, 1951; supplement 1958.

Spangler, Earl, Bibliography of Negro History, Selected and Annotated Entries: General and Minnesota. Minneapolis: Ross and Haines, 1963. About two thirds on Minnesota.

Stuckert, Robert D., and Irwin D. Rinder, "The Negro in the Social Science Literature: 1961," Phylon 23:111-127 (Summer 1962)..

"Studies in Race and Culture, 1962," Phylon 24:392-398 (Winter 1963). A list of 48 doctoral dissertations and 70 master's theses on race and culture.

Thompson, Edgar T., and Alma M. Thompson, Race and Region: A Descriptive Bibliography Compiled with Special Reference to Relations Between Whites and Negroes in the United States. Chapel Hill: University of North Carolina Press, 1949.

Tumin, Melvin M., and Robert Rotberg, Segregation and Desegregation: A Digest of Recent Research. New York: Anti-Defamation League, 1956. Articles in professional journals for the period January 1, 1951, to July 1, 1956, as well as data from public opinion polls and surveys.

Tumin, Melvin M., and Robert Rotberg, Supplement to Segregation and Desegregation: A Digest of Recent Research, 1956-1959. New York: Anti-Defamation League, 1960.

Tuskegee Institute Library, Washington Collection, 11,000 volumes.

U. S. Department of Health, Education, and Welfare Library. Contains some 700,000 items on all phases of Negro education.

Welsch, Erwin K., The Negro in the United States: A Research Guide. Bloomington: Indiana University Press, 1965. A brief but useful introduction to research.

Work, Monroe N., A Bibliography of the Negro in Africa and America. New York: Wilson, 1928; reprinted New York: Octagon Books, 1965. Over 10,000 items. Invaluable for older items.

Yale University Library, James Weldon Johnson Memorial Collection of Negro Arts and Letters.

Aaron, Benjamin, 74
Abbott, Walter M., 153
Aber, Elaine M., 115
Abraham, Henry J., 99, 109
Abrahamson, Julia, 93
Abrams, Charles, 58, 87, 89, 93, 136
Abramson, Marcia, 18
Abu-Laban, Baha, 21
Abu-Lughod, J., 90
Ackiss, T.D., 21
Adams, Frankie V., 93
Adams, M.S., 36
Adams, Russell L., 9
Adams, W. Thomas, 63
Ahmann, Mathew, 140, 155
Aikin, Charles, 127, 129
Alexander, Charles C., 148
Alexander, W.W., 155
Alexis, Marcus, 72
Alfange, Dean, Jr., 136
Allen, James Egert, 58
Allman, Reva White, 45, 109
Allport, Gordon W., 25, 45
Alpenfels, Ethel, 14
Altenderfer, Marion E., 37
Alter, S.M., 36
Amos, R.T., 115
Amos, William E., 76, 114
Anastasi, Anne, 25, 30, 115
Anderson, Archibald W., 106
Anderson, C. Arnold, 56, 109
Anderson, John Weir, 136
Anderson, Margaret, 115
Anderson, Martin, 90
Anderson, R.S., 36
Annella, Sister M., 24
Anthony, Daniel S., 58
Antonovsky, Aaron, 45, 76, 114
Appel, K.E., 38
Aptheker, Herbert, 5, 136, 140
Armstrong, C.P., 115
Armstrong, Robert G., 99
Arnez, Nancy Levi, 105
Asbury, Edith Evans, 73
Ashmore, Harry S., 105, 149
Atelsek, F.J., 96
Athey, K.R., 45
Atkinson, J.W., 29
Aurbach, Herbert A., 87
Ausubel, D.P., 25
Avins, Alfred, 87, 136
Axelrad, Sidney, 63
Axelrod, Morris, 45

Axelson, Leland, 27
Axline, Virginia M., 25
Ayres, P., 37

Babbit, Thelma W., 51
Babchuk, Nicholas, 21, 48
Babow, Irving, 37, 76, 124
Bachrach, Arthur J., 149
Back, Kurt W., 20
Bacon, Margaret H., 93
Bacon, Margaret K., 63
Bacote, C.A., 129
Bagdikian, Ben H., 71
Bailey, Kenneth K., 155
Bain, M., 81
Bakelman, W. Robert, 111
Baker, P.T., 33
Baldwin, James, 39, 62, 105, 140
Balfour, Brickner, 51
Balk, Alfred, 93
Ball, Brenda, 26
Ball, Edward D., 122
Ball, J.C., 25
Ball, William B., 155
Bamberger, Michael A., 74
Bancroft, Gertrude, 76
Bandure, A., 25
Banfield, Edward C., 58, 90, 92, 129, 133
Banks, Waldo R., 51
Banks, W.S.M., II, 45
Banton, Michael, 45
Bardolph, Richard, 18, 21
Barker, Gordon H., 63
Barker, J., 26
Barksdale, Richard K., 39
Barnes, Nicholas L., 72
Barnes, William W., 118
Barnett, Richard, 136
Barnicot, N., 14
Baron, Harold, 77
Baron, W., 119
Barrett, Russell, 120
Barrett, William E., 39
Barron, Milton L., 24, 46
Barry, H., III, 63
Bart, Peter, 66
Barth, Ernest A.T., 21, 46, 90, 95
Barton, Paul, 55, 118
Bass, B.M., 64
Bass, D.E., 33
Bass, L.N., 33
Batchelder, Alan B., 68, 71, 77
Bates, Daisy, 120

Bates, William, 63
Battle, Robert, III, 81
Bauer, Catherine, 90
Baumgartner, Leona, 36
Bayton, J.A., 24
Beach, Waldo, 149
Beale, Calvin L., 56
Beals, Carleton, 5
Beattie, R.H., 63
Beattie, Walter M., Jr., 21
Beck, Samuel J., 25
Becker, Gary S., 68, 77
Becker, William, 74
Beechwood, Mary, 39
Belfrage, Sally, 140, 141
Bell, Daniel, 21, 81, 141
Bell, E., 24
Bell, John L., 155
Bell, Odessa Khaton, 107
Bell, R.R., 16
Bell, Wendell, 62, 90
Bendix, Reinhard, 69, 73
Benedict, Roger W., 149
Benjamin, Lawrence, 47, 84
Bennett, John C., 155
Bennett, Lerone, Jr., 5, 9, 21, 24, 141
Bennett, Richard, 122
Bennett, William S., Jr., 27
Bensing, R.C., 63
Benson, Arthur L., 113
Benson, W.M., 55
Berdie, R.F.B., 25
Berelson, Bernard, 1
Berger, E.M., 25
Berger, Morroe, 74, 99, 136, 164
Berman, Daniel M., 136
Berman, Hyman, 6, 78
Bernard, Raymond, 149, 155
Bernard, Viola W., 34
Bernd, Joseph L., 127
Bernhard, B.I., 127
Bernstein, Barton J., 99
Berreman, Joel V., 115
Berry, Brewton, 14, 46
Berry, L.H., 36
Berscheid, E.S., 29
Bertrand, Alvin L., 56
Beshers, James M., 8, 58
Beth, L.P., 127
Bettelheim, Bruno, 46
Beynon, Erdmann Doane, 18
Bibbly, Cyril, 105
Bickel, Alexander M., 99, 100, 127, 136
Bickers, J.T., 90
Bidwell, C.E., 115
Billingsley, Amy Tate, 16
Billingsley, Andrew, 16
Bird, Alan R., 56
Bird, C., 83

Birnbaum, O., 74
Bittker, B.I., 87
Bittle, William E., 22, 120
Black, C.L., Jr., 100
Black, I., 14
Black, L.E., 72
Blackford, Staige, 127
Blackwell, Gordon W., 149
Blair, Lewis H., 1
Blalock, Hubert M., Jr., 22, 46, 59, 68, 77, 114
Blatt, B., 30
Blau, Zena Smith, 16
Blaustein, Albert P., 100
Blayton, J.B., 90
Bloch, Charles P., 136
Bloch, Herman D., 51, 77, 81, 83
Blood, Robert O., 16
Bloom, Benjamin S., 30
Bloom, R., 20
Blossom, Virgil T., 121
Blue, John J., Jr., 20
Bluford, Lucile H., 100
Blumberg, B.S., 16, 33
Blumberg, Leonard, 90
Blumer, Herbert, 46, 51
Blumrosen, A.B., 87
Bogardus, Emory S., 51
Boggs, James, 81, 141
Boggs, Marion, 155
Bogue, Donald J., 8, 59, 60
Bohannon, P., 63
Boldon, Wiley S., 113
Bond, Horace Mann, 30, 113
Bond, Marjorie H., 51
Bone, Robert A., 39
Bonfield, A.E., 127, 136
Bontemps, Arna Wendell, 9, 18, 39, 42
Booker, Simeon, 141
Borinski, Ernst, 100, 136
Boucher, Bertrand P., 105
Bouton, Ellen Naylor, 155
Bower, R.J., 121
Bowerman, Charles E., 109
Bowman, Garda W., 83
Bowman, M.J., 56
Boyd, Malcolm, 155
Boyd, William C., 14
Boykin, Leander L., 105, 111, 113, 114
Boylan, Francis T., 46
Boyle, E., Jr., 37
Boyle, Sarah Patton, 149
Braden, Anne, 141
Bradley, Gladyce H., 115
Brady, Tom P., 100
Brain, George B., 115
Braithwaite, William S., 39
Brameld, Theodore, 105
Branscomb, A.W., 87

Brazeal, Brailsford R., 121, 129
Brazziel, William F., 111, 113, 114, 121
Brecher, Edward, 83
Brecher, Ruth, 83
Breed, Warren, 22, 46, 121
Breitman, George, 165
Breman, Paul, 39
Bremner, Robert H., 71
Bressler, Marvin, 93
Breton, Gabriel, 142
Brewer, J. Mason, 18, 39
Brewster, Edward E., 25
Brickman, William W., 105, 106
Briggs, William A., 114
Brink, William, 141
Brinker, Paul A., 93
Brittain, Joseph M., 127
Britts, Maurice W., 155
Broadfield, George W., 71
Broder, David S., 129
Broderick, C.B., 24
Broderick, Francis L., 9
Brody, Eugene B., 16, 26, 34, 46
Brogan, Dennis W., 129
Brookover, William B., 106
Brooks, Albert N.D., 121
Brooks, Alexander D., 169
Brooks, Gwendolyn, 39
Brooks, Hugh C., 105
Brooks, Maxwell R., 24, 129
Brooks, Tom, 81
Broom, Leonard, 1
Brophy, Ira N., 46
Brotz, Howard, 164
Brown, Aaron, 109, 111
Brown, Aubrey N., Jr., 155
Brown, Bert, 30
Brown, Claude, 9, 62
Brown, Earl L., 66
Brown, Frank L., 40
Brown, Ina Corinne, 1
Brown, L.G., 37
Brown, L.P., 63, 164
Brown, Morgan C., 56
Brown, Robert, 68
Brown, Robert R., 155
Brown, Sterling A., 40
Brown, Warren, 24
Browne, V.J., 83
Bryant, Lawrence C., 111
Bryce, Harrington, 107
Buckley, Louis F., 77
Buder, Leonard, 119
Bullock, Henry Allen, 72, 127
Bullock, Paul, 75, 83, 107
Bullock, W.H., 33
Bunche, Ralph, 141
Burch, G.E., 37
Burchard, Peter, 5

Burgess, Ernest W., 51, 59
Burgess, M. Elaine, 22
Burma, John H., 24
Burns, W. Haywood, 141, 164
Burnstein, E., 46
Burr, Nelson R., 18
Burrus, Bernie, 55, 118
Burton, R.V., 16, 26
Bushnell, Paul E., 141
Buskirk, E.R., 33
Butcher, James, 26
Butcher, Margaret Just, 40
Butts, Hugh F., 26
Byrnes, James F., 100
Byrns, O'Meara, 46

Cadwallader, M.L., 65
Cahill, Edward, 149
Cahn, Edmond, 100
Calden, G., 27
Caldwell, Erskine, 1, 149
Caldwell, M.G., 63
Caldwell, Willard E., 32
Calef, Wesley C., 8
Caliver, Ambrose, 109
Callahan, K.R., 77
Calvet, Ivis J., 37, 83
Campbell, Byram, 46
Campbell, Ernest Q., 46, 51, 109, 155
Campbell, John D., 51, 55
Campbell, Will D., 155
Cannon, T.M., Jr., 52
Cantril, Hadley, 18
Canzoneri, Robert, 149
Caplan, Eleanor, 93
Carawan, Candie, 141
Carawan, Guy, 141
Carey, A.J., 100
Carey, James B., 81
Carl, E.L., 77, 124
Carleton, William G., 51, 129
Carmack, William R., 116
Carmichael, B.E., 110
Carmichael, Omer, 100
Carnegie, M.E., 37
Carnell, Edward John, 156
Carr, Warren, 156
Carson, Arnold S., 30
Carter, Barbara, 116, 127
Carter, Elmer, 51, 136
Carter, Hodding, III, 141, 149
Carter, Marion Elizabeth, 51
Carter, Robert L., 87, 100
Carter, Wilmoth A., 59
Cartwright, Colbert S., 156
Cash, W.J., 1
Cassell, Frank H., 83
Cassels, Louis, 160
Catchings, L. Maynard, 156

Cavan, Ruth Shonle, 16, 63
Cavusoglu, M., 36
Cayton, Horace R., 9, 18, 59, 82
Chaffee, John, Jr., 108
Chalmers, David M., 149
Chalmers, W. Ellison, 77
Chambers, Walter D., 58
Chapin, F. Stuart, 60
Chase, A.L., 52
Chastain, Thomas, 40
Chein, Isidor, 26, 63
Cherry, Gwendolyn, 9
Chickering, Arthur W., 51
Child, I.L., 63
Christie, Richard, 46
Christman, Henry M., 5
Christopher, Maurice, 83
Christopherson, W.M., 36
Churn, Browning, 32
Clark, Dennis, 51, 62, 93, 95, 116
Clark, Elmer T., 18
Clark, Henry, 24, 93, 156
Clark, Kenneth B., 26, 46, 49, 51, 62, 63, 66, 100, 108, 111, 116, 121, 141
Clark, Mamie P., 26
Clark, Michael, 164
Clark, Thomas D., 2
Clarke, Jacquelyne J., 141
Clarke, John Henrik, 40
Clausen, J.A., 34
Claye, Clifton M., 22
Clayton, Edward T., 129, 142
Cleaveland, Frederic W., 132
Clift, Virgil A., 106, 113, 116
Clinard, Marshall B., 26
Cloward, Richard A., 63
Clubok, Alfred B., 129
Cobb, W. Montague, 37, 77
Coe, Paul F., 60
Cogley, John, 156
Cohen, Albert K., 63, 77
Cohen, Melvin, 52
Cohen, Oscar, 93
Cohen, Richard, 108
Coke, James G., 59
Cole, Mildred Wiese, 2
Cole, Stewart G., 2
Coleman, A. Lee, 51, 114
Coleman, J.S., 22
Coleman, Joan E., 45
Coleman, John R., 87
Coles, Robert, 26, 40, 56, 63, 116, 119, 121, 142
Colley, N.S., 88
Collie, Robert, 156
Collier, Eugenia W., 40
Collins, Mary Evans, 93
Comings, Carolyn, 108
Comstock, G.W., 36

Conant, James B., 108
Congar, Yves M.-J., 156
Constable, John, 142
Conyers, James E., 26
Cook, Elaine, 51
Cook, Eugene, 100
Cook, James Graham, 149
Cook, Lloyd A., 51
Cook, Peggy, 46
Cook, Samuel DuBois, 5, 142, 149
Cook, Stuart W., 26, 55
Cooke, Paul, 121
Coombs, Philip, 106
Coon, Carleton S., 14
Cooper, A.J., 16, 33
Cooper, Joseph B., 46
Corey, John, 118
Cornely, P.B., 37
Cornwell, Elmer E., 129
Cothran, Tilman C., 40, 129, 142
Countryman, Vern, 137
Counts, S., 28
Courlander, Harold, 40
Cowgill, Donald O., 90, 108
Cowhig, James D., 56
Cowles, Wylda, 37
Cox, Archibald, 75
Cox, Harvey, 156
Cox, John H., 5
Cox, Oliver Cromwell, 2
Cox, T., 84
Cox, La Wanda, 5
Cozart, L.S., 106
Crain, Robert D., 91
Cramer, M. Richard, 54, 121, 149
Cranford, Clarence W., 111
Crawford, F.R., 34
Creger, Ralph, 156
Cressey, Donald R., 63
Crockett, Harry J., Jr., 119
Cromien, Florence, 88
Cronon, E.D., 9, 164
Crook, Roger H., 156
Cross, G.J., 63
Crowe, C. Lawson, 14
Crowther, Beatrice, 37
Crump, E. Perry, 31, 33, 37
Cruse, Harold W., 164
Crutchfield, Richard, 31
Culver, Dwight W., 156
Cummins, J.D., 24
Cuninggim, Merrimon, 121, 156
Cunningham, George E., 77
Curry, Andrew E., 46
Curry, J.E., 66
Cushman, Robert E., 137

Dabbs, James McBride, 51, 149
Dai, Bingham, 26

Daly, Victor R., 51
D'Amico, Louis A., 26, 111
Dandekar, D.P., 60
D'Andrade, R.G., 16
D'Angelo, Rita, 30
Daniel, Bradford, 142
Daniel, Vattel E., 18
Daniel, Walter C., 77
Daniel, Walter G., 63, 77, 116
Daniels, Jonathan, 156
Danzig, David, 142, 150
Danzig, Fred, 72
David, Martin, 71
Davidson, William, 20
Davie, Maurice, 2
Davis, Allison W., 2, 16, 113
Davis, Arthur P., 26, 40
Davis, Christopher, 40
Davis, James H., Jr., 162
Davis, John P., 169
Davis, Lloyd, 156
Davis, M.M., 37
Davis, Ossie, 40
Davis, Russell F., 40
Davis, Sammy, Jr., 9
Davis, T.W., 33
Davis, Wylie H., 103
Dean, John P., 51
Deasy, Leila C., 16
Deats, Paul, 161
Decker, Paul M., 77
DeCosta, Frank A., 111
Decter, Midge, 108
De Fleur, Melvin L., 51
De Grazia, Alfred, 127
Degrove, John M., 129
DeLacy, G.L., 124
Delavan, V., 142
Demby, William, 40
Demerath, Nicholas J., III, 31, 60, 121
DeMott, Benjamin, 62
Denison, Edward F., 69
Dent, Tom, 101
Dentler, Robert A., 96, 119
Derbyshire, Robert L., 17, 26, 34
Derthick, Martha, 129
Deschin, Celia S., 36
Deutsch, A., 34
Deutsch, E.P., 101
Deutsch, Martin, 30, 95, 113, 150
Deutsch, Morton, 93
Deutscher, Isaac, 26
DeVegh, Elizabeth, 40
DeVree, Charlotte, 142
Dewey, Donald, 77
Dicks, H.V., 46
Dienstfrey, Ted, 142
Diggs, C., Jr., 22
Diggs, Mary H., 64

Dingman, F., 35
Distler, Luther, 28
Dixon, R.G., Jr., 124
Dobbins, D.A., 64
Dobzhansky, Theodosius, 14
Doddy, Hurley H., 111, 121, 142
Dodson, Dan W., 94, 108, 116
Doherty, J.F., 24
Dollard, John, 2
Donahue, Charles, 75
Donahue, John W., 121
Donald, David, 5
Donavan, James B., 119
Dorfman, Elaine, 34
Dorman, Michael, 142
Dorsey, Nathaniel W., 77
Dorson, Richard M., 40, 41
Doss, George A., Jr., 142
Douglas, Paul H., 127
Douglass, Frederick, 9
Douglass, Joseph H., 64, 84
Dover, Cedric, 2
Dowd, Douglas F., 129
Downs, Anthony, 94
Doyle, William, 82
Drake, Merci L., 80
Drake, St. Clair, 2, 18, 59, 69
Dreger, R.M., 26
Drewry, G.N., 110
Drews, Elizabeth M., 33
Drinan, Robert F., 101, 124
Duberman, Martin B., 5
Dublin, T.R., 33
DuBois, W.E.B., 2, 22
Dugger, Ronnie, 150
Dulaney, William L., 59
Dummett, Clifton O., 37, 114
Dumond, Dwight L., 169
Dunbar, Ernest, 142
Dunbar, Leslie W., 142, 150
Duncan, Beverly D., 60, 77, 90
Duncan, Otis D., 60, 77, 90
Dunham, H.W., 34
Dunne, George H., 71, 121, 156
Dunnegan, Marjorie Lord, 108
Duplantier, Adrian G., 137
Dure, Leon, 101
Dworkin, Martin S., 84
Dwyer, Robert J., 78, 106
Dykeman, Wilma, 20, 142, 150

East, P.D., 150
Eastland, James O., 101
Eaton, Clement, 5
Eboine, Alvin E., 46
Echeruo, M.J.C., 41
Eddy, Elizabeth M., 52
Eddy, Mrs. George A., 150
Edmonds, William S., 30

Edmonson, Munro S., 4, 23, 29
Edmunds, Edwin R., 46
Edwards, Esther P., 106
Edwards, G. Franklin, 17, 20, 22, 78, 121
Edwards, Junius, 41
Edwin, Ed, 10
Eells, Walter Crosby, 111
Egan, John J., 59, 90, 156
Ehle, John, 142, 156
Ehrenzweig, A.A., 24
Ehrlich, Howard J., 46, 47
Eichner, Alfred S., 2
Elkins, Stanley M., 5
Elliot, O., 14
Ellis, Greeley H., Jr., 75
Ellison, Ralph, 41
Ellison, Virginia, 169
Elston, Wilbur, 156
Emerson, Rupert, 2
Engel, Gerald, 49
Engel, Leonard, 37
English, W.H., 62
Enion, R.A., 84
Epps, Edgar G., 21, 27
Epstein, Charlotte, 52, 64
Erikson, Erik, 17, 27
Ernst, Harry W., 150
Erskine, Hazel G., 47
Ervin, R.W., 125, 137
Ervin, Sam J., 101, 127
Essien-Udom, E.U., 164
Evans, James C., 84
Evans, John B., 156
Ezell, John Samuel, 8

Fair, Ronald L., 41
Fairman, Charles, 101
Falls, Arthur G., 78
Faris, R.E.L., 34
Farmer, James, 142
Farris, Charles D., 127, 129
Faubus, Orval, 101
Faulkner, William, 150
Fauman, S. Joseph, 94, 108
Fauset, Arthur H., 19
Feagans, Janet, 125, 142
Feibleman, Peter S., 41
Fein, Rashi, 2, 34, 69
Feinstein, Otto, 142
Feld, Shiela C., 29
Feldman, J. Arnold, 78
Fen, Sing-Nan, 52, 106
Fenton, John H., 130
Ferguson, Clarence Clyde, Jr., 100, 125, 137
Ferguson, Harold A., 106
Ferman, Louis A., 71
Fey, Harold E., 142, 156, 157

Fichter, Joseph H., 157
Fields, Uriah J., 143
Fineberg, S. Andhil, 47
Finestone, Harold, 64
Fischer, John, 143
Fischer, John H., 108, 116
Fischer, L.K., 33
Fisher, Burton R., 118
Fisher, Franklin M., 68
Fisher, Margaret, 88
Fisher, Miles M., 41
Fishman, Jacob R., 27
Fishman, Joshua A., 27, 47, 94, 95, 150
Fitzhugh, H. Naylor, 73
Fitzpatrick, Joseph P., 47, 157
Fleischman, Harry, 82
Fleming, G. James, 121, 130
Fleming, Harold C., 53, 84, 137, 143, 150
Fogel, David, 22
Foley, Albert S., 157
Foley, Eugene P., 73
Foley, M.M., 90
Fontaine, William T., 41
Fontinell, Eugene, 27
Foote, N.N., 90
Ford, Nick Aaron, 41
Forshey, Gerald, 157
Foster, Luther H., 47, 111
Fowler, Grady, 150
Fox, Vernon, 64
Frank, J.D., 35
Frank, John P., 52
Franklin, J.C., 64
Franklin, John Hope, 6, 127
Franklin, M., 101, 137
Frazier, E. Franklin, 2, 14, 17, 19, 20, 27, 47, 52, 59, 69
Freedman, Marcia K., 113
Freedman, Theodore, 116, 121
Freeman, Howard E., 90
Freund, Paul A., 101, 137
Frey, D.S., 88
Friedenberg, Edgar Z., 41, 106
Friedman, Leon, 137
Friedman, Murray, 121, 143
Friedrichs, Robert W., 91
Friedsam, N.J., 37
Frumkin, Robert M., 17, 20, 34
Fry, John K., 157
Fulk, Byron E., 30
Fuller, H.W., 143
Fuller, J.L., 33
Furnas, J.C., 2

Gabel, Hortense W., 129
Gaier, Eugene L., 27
Gaillard, S.P., 101
Gaines, Ernest J., 41

Gallagher, Buell, 157
Gallaher, Art, Jr., 78
Galtung, Johann, 150
Gamarckian, Edward, 130
Gandy, Samuel L., 121
Gandy, Willard E., 121
Gans, Herbert J., 91, 92
Gara, Larry, 6
Garai, Joseph, 136
Garfinkel, Herbert, 143
Garfunkel, F., 30
Garn, Stanley, 14
Garraty, John A., 6
Garrett, Henry E., 30
Garsand, Marcel, Jr., 101
Gasnick, Roy M., 157
Gates, Robbins L., 101
Gauntlett, John, 130
Gegan, B.E., 101
Geier, Woodrow A., 157
Geis, Gilbert, 22, 64
Geisel, P.N., 18
Gellhorn, Walter, 114
Genovese, Eugene D., 6
George, Wesley Critz, 14
Gerard, Donald L., 63
Gerber, Irwin, 22
Geschwender, J.A., 22
Gessell, John M., 121
Gibel, Inge Lederer, 119
Gilbert, Arthur, 150
Giles, E., 14
Giles, H. Harry, 116
Gill, Robert L., 101, 137
Gillard, John T., 19, 157
Gillespie, G.T., 157
Ginger, A.F., 88
Ginsburg, Gilbert J., 75
Ginzberg, Eli, 2, 6, 17, 69, 78, 106
Gipson, Theodore H., 17, 111
Gist, Noel P., 27, 59
Givens, R.A., 101
Glantz, Oscar, 130
Glass, Bentley, 14
Glazer, Nathan, 47, 59, 91, 119
Gleason, Robert W., 157
Glenn, Norval D., 1, 19, 20, 21, 78, 150
Glick, Paul C., 8
Gloster, Hugh M., 41
Glueck, Eleanor T., 64
Glueck, Sheldon, 64
Goddard, David, 47
Gold, M., 64
Goldberg, Milton S., 93
Goldblatt, Harold, 88, 108
Golden, Joseph, 24
Goldhamer, Herbert, 16
Goldman, Freda H., 111
Goldman, R.F., 33

Goldstein, Marcus S., 33, 36
Goldstein, R.L., 38
Goldston, Judith, 84
Golightly, Cornelius L., 108
Gomillion, Charles G., 130
Good, Paul, 150
Goodall, Merrill R., 121
Goode, Bill, 82
Goodman, George W., Jr., 67
Goodman, Mary Ellen, 109
Goodman, Paul, 143
Goodwyn, Larry, 150
Gordon, Albert I., 25
Gordon, D.N., 27
Gordon, Margaret, 121
Gordon, Milton M., 52, 102
Gordon, Vivian Verdell, 111
Gore, Pearl M., 27
Gosnell, Harold F., 130
Gossett, Thomas F., 14
Gould, Flo, 17
Gould, John, 84
Goyen, William, 41
Grabill, Wilson H., 33
Graham, Frank, 143
Grannum, E.S., 38
Grant, F.W., 36
Grant, George C., 111
Gray, J.S., 47
Gray, Kenneth, 130
Greeley, Andrew M., 91, 157
Green, Constance McLaughlin, 59
Green, Gordon G., 113
Green, Reginald H., 109
Green, Robert L., 113
Greenbaum, Charles, 28
Greenberg, Herbert, 47, 52
Greenberg, Jack, 102, 137, 138
Greene, James E., Sr., 109
Greene, Robert J., 52
Greenfield, Robert W., 94
Greenstone, David, 130
Greenwald, William, 78
Greer, Frank, 91
Greer, Scott, 82
Gregor, A.J., 102
Gregory, Dick, 9
Gregory, Francis A., 116
Gremley, William H., 125
Grier, Eunice, 59, 60, 91, 94, 115
Grier, George, 59, 60, 91, 94
Griffin, John A., 110
Griffin, John Howard, 9, 121
Griffin, Roscoe, 122
Grigg, Charles M., 22, 48, 59, 103, 151
Grigsby, William G., 95
Grimes, Alan P., 3
Grimshaw, Allen D., 67
Griswold, Erwin N., 138, 140

Griswold, Nat, 109
Grob, Gerald N., 82
Grodzins, Morton, 59, 62, 90, 91
Groff, Patrick J., 116
Groom, D., 36
Gross, Calvin E., 108, 119
Grossack, Martin M., 27, 35, 47, 52
Groves, H.E., 75
Guba, E.G., 115
Guillory, Barbara M., 78
Gulley, William H., 22
Gunter, Laurie M., 36, 38
Guralnick, Lillian, 33
Gurin, David, 143
Gurin, G., 29
Guscott, Kenneth I., 69
Gustafson, James M., 19
Gustafson, Lucille, 30
Gutman, D., 75, 88
Guzman, Jessie P., 3, 102, 109

Haber, Alan, 71
Hager, Don J., 52, 88, 116
Haggstrom, Warren C., 27
Halberstam, David, 130
Halbert, L.A., 59
Haley, Alex, 9, 164
Hall, Claude H., 72
Haller, Mark H., 14
Hamblin, Robert L., 47
Hamelett, Margaret L., 22
Hamilton, C. Horace, 56, 57, 60
Hamilton, Charles V., 102, 127
Hammer, E.F., 27, 31
Hammett, Richard, 84
Handlin, Oscar, 3, 22, 136, 143
Hannah, J.A., 138
Hansberry, Lorraine, 41, 143
Hansen, Carl F., 35, 113, 116, 122
Harbutt, Charles, 157
Hardwick, Elizabeth, 143
Hardy, Janet, 36
Hare, Nathan, 143
Hare, Nathaniel, 78
Hargrett, Andrew J., 111
Harlan, Louis R., 109
Harper, P.A., 33
Harper, R.M., 78
Harrell, Thomas W., 30
Harrington, Michael, 62, 71, 78
Harris, Abram L., 73
Harris, Louis, 141
Harris, Nelson H., 122
Harris, Robert J., 138
Harrison, E.C., 113
Harrison, Lincoln J., 78
Hart, Joe W., 78
Harte, Thomas J., 25, 157
Hartman, Chester W., 91

Hartman, Paul, 75, 102, 138
Hartnett, Robert C., 158
Harvey, Jerry, 27
Harvey, O.J., 54
Haselden, Kyle, 143, 158
Hatchett, John F., 164
Haubrich, Vernon, 113
Hauser, Philip M., 8, 34, 38, 60, 61, 78, 90
Havens, Charles W., III, 127
Havighurst, Robert J., 16, 108, 116
Hawkins, Hugh, 9
Hawley, Langston T., 78
Hayakawa, S.I., 27
Hayden, Robert, 41
Hayden, Tom, 150
Hayes, Charles L., 143
Haynes, Leonard L., 19
Haynes, Marion, 69
Hays, Brooks, 150
Hazel, David W., 118
Heard, Eliza, 151
Hechinger, Fred M., 106
Hedgeman, Anna Arnold, 10
Heer, David M., 22, 151
Heller, Ben I., 151
Hellerstein, W.E., 88
Hellins, G.W., 34
Henderson, E.B., 22
Henderson, G., 69
Henderson, George, 138
Henderson, Thelton, 138
Henderson, Thomas H., 111
Henderson, Vivian W., 69
Henkin, Louis, 88
Henry, A.F., 64
Henry, Anthony, 143
Hentoff, Nat, 38, 47, 78, 143, 164
Henton, Comradge L., 35, 64
Hepburn, Richard, 94
Herberg, Will, 158
Hernton, Calvin C., 15, 164
Hero, Alfred O., 3
Herring, B.D., 36
Herskovits, Melville J., 3, 15, 19
Heyman, Ira Michael, 102, 108, 128
Hickey, Neil, 10
Hickey, Philip J., 119
Hiestand, Dale L., 78
Higdon, Hal, 47
Higgins, C., 31
Highsaw, Robert B., 3
Hill, Haywood N., 151
Hill, Herbert, 41, 56, 69, 75, 78, 79, 82, 138
Hill, Mozell C., 21, 23, 64
Hill, Samuel, 75
Hill, Samuel S., Jr., 158
Hilleboe, H.E., 36

Hilliard, Robert L., 116
Hilsheimer, G. von, 56
Himelstein, P., 47
Himes, Chester B., 41
Himes, Joseph S., 17, 22
Hindman, Baker M., 27
Hines, Ralph H., 143
Hingson, R.A., 36
Hintz, August M., 160
Hirsch, E.F., 38
Hites, Robert W., 47
Hobart, Charles W., 31, 113
Hodges, Harold M., 77
Hoffman, Louis J., 113
Hokanson, J.E., 27
Holden, Anna, 122, 158
Holland, Lynwood M., 127
Hollingshead, A.B., 35
Holloway, Harry, 130
Holloway, Robert G., 115
Holmes, Bob, 91
Holt, Len, 143
Holt, Rackham, 10
Holte, C.L., 72
Holtzman, Wayne H., 52, 55, 118
Holzer, Henry Mark, 138
Holzer, Phyllis Tate, 138
Homan, H.L., 84
Homer, Dorothy R., 169
Hood, W.R., 54
Hope, John, II, 47, 79, 82, 84, 111
Hopkins, J.V., 138
Hopkins, L.L., 138
Horchler, Richard, 158
Horne, Frank S., 59, 94
Horsky, C.A., 128
Horton, Carrell P., 31, 33, 37
Howden, Edward, 76
Howe, Florence, 143
Howe, Irving, 41
Howe, John, 95
Howe, Mark DeWolfe, 138
Howell, Elva J., 110
Howells, William W., 15
Hronek, Mary Linda, 122
Hughes, Carl Milton, 42
Hughes, Emmet John, 69
Hughes, Everett C., 3, 15, 16
Hughes, Helen M., 90
Hughes, J.H., 27
Hughes, Langston, 6, 42, 143
Hugon, J., 34
Huie, William Bradford, 144
Hullfish, H. Gordon, 106
Hummel, Dean L., 114
Humphrey, Hubert H., 106
Hund, James M., 73
Hunt, Chester L., 94
Hunt, Edward E., 1ʹ

Hunt, J.M., 31
Hunter, David R., 62
Hunter, Floyd, 130
Hunton, Harold, 84
Hurley, Denis E., 158
Hurley, Phillip S., 113, 158
Hutto, Dolores, 52
Hyman, Herbert H., 52, 151
Hyman, J.D., 102
Hypps, Irene C., 64, 116

Iampietro, P.F., 33
Ingle, Dwight J., 15
Irving, Florence B., 102
Isaacs, Harold R., 3, 10, 15, 42, 144
Isaacs, Reginald R., 91
Iscoe, Ira, 27, 31, 32
Iskander, Michel G., 52
Ivins, S.P., 35
Ivy, A.C., 34

Jackson, Blyden, 42
Jackson, Esther Merle, 27
Jackson, Eureal Grant, 8
Jackson, Hubert M., 91
Jackson, P.W., 115
Jaco, E.G., 35
Jacob, B.R., 125
Jacobs, Paul, 82
Jacobson, Dan, 42
Jager, Melvin F., 102
Jahoda, Marie, 35, 46, 47
James, Beauregard, 144
James, J.H., 84
James, Weldon, 100
James, Willis Laurence, 19, 42
Janis, Irving L., 118
Janowitz, Morris, 46, 47
Jansen, Donald Orville, 102
Javits, Jacob K., 47
Jefferson, Miles, 79
Jenkins, Herbert T., 64
Jenkins, Iredell, 110
Jenkins, T.M., 102
Jenkins, Wesley W., 17,
Jennings, M. Kent, 130, 151
Jensen, Arthur R., 31
Jewell, Malcolm, 130, 151
Jocher, Katherine, 3
John, Vera P., 31
Johnpoll, B.K., 82
Johnson, Benton, 19, 158
Johnson, Charles S., 19, 22, 52, 56, 102
Johnson, Edwina C., 28
Johnson, Granville B., Jr., 31
Johnson, Guy B., 3, 47, 52, 64, 110, 116, 122
Johnson, Haynes, 144, 151
Johnson, J.B., 33

Johnson, James Weldon, 10, 19, 42, 59
Johnson, John H., 144
Johnson, Joseph P., 65
Johnson, Manning, 151
Johnson, Oakley C., 82
Johnson, Philip A., 94
Johnson, R.O., 110
Johnson, Reginald A., 91
Johnson, Robert B., 28, 52
Johnston, Ruby F., 19
Jones, Charles, 125, 144
Jones, Frederick, 108
Jones, Hubert E., 144
Jones, LeRoi, 42
Jones, Lewis W., 56, 128, 130, 151
Jones, Madison, 158
Jones, Major J., 79
Jones, Malcolm, 91
Jones, Raymond J., 19
Jones, W.B., 102
Jordan, Lawrence V., 122
Juvigny, Pierre, 106

Kahl, Joseph A., 61
Kahn, Tom, 82, 144
Kamii, Constance K., 18
Kane, J.L., Jr., 24
Kaplan, John, 102
Kaplan, M., 88
Kardiner, Abram, 28
Karon, Bertram P., 28
Karpinos, B.D., 34
Karrick, D.B., 15
Karst, K.L., 125, 140
Kasoff, Allen, 47
Katz, Irwin, 27, 28, 47, 52, 84
Katzenbach, Nicholas de B., 128
Kean, Charles D., 158
Kearney, John, 158
Keeler, Martin H., 35, 36
Keller, Suzanne, 62
Kelley, William Melvin, 42
Kellogg, Edward P., 47
Kelly, Alfred H., 102
Kelman, Herbert C., 48
Kelsey, George D., 158
Kempton, Murray, 144
Kenealy, William J., 116, 125, 158
Kennedy, T.H., 26
Kennedy, Wallace A., 31
Kenney, J.A., Jr., 38
Kenyon, Dorothy, 87
Kephart, William M., 64
Keppel, Francis H., 117
Kerckhoff, A.C., 28
Kerckhoff, Richard K., 17, 94
Kesselman, Louis C., 131
Kessler, Matthew A., 69
Kessler, S.H., 169

Key, V.O., Jr., 131
Keyes, Walter E., 91
Kiehl, Robert, 79
Killens, John O., 28, 42, 43, 84, 144
Killian, Lewis M., 22, 23, 48, 59, 147, 151
Kilpatrick, James Jackson, 102, 151
Kilson, Martin, 2
Kincheloe, J.B., 110
King, Charles E., 21
King, Glen D., 66
King, John Q. Taylor, 122
King, Marion, 144
King, Martin Luther, Jr., 144
King, Morton B., Jr., 48
King, Roberson L., 75
Kinzer, Robert H., 73
Kirk, W. Astor, 122
Kirkhart, Robert O., 23
Kirman, J.M., 164
Kirwan, Albert D., 6
Kiser, Clyde V., 33
Kistin, Helen, 91
Kitagawa, Daisuke, 158
Kitagawa, Evelyn M., 34, 38
Klausler, Alfred P., 110, 158
Klaw, Spencer, 119
Klein, Louise H., 95
Kleiner, Robert J., 21, 34, 35
Klineberg, Otto, 31
Klopf, Gordon J., 117
Knapp, P.H., 35
Knapp, Robert B., 61
Knobloch, Hilda, 31, 32, 35
Knoll, Erwin, 122
Koenig, Frederick W., 48
Kohler, Mary Conway, 79
Kohn, M.L., 52
Kolb, Avery E., 43
Konvitz, Milton R., 138
Kopp, R.W., 84
Korenvaes, P., 72
Korey, William, 122
Kornberg, Leonard, 113
Kornbluh, Joyce L., 71
Kornhauser, William, 82
Kosa, J., 69
Kotinsky, Ruth, 30
Kotler, Neil, 144
Kovarsky, Irving, 75
Kozol, L.H., 88
Kramer, Alfred S., 158
Kramer, B.M., 45
Kramer, S.A., 64
Krass, Elaine, 61
Krech, David, 31
Krosney, Herbert, 164
Krueger, A.O., 69
Kruuse, Elsa, 158

Ktsanes, Thomas, 46
Kuebler, Jeanne, 79
Kunstadter, Peter, 17
Kupferer, Harriet J., 117
Kutner, Bernard, 48
Kvaraceus, William C., 28, 65
Kyle, Keith, 128

Ladd, Everett C., Jr., 144
Ladd, W.M., 94
LaFarge, John, 158, 159
Lally, Francis J., 159
Lamanna, Richard, 53
Lampman, Robert J., 71
Lande, Bernard, 30
Landes, Ruth, 15, 115
Landry, Lawrence, 119, 164
Lane, David A., Jr., 84
Lane, Robert E., 69, 131
Laney, L.M., 102
Lang, Gladys Engel, 69, 79
Langer, E., 38
Lanier, L.H., 32
Lantz, Edna M., 36
Lapouse, Rema, 28
Larimore, B.W., 36
Larkins, John R., 23
Larsson, Clotye M., 25
LaSalle, Thomas, 123
Lasch, Robert, 119
Lash, John, 43
Laster, Israel A., 117
Laue, James H., 151, 164
Laurenti, Luigi, 94
Lavell, Martha, 35
Leacock, Eleanor, 95
Lee, Alfred McClung, 91
Lee, Anne S., 34
Lee, Everett S., 31, 34, 35
Lee, Frank F., 48, 106
Lee, J. Oscar, 19, 48, 159
Lee, Robert, 159
Lee, Robert S., 63
Lee, Ulysses, 40
Lees, Hannah, 21, 95, 144
Leflar, Robert A., 103
Leggett, John C., 72, 131
Lehman, W.W., 88
Lehrer, Stanley, 106
Lenox, G. Merrill, 159
Lenski, Gerhard, 19
Lerche, Charles O., 3, 151
Lerner, Melvin J., 76, 114
Lesesne, T.P., 37
Leskes, Theodore, 138
Levenson, Frances, 88
Leverett, E.F., 103
Levey, Robert, 108
Levin, David, 28

Levin, Nathan, 74
Levine, L.H., 36
Levitan, S.A., 75
Levy, Charles J., 151
Lewinson, Paul, 131
Lewis, Anthony, 25, 103, 128, 145
Lewis, Earl M., 131
Lewis, Hylan, 17, 23, 65
Lewit, S., 18
Lieberman, Myron, 106
Lieberson, Stanley, 8, 53, 59, 90, 91
Lief, Harold I., 48
Lincoln, C. Eric, 17, 21, 145, 164
Lindner, Ronald S., 31
Lippman, Leopold, 53
Lipset, Seymour M., 49, 69, 73, 81, 82
Lipsky, Roma, 131
Lissovoy, Peter de, 145
Litwack, Leon F., 6, 82
Liu, William T., 159
Livson, Norman, 48
Locke, Alain, 43
Loescher, F.S., 159
Logan, Rayford W., 6, 103
Lohman, Joseph D., 23, 65
Lohman, Maurice A., 120
Lomax, Louis E., 145, 165
Lombardi, Donald N., 53
London, Jack, 84
London, Nathaniel J., 65
Long, Heiman, 53
Long, Herman H., 53, 122, 145, 159
Long, Howard Hale, 31
Long, Margaret, 145, 151
Long, N.E., 151
Lord, Walter, 122
Lorwin, Lewis L., 76
Losos, J., 138
Loth, David, 53
Lott, Albert J., 53
Lott, Bernice E., 53
Lubell, Samuel, 131, 145
Lubin, Charlotte, 122
Luchins, Abraham S., 28
Luchins, Edith H., 28
Lunden, Leon E., 75, 84
Lurie, Ellen, 119
Lusky, Louis, 138
Lustig, Norman I., 151
Luthans, F., 86
Lyford, Joseph P., 62
Lymans, S.M., 8
Lynd, Staughton, 145

McCain, James T., 131
McCauley, Patrick, 122
McCloskey, Mark A., 65
McCloskey, R.G., 138
Maccoby, Eleanor E., 65

McConaughy, John B., 130
McConnell, Roland C., 111
McCord, Charles, 145
McCord, William M., 31, 145
McCormick, Ken, 65
McCormick, T.C., 28
McDaniel, Paul A., 48
McDermott, John, 95, 145
McDonald, Erwin, 156
McDonald, L.R., 96
McEntire, Davis, 88, 91
McGavern, John, 117
McGhee, M.L., 88
McGill, Ralph, 131, 151, 159
McGrath, Earl J., 111
McGraw, B.T., 88, 91
McGuinn, Henry J., 131
McGurk, Frank, 32
McIlwain, William, 43
MacInnes, Colin, 43
McIntyre, Thomas J., 151
McIntyre, William R., 103, 128, 152
McKay, Claude, 43, 62
McKay, Robert B., 103, 125, 138
McKee, James B., 53, 91
McKinney, Theophilus E., Jr., 125
Maclachlan, John M., 110
McLaughlin, Wayman B., 19
McLean, F.C., 38
McManus, Eugene P., 159
McManus, G.J., 85
McManus, George P., 65
McMillan, George, 67, 152, 159
McNeill, Robert, 159
McPeak, William, 73, 159
McPherson, James M., 6
McQueen, Robert, 32
McRae, Adie V., 46
McVey, Wayne W., 61
McWhinney, Edward, 103
McWilliams, Carey, 67
Mabee, Carleton, 145
Maddox, George L., 157
Maddux, Rachel, 43
Makdisi, Nadim, 165
Malcolm X, 9, 164, 165
Malev, William S., 152, 159
Mallery, David, 106
Maloney, W.H., Jr., 75
Malzberg, Benjamin, 35
Manderson, Marge, 152
Mangum, Charles S., Jr., 15
Manis, Francis, 122
Manley, Albert E., 111
Mann, John H., 48, 53
Mannix, Daniel P., 7
Mantinband, Charles, 159
March, Sue, 90
Marciniak, Edward, 53

Marcus, Lloyd, 48
Marcus, Steven, 43
Marcuse, Peter, 87
Margolis, Joseph, 145, 152
Marion, John H., 152
Marney, Carlyle, 48
Marrow, Alfred J., 53
Marsh, B.L., 53
Marshall, Burke, 139
Marshall, Paule, 43
Marshall, Ray, 75, 82
Marshall, Thurgood, 79, 100, 128
Martin, James G., 48
Martin, John Bartlow, 152
Martin, R.E., 130
Martin, Ralph, 43
Martin, Roscoe C., 59
Martin, William H., 117
Maslen, Sidney, 91
Maslow, Will, 103, 108
Mason, Philip, 48, 53
Maston, T.B., 159
Masuoka, Jitsuichi, 48
Mather, P. Boyd, 159
Matsuda, R., 37
Matthews, Donald R., 45, 131, 152
Matza, David, 66
Maund, Alfred, 43
Mausner, Bernard, 53, 87
Maxey, Alva, 53
Maxwell, Neil, 131
Mayer, Albert J., 95
Mayer, Martin, 108
Mayer, Milton, 15, 145, 152
Mayfield, Julian, 43, 145
Mayhew, Leon Hinckley, 75, 88
Mayo, Selz C., 56, 57
Mays, Benjamin E., 19, 53, 65, 159
Mays, Nebraska, 117
Mead, Margaret, 15
Meador, D.J., 103
Meadow, Kathryn P., 61
Meckler, Zane, 108
Medalia, Nahum Z., 48
Meenes, Max, 32, 46
Mehan, Joseph, 159
Meier, August, 7, 21, 146
Meltzer, Milton, 6
Mendelson, Wallace, 48
Mercer, N.A., 95
Merz, Louise E., 48
Metzger, Earl H., Jr., 95
Meyer, Agnes E., 106
Meyer, Sylvan, 154, 159
Meyerson, Martin, 92
Michael, Donald D., 79
Middleton, Russell, 17, 28, 48, 131
Mihlon, Lawrence F., 79
Milgram, Morris, 95

Millard, Thomas L., 146
Miller, Alexander F., 67, 92
Miller, Arthur S., 103, 122
Miller, C., 28
Miller, Carroll L., 65, 110
Miller, Helen Hill, 70, 110
Miller, Herman Phillip, 70
Miller, K.C., 112
Miller, K.S., 26
Miller, Loren, 61, 87, 88, 131, 139, 146
Miller, Mike, 92
Miller, Robert M., 159
Miller, S.M., 106, 107, 108
Miller, Vincent A., 61
Miller, Warren, 43
Miller, William Robert, 146, 159
Millstein, G., 28
Milner, Esther, 28
Milner, Jay, 43
Minnis, Jack, 131
Mirel, E., 57
Mischel, W., 28
Mitchell, George S., 82, 131
Mitchell, James J., 112
Mitchell, James P., 85
Mitchell, Lonnie E., 28, 29
Miyamoto, S. Frank, 48
Moffitt, Donald, 85, 88
Moland, John, 28
Monk, Mary A., 28
Montague, Joel B., 21
Montserrat, Joseph, 117
Moon, F.D., 122
Moon, Henry Lee, 131, 132
Moore, J.C., 47
Moore, R.E., 110
Moore, Truman E., 57
Moore, William P., 117
Morant, D.M., 15
Morgan, Charles, Jr., 65, 152
Morgan, Chester A., 75
Morgan, Frank, 70
Morgan, Gordon D., 79
Morland, J. Kenneth, 28, 117, 125
Moron, Alonzo G., 112
Morris, H.H., Jr., 38
Morris, J.P., 38
Morris, R.B., 85
Morris, R.G., Jr., 38
Morris, Robert, 90
Morris, Willie, 3
Morrison, Allan, 132
Morrison, J.L., 15
Morrow, Joseph J., 79, 85
Morse, H.T., 107
Morse, O., 103
Morsell, John A., 103, 152, 165
Mose, Ashriel I., 115
Motley, C.B., 38

Moynihan, Daniel Patrick, 17, 59, 79
Mphahlele, Ezekiel, 3
Muelder, Walter, 19
Mugge, Robert H., 61
Muhammad, Elijah, 165
Mulholland, Joseph A., 159
Murphy, J.W., 103
Murphy, Walter F., 103, 139
Murray, Florence, 19
Murray, Walter, 114
Muse, Benjamin, 15, 103, 117, 152
Mussen, Paul H., 28
Myers, Henry J., 28
Myers, Jerome K., 65
Myrdal, Gunnar, 3, 71

Nabrit, James M., Jr., 103, 117
Nash, Diane, 146
Nash, William, 92
Needham, Maurice d'Arlan, 70, 92
Nelson, Gaylord, 139
Nelson, Harold A., 48
Nelson, Howard J., 8
Nelson, J. Robert, 122, 160
Nelson, William Stuart, 146
Neprash, Jerry A., 48
Nesbitt, George B., 88, 92, 95
Newby, I.A., 15
Newfield, Jack, 146
Newhouse, W.J., Jr., 102
Newman, Dorothy K., 61
Newton, Eunice Shaed, 113
Newton, I.E., 80
Newton, I.G., 132
Nichaman, M.Z., 37
Nicholls, William H., 4, 70
Nichols, Lee, 53, 85, 160
Nichols, Thomas F., 48
Nicholson, Joseph W., 19
Nicol, Helen, 80
Niebuhr, H. Richard, 19
Niebuhr, Reinhold, 160
Nieburg, H.L., 67
Nilon, Charles H., 43
Nipson, Herbert, 147
Noble, Jeanne L., 107
Noel, Donald L., 26, 48
Nordlie, Esther B., 17
Norgren, Paul H., 75, 80
Norman, Arthur, 32
Norris, Hoke, 43, 152
North, Arthur A., 103
North, Robert D., 32
Northrup, Herbert, 80
Northwood, Lawrence K., 92, 95, 160
Nosow, Sigmund, 106
Novasky, V.S., 89
Nunn, C.Z., 69
Nuttall, Ronald L., 34

O'Connor, John J., 160
Odum, Howard W., 4
Ogburn, William Fielding, 53, 103
Ogden, Frederick D., 128
Ohlin, Lloyd E., 63
Oliver, Clinton, 44
O'Neill, Joseph E., 160
Opler, Marvin K., 17
Opotowsky, Stan, 152
Oppenheimer, Martin, 112, 146
Orshanksy, Mollie, 17, 71
Osborne, Irene, 122
Osborne, R.T., 32
O'Shea, Harriet E., 49
Osofsky, Gilbert, 62
Ostlund, Leonard A., 115
Ottenburg, Simon, 23
Ottley, Roi, 10, 24
Ovesey, Lionel, 28

Parenti, Michael, 146
Parenton, Vernon J., 57
Parish, Charles H., 122
Park, Robert Ezra, 4
Palermo, D.S., 29
Palley, Howard A., 57
Palmer, B.W., 103
Palmer, C.L., 103
Palmer, R. Roderick, 49, 103
Palmore, Erdman, 95
Papageorge, George T., 92
Papale, A.E., 103
Parker, Franklin, 107
Parker, J.E., 36
Parker, Robert A., 19
Parker, Seymour, 21, 35
Parks, Gordon, 44
Parsons, Howard L., 117
Parsons, Talcott, 4
Partee, Carter, 103
Pasamanick, Benjamin, 31, 32, 35
Passow, Harry A., 113
Patrick, T.L., 110
Patten, Thomas H., Jr., 85
Patterson, Fred D., 107, 112
Patterson, William L., 73
Payne, Joseph Arthur, Jr., 112
Payne, Raymond, 57
Payton, E., 37
Peabody, Malcolm E., Jr., 85
Pearlin, Leonard I., 48
Pearson, Leonard E., 85
Peck, James, 146
Pederson, H.A., 57
Peerman, Dean, 160
Pellegrin, Roland J., 57
Peltason, J.W., 104
Pennington, Stewart, 29
Perlmutter, Nathan 152

Perlo, Victor, 70
Perry, Jane, 76
Perry, John, 85
Peter, Emmet, Jr., 57
Peters, James S., II, 32
Peters, William, 152
Petersen, William, 49
Peterson, F.L., 37
Peterson, J., 32
Petrof, John V., 146
Pettigrew, Ann Hallman, 37
Pettigrew, Thomas F., 29, 32, 34, 37,
  48, 49, 53, 54, 65, 90, 110, 117, 155,
  160
Pfautz, Harold W., 23
Phillips, J.H., 37
Phillips, Waldo B., 115
Phillips, William M., Jr., 129, 146
Picott, J. Rupert, 122
Pierce, C.M., 54
Pierce, H.E., Jr., 38
Pierce, J.A., 73
Pierce, James E., 143
Pierce, T.M., 110
Pierce-Jones, John, 31
Pierson, Jerome, 47
Pinkney, Alphonso, 48, 49
Pittman, Joseph A., 114
Pittman, R.C., 139
Plaut, Richard L., 106, 107, 115
Plotkin, Lawrence, 32, 111
Podhoretz, Norman, 49
Pohlhaus, J. Francis, 160
Poinsett, Alex, 108
Polgar, Steven, 37
Polk, William Tarnahill, 152
Pollak, Louis H., 104, 139
Pollitt, Daniel H., 125, 139
Pollitzer, W.S., 15
Pomfret, John D., 57
Pool, Rosey, 44
Pope, Liston, 19, 20, 160
Popham, John N., 104
Porter, Dorothy P., 44
Porterfield, Austin L., 65
Posey, Walter B., 160
Potter, William I., 100
Powdermaker, Hortense, 20, 29
Powell, Edwin H., 81
Powledge, Fred, 117, 123
Prange, A.J., Jr., 35
Preu, James, 4
Price, Arthur Cooper, 29
Price, Daniel O., 109
Price, Hugh D., 129, 132
Price, Margaret, 132, 146
Procope, J.L., 38
Prothro, Charles E., 111
Prothro, Edwin Terry, 152

Prothro, James W., 29, 45, 131, 152
Proudfoot, Merrill, 146
Puryear, Mahlon T., 80
Puryear, Paul L., 104
Putnam, Carleton, 15
Putney, Snell, 17

Quarles, Benjamin, 7
Quinn, Olive W., 16
Quint, Howard H., 153

Raab, Earl, 49
Rabin, A.I., 30
Rabkin, Sol, 75, 89, 139
Radin, Norma, 18
Radzinski, J.M., 29
Rainwater, Lee, 18
Ramaker, Robert, 80
Rames, Jose, 61, 95
Ramsey, Paul, 160
Rand, E.W., 112
Randel, William Peirce, 153
Randolph, A. Philip, 82
Ranney, Austin, 132
Ransone, Coleman B., Jr., 153
Rapkin, Chester, 95
Raskin, A.H., 83
Rasky, Frank, 20
Ratchford, R.U., 70
Raubinger, Frederick M., 119
Ravitz, Mel J., 38, 92, 119
Ray, Eva, 26
Rayack, Elton, 80
Raymond, George M., 92
Read, F.T., 76
Record, Jane Cassells, 123, 153
Record, Wilson, 7, 21, 49, 57, 104, 115, 120, 123, 146, 165
Redden, C.L., 170
Reddick, Lawrence D., 10, 80, 112
Redding, Jay Saunders, 10, 44
Redding, Louis L., 123
Redfield, Robert, 15
Redlich, F.C., 35
Reed, Eugene T., 80
Reed, Roy, 146
Reed, Sheldon C., 17
Reedy, Sidney J., 120
Reid, Ira De Augustine, 4, 20, 61, 117
Reif, Janet, 110
Reimers, David M., 7, 160
Reiss, Albert, Jr., 65
Reiss, I.L., 18
Reitman, Audrey P., 45
Reitzes, Dietrich C., 23, 38, 49
Reitzes, H., 38
Reller, Theodore L., 109
Reston, James, 95
Reuter, George S., Jr., 160

Reuter, Helen H., 160
Rexroth, Kenneth, 44
Rhodes, Albert Lewis, 37, 65
Rhyne, Edwin Hoffman, 49
Rice, Arnold S., 153
Rich, J.C., 83
Rich, John Martin, 110
Richey, Elinor, 92, 95
Richmond, Anthony H., 49
Rider, R.V., 33
Riese, H., 35
Riessman, Frank, 114
Riley, L.H., 25
Rinder, Irwin D., 24, 170
Ring, H.H., 70
Rivkin, Malcolm D., 92
Rivlin, Harry N., 107
Roady, Elston E., 132
Robbins, Richard, 54
Robcock, Stefan H., 70
Roberts, Gene, Jr., 80
Roberts, H.J., 37
Roberts, Harry W., 49, 54
Roberts, Richard J., 89
Robinson, Jackie, 86
Robinson, James H., 49
Robinson, Mary L., 32
Robinson, Sophia M., 65
Robinson, William H., 117, 123
Robison, Joseph B., 109, 139
Roche, John P., 4
Rodell, Fred, 146
Roebuck, Julian B., 65
Rogers, Lettie Hamlett, 44
Rogers, W.W., 57
Rogers, William P., 104, 117
Rohrer, John H., 4, 23, 29
Rony, Vera, 83
Rooney, Isabel W., 120
Root, Robert, 54
Rorty, James, 82
Rose, Alvin W., 70, 83
Rose, Arnold M., 4, 7, 23, 35, 49, 95, 96, 153
Rose, Caroline, 49
Rose, G., 37
Rose, Harold M., 80
Rose, Stephen C., 146, 160, 161
Roseman, D.M., 89
Rosen, Alex, 51
Rosen, Bernard C., 24, 29
Rosen, David, 96
Rosen, Ellsworth E., 96
Rosen, H., 35
Rosen, Harry, 96
Rosen, S.R., 32
Rosenbaum, J.B., 123
Rosenfeld, Eva, 63
Rosenfeld, Stephen S., 96

Rosenthal, Jonas O., 117
Roshco, Bernard, 96
Rosner, Joseph, 117
Rossi, Peter H., 92, 96
Rostow, Eugene, 146
Rotberg, Robert, 55, 118, 170
Roth, Robert M., 112
Rothman, Jack, 92
Rothney, William B., 34
Rotter, J.B., 27
Rousseve, Ronald J., 49, 114, 115
Rovere, Richard, 18, 146
Rowan, Carl, 10, 146
Rowan, Richard, 80
Rowe, Allen S., 32
Rubin, Louis D., Jr., 153
Rubin, Morton, 57, 96
Ruchames, Louis, 76
Rudman, W.G., 125
Rudwick, Elliott M., 10, 49, 65, 67
Russell, A.L., 37
Russell, Beth Duvall, 44
Russell, James W., 115
Russell, R.D., 80
Russell, Ross, 44
Rustin, Bayard, 147
Rutledge, Edward, 96
Ruttan, Vernon W., 57
Ryan, Margaret W., 118
Ryan, William, 18

Sabagh, Georges, 35
Sagarin, Edward, 73
St. Antoine, T.J., 139
St. James, Warren D., 147
St. John, Nancy, 114
Saks, J.H., 89
Saleem, Betty, 107, 108
Salisbury, Harrison, 66
Samet, Elaine R., 153
Samuels, Gertrude, 66, 123, 147, 165
Sand, Mary E., 114
Sanders, Stanley, 67
Sargent, F.O., 57
Sass, Herbert Ravenal, 153
Sauer, H.I., 37
Saunders, Doris E., 147
Saundle, J.S., 112
Savage, Henry, Jr., 7
Savitz, Leonard, 66
Sawyer, Broadus E., 72, 112
Sawyer, David A., 86
Saxton, Alexander Plaisted, 44
Scales, Eldridge E., 114
Scheiner, Seth M., 7
Schermerhorn, R.A., 4, 35
Schickel, Richard, 120
Schietinger, E. Frederick, 96
Schiffman, J., 80

Schiltz, Michael E., 96
Schlivek, Louis B., 60
Schmid, Calvin F., 61, 66
Schneider, Louis, 15
Schnore, Leo F., 60, 61
Scholz, B.W., 38
Schomburg, Arthur Alfonso, 44
Schomer, Howard, 161
Schrag, Peter, 107
Schreiber, Daniel, 107
Schroeder, O., Jr., 63
Schulder, Daniel J., 82
Schultz, Leroy G., 66
Schultz, Raymond E., 32
Schultz, Theodore W., 70
Schutter, C.W., 104
Schuyler, Joseph B., 161
Schwartz, M., 18, 80
Schwartz, Raymond J., 92
Schwelb, F.E., 125
Sclare, A., 36
Scott, Barbara W., 92
Scott, R.B., 34
Scott, W.R., 90
Screiber, Harry N., 76
Searles, Ruth, 147
Seasholes, Bradbury, 132
Secord, P.F., 29
Secrest, A.M., 153
Sedler, R.A., 104
Seeman, Melvin, 29
Seidenberg, Jacob, 80
Selkow, Samuel, 104
Sellers, Charles Grier, 7
Sellers, James, 161
Seltzer, A.P., 37
Semer, Milton, 89
Semler, Ira J., 32
Senn, Milton, 161
Senser, Robert, 161
Setleis, Lloyd, 18
Sexton, Patricia Cayo, 62, 107, 120
Seymour, Robert, 161
Shack, William A., 165
Shaffer, Helen B., 25, 96, 117, 153
Shagaloff, June, 108, 120
Shanahan, T.J., 38
Shane, M., 36
Shannon, Lyle W., 61
Shapiro, Fred C., 67
Shapiro, Harry H., 139
Shapiro, M., 15
Sharp, Harry, 61
Sheatsley, Paul B., 49, 52, 151
Sheffield, Horace, 81
Shelley, J., 54
Shelton, E., 79
Sheppard, Harold L., 49
Sherif, Carolyn, 54, 66

Sherif, Muzafer, 54, 66
Sherman, Stanley, 47
Sherrill, Robert, 153
Sherwin, Mark, 165
Shirk, E.M., 76
Shoemaker, Don, 123
Short, James F., Jr., 63, 64, 66
Shostak, Arthur B., 76, 86
Shriver, Donald W., Jr., 161
Shuey, Audrey, 32
Shurman, Howard E., 139
Sibley, Mulford Q., 147
Siegel, Paul M., 70
Sigel, Roberta S., 132
Silard, John, 112, 139
Silberman, Charles E., 60, 62, 80, 147
Silver, James W., 153
Simkins, Francis Butler, 153
Simmons, Herbert, 44
Simms, David McD., 161
Simon, W.B., 49
Simpson, George E., 49, 54, 147
Simpson, George L., 3
Simpson, Ida Harper, 20
Simpson, Richard, 50
Singer, Herman, 70
Singer, S.L., 29
Singletary, Otis A., 7
Singleton, Robert, 107
Sisson, John P., 153
Sitton, Claude, 117, 139
Sivers, Cathryne, 31
Sloan, Irving, J., 7
Sloane, Martin, 89
Smalley, Webster, 44
Smart, Mollie S., 32
Smith, Bob, 110
Smith, Bulkeley, Jr., 96
Smith, Charles U., 23, 29, 54, 147
Smith, Earl B., 39
Smith, Frank E., 153
Smith, Howard K., 147
Smith, Howard P., 18
Smith, Lauren A., 161
Smith, Lillian, 54, 147, 153
Smith, P.M., 57
Smith, Ralph Lee, 92, 104
Smith, Robert C., 104
Smith, Samuel Stanhope, 15
Smith, Stanley H., 110, 128, 130
Smith, T. Lynn, 9
Smith, William Gardner, 44
Smuts, Robert W., 23
Smythe, H.H., 37
Smythe, Lewis S.C., 161
Snellings, Rolland, 165
Snowden, George W., 96
Snyder, J.D., 39

Snyder, Louis L., 16
Solomon, Benjamin, 120
Solomon, Frederic, 27
Solzbacher, Regina, 21
Southard, Samuel, 161
Southwick, Albert B., 165
Sovern, Michael I., 76
Spangler, Earl, 170
Sparkman, John, 89
Spearman, Walter, 154
Spellman, A.B., 165
Spergel, Irving, 66
Speroff, B., 86
Sperrazzo, Gerald, 33
Spicer, George W., 104, 128
Spiegel, Hans B.C., 96
Spier, Rosalind B., 65
Spike, Robert W., 161
Spitz, H., 76
Spock, Benjamin, 29
Spraggins, Tinsley Lee, 131
Sprey, Jetse, 115
Spruill, Albert W., 118
Spurlock, Clark, 104
Srole, Leo, 21, 55
Stafford, Douglas K., 117
Stallings, Frank H., 110, 114
Stamler, J., 37
Stampp, Kenneth M., 7
Stanton, William, 16
Star, Shirley, 50
Starke, Juanita G., 54
Steckler, G.A., 50
Steele, H. Ellsworth, 80
Steele, Kay, 150
Stefflre, B., 29
Steinberg, C., 128
Steiner, Gary A., 1
Steiner, P.E., 37
Stember, Charles Herbert, 54
Stennis, J.C., 104
Stephan, A. Stephen, 118, 123
Stern, Curt, 16
Sterner, Richard, 70
Stetler, Henry G., 54, 96, 109
Stevens, Rutherford B., 39
Stevenson, H.W., 29
Stewart, D.D., 36
Stewart, E.C., 29
Stokely, James, 20, 142, 150
Stone, Alma, 44
Stotts, Herbert E., 161
Stouffer, Samuel A., 50
Straetz, Ralph A., 132
Strayer, R., 36
Street, David, 72
Street, James H., 80
Stringfellow, William, 62, 161
Strodtbeck, Fred L., 18, 66

Strong, Edward K., Jr., 115
Stroud, Virgil C., 132
Strutt, Joseph W., 81
Stuart, Irving R., 50, 86
Stuckert, Robert D., 170
Stumberg, G.W., 100
Suchman, Edward A., 50, 54
Sullivan, James W., 67
Sullivan, Neil V., 123
Sullivan, Terry, 147
Sunderhauf, M.B., 97
Sussman, Marvin B., 96
Sutherland, Arthur E., 105
Sutherland, Elizabeth, 147
Sutherland, R.L., 34
Sutton, R.O., 92
Swanson, Ernst W., 110
Sweet, William W., 20

Tabachnick, B. Robert, 50
Taeuber, Alma F., 9, 61, 62, 93
Taeuber, Conrad, 9
Taeuber, Irene B., 9
Taeuber, Karl E., 9, 61, 62, 92, 93
Taft, Philip, 83
Talbert, Robert H., 65
Tanenbaum, Marc H., 161
Tang, Jenny, 45
Tannenbaum, Frank, 7
Tansill, C.C., 105
Taper, Bernard, 128, 132, 147
Tarjan, George, 35
Taylor, Dalmas A., 29
Taylor, H., 21
Taylor, W.L., 105
Teahan, John E., 33
Teeters, Negley K., 66
Terrell, Mary, 113
Terrett, Barbara, 92
Terte, Robert H., 118
Thayer, V.T., 118
Thomas, Mary S., 161
Thomas, Rose C., 66
Thomas, Ruby, 9
Thompson, A.J., 47
Thompson, Alma M., 170
Thompson, Charles H., 107, 112, 118
Thompson, Daniel C., 23, 50, 81, 118, 140, 147
Thompson, Edgar T., 16, 50, 170
Thompson, Era Bell, 147
Thompson, G.C., 27
Thompson, Lorin A., 110
Thompson, Ralph V., 21
Thompson, Richard, 54
Thompson, Robert A., 93
Thompson, W.A., 39
Thompson, W.R., 33
Thorne, Richard, 165

Thorpe, Earl E., 7
Thurman, Howard, 20, 107, 147, 161
Tietze, C., 18
Tillman, James A., Jr., 96, 97, 120
Tilson, Everett, 161
Tindall, George B., 154
Toal, Robert, 33
Tobin, James, 70
Toby, Jackson, 147
Tower, John, 76
Towler, Juby E., 66
Travis, Fred, 132
Trent, Richard D., 29, 50
Trent, William J., Jr., 73, 112
Trewhitt, Henry L., 83
Triandis, Harry C., 50
Triandis, Leigh Minturn, 50
Trigg, Martelle D., 25
Trillin, Calvin, 123
Trueblood, Dennis L., 115
Tucker, Shirley, 154
Tuckman, Jacob, 35
Tuddenham, R.D., 33
Tufts, Edith Miller, 66
Tumin, Melvin M., 33, 54, 55, 118, 123, 170
Turman, James A., 118
Turner, Francis A., 120
Turner, John B., 147
Turner, Ralph H., 81
Tussman, Joseph, 4
Tyler, Gus, 83
Tyler, Leona E., 16
Tyre, Nedra, 154
Tyson, Cyril, 108, 118

Ulmer, S. Sidney, 140
Ungar, Andre, 161
Upham, Judith, 156

Valien, Bonita, 122
Valien, Preston, 9, 118, 122, 132, 147
Van Alstyne, W.W., 89, 125, 140
Vance, Rupert B., 3, 60
Van Den Berghe, Pierre L., 16
Van Den Haag, E., 105
Vanderburgh, Charles, 147
Vander Zanden, James W., 50, 110, 118, 123, 147, 154
Vandiver, Frank E., 154
Vaughan, Graham M., 29
Vax, John J., 93
Veroff, J., 29
Verst, Edward C., 125
Vespa, Marcia Lane, 120
Vincent, Clark, 18
Vincent, M., 34
Vincent, William S., 120
Vines, Kenneth N., 130, 132, 140

Viorst, J., 81
Visser't Hooft, W.A., 161
Vitols, Mintauts M., 35, 36
Volakakis, Joann, 64
Volkan, U., 29
Von Eckardt, Wolf, 93
Vontress, Clemmont E., 30, 66
Vorspan, Albert, 162
Vose, Clement E., 89, 147

Wade, Richard C., 7
Wagley, Charles W., 4
Wakefield, Dan, 148
Wakin, E., 18
Walker, George W., Jr., 118
Walker, Gerald, 120
Walker, H., 121
Walker, H.J., 5
Walker, Jack L., 23, 132
Walker, LeRoy T., 110
Walker, Wyatt Tee, 148
Walkley, Rosabelle Price, 55
Wall, Marvin, 123
Wallace, Mike, 165
Walter, Norman W., 148
Walters, R.H., 25
Walton, Edmund L., 25
Walton, O.M., 162
Waltz, Alan K., 162
Wambach, Helen S., 27
Waring, Thomas R., 105, 154
Warner, A.E., 93
Warner, Bob, 154
Warner, W. Lloyd, 21, 55
Warren, Earl, 140
Warren, Richard L., 148
Warren, Robert Penn, 148, 154
Washburn, Sherwood L., 16
Washington, Booker T., 10
Washington, Charles, 64
Washington, Joseph R., Jr., 20
Waskow, Arthur L., 67
Waters, Enoc P., 24
Waters, H.G., 36
Watkins, Sylvester C., 44
Wattenberg, Ben, 9
Watts, Lewis G., 55, 90
Watts, Marzette, 148
Weatherford, Willis Duke, 20
Weaver, E.K., 30
Weaver, Robert C., 55, 60, 62, 71, 81,
    93, 97, 112, 129, 148
Webster, Staten W., 55
Wechsler, Herbert, 105
Wedge, E. Bruce, 93
Weeks, O. Douglas, 154
Weinberg, Meyer, 118
Weinberger, Andrew D., 25
Weiner, Max, 114

Weinstein, E.A., 18
Weintraub, Robert E., 78, 86
Weisberger, Bernard A., 8
Weisbord, Marvin, 97
Weiss, L., 76
Weiss, Shirley F., 60
Weiss, Walter, 50
Weissbourd, Bertram, 60
Welsch, Erwin K., 170
Wennerberg, C.H., 120
Werdegar, Kathryn Mickle, 129
Werthman, Carl, 92
Wertz, C., 28
Wertz, R.C., 97
Wesley, Charles H., 8
West, Earle H., 107
Westfeldt, Wallace, 148
Westie, Frank R., 50, 51
Westie, Margaret L., 50
Westin, Alan F., 148
Wey, Herbert, 118
Weyl, Nathaniel, 5
Whatley, C.D., 37
Wheaton, William, 92
Wheeler, J.H., 86
Wheeler, Keith, 44
Whelpton, Pascal K., 33
White, B.J., 54
White, Lewis W., 148
White, Theodore H., 60
White, Walter, 10
Whiteman, Maxwell, 44
Whiting, J.W.M., 16, 26
Whitman, Frederick L., 162
Whitson, Edmund R., 93
Whyte, William H., Jr., 60
Wiley, Bell Irvin, 8
Wilkerson, Doxey A., 110, 123
Wilkins, Carol, 48
Wilkins, Roy, 50, 148
Wilkins, Walter L., 33
Willhelm, Sidney M., 81
Williams, Avon, 23
Williams, Franklin H., 140, 154
Williams, J. Allen, Jr., 147
Williams, John A., 10, 42, 44
Williams, Lorraine A., 55
Williams, Martha, 27
Williams, Philip F., 39
Williams, Robert, 148
Williams, Robin M., Jr., 50, 52, 55, 118
Williamson, E.M., 162
Williamson, Stanford W., 63
Willie, Charles V., 34
Willis, Ernest M., 62
Willis, Pauline, 9
Wills, Garry, 50
Wilmore, Gayraud S., Jr., 162
Wilner, Daniel M., 55

Wilson, C.E., 81, 148
Wilson, D.C., 36
Wilson, James Q., 23, 66, 129, 132, 133
Wilson, Neill Compton, 44
Wilson, P.E., 105
Wilson, R.B., 140
Wilson, Robert L., 162
Winder, Alvin, 55
Winnick, L., 90
Winsborough, H.H., 90
Winter, Gibson, 20
Winter, William F., 105
Wirth, Louis, 16, 63
Witcover, Jules, 67
Witmer, Helen, 30
Wogaman, Philip, 162
Wolf, Eleanor P., 93, 97
Wolfe, Deborah Partridge, 114
Wolfe, Donald M., 16
Wolfe, John B., 50
Wolff, Max, 109, 118, 120
Wolfgang, Marvin E., 66
Woll, J. Albert, 76
Wollett, Donald H., 140
Wood, David G., 86
Wood, Robert C., 133
Woodring, Paul, 33
Woods, Sister Frances Jerome, 18
Woods, Walter, 33
Woodson, Carter G., 8, 20, 23
Woodward, C. Vann, 8, 133, 140, 154
Woofter, Thomas J., 8, 154
Work, Monroe N., 170
Workman, P.L., 16
Workman, William D., 154
Works, Ernest, 50, 97
Woronoff, Israel, 30
Worsnop, Richard L., 50, 129

Worthy, William, 165
Wortman, M.S., Jr., 86
Wright, Charles, 44
Wright, Charles Allen, 118
Wright, Dale, 57
Wright, J.S., 105
Wright, M.A., 125
Wright, Marion A., 148, 154
Wright, Richard, 8, 10, 44, 50
Wright, Stanley W., 35
Wright, Stephen J., 112, 148
Wrightstone, J. Wayne, 114
Wyant, William K., 97

Yaghmai, H.B., 33
Yankauer, Marian P., 95, 97
Yarrow, Leon J., 51, 55
Yarrow, Marian R., 30, 51, 55
Yarrow, Penny R., 48
Yellin, Carol Lynn, 123
Yinger, J. Milton, 49, 54
Yochelson, Leon, 28
Yoshino, I. Roger, 107
Young, Andrew J., 162
Young, Harding B., 73
Young, Harrison, 165
Young, Merrill Orne, 162
Young, R.K., 55
Young, Whitney M., Jr., 21, 93, 143, 147, 148

Zabel, William D., 25
Zeigler, L. Harmon, 130
Zeitz, L., 66
Ziegler, Benjamin Munn, 105
Zietlow, Carl P., 148
Zimmer, Basil G., 61
Zinn, Howard, 133, 148, 154